*CULTURAL PSYCHOLOGY*

This book has been awarded Harvard University Press's annual
prize for an outstanding publication about education and society,
established in 1995 by the Virginia and Warren Stone Fund.

D0113280

# Cultural Psychology

## A ONCE AND FUTURE DISCIPLINE

Michael Cole

*The Belknap Press of Harvard University Press*
Cambridge, Massachusetts, and London, England

Third printing, 1998

First Harvard University Press paperback edition, 1998

*Library of Congress Cataloging-in-Publication Data*

Cole, Michael, 1938–
    Cultural psychology : a once and future discipline / Michael Cole.
        p.   cm.
    Includes bibliographical references and index.
    ISBN 0-674-17951-X (cloth)
    ISBN 0-674-17956-0 (pbk.)
    1. Ethnopsychology.   2. Social psychology.   3. Cognition—Social
    aspects.   I. Title.
    GN273.C65   1996
    155.8'2—dc20
    96–8234

I dedicate this book to my two mentors, William Estes and Alexander Luria, whose lessons in how to conduct one's life as a member of the community have been no less significant to me than their lessons in how to conduct psychological inquiry.

# Contents

# Foreword
*by Sheldon H. White*

MICHAEL COLE'S research projects and writings—multitudinous, adventurous, at times deeply searching and thoughtful—have done much to stimulate the growth of developmental psychology in the past three decades. This is a book of reflection and consolidation in which Cole takes the measure of what he has learned through his efforts, and in which he spells out a program for developmental psychology as a cultural-historical science. Cole addresses some fundamental questions. What does it mean to study a human's development scientifically? What kind of science do you arrive at? How broadly does it apply? What use can be made of it?

Developmental psychology came to life as a field of research at the turn of this century. There had been a rising tide of nineteenth-century writings about children, with authors examining their lives and circumstances philosophically, pedagogically, medically, politically, autobiographically, statistically, didactically, sentimentally, apocalyptically. Now there was to be a scientific approach to child development. At the beginning, the approach stood insecurely on scattered facts strung together with much theorizing. Followers of Darwin put together observations of children, animals, cross-cultural beliefs and practices, psychopathology, and so on, to sketch out an evolutionary picture of the human mind. It was risky, speculative science; William James, in *The Principles of Psychology,* called it "wild work":

> So it has come to pass that instincts of animals are ransacked to throw light on our own; and that the reasoning faculties of bees and ants, the minds of savages and infants, madmen, idiots, the deaf and blind, criminals, and eccentrics, are all invoked in support of this or that special theory about some part of our own mental life. The history of sciences, moral and political institutions, and languages, as types of mental product, are pressed into the same service . . . There are great sources of error in the comparative method. The interpretation of the "psycho-ses" of animals, savages, and infants is necessarily wild work, in which the personal equation of the investigator has things very much its own way. A savage will be reported to have no moral or religious feeling if his actions shock the observer unduly. A child will be assumed without self-consciousness because he talks of himself in the third person, etc., etc. No rules can be laid down in advance . . . the only thing then is to use as much sagacity as you possess, and to be as candid as you can.

The hope was that comparative studies of mental development would reveal the plan of the child's growth, giving guidance to educators, parents, pediatricians, social workers, and others with responsibilities for children. And the natural history of the child's development would fit together with the data of comparative neurology, animal psychology, abnormal psychology, and cross-cultural studies in principled ways to yield an evolutionary psychology. The evolutionary psychology given by the comparative method at the turn of the century was thin and marred by Western ethnocentric biases, but it did offer the skeleton of a universal account of children's mental development. Given a somewhat Wagnerian rendition by Freud, it initiated an intriguing, influential, but ultimately quite controversial body of psychoanalytic writings. Could one go beyond facts strung together to make plausible theories? One could if one had systematic, rich, constructive research programs. The history of psychology is a history of the struggle to build such programs.

The late nineteenth and early twentieth centuries brought organized cooperative research enterprises to psychology, scientific programs modeled on those of the natural sciences. Why did psychology follow the natural sciences? Psychology is occasionally pictured as a discipline haunted by a hapless, hopeless yearning for status as a *real* science. Without denying that there are touches of physics-envy to be found in some psychologists' writings, I think there is more to the problem than that. At the turn of this century, the physical sciences were well-formed, producing findings that were intellectually interesting and practically useful. There was good reason for psychologists to try to follow their pattern of cooperative activity, if only to see how far that pattern would take them. By concentrating on naturalistic questions and methods, psychologists sidestepped some tricky and risky issues. The twentieth-century scientific psychology of the universities, it must be remembered, emerged out of the nineteenth-century moral philosophy courses of the old-time American college. For a time, at least, the new psychologists of the universities (and those who hired them and provided resources to support their research) cherished the hope that a purely naturalistic, value-free enterprise of scientific psychology could yield data that would be used to provide easy, uncontroversial resolutions of the dilemmas, choices, and political confrontations of people living in the institutions of modern society.

But the science of the new psychology would prove to have hidden and awkward restrictions. The methods of a naturalistic scientific program would reveal patterns of organization of human perception, learning, and development, and the rhetoric of that program would assert that such patterns must be true for everyone everywhere. Michael Cole's point of entry into the problems of twentieth-century psychological science was the discovery that part of that assertion was not true. He took part in an effort to export the "new mathematics" to the Kpelle in Africa in the 1960s. He used Western research methods to study the cognitive development of Kpelle children living in a traditional society, and he came face to face with the fact that although tribal children classify, learn, remember, form concepts, and reason in everyday life, they do not perform in a sophisticated manner on experimental procedures designed for the study of age changes in those faculties. Western research procedures are grounded in a world in which children go to school at six years of age and are surrounded by the life, language, and thought of a modern society. Much of what we consider to be normal to child development is simply a recognition of what usually happens when children grow up in such a world.

In this book Cole reviews the generality of his observations. He discusses the findings of a number of cross-cultural research projects and shows that there are always great difficulties in using traditional natural-scientific inquiries to compare peoples across cultures.

The fact that some twentieth-century psychology has produced findings that are only true within situational boundaries is not completely surprising. Before this century, a number of distinguished philosophers argued that in order to fully understand how the human mind works we will require two psychologies of different orders. We will need the kind of naturalistic psychology with which we are familiar, analyzing mental phenomena as constructions built out of sensations, ideas, associations, reflexes, or sensorimotor schemes. We will need also a less-familiar "second psychology" describing higher-level mental phenomena as entities given form by the language, myths, and social practices in which the individual lives. Such a second psychology would not be expected to yield universal findings. Since higher mental processes are formed by culture, they differ from one society to another.

Cole traces the lineage of proposals for a second psychology through the writings of Vico, Herder, von Humboldt, John Stuart Mill, and Dilthey and, among contemporary writers, through Toulmin, Price-Williams, Boesch, Shweder, and Bruner. There is a lineage of *cultural psychologists*, he says, that has consistently argued for an emphasis on mediated action in a context; the use of the "genetic method" understood broadly to include historical, ontogenetic, and microgenetic levels of analysis; the grounding of analysis in everyday life events; the assumption that mind emerges in the joint activity of people and is in an important sense, "coconstructed"; the assumption that individuals are active agents in their own development; rejection of cause-effect, stimulus-response, explanatory science in favor of a science that emphasizes the emergent nature of mind in activity and that acknowledges a central role for interpretation in its explanatory framework; methodologies that draw upon the humanities as well as the social and biological sciences (Chapter 4).

We have to see this lineage of cultural psychology not simply as an exercise in intellectual history but as an achievement, ideas about principles slowly and with care and creativity being realized in a set of social practices. The effort to put a programmatic second psychology on the ground began in the 1920s, when the brilliant young Soviet psychologist L. S. Vygotsky reacted to a fractionation of psychology into schools, or a "crisis," that was being described with varying degrees of alarm by psychologists around the world. At the heart of psychology's crisis, Vygotsky believed, was the emergent recognition of the need for a human science of psychology to stand beside the existing natural science of the time. It is one thing to set forth an in-principle need for such a science as philosophers have done in the past, quite another to find the methods, ideas, and organizational mechanisms that will allow human beings acting together to create such a science.

At the very beginning of the road, Vygotsky recognized, there is the need to come to terms with the reality such a human science must deal with. Vygotsky argued that we must understand human mental life as deeply connected to the objects of human manufacture in the world around us. Human beings live in a world of human artifacts—tools, words, routines and rituals—changeling objects that are at one and the same time things the individual must deal with and repositories of prior human thought and judgment. When children learn the sequence "January-February-March-April-May-June-July-August-September-October-November-December," are they learning about the rhythms of the natural world or about an organized social practice by which people deal with such rhythmicity? They are learning both, of course, in the same activity. It is extremely difficult for the empiricist epistemology on which ordinary American psychology is grounded to come to terms with that.

At the heart of Michael Cole's work since the 1960s, I believe, has been the long, slow realization of cultural-historical psychology as a cooperative human enterprise. No one has done more to make that psychology a reality. Understanding, as only a well-trained experimental psychologist can understand, that psychology comes to life only when there are research procedures through which people can experience and know the world together, Cole has sought to find such procedures. There was a great hill to be climbed at the beginning. The reality human psychological scientists explore is different from the reality of the natural scientists. Cole traces the personal experiences that brought him, step by step, towards an understanding of Vygotsky's psychology with its grounding in German idealistic epistemology. He asserts a philosophical position in a clear, circumstantial, and anecdotal discourse: "An artifact is an aspect of the material world that has been modified over the history of its incorporation in goal-directed human action. By virtue of the changes wrought in the process of their creation and use, artifacts are simultaneously ideal (conceptual) and material"(Chapter 5).

Artifacts are the fundamental constituents of culture. The growth of the human mind, in ontogeny and in human history, must properly be understood as a coevolution of human activities and artifacts. The words we speak, the social institutions in which we participate, the man-made physical objects we use, all serve as both tools and symbols. They exist in the world around us; they organize our attention and action in that world and, in the aggregate, they create "alternative worlds." In the formation of a human culture across historical time, cultural mediation produces a mode of developmental change in which the activities of prior generations are cumulated in the present as the specifically human part of the environment. The social world influences the individual not only through the agency of flesh-and-blood people who converse, communicate, model, or persuade, but through the social practices and objects unseen people have built up in the world around that individual. There are the prescribed forms of social interaction: routines, schemas, scripts, games, rituals, cultural forms. There are the manufactured objects that silently impregnate the furniture of the world with human intelligence: words, maps, television sets, subway stations.

Ultimately, Cole's cultural-historical approach to the study of mind dictates that when we study human development we must make the study of surrounding social practices part and parcel of our inquiry. Similarly, if we want to change the pattern of a human being's activities, we need to address the surrounding situations in which those activities live.

Particularly interesting examples of Cole's developed psychology are to be found in Chapters 9 and 10 of this book—chapters in which his cultural-historical psychology is applied. In Chapter 9, Cole reports on a cultural-mediational approach to the teaching of reading. His Question-Asking-Reading approach to the teaching of reading was based on the Vygotskian principle that in human development the interpsychological (transactions between people) precedes and sets the stage for intrapsychological (complex mental processes within one child's mind). Group discussions of passages of reading were organized so that individual children "played" distinct lines of inquiry. An interpersonal world of interpretative discussions of texts was created. "The person who asks about words that are hard to say" talked with "the person who asks about words that are hard to understand" and "the person who asks a question about the main idea of the passage," and so on. Children played these roles in an environment designed to be engaging to children and to promote goals associated with reading. The intellectual dramaturgy worked. "Overall," Cole says, "I judge Question-Asking-Reading to be a successful application of cultural-historical theory to the problem of differential diagnosis and remediation of reading difficulties."

Cole's program, as a distinct and organized entity, is over now. Yet the principle of teaching reading comprehension by personifying thought processes is coming into wider use in the schools—becoming, appropriately enough, part of the "buried intelligence" of school procedures. Not only does the second psychology use methods distinct from those of naturalistic psychology, but its findings enter into ordinary life, are useful to people, in distinctly different ways.

In this intervention project, and even more in the series of Fifth Dimension projects described in Chapter 10, Cole reveals an imaginative ability to weave together intellectual and social elements to create a principled educational intervention within an artfully designed and appealing microculture. It took the second psychology to create the Fifth Dimension projects and, beyond that, it took some empathy and some flair.

Part of what Michael Cole has contributed to contemporary psychology is a cultural-historical psychology, a second psychology on the ground. Part of what he has offered is the *romantic science* he learned from the man with whom he did his post-doctorate, the late great Alexander Luria. Luria's romantic science, "the dream of a novelist and a scientist combined," looks at people alternately in terms of scientific categories and diagnostic nomenclature and as whole human beings. Another contemporary follower of Luria's practices romantic science—Oliver Sacks, the neurologist, in whose case studies brain-damaged people, autistic individuals, retarded people, idiots savants, come to life as sympathetic figures who struggle to live within their limitations just as we struggle to live within ours. Perhaps it is the methods of cultural-historical psychology and the spirit of romantic science that will allow us all some day to have a psychology within which human beings can live and breathe.

# Introduction

IN THIS BOOK, in the spirit of its title, I explore the origins and possible future of the field of cultural psychology, the study of the culture's role in the mental life of human beings. I begin with a seeming contradiction. On the one hand, it is generally agreed that the need and ability to live in the human medium of culture is one of the central characteristics of human beings. On the other hand, it is difficult for many academic psychologists to assign culture more than a secondary, often superficial role in the constitution of our mental life.

This situation brings me to my first question: *Why do psychologists find it so difficult to keep culture in mind?*

My efforts to answer this question take me into the history of psychology to discover how culture came to be so marginal to the discipline. I then review earlier efforts that relied primarily on cross-cultural methods to include culture within psychology's scientific program. My focus is on both the difficulties these efforts encountered and the successes they achieved.

Once I have explained why it has been so difficult for psychologists to keep culture in mind, despite many decades of effort by many

talented researchers, I address a second question: *If you are a psychologist who believes that culture is a fundamental constituent of human
thought and action, what can you do that is scientifically acceptable?*
My goal is to describe one principled way to create and use a culture-
inclusive psychology.

Of course, this goal is by no means original. In recent decades
many scholars whose work I discuss have sought to make the case
for a culture-inclusive psychology. They argue that so long as one
does not evaluate the possible cultural variability of the psychological
processes one studies, it is impossible to know whether such processes are universal or specific to particular cultural circumstances.

For example, John and Beatrice Whiting, anthropologists with a
long-term interest in human development, wrote: "If children are
studied within the confines of a single culture, many events are taken
as natural, or a part of human nature and are therefore not considered
as variables. It is only when it is discovered that other peoples do not
follow these practices that have been attributed to human nature that
they are adopted as legitimate variables" (1960, p. 933).

More recently the same argument has been made by Marshall Segall, John Berry, Pierre Dasen, and Ypes Poortinga, four psychologists
who have spent decades engaging in cross-cultural work: "given the
complexities of human life and the importance of culture as a behavioral determinant, it obviously behooves psychologists to test the
cross-cultural generality of their principles before considering them
established. It is obvious, then, that the scientific study of human
behavior requires that they employ a cross-cultural perspective"
(1990, p. 37).

This line of argument seems so commonsensical that it may be
difficult to understand why such a patently correct point of view does
not have the corresponding effect on the discipline. Why isn't cross-
cultural research fully integrated into psychology's project of establishing basic principles of human behavior? A simple answer, the
complexities of which I will spend a good deal of time deconstructing
in this book, is that general psychology does not know what to make
of a good deal of the data that cross-cultural psychologists produce
because the research does not live up to the methodological requirements of the discipline.

Among those interested in exploring the role of culture in mind,

a rather sharp and well-articulated division of opinion has developed
in response to the dual facts that cross-cultural research is widely
ignored and that its findings are difficult to interpret. Many cross-
cultural psychologists believe that increased attention to problems of
methodology will eventually lead to cross-cultural psychology's integration into the mainstream of psychological research (for example,
Segall et al., 1990). From this perspective, the problem can be solved
by rigorous application of known methods. In place of the all-too-
prevalent one-shot experiments, what is needed are multicultural
comparisons that allow the "unpackaging" of culture as a variable so
that firmer causal conclusions can be reached. The effort to "unpackage" culture leads the psychologist naturally into interdisciplinary
work with anthropologists, sociologists, and linguists, both as a
source of methods for making the appropriate observations and as a
source of theoretical ideas about how to handle the resulting complexities.

A second group believes that not only cross-cultural psychology,
but the entire enterprise of scientific psychology from which it de-
rives, is so deeply flawed at its foundation that an entirely new discipline for the study of culture in mind must be formulated. This
opinion is expressed forcefully by Richard Shweder, who writes that
for the general psychologist "there is no theoretical benefit in learning more and more about the quagmire of appearances—the retarding
effects of environment on the development of the central processing
mechanism, the noise introduced by translation of differences in the
understanding of the test situation or by cultural variations in the
norms regulating the asking and the answering of questions . . .
Rather, if you are a general psychologist, you will want to transcend
those appearances and reach for the imagined abstract forms and
processes operating behind intrinsic crutches and restraints and distortions of this or that performance environment" (Shweder, 1990,
p. 12).

In effect, Shweder is asserting that the cross-cultural strategy for
introducing culture into psychology is simply misguided. No amount
of increased methodological sophistication can rescue the enterprise.
In its place he proposes not a refurbished new subdiscipline of psychology but a new discipline, which he calls *cultural psychology*.
Rather than seeking to understand the mind as a general processing

*how cult psych sees mind*

device, Shweder argues, cultural psychology sees the mind as "content-driven, domain-specific, and constructively stimulus-bound; and it cannot be extricated from the historically variable and culturally diverse intentional worlds in which it plays a coconstitutive part" (ibid., p. 13). Shweder looks to interpretive branches of the social sciences and to the humanities for the methodological foundation of this new discipline.

As will become clear, I have a great deal of sympathy for Shweder's critique of general psychology and his attempt to formulate an alternative which places culture at its core instead of at its periphery. I am also convinced that in formulating an alternative way to think about culture in mind, it is important to integrate knowledge from all of the humane sciences, which, as I will show, are part of psychology's birthright.

However, I am not entirely clear on the shape that an alternative discipline would take. The reasons for my ambivalence will become clearer as the presentation proceeds.

I begin in Chapter 1 by looking at the prehistory of psychology as a discipline, adhering to the principle that to understand something it is important to know its history. Chapter 1 inquires into the ways in which culture's relation to thinking was dealt with before psychology came into being. In an important sense, cultural psychology was there "in the beginning." Of special interest is the link between the advent of psychology-as-science and the way cross-cultural research was conceived and conducted. In Chapter 2 I trace major attempts to apply the strategy of standardized cross-cultural research, emphasizing both the problems of interpretation it calls down on itself and its accomplishments. Chapter 3 focuses on development. In it I describe attempts to improve standard methodologies by conducting multidisciplinary research on cognitive development that takes people's everyday experiences as a starting point. This approach can be viewed either as a "reform" of the standard experimental method or as an alternative methodology. It leads necessarily to coalitions with anthropologists, sociologists, and field linguists, to find not only "native versions" of existing tasks but "native tasks" that are then modeled in experiments. At the time when I was carrying out research in that tradition I referred to my work as "experimental anthropology and ethnography psychology."

Such an approach must own up to undoubted shortcomings. There are often unbridgeable gaps between an anthropologist's or native's description of "native tasks" and what psychologists know how to experiment on. In addition, theoretically, such work is forced to assume the existence of a common, universal core of human nature, which, after all, is one of the questions that cross-cultural research is supposed to resolve. Despite its difficulties, this strategy has proven extremely fruitful as a means of decoupling various kinds of culturally organized experience and as a way to provide an experimental critique of overgeneralizations based on work restricted to modern, industrialized societies.

Beginning with Chapter 4 I turn to the search for an alternative formulation of the issues and the paths to their resolution. I take as my starting point the Russian cultural-historical approach to psychology and sketch out the challenges such an approach must meet if it is to be useful for guiding psychological research. Chapter 5 begins the job of elaborating the Russians' approach by proposing a conception of culture that, while consistent with their views, brings those views into line with contemporary ideas in anthropology and cognitive science. In Chapter 6, using the notion of culture developed in Chapter 5, I reexamine the question of culture's role in human origins and historical change. In Chapter 7 I apply the elaborated notion of culture to current evidence on child development.

Chapters 8, 9, and 10 focus on work my colleagues and I have conducted over the past decade and a half. Chapter 8 addresses a key methodological problem confronting cultural-historical approaches to cognition: how to ground one's psychological analysis in the culturally organized activities of everyday life. In Chapter 9 I build on the ideas presented in Chapters 4–8 and seek to demonstrate their utility by using them to create specially designed forms of reading instruction. In Chapter 10 I introduce a new methodology in which small cultural systems are created and studied in their institutional context over a period of years.

In Chapter 11 I return to the two questions with which I began. I summarize my current understanding about what makes the study of culture in mind difficult and discuss various lines of theory and research that can serve as tools for psychologists who seek a deeper understanding of how culture and mind create each other.

I have no particular hope that my ideas will lead to a coup in psychology, even if they were to convince many people. Psychology is a deeply entrenched social institution that will not humbly assent to being usurped by a view that holds *all* psychology to be part of cultural psychology. Perhaps those who argue for a new, postmodern discipline of cultural psychology are correct, and cultural psychology will emerge along with other "mixed-genre disciplines" such as cognitive science, history of consciousness, and communication. If so, then I am offering one methodology and set of theoretical precepts for such a science. If not, I am offering a program of positive critical research for psychologists who choose to use it.

# 1 ⑥

# Enduring Questions and Disputes

Culture might be precisely that condition that excludes a
mentality capable of measuring it.   *Theodore Adorno*

ACCORDING TO the mythology propagated in standard American
textbooks, the discipline of psychology began in 1879 when Wilhelm
Wundt opened a laboratory in Leipzig.[1] What was new about the
"new" psychology of the 1880s was experimentation. Students of human psychological processes in laboratory settings used ingenious
"brass instruments" to present people with highly controlled physical
stimuli (lights of precise luminance, sounds of precise loudness and
pitch, and so on) and to record the content, magnitude, and latency
of their responses with split-second accuracy. Mind, it was believed,
could now be measured and explained according to the canons of
experimental science.

Less often noted—the topic received only a single sentence in
Boring's (1957) tome on the history of psychology—was that Wundt
conceived of psychology as necessarily constituted of *two* parts, each
based on a distinctive layer of human consciousness and each following its own laws using its own methodology.

In recent years interest has grown in Wundt's "second psychology,"
the one to which he assigned the task of understanding how culture
enters into psychological processes (Farr, 1983; Toulmin, 1980). My
basic thesis is that the scientific issues Wundt identified were not

adequately dealt with by the scientific paradigm that subsequently dominated psychology and the other behavioral-social sciences. As a consequence, attempts by psychologists working within the paradigm of twentieth-century experimental psychology to reintroduce culture as a crucial constituent of human nature face insuperable, unrecognized, difficulties.

Later in this book I will describe how twentieth-century psychology has sought to deal with Wundt's legacy in attempting to create a more adequate theory of culture in mind. But first I must look into the prehistory of scientific psychology to make clear why culture-inclusive psychology has been such an elusive goal.

## In the Beginning

It has long been recognized that culture is very difficult for humans to think about. Like fish in water, we fail to "see" culture because it is the medium within which we exist. Encounters with other cultures make it easier to grasp our own as an object of thought.

Some of the earliest evidence of culture's becoming a self-conscious phenomenon can be traced back to the Greek historian Herodotus (Myers, 1953). The problem Herodotus set himself was a perfect vehicle for discovering culture. He wanted to know about origins: Who had initiated the hostility between the Greeks and Persians, and why? To answer this historical question, he traveled to more than fifty societies known to the Greeks of his day. In the process of recording their accounts of their origins, he obtained knowledge about the worlds they inhabited, as expressed in their religion, art, beliefs about gods, and everyday practices. What emerged were portraits of distinctive ways of life, which today we would call different cultures.

Herodotus's inquiry also raised in acute form the question of how cultural differences should be evaluated. When he wrote down the histories and lifeways of other peoples, the generic name he gave to the subjects of his inquiry was *barbarian*. In early fourth-century Greece, barbarian was a descriptive term for people whose language, religion, ways of life, and customs differed from those of classical Greek culture. In effect, for Herodotus, barbarian meant "people who are different," and his *History* is an inquisitive catalog of human variability that is relatively free of strong value judgments.

However, it was not long before difference became deficiency. Later Greeks used barbarian to mean "outlandish, rude, brutal." Both senses of barbaric, as different and as deficient, were retained when the term was appropriated into Latin. Subsequently it came to mean "uncivilized" or "uncultured," and later "non-Christian." The increasingly unflattering meanings attached to the word reached their apex when it was taken into English, where it is equated with "savage, rude, savagely cruel, inhuman" (OED).

Greek scholarly opinion was divided concerning the origins of the group differences they observed. (Aristotle believed that slaves and barbarians were *by nature* bereft of the powers of planning and reasoning, while Hippocrates held that group differences arose from differences in climate and social institutions.) Similar disagreements can be found in the scholarship of the Roman era and the Middle Ages (see Jahoda, 1992, for a summary and additional sources).

As Margaret Hodgen (1964) points out in her study of the origins of anthropology, the wide-ranging travels of fifteenth- and sixteenth-century explorers enormously increased both scholarly and popular interest in the varieties of humankind and culture. For a thousand or more years following the fall of Rome, European contact with "barbarians" had been very limited. Although descriptions of the life and customs of far-off people were available in reports by traders, soldiers, and missionaries, a vast folklore had grown up about the humans who lived beyond the fringes of the European world.

The difference between first-hand observation and second-hand mythologizing is illustrated by the beliefs that accompanied Christopher Columbus's voyages. Columbus's journal portrayed the people he met in the western hemisphere in relatively objective terms. He admired their generosity, moral character and intelligence, while finding their material circumstances lamentable. However, the second-hand accounts that began to proliferate as soon as Columbus returned to Europe built up a fantastic image of the newly discovered lands and their people which drew heavily on the mythical creatures of medieval imagination. The catalog was truly fantastic, including people who squeaked instead of speaking, people who were headless with their eyes and mouths located in their chests, people who went naked, had no marriage rites, lived in total promiscuity, and so on (Hodgen, 1964).

Even following a century of exploration and contact, one could encounter descriptions of the people living along the west coast of Africa as "dog faced, dog toothed people, satyrs, wild men, and cannibals," and the people of the New World were said to be "liars, thieves, perverts, and obstinate idolaters" who seemed to lack any semblance of "reason peculiar to man." "By this process of condemnation, New World man or the naked and threatening savage took that place in thought which, during the Middle Ages, had been reserved for human monsters. If human, theirs was a degraded humanity" (ibid., p. 363).

These images entered into the popular European conception of the world's inhabitants, coming down to us today in such forms as Shakespeare's Caliban, a creature "not honour'd with a human shape," who, like the troglodyte cave dweller of antiquity, was incapable of human speech. Some Europeans seriously questioned whether creatures deemed so different were members of the human species at all.[2]

Hippocrates' belief that geography and climate are the source of human variations was widely held in later centuries. Whatever its shortcomings, this view assumed all creatures we now recognize as human beings to be of a single species. In the sixteenth and seventeenth centuries geography and climate were thought to explain the darker skins of Africans and Amerindians. This tradition of environmental explanation came in for severe criticism (the sun kept shining on the Greeks and Romans, and yet their characteristic traits changed dramatically over time), and did not survive extensive European contact with third world peoples.[3]

Europeans assigned so-called savages (that is, non-Europeans) to an intermediate status between humans and animals. Pygmies, Laplanders, and others were claimed as "missing links" in the chain of being between animals and human beings. Carolus Linnaeus, in his *System of Nature* (1735) took the additional and decisive step of dividing human beings into two species, *Homo sapiens* and *Homo monstrous*, as follows:

*Homo sapiens*, varying by education and situation, was composed of

1. Wild man: four-footed, mute, hairy.
2. American: copper-colored, choleric, erect. Paints self. Regulated by custom.

3. European: fair, sanguine, brawny. Covered with close vestments. Governed by laws.
4. Asiatic: sooty, melancholy, rigid. Covered with loose garments. Governed by opinions.
5. African: black, phlegmatic, relaxed. Anoints himself with grease. Governed by caprice.

*Homo monstrous,* varying by climate and art, included

1. Mountaineers: small, inactive, timid.
2. Patagonians: large, indolent.
3. Hottentots: less fertile.
4. American: beardless.
5. Chinese: head conic.
6. Canadian: head flattened.

Linnaeus's scheme is clearly a hodgepodge of mixed criteria, including skin color, dress, and political organization. However, it set an influential precedent for the later division of humanity into separate races. Subsequent advances in biological knowledge brought with them increasingly refined attempts to justify a purely biological account of human variability (Gossett, 1965; Harris, 1968), paving the way for racial explanations of what had previously been conceived of as cultural variations.[4]

Such beliefs, although subsequently discredited, helped to sustain the nineteenth-century intellectual climate in which the idea that national variations among human beings were the result of *racial constitution* became as widespread as the earlier idea that non-Europeans were at a lower level of the great chain of being. These beliefs helped to justify slavery and colonialism at a time when both practices were under heavy attack (Haller, 1971). Hence in 1849 Benjamin Disraeli could stand before the British House of Commons and declare that "race implies difference, difference implies superiority, and superiority leads to predominance," confident that he was adopting a purely scientific point of view (quoted in Odom, 1967, p. 9).

## Sociocultural Evolutionism

Whether one believed that in some primeval time human beings sprang from a single source (and hence that we were once "all alike") or that morphologically distinct human groups represented distinct species (and hence that we were different to begin with) it was still necessary to explain the process of change over time. It was clear from the written record that during the sixteenth and seventeenth centuries the inhabitants of Germany, France, and England (for example) would have been firmly counted among the barbarians had the ancient Greeks been around at the time. How had the inhabitants of these countries, in the course of history, come to be transformed from barbarians into the apex of humanity?

Two explanations offered themselves. First, one could reinterpret the relation of environment to development and claim that northern peoples had advanced precisely because of constant challenges from their environment while their southern cousins lounged around indolently eating breadfruit. Or, one could claim that the northerners' innate intellectual endowment was such that they simply thought their way out of a state of nature more rapidly. Whichever explanatory mechanism one invoked, in the decades preceding the founding of scientific psychology, the mainstream of both scholarly and popular opinion in Europe and the Europeanized areas of North America took it for granted that societies had undergone a process of sociocultural development with profound implications for psychological functioning.

E. B. Tylor, one of the founders of modern anthropology, captures the spirit of such thinking in his hyperbolic personification of Civilization:

> We may fancy ourselves looking on Civilization as in personal figure she traverses the world; we see her lingering or resting by the way, and often deviating into paths that bring her toiling back to where she had passed long ago; but direct or devious, her path lies forward, and if now and then she tries a few backward steps, her walk soon falls into a helpless stumbling. It is not according to her nature, her feet were not made to plant uncertain steps behind her, for both in her forward view and her onward gain she is of truly human type. (1871/1958, p. 69)

Although enthusiasm for the equation of evolution and progress has subsided considerably in the century since Tylor wrote, the idea of sociocultural evolution has retained its importance in the social sciences (see Ingold, 1986; Hallpike, 1986; Harris, 1968; Sahlins and Service, 1960; White, 1959).

Tylor conceived of culture as what Melville Herskovitz (1948) later called the "man-made part of the environment," in which he included knowledge, belief, art, morals, law, custom, and so on. Insofar as these elements are conceived of as adhering in a "complex whole," claims about cultural variations in level of development could draw on any of them. Tylor reckoned levels of cultural evolution using the level of achievement in a variety of areas, particularly "the extent of scientific knowledge, the definitions of moral principles, the conditions of religious belief and ceremony, the degree of social and political organization (1874, p. 27)."[5]

In addition, Tylor was typical of other nineteenth-century scholars in assuming a close affinity between the level of sociocultural development and the level of mental development of the people constituting various social groups: "the condition of culture among various societies of mankind," he wrote, ". . . is a subject apt for the study of laws of human thought and action" (1874, p. 1).

As an example of how natural this packet of assumptions seemed, consider Herbert Spencer's thought experiment about the link between social and mental progress in which he drew an analogy between cultural development on the one hand and mental development on the other. Spencer assumed that the earliest humans lived such simple lives that they did not have basic materials from which to build complicated mental structures. He invites us to consider the most extreme case as a starting point.

> Suppose perpetual repetition of the same experience; then the power of representation is limited to reproduction of this experience in idea. Given two often repeated different experiences, and it thereupon becomes possible to discern in the representations of them what they have in common; to do which, however, implies that the representative faculty can hold the two representations before consciousness; and the ability to do this can arise only after multitudinous recurrences. In like manner it is clear that only after there have been received many experiences which differ in their kinds but present some relation in common, can the first step be taken towards the concept of a

truth higher in generality than these different experiences themselves. (Spencer, 1886, p. 521)

Spencer goes on to suggest that as experiences become more varied
in their character there are concomitant increases in "the power of
representation":

> It follows, therefore, that in the course of human progress gen-
> eral ideas can arise only as fast as social conditions render ex-
> periences multitudinous and varied; while at the same time it
> is to be observed that these social conditions themselves pre-
> suppose some general ideas. Each step towards more general
> ideas is instrumental in bringing about wider social co-opera-
> tions . . . And then, when correlative experiences have become
> organized, there arises the possibility of ideas yet higher in gen-
> erality, and a further social evolution. (1886, p. 522)

Spencer links these ideas to the concept of evolution proposed by
Darwin by assuming that over time the mental traits and sociocultural environments of different peoples of the world diverged. When
different groups came into conflict, the "better adapted" drove the
"inferior varieties" into "undesirable habitats" and occasionally exter-
minated them. Since, at the time he was writing, European societies
were manifestly vanquishing other peoples, European mentality and
society were the most highly evolved, providing a standard against
which to judge others.

There are three widespread assumptions implied in these passages.
The first is the general notion of social evolution as a process of
increasing differentiation and complexity of social life. The second is
that the basic mental operations of people, whatever the complexity
of the society they participate in, are universal in the sense that they
are built up according to a single set of laws, which for Spencer meant
a gradual accumulation of knowledge leading to broader and more
valid generalizations. The assumption of a core of mental characteristics common across all cultural groups is referred to in anthropology as the "psychic unity" of humankind. In psychology it is the idea
that "surely at some level of abstraction we are all alike, all human"
(Segall et al., 1990, p. 53). The third key assumption is that there is
an intimate relationship between culture and mind. All three ideas
continue to have their adherents down to the present day.

## Primitives and Children

The combination of a belief in psychic unity of basic psychological processes, sociocultural evolution, and a close correspondence between culture and mind leads almost inevitably to the conclusion that the thinking of adults living in modern, industrial societies is superior to that of the thinking of people living in less developed societies (however the criteria of more and less are decided upon). Furthermore, since it is assumed that the basic psychological processes are universal but their level of development depends upon the extent of one's experiences, it is a natural step to assume that there is a serious analogy to be drawn between the thinking of primitive adults and that of "modern" children, by virtue of their shared lack of complex experiences.

While Spencer cannot be said to speak for all of nineteenth-century thought on the subject, the line of reasoning he provides in the passages quoted above is broadly representative of sociocultural-evolutionary thinking, and it illustrates with particular clarity how the belief that primitive adults think like the children of advanced civilizations is virtually a reflexive conclusion. The following statement by Schiller (who, ironically, is probably best known today as the author of the "Ode to Joy" which serves as the text for the choral movement in Beethoven's Ninth Symphony), is typical:

> The discoveries made by European travelers in far-off seas and distant coasts show us a picture as instructive as it is entertaining of peoples of various stages of civilization in our world standing round us, just as we may see the children of various ages in a family standing round an elder brother, and by their condition reminding him what he was formerly, and through what stages he has come to man's estate. An overruling Providence seems to have reserved these immature races for our learning until we were wise enough to profit by the lessons set before us and to be able to reconstruct from these examples the lost history of the beginnings of mankind. The picture of the child of our race is sufficiently depressing and humiliating but we must remember that farther back our forebears were much less rational than the lowest of these. (quoted in Müller-Lyer, 1920, p. 32)

The variety of characteristics presumed to be shared by primitive adults and European children was quite impressive: an inability to control the emotions, animistic thinking, inability to reason about causes or to plan for the future, conservatism, love of analogy and symbolism, and so on. Chamberlain (1901) and Tylor (1865) contain representative claims. Tylor, for example, suggests that "the idol answers to the savage in one province of thought the same purpose as its analogue, the doll, does to the child. It enables him to give a definite existence and a personality to the vague ideas of higher beings, which his mind can hardly grasp without material aid" (1865, p. 94).

Although he wrote several decades later, the ideas of the French philosopher-sociologist Lucien Levy-Bruhl require mention at this point because he is often associated with the notion of primitive mentality and the idea that children raised in industrialized societies think like primitive adults. While the first characterization of Levy-Bruhl's ideas is true, the second is not.

Drawing on the same general corpus of evidence used by Tylor, Spencer, Wundt, and others (for example, reports from missionaries, travelers, and government officials), Levy-Bruhl objected to the idea that characteristics of the thinking of primitive peoples could be derived from presumably universal laws of individual thought. The ideas of primitive peoples, he argued, *because they are collective,* "force themselves upon the individual; that is, they are to him an article of faith, not the product of his reason" (1910, p. 15).

Levy-Bruhl went on to develop the thesis that a qualitatively distinct form of collective representation exists in primitive societies, in which emotion is fused with cognition and relationships between events are experienced as mystical fusions rather than causal sequences. Strictly speaking, Levy-Bruhl did not consider this form of thought an inferior precursor of civilized thought, nor did he equate it with the thought processes of European children. Rather, he considered it a qualitatively different mode of thought altogether. For example, he explicitly warns that social scientists should "no longer endeavor to account for these connections either by the mental weakness of primitives, or by the association of ideas, or by a naive application of the principle of causality . . . ; in short, let us abandon the attempt to refer their mental activity to an inferior variety of our own" (1910, p. 61). He also claims that in their everyday activity, when they are not being influenced (misled) by their collective representations, "they" think as "we" would, drawing the same conclusions from the same kinds of evidence.

By and large these caveats were ignored by Levy-Bruhl's readers, who assimilated his ideas to the generally held belief that historical change reflects a process of cultural evolution from lower-inferior to higher-better. They then supported him or criticized him depending upon their own beliefs about the evolution of culture and the evolution of mind. Typical is the reaction of F. C. Bartlett, who ascribed to Levy-Bruhl the opinion that "the psychology of primitive peoples represents a kind of mystical, pre-logical, lawless phase of mental development which set the early man at a very far distance indeed from ourselves" (1923, pp. 281–282).

To be sure, Levy-Bruhl is vulnerable to such interpretations because at many points in his text he lapses into language that is very difficult to interpret without drawing parallels to similar claims about children. However, his general point of view, that qualitatively different societies are characterized by qualitatively different modes of thought, is by no means generally rejected by social scientists. Levy-Bruhl will appear later in this narrative as he figures in more modern attempts to understand cultural variations in the development of thought.

## The Biological Recapitulation Hypothesis

The equation of primitive adults with European children could be based either on biological evolution or on differences in "education," that is, sociocultural evolution. Often the two sets of beliefs were mixed in an unrecognized and difficult-to-disentangle manner because the concept of "race" was not well delineated (see Tylor's use of the term above). Race was seen by some as a biological phenomenon and by others as a cultural one.

A popular biological explanation of the presumed fact that non-European peoples fail to develop as fully as Europeans is the "biogenetic" doctrine according to which individual development recapitulates the history of the species (ontogeny recapitulates phylogeny). Stephen Jay Gould traces the biogenetic doctrine back to the

race &
socio cult
evolution

biogenetic
doctrine

nineteenth century, when an early embryologist made the claim that there are "certain traits, which seem, in the adult African, to be less changed from the embryonic condition than in the adult European" (quoted in Gould, 1977, p. 126).

Its adherents supported this doctrine on both anatomical and ethnological grounds, providing an apparently iron-clad justification for a paternalistic approach to native peoples and the right to punish them, like errant children, when they misbehaved. An example of anatomical justification is found in Carl Vogt's work. Vogt (1864) claimed that the presumed differences between white and Negro development were to be explained by the fact that the brains of black adults resembled those of seven-year-old white children.

Ethnographic claims for the presumed early end to development among non-European peoples were no less numerous. A typical example is provided by Dudley Kidd (1906) in his book on childhood among the tribes of South Africa: "As a matter of fact the savage is at his best, intellectually, emotionally, and morally, at the dawn of puberty. When puberty is drawing to a close a degenerative process seems to set in, and the previous efflorescence of the faculties leads to no adequate fruitage in later life . . . In nothing is this more marked than in the case of imagination. Not a few observers have pointed out that the imagination in the Kafirs runs to seed after puberty: it would be truer to say that it runs to sex" (1906, pp. viii–ix). Like ideas about differences in levels of social development, the idea of the primitive-as-child was a part of the everyday belief systems of a great many Europeans, entering into the popular culture, where it remains to this day.[6]


## Scholarly Disputes

All during the centuries in which such popular views were developing in conjunction with the expansion of European power and the subjugation of peoples native to other parts of the world, scholars debated the scientific validity of different approaches to understanding the sources and significance of group differences in modes of life and modes of thinking.

## Two Kinds of Knowledge

In light of the way psychology, when the discipline came into being in the late nineteenth century, eventually marginalized culture, it is useful to think about the development of scholarly theories of culture and mind in terms of two distinctive paradigms which organized much of this discourse. The terms of the arguments for both paradigms were set by the Greeks, whose influence on European scholarly thought at the end of the Renaissance was enormous.

Common to the two paradigms is a quest for certain knowledge; they differ with respect to how and where they seek it. The first paradigm, which follows in Plato's path, emphasizes stable, universal processes of mind that are timeless in their operating principles. The second paradigm follows the lead of Herodotus, who believed that in order to understand the truth of past events it is necessary to understand the organization of people's current ways of life, which shape their thinking, which in turn influence their beliefs about the past.

In one of history's most famous thought experiments, Plato questioned the certainty of knowledge about objects and events "right before one's eyes." By likening the problem of the individual knower to the situation of a prisoner in a cave who can know the world only through the images its shadows cast upon the wall in front of him, Plato challenged us to explain how we can ever attain certain knowledge, given that we experience the world as re-presented, not as presented, even when the evidence is "right before our eyes." It is a universal problem that applies equally to all humans at all times. Any solution, should it be found, would rely on the universal properties of the knowing organism (or what has been referred to as the "universal central information processing mechanism": LCHC, 1983, Shweder, 1991).

## Science versus History

From at least the seventeenth century on, the dichotomy between ahistorical, universal theories of mind and historical, locally contingent theories has been bound up with another dichotomy, the opposition between "natural" and "cultural-historical" sciences. The Platonic view served to underpin "natural" theories of mind, while

cultural-historical theories of mind have followed in the footsteps of
Herodotus.

Isaiah Berlin (1981) contrasts the assumptions of the natural science and cultural-historical approaches to human nature in terms of
three issues. According to the assumptions of natural science: (1) any
real question has a single true answer; unless this is so, there is some
confusion in the posing of the question or the logic used in arriving
at an answer; (2) the method of arriving at the answers to genuine
problems is rational and universally applicable; and (3) solutions to
genuine problems are true universally, for all people at all times in
all places.

For the cultural-historical sciences the answers to real questions
depend upon the particular assumptions and point of view afforded
by the culture in question, and both the method of arriving at an
answer and what constitutes a problem or an answer are locally contingent, not universal. It is often suggested that cultural-historical
understanding requires a process of empathic understanding which,
while present in all people, is not the product of universally applicable rational problem solving. Also essential to distinguishing the
two ways of knowing is history's fascination with the unique instance,
the individual case, in strong contrast with natural science's reliance
on the analysis of repeated phenomena (Valsiner, 1987).

The dialogue between these two viewpoints continued through the
eighteenth and nineteenth centuries, up to and beyond the founding
of psychology and the other "social-behavioral" sciences. I'll present
a brief overview of this dialogue because it resonates clearly in today's
discussions about how psychologists may most profitably think about
culture and mind.

## The Path of Science

For purposes of the current discussion, Descartes's *Discourse on
Method,* published in the middle of the seventeenth century, provides
a useful starting point, because the links between Descartes and modern psychology are well known (Bakhurst, 1991; Gardner, 1985).
Descartes argued that true science is based on axiomatic premises
from which irrefutable conclusions can be deduced by the application
of reason. Quantifying the measurable properties of matter in motion

makes it possible to understand the world and its contents in terms of mathematical laws. Experimentation is an essential adjunct to quantification and rigorous deduction.

Descartes's prescriptions were based on an idealized form of the pathbreaking work by the seventeenth-century physicists Kepler, Galileo, and Newton, each of whom had discovered physical principles which became the hallmark of natural law. Natural laws were those which held for all times and all places; knowing the location of an object at time $n$, it was possible to determine its location at any arbitrarily chosen time in the past or the future.

(It was Descartes's belief that natural scientific methods, so conceived, could be applied far beyond the realm of physics. Of special relevance to psychology was his claim that all of organic life, including the operations of the human body, fit within the domain of natural science, but that the study of the human mind/soul (*l'âme*) did not. Hence, only that part of human nature shared with other animals (who have no souls) could be a part of natural science; uniquely human characteristics could not.

Descartes clearly excluded from "true" science phenomena which were contingent on specific historical circumstances. He had little use for the study of the humanities in general, and history in particular, because they could not yield precise definitions, quantifiable data, axioms, or clear rules of evidence, all of which were necessary to the deduction of general laws.

In part this extremely negative attitude toward historical research was a reaction against the discredited historiography of the times. In Descartes's era, world history was divided into periods based on the holy scriptures, with the most recent period beginning with the crucifixion of Christ. According to this scheme, no basic differences existed between the way of life of the apostles and the contemporary world of the seventeenth century. Such a simplistic account lost its credibility for post-Renaissance scholars who had become acquainted with Greek and Roman writings and were constantly bombarded with new scientific and technological innovations. As Berlin comments, the inferiority of historical research to the natural sciences must have seemed obvious.

However, it would be a mistake to attribute the split between natural science and humanities entirely to weaknesses of the latter at the time when the natural sciences began to blossom. The issue of historical laws is inextricably mixed together with the issue of the distinctiveness of human nature, particularly that part of human nature which Descartes excluded from scientific inquiry—the human mind. History is, in part, the product of the human mind; other animals do not have a history in the same sense as do human beings. Humans, like other creatures, are subject to laws of phylogeny and ontogeny, but in addition, as a result of the capacity to communicate experiences between generations (a capacity constitutive of "mind/ soul") we are the products of history in a way different from other creatures. According to this line of reasoning, history falls outside the realm of science precisely because the human mind has played a role in it.

In the two centuries following Descartes, scholars writing in the tradition of the European Enlightenment accepted his characterization of the nature of science but rejected his view that the study of the mind falls outside the realm of science, claiming instead that scientific methodology could be applied to the study of both history and mental phenomena (which they held to be intimately related). In his *Sketch for a Historical Picture of the Progress of the Human Mind*, for example, Condorcet not only proposed laws to account for past historical epochs but claimed that the uniformity of nature was so great that it would be possible to predict the future: "If man is able to predict with almost complete certainty the phenomenon whose laws are known, why regard it as a chimerical enterprise to foretell the future destiny of the species?" (Condorcet, 1822, p. 262).

## The Path of History and Culture

The leading opponent of Descartes's vision of science and the champion of a distinctive historical science was the Neapolitan scholar Giambattista Vico. In his *Scienza Nuova* (The New Science, 1725/ 1948) Vico accepted the qualitative distinctiveness of human nature and human history but drew very different lessons from it than did Descartes. His "new science" denied the applicability of natural science models to human nature and declared that the scientific study of human nature must be based upon specifically human forms of interaction and understanding.

In Vico's view there is an unbridgeable gulf between the man-made and the natural, between what human beings have constructed and what is given in nature. Not only works of art and laws, but history itself falls into the category of the humanly constructed. Up to this point Descartes might well be in agreement. Where Vico differed radically from Descartes and those of Descartes's heirs who sought a unified science based on the model of the physical sciences was in claiming that, precisely because they are constructed by human beings, the products of human activity, such as art and law and history itself, can be understood better than the physical world, which is unalterably "other" and ultimately unknowable. Berlin summarizes Vico's argument as follows:

> If anthropomorphism was falsely to endow the inanimate world with human minds and will, there was presumably a world which it was proper to endow with precisely these attributes, namely, the world of man. Consequently, a natural science of men treated as purely natural entities, on a par with rivers and plants and stones, rested on a cardinal error. With regard to ourselves we were privileged observers with an "inside" view: to ignore it in favor of the ideal of a unified science of all there is, a single, universal method of investigation, was to insist on wilful ignorance. (1981, p. 96)

Vico suggested that human nature must necessarily be understood through an historical analysis of language, myth, and ritual. His "new science," he believed, could arrive at a universal set of principles of human nature because even societies which had no contact with one another confronted the same problems of existence.

Toward the end of the eighteenth century, Johann Herder advanced Vico's line of thinking by arguing that the traditions coded in language and custom constitute an organic unity which gives human groups their sense of identity. It was Herder who introduced the notion of *Volk*, a community of people whose shared language and historical traditions shape the mental processes of its members and provide essential resources for the process of their development. Herder is often credited with the earliest formulation of the modern concept of cultural relativism, for he believed that the diversity of *Volk* is to be valued, and he explicitly asserted that each should be evaluated in its own terms: "Thus nations change according to place, time, and their inner character; each carries within itself the measure of its perfection, incommensurable with others" (1785/1966, vol. 4, p. 362).

In the early nineteenth century Wilhelm von Humboldt introduced the term *Völkerpsychologie,* to refer to the scholarly study of national *Geist,* the "spirit of the people"—what today we would call the study of national character.[8] Consistent with Herder's emphasis on the fusion of language, custom, and mentality in a *Volk,* von Humboldt argued that language and thought are intimately related, implying that modes of thought will differ fundamentally when encountered in each distinctive cultural group—a position that later gained fame as the Sapir-Whorf hypothesis.

## Proposals for Reconciling Science and History

By the middle of the nineteenth century one begins to see a number of efforts to reconcile the conflicting claims of natural science and human science. Owing to the increasing prestige of the natural sciences, the proposed reconciliations were likely to be biased toward suggestions for how scientific status could be extended to the study of the processes and products of mental life. However, the importance of historical studies for understanding the contemporary mind also gained wide acceptance. As a result, in the decades prior to the establishment of psychology as a distinct discipline one begins to encounter suggestions for a bifurcated psychology which incorporates both world views within a single discipline.

*Mill's version of a dual psychology.* In *A System of Logic* (1843) J. S. Mill argued that—contrary to received opinion—thoughts, feelings and actions could indeed be the subject of scientific study.[9] Mill likened the laws of psychology to the laws of "Tidology," the study of tides. In the case of tides, general laws are known concerning gravity and the action of the sun and moon, from which the local tides in any given locale may be deduced. But the specific laws so derived will be only approximate, since local factors such as wind and the configuration of the ocean bottom will determine the precise outcome in individual cases.

In psychology the laws in question concern the ways in which one mental state follows another. Mill believed that the laws of association (for example, when two ideas have occurred frequently together one will evoke the other in the future; or, the greater the intensity of two co-occurring ideas, the more likely they are to evoke each other) represent elementary psychological laws analogous to the laws of gravity and the attraction of bodies in physics. These laws, he claimed, "have been ascertained by the ordinary methods of experimental inquiry; nor could they have been ascertained in any other matter" (1843/1948, p. 173).

Trouble sets in, however, when we try to move from the demonstration of presumably universal elementary laws of mind to the prediction of actual behavior in particular circumstances. Two difficulties are especially important. First, while complex ideas may be generated by simple laws, in the act of combining, the whole is not equivalent to the sum of its parts. Mill referred to the combination of associations as "mental chemistry." Second, the outcome obtained from the combination of elementary laws is not universal and timeless. Rather, the actual combinations of elementary laws depend upon the local conditions of their combining, because "the actions of individuals could not be predicted with scientific accuracy, were it only because we cannot foresee the whole of the circumstances in which those individuals will be placed" (p. 170).

Mill referred to the emergent product of elementary thoughts combined with local, individual circumstances as *character.* The study of character, he wrote, should be "the principal object of scientific inquiry into human nature." Neither deduction nor experimentation ("the only two modes in which laws of nature can be ascertained") can be applied to the study of character. Deduction fails because character is an emergent phenomenon, not reducible to its antecedents. Experimentation is both impossible and inadequate. It is impossible because "no one but an Oriental despot" would have the power to gain total control over a person's experiences from birth. It is inadequate because even if total control were attempted, it would be insufficient to prevent undetected experiences from sneaking in and generating emergent combinations that would forever pollute later analyses.

Mill's solution was to create a dual science: "we employ the name Psychology for the science of the elementary laws of mind, Ethology [from the Greek *ethos*, "character"] will serve for the ulterior science which determines the kind of character produced in conformity to those general laws" (pp. 176–177).

This dual science required a dual methodology. Psychology would use experimentation and deduction to yield elementary mental laws. Ethology, the study of character, would be based on "approximate generalizations" from the elements to the whole. Mill adds that there is a close link between ethology and education; even in the absence of precise causal knowledge, it should be possible, he suggests, to shape the circumstances in which individuals or nations develop "in a manner much more favorable to the ends we desire than the shape which they would of themselves assume" (p. 177). Hence the domain of education, whether of individuals or nations, could provide a testing ground for what he calls "the exact science of human nature."

*The Völkerpsychologie movement.* Mill's ideas, along with those of von Humboldt, were seized upon by Moritz Lazarus and Heymann Steinthal, two German scholars. In 1860 Lazarus and Steinthal began to publish the *Zeitschrift für Völkerpsychologie und Sprachwissenschaft* (Journal of Cultural Psychology and Philology), which presented itself as a forum for reconciling the natural and cultural/historical sciences (Jahoda, 1992; Krewer and Jahoda, 1990; Whitman, 1984). They were strongly influenced by von Humboldt and explicitly noted the similarity between their version of Völkerpsychologie and Mill's concept of Ethology. The pages of the *Zeitschrift* contained articles by leading historical, philological, and anthropological scholars of the day.[10] These contributions provided analyses of language ("Exclamation, question and negation in the Semitic languages"), myth ("On the relation between myth and religion"), and other cultural phenomena (arithmetic systems, proverbs, calendrical devices, folk medicine, and so on). All were intended to contribute to explaining differences in "Volksgeist" in a manner that was simultaneously scientific and historical.

Lazarus and Steinthal's effort to reconcile the schism between the natural and cultural sciences was heavily criticized because they ignored the idea of mental chemistry and began to claim that it was possible to apply data obtained from the study of individual minds to the formulation of strict explanatory laws of culture and historical phenomena, precisely the move that Mill had shown to be flawed.

*Descriptive psychology.* Wilhelm Dilthey, whose work continues to influence a vast range of contemporary scholarship in what can be broadly characterized as cultural studies, sought to reconcile the natural and cultural sciences. Psychology, he believed, should serve as the foundational science for all of the human sciences (philosophy, linguistics, history, law, art, literature, and so on). Without such a foundational science, he claimed, the human sciences could not be a true system (1923/1988).

Early in his career, Dilthey considered the possibility that experimental psychology might provide such a foundation science. However, he gradually came to reject this possibility because he felt that in attempting to satisfy the requirements of the *Naturwissenschaften* for formulating cause-effect laws between mental elements, psychologists had stripped mental processes of the real-life relationships between people that gave meaning to their elements. He did not mince words in his attack on the academic psychology of the late nineteenth century: "Contemporary psychology is an expanded doctrine of sensation and association. The fundamental power of mental life falls outside the scope of psychology. Psychology has become only a doctrine of the forms of psychic processes; thus it grasps only a part of that which we actually experience as mental life" (quoted in Ermath, 1978, p. 148).

Dilthey proposed a different approach to the study of psychology, one which harks back to Vico's prescriptions for the study of human nature as an historically contingent phenomenon. Dilthey believed that since it encompasses only a part of mental life, explanatory psychology must be subordinated to an historical-social approach that studies individuals in relation to their cultural systems and communities (Dilthey, 1923/1988). He called this approach *descriptive psychology.* It was to be based on an analysis of real-life mental processes in real-life situations, including both the reciprocal processes between people and individuals' thoughts. As a method for carrying out this kind of analysis, Dilthey suggested the close study of the writings of such "life-philosophers" as Augustine, Montaigne, and Pascal, because they contained a deep understanding of full experiential reality.

*Wundt's compromise.* The system of psychology proposed by Wundt adopted Mill's strategy: recognize that two different orders of reality are involved, and create two psychologies, one appropriate to each. On the one hand there is "physiological psychology," the experimental study of immediate experience. The goal of this half of the discipline was to explicate the laws by which elementary sensations arise in consciousness and the universal laws by which the elements of consciousness combine. The label "physiological" for this half of Wundt's enterprise is somewhat misleading, because experiments carried out in its name rarely involved physiological measurement. Rather, it was believed that the verbal reports of subjects who were carefully trained in methods of self-observation (introspection) would yield results that could eventually be traced to physiological processes. Experiments conducted with this goal in mind concentrated on *elementary* psychological functions, meaning the qualities of sensory experience and the components of simple reactions.

Wundt also initiated a mammoth investigation of *higher* psychological functions, those resulting from the fusing and concatenation of elementary functions. Higher functions include processes such as deliberate remembering, reasoning, and language. Wundt, following von Humboldt, called this second branch of psychology *Völkerpsychologie*. He argued that Völkerpsychologie could not be studied using laboratory methods of trained introspection that focus on the contents of consciousness because the higher psychological functions extend beyond individual human consciousness. So, for example, one could not understand the psychology of language use because "A language can never be created by an individual. True, individuals have invented Esperanto and other artificial languages. Unless, however, language had already existed, these inventions would have been impossible. Moreover, none of these has been able to maintain itself, and most of them owe their existence solely to elements borrowed from natural languages" (Wundt, 1921, p. 3).

According to this view, higher psychological functions had to be studied by the methods of the descriptive sciences, such as ethnography, folklore, and linguistics. Wundt's volumes on this topic are full of data derived from a broad range of historical and anthropological accounts about the languages and customs of the world's cultures (Jahoda, 1992; Wundt, 1921). This branch of psychology, he wrote, was supposed to combine "into a unified whole the various results concerning the mental development of many as severally viewed by language, religion, and custom" (ibid., p. 2).

Wundt believed that the two enterprises, physiological psychology and Völkerpsychologie, must supplement each other: only through a synthesis of their respective insights could a full psychology be achieved. To those who would claim that Völkerpsychologie could be entirely subsumed under experimental psychology Wundt replied: "Its problem relates to those mental products which are created by a community of human life and are, therefore, inexplicable in terms merely of individual consciousness, since they presuppose the reciprocal action of many . . . Individual consciousness is wholly incapable of giving us a history of the development of human thought, for it is conditioned by an earlier history concerning which it cannot of itself give us any knowledge" (p. 3).

In this connection, Wundt made an additional methodological claim which is central to the history and current practice of the study of cultural psychology: Völkerpsychologie is, in an important sense of the word, genetic psychology; that is, the study of higher psychological functions requires the use of a developmental-historical methodology. For this reason he believed that Völkerpsychologie must involve the methods of ethnology, conceived of as "the science of the origins of peoples."

Wundt himself did not study ontogeny (the genesis of an individual life), sticking instead to the study of cultural history, so he had little to say about how these two levels of genetic analysis are related. But he believed the results of such historical research would yield evidence about "the various stages of mental development still exhibited by mankind" (p. 4). In reaching such conclusions, Wundt was inheriting the German tradition of cultural-historical philosophy. Völkerpsychologie, he declared, would "reveal well-defined primitive conditions, with transitions leading through an almost continuous series of intermediate steps to the more developed and higher civilizations" (p. 4).

Wundt adopted a cultural, not racial, theory of the perceived inequalities in mental products separating primitive and civilized peoples. He was convinced *both* of the superiority of European culture *and* that the intellectual endowment of primitive peoples is equal to that of Europeans. Like Spencer, Wundt believed that it is not intellectual endowment that differentiates primitive and civilized people, but the range of world experiences: "Primitive man merely exercises his ability in a more restricted field" (p. 13). This narrow range of experiences coincided in Wundt's mind with the image of the primitive person living in the tropics where there is food and fun always at hand, so that the native peoples were not motivated to move outside of "a state of nature."

## Whither Culture?

As many commentators have noted (for example Danziger, 1990; Farr, 1983; Van Hoorn and Verhave, 1980) no sooner had Wundt been anointed as the founder of scientific (experimental) psychology than psychologists began rejecting his approach and proposing alternatives.

The only part of Wundt's scientific system to win broad acceptance was his advocacy of the experimental method as the criterion of disciplinary legitimacy. Unfortunately for Wundt, his successors used the scientific method against him. Some, such as adherents of the Würzburg school, claimed to have discovered laws of mind, using Wundt's methods, that contradicted his claims about the relationship between elementary and higher psychological functions. Gestalt psychologists reported experimental evidence undermining Wundt's belief that lower psychological functions were built out of sensory elements. They argued against the distinction between elementary and higher psychological functions and for the idea that perception is inherently structured by principles of form. Others rejected Wundt's approach on the grounds that his evidence, insofar as it was dependent on introspective methods, was unscientific and unreplicable.[11] At the hands of behaviorists, Wundt's claims about features of mind were transformed into claims about the laws by which elements of behavior combine according to reflex principles.

Contrary to Wundt's explicit warnings, the experimental method, supplemented by psychometric tests and standardized questionnaires, were used to study all psychological functions. A unified science needs a unified methodology, and the natural sciences provided the model.

In their discussion of the fate of Wundt's ideas about two psychologies, Emily Cahan and Sheldon White (1992) summarize some of the main characteristics of the unified methodology that psychology adopted in place of Wundt's dual psychology:

1. Methodological behaviorism—use of laboratory studies of perceptual and learning mechanisms as the basis for a unified science of psychology.
2. Reliance on experimental procedures that take "collective subjects," or groups of people, as the basis for inferences about individual psychological processes.
3. The use of inferential statistics applied to group data, as, for example, in correlational studies based on psychometric tests or analysis of variance procedures applied to classical treatment-control experiments.

As Cahan and White remark: "Behavior theory, experimental psychology, and inferential statistics were brought together to form a new image of psychology . . . a framework for psychology based on analysis of the 'more mature' physical sciences" (p. 8).

When focusing specifically on the question of how general psychology incorporates culture into its laws, other important characteristics of the dominant psychology can be seen to accompany its interpretation of correct scientific methods:

4. The functional relations ("psychological laws") produced by this research underpin human behavior in general, not just in the peculiar laboratory circumstances or the specific historical period and culture in which the data were collected.
5. The major tools for laying bare the universal mechanisms of mind are the psychologist's experimental procedures, which, in effect, operate by analogy with the use of vacuum tubes in physics. In the real world, leaves and pellets of the same weight drop at different speeds and follow different pathways, but in a vacuum tube, where the "noisy" elements have been removed, the underlying gravitational laws will be shown to be operative.
6. Universality of the laws obtained by general psychology is generally claimed not just across contexts but across species as well. This kind of claim rested on faith in Darwin's assertion

that the difference between *Homo sapiens* and our near phylogenetic neighbors is "one of degree, not of kind."[12]

The fact that general psychology took as its task the discovery of
universal features of human psychological makeup does not mean it
ignored culture. However, as one can establish by examining any
current introductory textbook in the field, culture is accorded a distinctly minor role, and when it does appear, it refers to cultural difference.

Discussing the role of culture in general psychology, Richard
Shweder argues that even when they seem to attribute a great deal of
influence to culture, psychologists assume that this works through
universal mechanisms which are the real object of the psychologist's
interests: "The main force in general psychology is the idea of a central processing device. The processor, it is imagined, stands over and
above, or transcends, all the stuff upon which it operates. It engages
all the stuff of culture, context, task and stimulus materials as its
content" (1991, p. 80).

By and large, early attempts to take account of culture within the
dominant paradigm of general psychology did not generate research
explicitly designed to test propositions about cultural influences.
When culture did become the topic of research, it was in the form of
*cross*-cultural research. Most of this work proceeded within the
framework of methodological behaviorism, where culture is accorded
the status of an independent variable. Different cultural circumstances provide different stimuli to their members, who, in consequence, learn different kinds of responses. The sum total of that
learned behavior in a particular time and place serves as the working
definition of culture.

## The Fate of the Second Psychology

Although Wundt's ideas about Völkerpsychologie were not generally
taken up by methodological behaviorism, they were not entirely ban-
ished from the stage (Cahan and White, 1992; Jahoda, 1992; Judd,
1926; Farr, 1983). In various ways and in various places, objections
were raised against one or another aspect of the dominant paradigm
of general psychology.

Early in this century, Hugo Münsterberg (a Harvard psychologist who came from Germany) attempted to convince Americans to retain Wundt's distinction between physiological psychology and Völkerpsychologie. Münsterberg (1914) referred to the experimental half of Wundt's program as a *causal* psychology that seeks to explain the content of mental states, which he contrasted with *purposive* psychology, an interpretive science concerned with meaning and the self.

Following the path of causal psychology, he wrote, "We shall resolve the personality into the elementary bits of psychical atoms and shall bring every will act into a closed system of causes and effects. But in the purposive part we shall show with the same consistency the true inner unity of the self and the ultimate freedom of the responsible personality. *Those two accounts do not exclude each other;* they supplement each other, they support each other, they demand each other" (p. 17). At the same time, he emphasized that because each aspect of psychology has its own special methods, concepts, and principles, it is "extremely important to keep them cleanly separated and to recognize distinctly the principles which control them" (pp. 16–17). Münsterberg believed the two kinds of psychology could be united only in those cases when the psychologist seeks to apply facts about mental life in the service of human purposes, that is, in applied psychology.

Wundt, of course, had not made a link between Völkerpsychologie and the applications of psychological knowledge. But Münsterberg made a sage point. Purposeful human activity has all of the characteristics that Wundt identified as involving higher psychological functions. It is mediated by human language and draws on the beliefs and customs of the group. An involvement in practice meant, de facto, an interest in psychological processes that depended upon time and place. It seems natural, therefore, as Cahan and White note, that many of those who objected to general psychology's claims about universal principles of behavior believed that psychological analysis should begin with an analysis of people's everyday activities, rather than with abstract principles embodied in experimental procedures.

It is but a short step from starting psychological analysis with people's engagement in purposeful activity to the idea that psychological processes do not stand apart from activity but, rather, are constituted by the activities of which they are a part. In terms of the Gestalt formula, the structure of the whole determines the operation of its parts.

Another characteristic shared by many of those who identified with a second psychology was rejection of a strong position with respect to continuity of species. Without questioning Darwin's general theory of descent, many scholars believed that *Homo sapiens* is different from other species in both degree and kind: that the new level of evolutionary organization which results in our species also results in new principles of psychological functioning.

The criteria for this qualitative change varied from one writer to another, but they generally focused on human language and the ability to make tools, which together constituted a specific form of life. The reproduction of this way of life, it was assumed, is both the producer and product of history. Insofar as thinking is also involved in the production and reproduction of culture, human thinking and human culture must be assumed to be intrinsically intertwined.

Other characteristics of the second psychology could be mentioned, but we will have ample opportunity to consider them later. The major point I wish to make at this juncture is that Wundt's insistence on the importance of including the cultural products of prior human activity in psychology did not entirely disappear from American psychology.

One sees outcroppings of the second psychology in many national traditions. In Germany, where cultural-historical theory was perhaps strongest, many scholars sought to reformulate Wundt's ideas about Völkerpsychologie in terms of their own theoretical paradigms. Although the Gestalt psychologists first came to prominence for their work on perception, they also engaged in comparative research on adults in small groups of different kinds. They also studied language, problem solving, and other "higher psychological functions" among children, primitive peoples, people with brain damage, and chimpanzees. Their theorizing in these domains had a decidedly developmental-historical cast to it.

In France, Emile Durkheim and his student Lucien Levy-Bruhl argued the primacy of social life in creating specifically human forms of consciousness; their focus was primarily on mediation through shared cultural symbols (Durkheim, 1912). Jean Piaget (1928), early in his career, speculated on ways in which the cultural organization of intergenerational relations in primitive cultures might impede development of autonomous moral thinking.

In the United States a great many of the leading psychologists of the turn of the century had received their doctoral training in Germany. Consequently, it is only natural that some developed sympathy for the historical orientation of Völkerpsychologie and were critical of the wholesale application of methodological behaviorism to theories of mind.

For example, Charles Judd (1926), who is best known as an educational psychologist, wrote a book on social psychology. He explicitly followed Wundt in arguing that language, tools, number systems, the alphabet, art, and so on are forms of "accumulated social capital" that developed over the millennia. Individuals have to adapt to such social institutions; individual minds are actually formed in the process of socialization. Consequently, it would be an egregious error to think it possible to develop a social psychology based on properties of the individual mind. Rather, social psychology (Judd's translation of the term Völkerpsychologie) must be a totally independent science which uses methods from anthropology, sociology, and linguistics.

ⓖ This was also the period when American pragmatism flowered, a philosophy which followed Hegel in locating the source of knowledge within the everyday, culturally organized, historically evolving activities of the social group (Mead, 1935; Dewey, 1938). This version of a second psychology will become an important part of my narrative in later chapters.

It was characteristic of various branches of this second psychology to be rather fragmented in comparison with the dominant paradigm; they found it easier to say what they did not like in the old paradigm than to agree on methodological and theoretical principles of a systematic alternative. They were sufficiently divided among themselves that there was a continuing dialogue about "the crisis in psychology" owing to its fragmented nature and the inability of different schools to reconcile their ideas with each other. They were also politically weak because the topics on which they focused—development, education, social life, psychopathology—were considered soft and un-scientific.

The one country in which a version of the second psychology came to prominence as a successor to Wundt's dual psychology was the Soviet Union. The paradigm worked out by Lev Vygotsky, Alexander Luria, and Alexei Leontiev was not intended as either a special branch of or a particular approach to psychology. It was conceived of as a resolution of "the crisis in psychology," a comprehensive psycholog-ical framework within which the various traditional sub-areas of psy-chology represented a principled division of labor, rather than com-peting approaches to the same object of study.

Their formulation of a cultural historical theory and its associated methodology was by no means an independent invention, carried out in splendid isolation. Vygotsky and his colleagues read widely in the psychology of their day, translating and writing prefaces to the works of Dewey, James, Janet, Piaget, Freud, Levy-Bruhl, Durkheim, the Gestalt psychologists, and many more. At the same time, they accom-plished (at least temporarily) what others did not: they institution-alized a cultural psychology that could accommodate both sides of Wundt's two psychologies. They adopted a methodology that could guide theory in various domains of social practice in a manner that won social approval (Van der Veer and Valsiner, 1991).

## A Look Ahead

My own relationship to these competing paradigms for understand-ing the relationship of culture to mind is a complicated one. I began my career as an advocate of that part of general psychology which seeks to use experiments as sources of quantifiable data describable in the language of mathematics. When I first became involved in the study of culture in mind, the theories and methods of general psy-chology were my basic tools. As a consequence of my involvement in cross-cultural research, I came gradually to question key assump-tions on which my methods were based. My dissatisfaction motivated attempts to improve on those methods. The search for improvement led me to borrow from the repertoire of other disciplines. Eventually I sought a theoretical framework that would allow me to make better sense of the data I collected. That framework draws heavily on the ideas of the Russian cultural-historical school of psychology, early-twentieth-century American pragmatism, and a hybrid of ideas borrowed from other disciplines.

Later I will present my version of a cultural-historical theory of mind. In doing so, it would be nice if I could simply "cut to the chase" and summarize current wisdom, the "correct theory." But what is "really there" and how we come to know it (ontology and epistemology) constitute two sides of a single process of knowing, and I will have to deal with the two of them together.

My narrative will focus on questions about culture and human development. This topical focus is a natural one because, as we have seen, questions about culture and mind were intricately bound up with arguments about historical change and development in the nineteenth century. As we shall see, these issues have remained intertwined in the succeeding century.

Within the general domain of culture and development, I will pay particular attention to the developmental significance of education, particularly formal schooling as an important sociocultural institution. As most of my research has been carried out in this domain, I can draw on personal experience to complement what can be learned from the research of others.

# 2 ⑥

# Cross-Cultural Investigations

VARIOUS researchers have sought to implement a scientific approach to the study of culture in mind based upon cross-cultural comparisons. I shall discuss three such research programs; each sheds light on the impulse to study culture in mind through cross-cultural studies, and each illustrates the difficulties that this strategy entails. The first focuses on sensation and perception, which correspond to elementary psychological functions in Wundt's approach. These are the functions considered universal, potentially reducible to their physiological substrata, and hence suitable for experimental study. The second is about intelligence, which is generally believed to involve "higher" psychological functions of a kind that Wundt denied could be studied experimentally, even in his own culture. The third focuses on memory, which is widely believed to involve both higher and lower psychological functions.

In the early years of this century popular opinion accepted as fact the existence of cultural differences at all three levels of psychological function. But beliefs differed concerning which psychological functions were most highly developed in which societies. Perceptual capacities and memory were thought to predominate among primitive peoples, while intelligence, the essence of higher psychological functioning, was thought to be greater among peoples of advanced technological societies, namely those in Europe and the United States.

Research on these topics began not long after psychology established itself as a scientific discipline, so it is possible to compare the findings and conclusions produced at two different stages in the development of psychological theory and methodology in the discipline. By comparing early and later efforts, we should be able to shed some light on the degree to which general psychology's lack of interest in cross-cultural research is the result of shortcomings of early research or of more enduring problems with this strategy for studying culture in mind.

The internal logic of the three research programs, narrowly speaking, is important for our understanding of their usefulness as examples of how general psychology sought to understand the role of culture in mind. But it is also important to consider, at least schematically, the sociocultural circumstances that shaped the world view of the researchers themselves. As we will see, the scientific judgments of the investigators bear the imprint of the dominant beliefs in their societies at the times in which they lived.

## Sociohistorical Context

As Emily Cahan and Sheldon White point out, the rise of psychology as a discipline was associated with the rise of research universities and a division of labor among the former humane sciences. In a thirty-year period one witnesses the emergence of psychology, sociology, anthropology, economics, political science, and other disciplines grouped around the idea of a *behavioral* science.[1] Outside of academia it was a time of growth of large bureaucratic and commercial structures and demands for people who could make those new structures run efficiently; schools, factories, and the armed forces all sought help in dealing with the social and economic problems associated with mass-mediated, industrial societies. On the international scene it was a time when European presence and influence on the continents of Asia, Africa, and South America was at its zenith. In this respect, despite the jolt dealt to romantic ideas about human progress by World War I, the early generations of twentieth-century psychologists were still steeped in the dominant world view of the late nineteenth century. Neither as scientists nor as citizens had they solved the fundamental questions of their grandparents' generation.

This was the period when American life underwent an intensification of the fundamental shift from a rural, mostly agricultural, society to one in which people lived in crowded cities, where electricity and gasoline were fueling vast changes in everyday life experiences. It was a period when African Americans were legally segregated and large influxes of central and southern Europeans were flooding the streets of America's large cities. It was a time of vast enthusiasm for the ability of science to solve human problems.

Scientifically, psychology may have put issues of social relations and social context into neat analytic categories, but in everyday beliefs about such matters as culture, race, evolution, and historical change, the scientists no less than ordinary citizens found it impossible to put their leading values "out of mind." As we shall see, in this respect, psychology has not changed much in the course of this century.

## Perceptual Processes and Culture

The first technically sophisticated experimental studies of cultural variations in perceptual processes were carried at the turn of the century, when scientific psychology was still in its infancy (Haddon, 1901). Half a century later, one aspect of this early work became the subject of a meticulous series of studies designed to clarify its cultural underpinnings (Segall, Campbell, and Herskovitz, 1966).

In 1895 a well-equipped expedition from Cambridge University, headed by A. C. Haddon, went to the southeastern coast of what was then British New Guinea and the islands of the Torres Straits. Haddon (subsequently chair of the newly founded department of anthropology at Cambridge) had previously studied marine zoology in the region. When he organized an ethnographic investigation, he followed the natural scientific tradition, declaring that "no investigation of a people was complete that did not embrace a study of their psychology" (1901, p. v).

The expedition's expert on experimental psychological methods was W. H. R. Rivers, who went on to a distinguished career in anthropology (Slobodin, 1978). Trained in medicine, Rivers had become interested in experimental psychology and taught it at University College, London, before moving to Cambridge in 1897. He enlisted two students, C. S. Myers and William McDougall (both of whom later became prominent psychologists), to assist in the research. True to Wundt's tradition of laboratory research, Rivers and his colleagues concentrated on *sensory* capacities (that is, elementary psychological functions). For this purpose they took with them an impressive array of apparatuses and techniques designed to be used to study visual, tactile, and olfactory sensations following accepted laboratory methods.

A central focus of their work was to test the validity of the claim, made by Europeans who had traveled to "uncivilized parts of the world," that "savage and semi-civilized races [manifest] a higher degree of acuteness of sense than is found among Europeans" (Rivers, 1901, p. 12). As examples of primitive prowess, Rivers quotes the following reports: "The men of San Christoval in the Solomon Islands had 'eyes like lynxes, and could discover from a great distance, though the day was anything but clear, the pigeons which were in the trees hidden by the leaves . . . the natives of New Ireland . . . could discover land which we were unable to make out with good glasses, and they would find out small boats 6 or 7 miles off in bad weather which we were unable to do with binoculars or telescopes' " (p. 13).

In the 1880s a controversy over the interpretation of such reports had appeared in the scientific journal *Nature*. Some believed that "savages" possessed greater visual acuity than "civilized man." Others believed the reported differences arose because savage peoples paid great attention to the minutiae of their environments and hence were highly practiced in making the relevant discriminations.

The researchers tested these alternative views by conducting studies of sensory acuity for each of the basic senses. Rivers himself studied visual acuity, color vision, and visual spatial perception (including susceptibility to visual illusions); Myers studied auditory acuity, smell, and taste; while McDougall studied tactile sensitivity, weight discrimination, and the size-weight illusion.

One of Rivers's most widely cited results was obtained from a test of visual acuity similar to the one that is administered to driver's license applicants. Subjects were shown a chart with the single letter *E* arrayed on it in descending sizes. On each line of the chart, the *E*'s were placed in different orientations. The subjects were given a card with an *E* on it and asked to hold their card so that their *E* matched the spatial orientation of the one pointed to by the experimenter. These simplifications allowed the procedure to be used with non-literate subjects. From the evidence Rivers provides, people seemed to understand what was intended; their accuracy decreased in a regular way as the target stimuli became smaller and smaller or as their distance from the target increased.

Rivers collected data from 170 Torres Straits natives, who were tested in the open air to ensure adequate lighting. The results were expressed as a ratio of the distance at which the stimulus can be identified to its size: the greater the ratio, the greater the visual acuity. Overall, he obtained a "visual acuity score" of 2.1:1.

In order to determine whether this performance was extraordinary, Rivers needed data for comparison. This requirement posed some difficulties, for as he noted, "the true European normal, the average vision of Europeans with normal eyes, has not yet been satisfactorily determined" (p. 14). Nor was there a single accepted technique for measuring visual acuity.

At this point, many of the difficulties of cross-cultural experimentation reveal themselves. It would not be appropriate to use data collected by some other technique, so equivalent application of the *E*-technique was sought. This equivalence could not be restricted to the actual materials used; it had to be extended to the procedures and conditions of testing as well. His selection of comparison data and the criteria he focused on in his choice show the difficulties involved.

The key data upon which he based his comparisons were collected in Helgoland, an island off the German coast. These data were considered especially useful because the sample consisted of 100 men from a wide age span and hence assumed to be representative of the community. These men engaged in fishing for a living, as did the people of the Torres Straits, and were not highly educated, further enhancing their comparative value. The average acuity for this group was 1.77:1.

Although Rivers believed these results to be reliable, the magnitude of the differences between the two test groups did not impress him. After going over these data and results from alternative techniques for measuring visual acuity he declared: "The general conclusion which may be drawn . . . is that the visual acuity of savage and half-civilized people, though superior to that of the normal European, is not so in any marked degree . . . The races which have so far been examined do not exhibit that degree of superiority over the Europeans in visual acuity proper which the accounts of travelers might have led one to expect" (1901, p. 42).

The results from studies of the other senses by and large sustained this verdict, although not always. Rivers reports that in addition to an impoverished color vocabulary, his subjects displayed somewhat diminished sensitivity to the color blue, and were less susceptible than European subjects to certain visual illusions. In his studies of the ability to distinguish small distances between two points on the skin touched simultaneously, McDougall found that the Torres Straits natives could detect a gap between two points roughly half the size of that reported for three different European samples. He also found that the Torres Straits natives had a lower threshold for detecting the difference between two weights. Myers, however, found that auditory sensitivity was somewhat greater for European samples while there was no apparent difference in sensitivity to odors.

Various questions could be, and were, raised about this research. E. B. Titchener, a major American champion of Wundtian experimental methodology, accepted as legitimate the goal, as he put it, of seeking "to obtain psychological data which shall enable [the field worker] to rank a primitive race in relation to the various strata of his own civilized community" (1916, p. 235). He was also sympathetic to the difficulties of conducting experiments in the field and went out of his way to commend the Torres Straits researchers for their labor and ingenuity. Nonetheless, his judgment is severe: "the tests were inadequate to their purpose." Titchener's criticisms apply to many, if not all, later experimental cross-cultural comparisons as well.

One problem with such studies is obvious, but often overlooked. It is usually impossible to replicate an experiment conducted in primitive societies. The costs of getting to the field are considerable, and the conditions of the people involved are constantly changing.[2] To reduce the severity of this problem, Titchener made what he called "parallel and illustrative" experiments to test rival hypotheses. This expedient rests on shaky logical grounds. As Titchener noted, replication in psychological laboratories means repeating experiments with subjects who have been trained in similar ways using similar methods and instruments. Instead, he fell back on the *assumption* of psychic unity to give plausibility to his results. He tells us, for example, that the descriptions of the Torres Straits group

> remind us, time and again, that human nature is much the same the world over. The old lady on Murray Island who, "by associations of some kind," gave her own and her friends' names when she was asked to name a set of colored papers, have we not met her—with all respect be it spoken—in our summer session? The man who was asked to arrange colors in the order of his liking, and who handed them back in almost exactly the order in which they had been presented by the experimenter in an earlier test, is a fairly familiar figure in our laboratories. If, then, I presently compare the observations of my colleagues with those of a Papuan chief, I am not necessarily falling into absurdity. (1916, p. 206)

Titchener provided a meticulous criticism of two of the experiments reported by the Torres Straits group: McDougall's study of tactile discrimination and Rivers's work on color perception. Both are of special interest because they appear to reveal group differences in basic psychological processes where Wundtian theory (and Rivers' own interpretation of visual sensitivity differences) would lead one to expect pan-human universals.

The McDougall experiment demonstrating apparently greater two-point touch sensitivity among the Torres Straits natives would appear to be on relatively safe ground, since his conclusions are based on a comparison of data he himself collected in both the Torres Straits and in England. But that too was vulnerable to reinterpretation.

Titchener began by quoting McDougall to the effect that "the procedure should be, as far as practicable, without knowledge on the part of the subject" and then declared that in reality the procedure was subject to all sorts of suggestion effects which would have influenced how the task was interpreted. Second, he noted that while the average score for English subjects was higher (indicating less sensi-tivity) the variation of the scores within each of the two groups was very large, suggesting that different subjects may have been engaging in different tasks. Then he zeroed in on the instructions (I quote because in the interpretation of experimental results, such details are often crucial, precisely Titchener's point): "The limen [difference threshold] sought by McDougall was, it will be remembered, 'not that distance at which two points can be distinctly felt, but . . . that dis-tance at which they yield a sensation perceptibly different from that yielded by a single point' " (pp. 207–208).

From this seemingly insignificant point, Titchener went on to make a very plausible case that the cultural differences observed by McDougall were differences in the way subjects in the two cultures were inclined to interpret the instructions and subsequently, how they interpreted the stimuli with which they were presented. First, he concluded from research in his laboratory that between the sen-sation of one point and that of two points there are intermediate sensations. Some subjects report feeling a "dumbbell" (two points connected by a line), and others feel a "line." These sensations are discriminably different from one point, but they are not two distinct sensations. Here, Titchener wrote, was the explanation for the wide range of results in McDougall's study: some of his observers judged "two" as soon as the impression of the points differed in the slightest degree from "one"; others judged "two" only when the points were on the brink of falling apart or had actually done so.

He then conducted what he called "a venturesome experiment" to determine whether McDougall's comparative results were "null and void." He replicated McDougall's experiment on himself using a sim-ilar instrument, and instead of judging when he distinctly sensed two impressions, he judged when he was feeling more than one distinct point (but not necessarily two distinct points). Under these condi-tions, his performance was almost perfect. Consequently, he argued that McDougall's English subjects did not have less delicate sense of touch; rather they interpreted the task differently, and their interpre-tation worked to increase estimates of their sensory thresholds.

In making this argument, Titchener did not claim to have proven that the sensory thresholds are the same for the two groups, but simply that McDougall had not proven they are different. As an alternative to the real state of affairs, he adopted the argument from experience: "[The English subjects were] less interested in the minutiae of stimuli than the savages; their power of sensory interpretation was less; they paid, we may suppose, more attention to the particular instrument used, and to its probable effect on the skin. They looked for a sensibly dual impression" (p. 211). Titchener attached special importance to McDougall's report that the more educated Englishmen in his experiment had the highest thresholds. "The farther we go from the savage's sensory interest," he wrote, "the larger do our limens become!" (ibid.).

He went on to provide further criticisms of this experiment and then an equally detailed refutation of Rivers's conclusions concerning the relatively weak perception of blue among Torres Straits natives. In the latter case he noted the influence of illumination on color perception and replicated some of Rivers's more unusual procedures, again producing results that undermine the conclusion of cultural variation in elementary psychological processes.

### The Torres Straits Project: An Evaluation

A number of points could be made about the lessons of the Torres Straits expedition and Titchener's critique of its conclusions. At a general level, almost a century of subsequent research has generally sustained the conclusion that cultural differences in the sensory acuity are either minimal or absent; cultural differences are most likely to appear when complex materials, particularly pictorial materials, are the stimuli (for reviews see Berry, Poortinga, Segall, and Dasen, 1992; or Segall, Dasen, Berry, and Poortinga, 1990). This is just the trend one would expect on the assumption that elementary psychological processes are not influenced by cultural variations, while processes that depend upon the use of cultural conventions (such as linear perspective in two-dimensional drawings) are.

Nonetheless, the research by the Torres Straits group and Titchener indicated that even in the study of so-called elementary (and presumably universal) psychological processes it is very difficult to get around the fact that culturally organized ways of interpreting the task influence performance. Titchener did not *remove* cultural influences through his modifications in procedures—he manipulated them and thereby demonstrated that they existed in the first place.[3]

An additional aspect of Rivers's report casts a slightly different light on the difficulty of maintaining a strict distinction between elementary and psychological functions. It also illustrates how widely held cultural beliefs rush in to fill the gap that arises when data do not yield to unambiguous conclusions on scientific grounds.

Having demonstrated to his satisfaction that residents of the Torres Straits did not have special powers of visual acuity as measured by carefully controlled tests, Rivers nonetheless had to acknowledge that they sometimes astounded him by their visual sensitivity. On one such occasion he was sailing from one island to another when the three men he was with suddenly exclaimed that a boat was in the harbor on the other side of the island toward which they were sailing. Rivers had already measured their visual acuity, which was good but not extraordinary. Yet he reckoned that they had been able to see the *tops* of the ship's masts that were visible over the low-lying island well before he could. This kind of evidence (bolstered by similar accounts from other scholars) is sufficient, Rivers wrote, "to illustrate the special nature of the visual powers of those who live in a state of nature" (p. 43). He continued: "so far as our data go it seems that the savage starts with visual acuity which is but slightly superior to that of the average normal-sighted European. By long-continued practice, however, in attending to minute details in surroundings with which he becomes extremely familiar, the savage is able to see and recognize distant objects in a way that appears almost miraculous" (1901, p. 43).

He went on to say that this ability is extremely context-specific, drawing on evidence that Australian trackers are inept outside of their own habitat. This line of reasoning, as we shall see, has a very modern ring. The idea as proposed by Rivers does not rest on experimental evidence, however, nor does it necessarily implicate cognitive functioning outside of the narrow skill involved: the experimental evidence showed, in fact, that natives who have acute visual skills may have dull auditory skills.

Another interesting way in which Rivers attempted to go beyond the limits imposed by the restriction of observations to elementary

psychological functions was to put forward what might be called a
*zero-sum* or *compensation* theory of culture and mind, a tradeoff between the degrees to which lower and higher functions could be
developed. He reasoned as follows:

> We know that the growth of intellect depends on material which
> is furnished by the senses, and it therefore at first sight may
> appear strange that elaboration of the sensory side of mental
> life should be a hindrance to intellectual development. But on
> further consideration I think there is nothing unnatural in such
> a fact. If too much energy is expended on the sensory founda-
> tions, it is natural that the intellectual superstructure should
> suffer. (pp. 44–45)

Rivers endorsed the view that "the predominant attention of the
savage to the concrete things around him may act as an obstacle to
higher mental development" (p. 45).

Whatever other objections I might want to raise against such an
idea, the most relevant for judging the adequacy of this way of combining theory and data is methodological. Rivers and his group nowhere conducted experimental research on higher psychological
functions. Since they had effectively overturned incorrect conclusions about the high sensory capacities of native peoples (with a
helping hand from Titchener), one might have thought they would
take a skeptical view about claims of low reasoning abilities from the
same kinds of sources. Unfortunately, they did not address the latter
claims, in part because no accepted techniques existed for doing so
and the accepted dogma of Wundtian-influenced experimental psychology said it couldn't be done, and in part because prior convictions
about "native mentality" made the work involved seem unnecessary.

Overall, the lessons of the Torres Straits expedition were ambiguous. On the one hand, the experimental method had demonstrated
its power to contribute usefully to a narrow range of scientific disputes about culture and cognition (albeit with residual doubts). On
the other hand, restricting oneself to experimental methods deemed
appropriate to elementary psychological functions left major issues
untouched and tempted even sophisticated researchers into spurious
lines of reasoning.

## Susceptibility to Visual Illusions: Modern Data

One of the lesser-known results of Rivers's studies concerned susceptibility to visual illusions. The same folklore that attributed great sensory acuity to peoples considered primitive generated the idea that such people would be easily fooled by illusions such as those shown in Figure 2.1.

Rivers found that peoples native to the Torres Straits and a rural area in India were actually *less* susceptible to the Müller-Lyer illusion than a European comparison group, but more susceptible to the horizontal-vertical illusion. Although his results burst the bubble of expectations based on European mental superiority, it was not clear what factors produced these cultural differences.

In the 1960s, Marshall Segall and his colleagues returned to some of the core issues investigated by Rivers. The modern group were a good deal more experienced in both experimental psychological re-

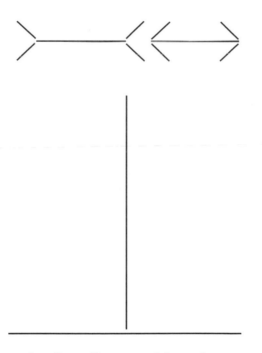

Figure 2.1.   Examples of two illusions widely used in cross-cultural research: (top) the Müller-Lyer illusion; (bottom) the horizontal-vertical illusion. In each case, line segments of equal length are seen as unequal because their contexts differ.

search methods and ethnographic fieldwork than their predecessors. They formulated their work as an attempt to resolve the influence of environmental circumstances on visual perception.[4] Their means was the study of visual illusions.

Their basic hypothesis was that different culturally organized environments foster different habits of visual interpretation that give rise to erroneous interpretations when subjects are presented with a stimulus unlike the ones they are used to encountering. For the Müller-Lyer illusion the researchers expected people living in "carpentered environments" to interpret the drawings in terms of three-dimensional objects more than people from less carpentered (rural) environments. They expected people who habitually saw long visual vistas to be more susceptible to the horizontal-vertical illusion.

Segall and colleagues undertook a variety of measures to increase the power of their data-gathering techniques. In place of a two-point contrast between a group of natives and a group of university students, their study included people from 14 non-European groups (13 African, 1 Filipino) and 3 groups of European origin (1 in South Africa, and 2 in the United States that differed markedly in social class and educational background). The number of people in a group varied from 30 to 344; altogether almost 1,900 people participated.

Concerned about failures to communicate adequately, the investigators began each session by asking people to compare several pairs of lines of very different lengths to ensure that they understood the instructions. They also colored the different segments differently and made sure the line segments did not touch to enhance communication. Once they were sure their subjects could understand the task and communicate their judgments, they presented the illusions and asked for judgments of line length.

As expected, the European samples were significantly more susceptible to the Müller-Lyer illusion than the generally rural, non-European samples. And, as expected, susceptibility to the horizontal-vertical illusion varied across groups in a different way. People from groups accustomed to seeing long vistas were more susceptible to this illusion than people who lived in rain forests or modern European cities. Consequently, the authors could conclude that they had shown that culture influences perception by shaping habits of perceptual inference that operate in ambiguous circumstances.

As Segall and colleagues (1990) comment, the fact that the outcomes generally fit the theory did not mean they ruled out other interpretations. Robert Pollack (1970; Pollack and Silvar, 1967), who had shown that susceptibility to illusions declined when pigmentation of the retina declined, suggested that it was really race, not the degree of "carpenteredness" of the cultural environment, that caused group differences in susceptibility to illusions. His speculation seemed to be confirmed when Berry (1971) reported that when groups of people who differed along both dimensions were tested, skin pigmentation was a better predictor of susceptibility to illusions than was the degree of carpenteredness of the environment. However, this and similar studies turned up inconsistent results: sometimes skin pigmentation seemed to predict susceptibility to illusions, and sometimes it did not (see Deregowski, 1989; Pollack, 1989; and Segall et al., 1990, for summaries of the range of findings).

Considerable ingenuity has been devoted to trying to obtain a clear test of the hypothesis that culture influences perception. For example, Bolton, Michelson, Wilde, and Bolton (1975) studied susceptibility to illusions among two Peruvian groups living at 4,500 and 13,000 feet in the Central Andes. They reasoned that if the pigmentation hypothesis was correct, the people living at the higher altitude would be less susceptible to the illusions because they had been more exposed to sunlight (which promotes pigmentation). But what they found fit an ecological hypothesis better: there were no differences with respect to the Müller-Lyer illusion, but people living at high altitudes showed less sensitivity to the horizontal-vertical illusion, presumably because they lived in open vistas, not closed mountain passes.

Reviewing these data in the late 1980s, Segall and his colleagues commented that "the empiricist hypothesis is as tenable today as it was at the outset of this research project." And just how tenable is that? In the discussion that follows Jan Deregowski's (1989) review of this literature, Pollack remains unconvinced that differences in pigmentation cannot account for differences in susceptibility to illusions, while a good many of the commentators whose work is included in the discussion dispute his interpretations of the data. My own conclusion is that despite the enormous amount of effort that went into this work, it has taught us very little about perception that was not already known from general psychology. Moreover, many key questions about causality remain problematic.

## Intelligence and Culture

Little more than two decades after the founding of psychology laboratories and the advent of scientific psychology in several European countries and the United States, a major push for psychologists to conduct research into complex human problem solving came from a source seemingly outside the scientific community, although respected psychologists were involved. Early in this century Alfred Binet and Theophile Simon were asked to deal with a practical social problem. With the growth of public education in France, there was a growing problem of school failure. Some children learned more slowly than others, and some children, who otherwise appeared perfectly normal, did not benefit from instruction at all. Binet and his colleagues were asked to try to find a way to identify slow-learning children at an early stage in their education. If they could be identified, special education could be provided for them, allowing the remaining children to be taught more efficiently. The subsequent history of IQ testing has been described too frequently to bear repetition here, but a sketch of the basic strategy of research is necessary as background to an understanding of why cross-cultural strategies are a problematic means for discovering how culture influences the development of intelligence.

To begin with, Binet and Simon offered a definition of the quality they sought to test for: "It seems to us that in intelligence there is a fundamental faculty, the alteration or lack of which is of the utmost importance for practical life. This faculty is judgment, otherwise called good sense, practical sense, initiative, the faculty of adapting oneself to circumstances. To judge well, to comprehend well, to reason well, these are the essential activities of intelligence" (Binet and Simon, 1916, p. 43).

Next they had to decide how to test for it. The decision seemed straightforward. They wanted to test children's ability to perform the kinds of tasks required "for practical life." But practical life for children at the start of the twentieth century meant life in schools. Binet and Simon observed classrooms, looked at textbooks, talked to teachers, and used their intuition to arrive at some idea of the many kinds of knowledge and skills that children are expected to master in school. What they found was not easy to describe briefly, as anyone who has looked into a classroom can testify.

There was an obvious need to understand graphic symbols, such as alphabets and number systems. So recognition of these symbols was tested. But recognition was not enough. Children were also expected to manipulate these symbols to store and retrieve vast amounts of information, to rearrange this information according to the demands of the moment, and to use the information to solve a great variety of problems that had never arisen before in their experience. Thus, children's abilities to remember and carry out sequences of movements to define words, to construct plausible event sequences from jumbled picture sequences, and to recognize the missing elements in graphic designs were tested, along with many other components of school-based problems.

It was also obvious that to master more and more esoteric applications of the basic knowledge contained in alphanumeric writing systems, pupils had to learn to master their own behavior. They had not only to engage in a variety of "mental activities" directed at processing information; they also had to gain control over their own attention, applying it not according to the whim of the moment but according to the whim of the teacher and the demands of the text.

It was clearly impossible to arrive at a single sample of all the kinds of thinking required by "the" school. Not only was there too much going on in any one classroom to make this feasible; it was also clear that the school required different abilities from children of different ages. Binet and Simon realized that estimates of "basic aptitude" for this range of material would depend upon how much the child had learned about the specific content before arriving at school, but they believed that knowing a child's current abilities would be useful to teachers anyway.

They decided to construct a sample of school-like tasks appropriate for each year of education, starting with the elementary grades and reaching into higher levels of the curriculum. They would have liked to include all essential activities in their test and in such a way that tasks at one level of difficulty would be stepping-stones to tasks at the next-higher level. But because no firmly based theory of higher psychological functions existed, they had to rely on a combination of their own common sense and a logical analysis of tasks that classrooms seemed to require (for example, you have to be able to re-member three random digits before you can remember four; you have to know the alphabet before you can read).

Binet and Simon also hit on the handy strategy of letting the children themselves tell them when an item selected for the test was appropriate. Beginning with a large set of possible test questions, they hunted for items that half the children at a given age level could solve. An "average" child would then be one who solved problems appropriate to his or her age level. Keeping items that discriminated between children of different ages (as well as items that seemed to sample the activities demanded in classrooms), they arrived at the first important prototype of the modern IQ test. Of course a great deal of work has gone into the construction of tests since these early efforts, but the underlying logic has remained pretty much the same: sample the kinds of activities demanded by the culture (reduced in practice to the culture of the school). Children who have mastered far less than the average for their age are those who will need extra help if they are to reach the level expected by the culture.

This strategy is perfectly reasonable, so long as we stay within the framework that generated the item-selection procedures in the first place. However, people did not stay within the methodologically pre-scribed limits. Although Binet and Simon specifically warned against the procedure, their test, and tests like it, began to be used as mea-sures of an overall aptitude for solving problems in general, rather than samples of problem-solving ability and knowledge that are important to formal education in particular. They also ignored Binet and Simon's warnings about the problems of dealing with children from different cultural backgrounds.

Those engaged in such extrapolations often acknowledged that in principle it is important to make certain that everyone given the test has an equal opportunity to learn the material that the test demands (Oliver, 1933a, 1933b; Woodworth, 1910). But in practice there was no way to guarantee this essential prerequisite for making comparative judgments about basic abilities. More important, perhaps, the belief that such tests tap into inherited capacities that are more or less impervious to particular forms of experience created a climate in which otherwise sober-minded researchers seemed to throw caution to the winds.

Quotations could be culled from a number of prominent psychologists (Goddard, Terman, Yerkes—see Gould, 1981) but Cyril Burt's judgment captures the general tone:

> By intelligence the psychologist understands inborn, all-around intellectual ability. It is inherited, or at least innate, not due to teaching or training; it is intellectual, not emotional or moral, and remains uninfluenced by industry or zeal; it is general, not specific, i.e., it is not limited to any particular kind of work, but enters into all we do or say or think. Of all our mental qualities, it is the most far-reaching. (quoted in Carroll, 1982, p. 90)

Confidence in the universal validity of IQ tests as measures of an inborn trait called intelligence that possessed the same qualities in all cultures and all places led to a flood of cross-cultural applications of IQ testing (Gould, 1977, 1981; Wober, 1975).

Remarking upon this state of affairs at a meeting of the American Anthropological Association in 1935, Florence Goodenough, a psychologist whose "draw a man test" had been used for making cross-cultural comparisons, commented that "the rising wave of interest in intelligence tests swept away the banks of scientific caution" (1936, p. 5). Goodenough estimated that about two-thirds of all publications dealing with racial (sic) differences in mental traits used materials that had been standardized on American or European whites, and that the vast majority of the remainder had to do with "the even more hazardous problem of comparing races with respect to traits of temperament and personality as indicated by their scores on tests designed to measure these qualities but of very doubtful validity, even for whites" (ibid.).[3]

Robert Woodworth, one of the most influential American psychologists of the first half of this century, had initiated this dubious enterprise by administering an intelligence test to people from various primitive tribes who were assembled at the St. Louis Exposition in 1904 (Woodworth, 1910). Woodworth, while sympathetic to the idea that different test results reflected deep underlying differences in intelligence, was nonetheless circumspect in his conclusions on methodological grounds. Others were not. For example, Stanley Porteus carried a board with a labyrinth on it all over the world attempting to construct a hierarchy of races based on the assumption that his "maze test" was a valid, culture-free measure of general intelligence—despite the fact that among his South African samples one group that already knew a "labyrinth game" outscored all neighboring groups that did not know the game (Porteus, 1937, p. 256).

Goodenough identified the crucial shortcomings of the logic of this enterprise in a way that has very broad, if rarely recognized, implications when she wrote: "the fact can hardly be too strongly emphasized that neither intelligence tests nor the so-called tests of personality and character are measuring devices. They are sampling devices" (1936, p. 5). Goodenough argued that when applied in American society, IQ tests represent a reasonable sampling device because they are "representative samples of the kind of intellectual tasks that American city dwellers are likely to be called upon to perform" (ibid.); but that such tests are *not* representative of life in other cultural circumstances, and hence their use as measuring devices for purposes of comparison is inappropriate. This injunction applies no less, of course, to variations among subgroups living in the United States than to peoples living in economically less developed societies.

It might be thought, on the basis of Goodenough's critique, that attempts to discover the influence of culture on the development of intelligence would have been long ago abandoned. However, the utility and theoretical implications of cross-cultural IQ testing continue to be heatedly debated (Irvine and Berry, 1983, 1988; Segall, Dasen, Berry, and Poortinga, 1990).

So far as I can see, the only way to obtain a culture-free test is to construct items that are equally a part of the experience of all cultures.[6] Following the logic of Binet's undertaking, this would require us to sample the valued adult activities in all cultures (or at least two!) and identify activities equivalent in their structure, their valuation, and their frequency of occurrence. I probably do not have to belabor this point further. No one has carried out such a research program.

The simple fact is that we know of no tests that are culture-free, only tests for which we have no good theory of how cultural variations affect performance. Contemporary proponents of cross-cultural intelligence testing continue to work at developing appropriate research instruments and theoretical models. Vernon (1969), for example, has suggested that one must assume that three kinds of intelligence contribute to test scores: "native intelligence," something like a general, inherited component; a cultural component which has to do with the ways in which cultures foster native intelligence; and a task component which reflects the individual's experience with the particular kinds of tasks sampled.

My own belief is that such efforts will be of limited theoretical value because we lack just that which we are seeking, guidelines that would permit us to specify clear connections between cultural experience and performance. Without such guidelines, separation of the components of variance in a unique way is extremely unlikely.

This is not to say that, treated as prognostic devices or samples of performance, IQ tests are necessarily devoid of social utility. A great many contemporary researchers who reject the use of standardized IQ tests as a way to measure cultural differences in intelligence recognize that IQ testing may be an expedient way to identify people who may accomplish tasks valued in modern industrialized socio-economic conditions with a minimum of training (see Segall, Dasen, Berry, and Poortinga, 1990, for a review; see Ord, 1970, for an example of pragmatic uses of IQ tests to select people for the army and jobs in the bureaucracy). However, as Serpell (1993) points out, even this conservative, pragmatic use of tests rests on the problematic assumption that schools and bureaucratic institutions of industrialized countries should be appropriated by developing countries without alteration. Insofar as such institutions are selectively appropriated, different kinds of tests would have to be constructed.

Although I have a dim view of cross-cultural IQ testing as a way of finding out about culture in mind, I do find IQ tests interesting as models of intellectual activities related to formal education. The reason for this is very simple: Binet based his test items on school practices. Whatever IQ test performance is not related to, it most certainly *is* related to schooling.

## Memory and Culture

Early twentieth-century researchers who studied culture and memory commonly believed that primitive peoples are capable of unusual, or in some cases spectacular, feats of memory. For example, Galton (1883, p. 72) wrote about the astounding memory of an Eskimo observed by one Captain Hall. This man, using no external memory aids, was said to have drawn a map of a coastline some six thousand jagged miles long with a surprising degree of accuracy, as determined by comparison with an English map of the same territory. More recently, Warren D'Azevedo, an anthropologist who worked among the Gola people of Liberia, reported that "an elder with a poor memory, or 'whose old people told him nothing' is a 'small boy' among the elders and might well be looked upon with contempt by younger persons" (1962, p. 13).

The first experimental psychologist to take up the question of culture and memory in a controlled fashion was F. C. Bartlett (1932). Bartlett proposed that memory is organized in terms of two principles. The first is the process of constructive remembering. He assumed that cultures are organized collectivities of people with shared customs, institutions, and values. People form "strong sentiments" around valued, institutionalized activities. These values and their expression through culture shape psychological tendencies to select certain kinds of information for remembering. Knowledge assimilated through their operation constitutes the schemas upon which the universal process of reconstructive remembering operates. In content domains where the schemas are richly elaborated, recall will be better than in domains which are less valued, where there are few strong sentiments, and hence in which fewer schemas are available to guide recall.

As an example of this principle, Bartlett recounts an informal experiment he conducted among the Swazi of East Africa. A farmer proposed that Bartlett query his herdsman, who had been present when he bought some cattle a year before. The farmer had recorded each purchase with a description of the cow in a book, which was used as evidence to test the herdsman's memory. Bartlett asked the herdsman to list the cattle bought, with any details he cared to give. The man recalled all the purchases—their prices, their markings, and their previous owners—with only two errors on details. Typical descriptions included these: "From Gampoka Likindsa, one young white bull with small red spots for 1 pound; From Lolalela, one spotted five year old cow, white and black, for 3 pounds, which was made up of two bags of grain and 1 pound" (Bartlett, 1932, p. 250).

Although this performance was quite impressive (the man provided information on about a dozen cows although he had not been responsible for the transactions), Bartlett treats it as in no way extraordinary: "The Swazi herdsman has a prodigious retentive capacity to recall the individual characteristics of his beasts. An animal may stray and get mixed up with other herds. It may be away for a very long time. However long the interval, if the owner comes with a description of the missing beast, his word is almost never questioned, and he is peaceably allowed to drive the animal back" (ibid.).

Bartlett also hypothesized the existence of a second kind of recall in which temporal order serves as the organizing principle: "There is a low-level type of recall which comes as nearly as possible to what is often called rote recapitulation. It is characteristic of a mental life having relatively few interests, all somewhat concrete in character, and no one of which is dominant" (p. 266).

His evidence for rote recapitulation came from the transcripts of a local law court. In the following example, a man was being examined for the attempted murder of a woman, and the woman herself was called as a necessary witness.

*The Magistrate:* Now tell me how you got that knock on the head.

*The Woman:* Well, I got up that morning at daybreak and I did . . . (here followed a long list of things done, and of people met, and things said). Then we went to so and so's kraal and we . . . (further lists here) and had some beer, and so and so said . . .

*The Magistrate:* Never mind about that. I don't want to know anything except how you got the knock on the head.

*The Woman:* All right, all right. I am coming to that. I have not got there yet. And so I said to so and so . . . (there followed again a great deal of conversational and other detail). And then after that we went on to so and so's kraal.

*The Magistrate:* You look here; if we go on like this we shall take all day. What about that knock on the head?

*The Woman:* Yes; all right, all right. But I have not got there yet. So we . . . (on and on for a very long time relating all the initial details of the day). And then we went on to so

>and so's kraal . . . and there was a dispute . . . and he
>knocked me on the head, and I died, and that is all I
>know. (p. 265)

Bartlett was not an ethnographer, and his judgments about Swazi culture and thought in cases such as this must be viewed with a great deal of skepticism. In defense of his claim that Swazi culture might lend itself to rote recapitulation he speculated, for example, that in Swaziland

>news travels among the native population with great rapidity.
>There is no native system of signals for its transmission, but,
>whenever two wanderers on a pathway meet, they make a clean
>breast one to another of all that they have lately done, seen, and
>learned. Rote recital is easily the best method. The same style
>is exploited in the leisurely and wordy native councils. There is
>behind it the drive of a group with plenty of time, in a sphere
>of relatively uncoordinated interest, where everything that hap-
>pens is about as interesting as everything else, and where, con-
>sequently, a full recital is socially approved. Thus the individual
>temperament and the social organisation play one upon the
>other, and both perpetuate a particular manner of recall.
>(pp. 265–266)

In this sort of speculative ethnography, Bartlett falls prey to the same temptation as did Rivers—to use Europeans' cultural stereotypes to justify conclusions that go far beyond the data and far beyond what he would have been likely to conclude under less ideologically loaded circumstances.

To his credit, Bartlett realized (although he did not apply this re-alization to his work in Swaziland) that the exaggeratedly sequential recall he dubbed rote recapitulation may have been as much a prod-uct of the social situation of its evocation as of any enduring psy-chological tendencies associated with culture. "Change the audience to an alien group," he wrote,

>and the manner of recall again alters. Here the most important
>things to consider are the social position of the narrator in his
>own group, and his relation to the group from which his audi-
>ence is drawn. If the latter group are submissive, inferior, he is

confident, and his exaggerations are markedly along the lines of the preferred tendencies of his own group. If the alien audience is superior, masterly, dominating, they may force the narrator into the irrelevant, recapitulatory method until, or unless he, wittingly or unwittingly, appreciates their own preferred bias. Then he will be apt to construct in remembering, and to draw for his audience the picture which they, perhaps dimly, would make for themselves. Every anthropologist at work in the field knows this, or ought to know it; and yet the details of the social determination of the manner of recall and the recoil of manner upon matter of recall have so far never been carefully studied. (p. 266)

Bartlett's ideas on the cultural organization of constructive recall were soon tested by an anthropologist, S. F. Nadel (1937b). Nadel had conducted fieldwork among both the Yoruba and Nupe of Nigeria. He was impressed that they were strikingly different in many respects although they lived side by side in the same material environment under the same general conditions, had similar economic systems and forms of social organization, and spoke similar languages.

According to Nadel, the Yoruba religion was characterized by an "elaborate and rationalized hierarchical system of deities" (p. 197), each with its own specific duties and functions. The Yoruba had developed realistic plastic arts and drama. By contrast, Nupe religion centered around a "vague, abstract, impersonal power and their art forms were most highly developed in the decorative arts and they had no tradition of drama akin to that of the Yoruba" (p. 197).

Nadel constructed a story which could be used to test remembering in both groups. The story told of a couple who had two sons. The sons fell in love with the same girl, who preferred the younger son. The older son killed the younger and the broken-hearted girl left, never to be seen again. Woven into this simple narrative were a number of elements that Nadel predicted would be remembered differently by people from the two cultures. These included set phrases ("God will revenge it"), and logical linking phrases ("when these sons had grown up"). He expected the Yoruba to emphasize the logical structure of the story and the Nupe to emphasize circumstantial facts and details, because these two emphases fit their respective dominant social tendencies and associated schemas. He read this story to groups of Yoruba and Nupe boys aged 15–18 and then asked them to recall the story several hours later, with no prior warning.

Nadel's results confirmed his expectations. The Yoruba subjects recalled more about the logical structure of the story, the Nupe about circumstantial facts and details. For example, only three of twenty Nupe subjects recalled the sentence beginning with "When these sons had grown up" while seventeen of twenty Yoruba did. Few Nupe but most Yoruba included the quarrel between the two brothers, a crucial element in supplying the motive for the murder.

By contrast, most of the Nupe but few of the Yoruba recalled set phrases precisely, and the Nupe were more likely to add situational and temporal details in their renditions, contributing to what Nadel calls "a vivid, concrete picture of the happenings of the story" (p. 201). For example, one subject added the idea that the two brothers were "traveling about" when they met the girl, another said they met her "in town." The Nupe also imported more context into the conditions of the killing, adding such phrases as "Then it became night."[7]

No one in either culture remembered the story perfectly, contrary to the notion of fabulous memories among primitive peoples. In the present context, however, what seems most noteworthy is that the experiment is concerned with qualitative (cultural contingent) differences in experience and its associated schemas. It is not relevant to ask "who remembered better, the Yoruba or the Nupe?" The point is that they remembered differentially in line with the "persistent interests" of their cultures, as Bartlett's theory predicted.

Anthropological data were also brought to bear on Bartlett's ideas about rote recapitulation. As a part of his research on the cognitive aspects ("eidos") of Iatmul (a group in New Guinea), Gregory Bateson found that learned men among them appeared to be veritable storehouses of totems and names which are the content of "name songs" and used in debating. Considering the number of name songs possessed by each clan and the rough number of names per song, he reasoned that learned men carry 10–20,000 names around in their heads.

This material seemed to provide an excellent case in which to test rote-memory capability, and Bateson did so by recording the order in which informants offered names on different occasions. He reports that people generally altered the order of the names from one occasion to another and were never criticized for doing so. When they got stumped at some point in recalling a particular set of names they did not go back to the beginning of the series in the manner that signifies rote recapitulation. Nor, when asked about some event in the past, did informants launch into a series of chronologically related events in order to lead up to the event in question. Speaking directly to Bartlett's idea of rote recapitulation, Bateson concludes that "though we may with fair certainty say that rote memory is not the principal process stimulated in Iatmul erudition, it is not possible to say which of the higher processes is chiefly involved" (1936, p. 224).

## Modern Studies of Memory and Culture

Three decades after the pioneering work of Bartlett, Bateson, and Nadel, my colleagues and I conducted a series of studies of memory performance among Kpelle rice farmers of central Liberia (Cole, Gay, Glick, and Sharp, 1971). This work had several purposes, but one was to test Bartlett's notion that nonliterate African tribal people are prone to using rote recapitulation when confronted with a memory task for which they have no "strong sentiments."

The memory task we used most frequently is referred to in the psychological literature as "free recall": a list of items to be remembered is presented and subjects are free to recall them in any order they choose. This procedure became popular in the 1960s because it was found that when presented a set of items belonging to recognizable categories (clothing, food, utensils, tools) in a random order, adults do not tend to remember in the order items are presented; instead they "cluster" their recalled items into the categories constituting the list (Bousfield, 1953). Among American (educated) adults both the total number of items recalled and the amount of clustering increases with repeated trials; young children are less likely to cluster their recall and show little improvement with practice (see Kail, 1990, for a review of this literature).

We reasoned that such free-recall lists are unlikely to evoke strong social sentiments, so that if nonliterate Kpelle rice farmers have a proclivity toward rote remembering, it would appear when asked to remember the list of words. Once we established that the items we presented for learning and recall were familiar and readily categorizable in local terms, we used them in a set of studies.

Although procedures varied slightly from one study to another, people were usually presented with items one at a time at approximately two-second intervals and asked to try to remember them. When the entire set had been presented, they were told to say what they remembered. This procedure was repeated for five or more passes through the list.

Contrary to expectations based on Bartlett's early work, we found no evidence for rote-recapitulatory remembering. In fact, it was difficult for us to discern *any* organized pattern in the way people recalled the lists. People neither recalled in the order in which we presented the items (even when that order remained constant from one presentation of the entire set to the next) nor seemed to be mentally regrouping items according to the cultural categories that constituted them.

Contrary to the folklore emphasizing the remarkable memories of nonliterate peoples, performance levels were low according to standards based on research in the United States. Nor did repeated practice with the same list of words appear to result in much learning. Even when the same set of twenty items was presented as many as fifteen times, people recalled only one or two more items following the fifteenth presentation than they did following the first.

These low levels of performance and lack of improvement with practice motivated us to initiate a series of experiments to determine if there are ways of presenting the task that would lead to higher levels of recall and evidence of conceptual organization:

1. We tried paying people for each word they recalled to test the idea that they were not really trying to remember. People *said* a lot more words at recall time, but their recall did not improve.

2. We presented the same items in the form of spoken lists and as physical objects to test the idea that concrete items would be easier to recall. Presentation of objects did in fact improve recall slightly, but no more than it did when the same procedures were used with Americans.

3. We tried a variety of manipulations to make the conceptual structure of the list salient (by including category names with

the items, or by presenting items in different physical locations), but recall was largely unaffected.

4. Instead of asking people to recall the items, we asked them to recall the physical locations (a line of four chairs) where different categories of items were placed. If items were placed on the chairs according to their category membership, people learned rapidly and clustered their recall, indicating again that *when category structure was made sufficiently explicit* Kpelle people had the ability to use category information in the service of remembering.

In light of our earlier discussion about the extent to which IQ test items appropriate to one culture can be appropriate to a markedly different one, an obvious question to ask about these studies is whether they represent reasonable tasks for assessing the way Kpelle people remember. When, if ever, would these people encounter a task where they were required to commit a list of words or objects to memory simply for the purposes of remembering? Might we not obtain different results if we used a task more representative of the memory tasks that Kpelle people ordinarily encounter?

We tested this idea in two studies, both of which used narrative stories as their materials. The first experiment stuck close to the materials used in those I have just described: the same set of twenty words belonging to four prominent categories were used, except that this time the items were embedded in a traditional story frame in different ways to highlight different potential principles of categorization.

Common to each version of the procedure was a narrative in which suitors offered the to-be-remembered items as bridewealth for the daughter of a town chief. Two extreme versions of the story give the flavor of the idea. In one story, the first suitor offers all of the clothing; the second, all of the food; the third, all of the tools; and the fourth, all of the utensils. In a second story a man attempts to kidnap the girl, who drops items along the path as she goes; she drops them in an order that bears no relation to category membership but makes sense in the sequence of events.

Under these conditions, the ways the to-be-remembered items fit into the story powerfully influenced the ways they were recalled. In the case of the suitors who brought whole categories of items, those categories were recalled as a cluster. In the case of items presented as part of a sequential narrative, they were recalled according to the story sequence. So powerful was the story framework in organizing recall, in fact, that in some cases where different men brought different categories of items as the brideprice, people only named one category of items at the time of recall—the category associated with the items that were judged most attractive for winning the girl. When we inquired about this we were told that this was the person who should win the girl, so naming the other gifts was superfluous!

In a later study, which was conducted among a neighboring Liberian tribal group, the Vai, we assessed the level and pattern of recall for a number of stories that had been used extensively in research on the development of recall for stories in the United States (Mandler, Scribner, Cole, and DeForest, 1980). These materials were only minimally modified to use local names for people and animals, yet both the overall levels of recall and the patterns of recall for different elements in the stories were almost identical for Vai and American adults.[8]

## Evaluating the Standard Cross-Cultural Approach

This selective review of research on three psychological processes can by no means provide a comprehensive picture of the accomplishments and problems of cross-cultural research conducted according to the methodological standards of general psychology. But these examples provide an excellent sample of the enduring questions that occupy cross-cultural psychologists.

If we combine the major lessons of the Torres Straits expedition and research on visual illusions, it appears that the cultural environment does not influence visual acuity, but does establish habits of interpreting the visual world that influence the way ambiguous stimuli such as visual illusions are interpreted. Assuming that visual acuity is based on an elementary psychological process and that "perceptual inferences" are higher psychological functions (reasonable assumptions in a Wundtian framework, I think), these results are what one would expect. We have to remain uncertain about the conclusions, however. It may be that the evidence of cultural invariance of sensory thresholds is contaminated by differences of interpretation between cultures that make the processes generating the dependent variable (threshold magnitude) uncertain. The evidence based on visual illusions appears firmer, but it, too, is in dispute. In this case, dispute centers on culture as the independent variable. Groups differing in their cultural locations also differ in their global locations and in the degree of pigmentation in the irises of their eyes. The fact that culture is not really an independent variable because it is not under experimental control and subjects are not assigned at random with respect to it haunts all such efforts.

Cross-cultural research using IQ-test technology has taught us almost nothing about the nature of intelligence, serving instead to reinforce doubts about the appropriateness of cross-cultural testing using such instruments. That IQ tests can be used to select people who will be able to move into socially valued jobs in contemporary industrialized societies is an important fact, but one whose psychological significance is not at all clear.

In apparent recognition of these limitations, cross-cultural studies using standardized IQ tests as a tool for resolving disputes about nature and nurture has given way to intra-national studies seeking approximation to the random assignment of subjects to conditions (for example, studies of twins separated at birth and similar strategies for teasing apart genotype and phenotype; see Plomin, 1990, and Scarr, 1981, for summaries). This literature, too, is subject to continuing controversy in part because the logically appropriate experimental designs are ethically abhorrent.

The research on memory, like that on sensory acuity, speaks strongly against the idea that people in nonliterate ("primitive") societies have extraordinary powers of memory. Beyond that, it turns out to be interesting not because it shows that nonliterate, traditional peoples remember better or worse than their literate counterparts (depending upon the particular study, they remember better, no different, or worse). Rather, it locates cultural differences in the organization of activity in everyday life. Where the structures of activity are similar across social groups, cultural differences in processes of remembering appear to be minimal. Where one society has significant, institutionalized practices involving remembering that another does not have (such as formal schooling) we can expect cultural differences in memory processes in terms of specialized forms of remembering appropriate to that activity (such as an ability to recall lists of words).

Assuming that my assessment of these three examples more or less characterizes accomplishments in other psychological domains, the marginality of cross-cultural research to mainstream psychology is not difficult to understand. Its substantive offerings appear modest, and the evidence on which they are based is suspect.

But this conclusion leaves scientific psychology in the uncomfortable position of founding its claims about the "laws of behavior" on methods of observation which make it impermissible, in principle, to test for significant cultural variations. Such a position is uncomfortably reminiscent of the man who searches for his lost car keys only within the arc of light provided by the street lamp, except that psychologists who fail to encounter culture in their carefully designed experiments declare, in effect, that the keys have ceased to exist because they are not under the lamppost.

It is not surprising then, that psychologists who believe culture to play a central role in human nature should seek out approaches that enlarge the "circle of light" available in which to look for the keys to relationships between culture and cognition. In the next chapter I will explore cross-cultural work on cognitive development, which has received especially close scrutiny in recent decades. Both the promise and problems of contemporary cross-cultural approaches to cognition are clearly manifested in this work.

# 3 ⑥

# Cognitive Development, Culture, and Schooling

IN LIGHT OF what we learned about nineteenth-century theories of mind in the decades before psychology was institutionalized as a scientific discipline, it is notable that none of the three lines of research discussed in Chapter 2 addressed the problem of mental development. Developmentally oriented research would seem a natural way to address relations between culture and cognition, as well as the widespread belief that European societies were in some fundamental sense *more developed*, both cognitively and economically, than non-Europeans. Yet, with a few exceptions (a study of the development of animistic reasoning by Margaret Mead, 1932, and some research by Russian psychologists such as Luria, 1931, 1976), developmental cross-cultural research was notable by its absence in the decades preceding World War II.

There are probably many reasons for the early cross-cultural psychologists' focus on adults. To begin with, mainstream scientific psychology was decidedly nondevelopmental in its approach. It was in search of laws of mind so general that they could encompass rats, monkeys, and human beings. The choice of subject populations was determined primarily by convenience rather than by some principled psychological difference assumed to distinguish them. In addition, developmental comparisons add special methodological pitfalls to the already severe problems of cross-cultural comparisons (Cole and Means, 1981). It is difficult enough to deal with the problems of communication and experimental control that accompany cross-cultural research with adults; why add to these difficulties by requiring that one communicate clearly with children as well?

Despite such problems, developmental studies became the most popular form of cross-cultural research in the 1960s and later decades. Central to the rise of cross-cultural developmental research was the international context provided by the efforts to reconfigure world power in the wake of World War II.

In the early years of World War II a number of social scientists participated in planning for the postwar world in collaboration with various United Nations agencies, particularly UNESCO (Lipset, 1980; UNESCO, 1951) It was clear that postwar reconstruction would have to include independence for the colonial empires, and that the former colonies should be brought into more equitable interaction with countries in the industrialized world. This change was conceived of as a process of development at the social, political, economic, and psychological levels.

Reading through the UNESCO documents of the 1940s and 1950s produces an overwhelming impression that nineteenth-century ideas about culture and mind had survived unscathed. The basic premise in UNESCO's planning documents was that low levels of economic, political, and cultural development are associated with ignorance that blocks the economic changes these architects of the future were imagining for the world.

Much in the same spirit, economist Daniel Lerner argued that a key attribute of modern thinking is the ability to take another person's perspective and to empathize with that person's point of view (Lerner, 1958). Lerner was quite specific about the relationship between psychological modernity and modern economic activity. The ability to take another's point of view, he wrote, "is an indispensable skill for moving people out of traditional settings . . . Our interest is to clarify the process whereby the high empathizer tends to become also the cash customer, the radio listener, the voter" (Lerner, 1958, p. 50). The uneducated, primitive person, according to Lerner, lacked this form of empathy and as a consequence could not enter into modern economic and political relations.

A cornerstone of the strategy to "bring culture" to the non-European world and to raise people out of poverty and ignorance was to provide them with a modern education. There were two views about how best to accomplish this task. The first was to provide people with a "fundamental" education. At the core of the idea of fundamental education was a sort of "literacy-in-practice" intended to give people greater control over their local environment and to provide them with more information about the world events affecting their lives (UNESCO, 1951; Van Renberg, 1984). Fundamental education did not necessarily imply a system of formal education. Many argued that it would be best to teach literacy informally, in the context of everyday activity (UNESCO, 1951).

Fundamental education is a culturally *conservative* strategy of literacy inculcation because it assumes that literacy will be in the service of people's existing values and that people will continue to live in the same places, doing more or less the same kinds of work, as before. Formal education, in contrast, assumes that children will experience a new way of life outside their traditional communities (Serpell, 1993). Despite its appeal to educational reformers, the ideas underpinning the fundamental education approach failed to survive the transition from UNESCO headquarters to the hallways of local ministries of education. What occurred instead was the spread of formal education modeled roughly on a European or American style, depending upon who the former colonial power was. One encountered children in schools, packed fifty or more to a classroom, reading textbooks that had been discarded in Minneapolis a decade earlier.

It was in the 1960s and 1970s that psychology as a whole and cross-cultural psychological research on development in particular really took off.[1] The question of the impact of education on development was an important focus of cross-cultural effort because of education's presumed ties to economic as well as cognitive development.

The research programs that flowered in the middle 1960s differed with respect to their basic units of analysis for the study of development, their theoretical claims about cultural influences on cognitive development, and their approaches to methodological problems (see Berry, Poortinga, Segall, and Dasen, 1992; LCHC, 1983; and Se-

gall, Dasen, Berry, and Poortinga, 1990, for summaries and biblio-
graphic materials concerning these endeavors). I shall summarize and
compare some of the main lines of research.

## The New Mathematics Project in Liberia

Efforts to use education as the engine of rapid economic and social
development in what are now called the "less developed countries"
were what brought me into cross-cultural research. During the 1960s,
with support from the UN as well as national programs such as the
Agency for International Development and the Peace Corps, many
African countries expanded their educational systems. Despite a good
deal of external support, these efforts ran into a variety of problems,
not the least of which was endemically low levels of student performance. Psychologists, among other professional groups, were called
upon to give advice and assistance.

In 1963 I was asked to consult on a project to improve the educational performance of children living in the West African country
of Liberia. The initiator of the project was John Gay, who taught at
Cuttington College, a small Episcopal college in an interior area occupied by members of the Kpelle tribe. In a decade of teaching both
in the college and in a nearby village, John had noted that local youth
had far more trouble mastering mathematics than did students in the
United States. At a mathematics teaching workshop that brought together educators from all over sub-Saharan Africa, he encountered
scholars interested in applying the then-fashionable "new mathematics curriculum." John argued that more than cosmetic changes would
be needed to make such curricula successful for the children he
taught. He won support to bring a group of scholars to Liberia to
investigate indigenous mathematical knowledge and practices in the
hope that he could design a curriculum built upon local knowledge.
I was the psychologist on the team sent to help him.

It was an odd choice, governed more by my availability than by
any special expertise. My graduate training was in a branch of psychology known as mathematical learning theory, which used algebra
and probability theory to construct models of learning. This form of
theorizing was based upon data from experiments that modeled simple learning and problem-solving tasks. I had taken an introduction

to anthropology as an undergraduate, but nowhere in my education had I been exposed to methods of field research or to the study of human development or education. I was sent to Liberia with two weeks' notice, hardly enough time to do more than arrange for the needed vaccinations and to locate Liberia on the map.

When I arrived, I made it a point to ask people who spent a lot of time around children about the difficulties that the local children displayed in school, especially their difficulties with mathematics. The list of intellectual difficulties that tribal children were said to encounter was a long one. They had difficulty distinguishing between different geometrical shapes because, I was told, they experienced severe perceptual problems. This made it virtually impossible for them to solve even simple jigsaw puzzles, and I heard several times that "Africans can't do puzzles." I also learned that Africans didn't know how to classify and that when faced with a choice between thinking and remembering they would resort to rote remembering, at which they were said to excel.

These assertions—which echo more than a century of European claims about the primitive mind, although I did not realize this at the time—are based upon a deficit model of cultural variations. A person who can't do a jigsaw puzzle must have perceptual problems; a child resorts to rote remembering not in response to the form of instruction in school but as a result of presumed culturally ingrained habits. On a purely intuitive basis, I found these generalizations difficult to credit. It's a long way from inability to do jigsaw puzzles to general perceptual incapacities.

Visits to schools showed me the basis for some of these assertions. In many classrooms I saw students engaged in rote remembering. Not only were children required to recite from memory long passages of European poetry that they could not understand; they seemed firmly convinced that mathematics, too, was strictly a matter of memorizing. Teachers complained that when they presented a problem like $2 + 6 = ?$ as an example in a class lesson and then asked $3 + 5 = ?$ on a test, students were likely to protest that the test was unfair because it contained material not covered in the lesson. While such scenes are not unknown in American classrooms, they were all-pervasive in the Liberian classrooms I observed.

In encounters with local people whose lives were organized in

terms of indigenous cultural practices and not the modern economic
sector that schooling had been introduced to support, I got a quite
different impression of Kpelle intellectual skills. In the crowded marketplace, people were trading all manner of goods, ranging from traditional items such as rice, butchered meat, and cloth to modern
goods such as infant formula, hardware, and building supplies. On
taxi-buses I was often outbargained by the cabbies, who seemed to
have no difficulty calculating miles, road quality, quality of the car's
tires, number of passengers, and distance in a single formula that
worked to their advantage.

The questions aroused by these observations remain with me to
this day. Judged by the way they do puzzles or study for mathematics
in school, the Kpelle appeared dumb; judged by their behavior in
markets, taxis, and many other settings, they appeared smart (at least,
smarter than one American visitor). How could people be so dumb
and so smart at the same time?

Our initial research efforts were based on two simpleminded assumptions. First, we believed that although Kpelle children might
lack particular kinds of experience, they were not generally ignorant.
Second (and closely related), we assumed that practice makes profi-
cient if not perfect: that people become highly skilled in performing
tasks they engage in often.

Consequently, if we wanted to understand why Kpelle children
have difficulty with the kinds of problem-solving tasks we consider
relevant to mathematics, we needed to examine the circumstances in
which Kpelle people encountered something recognizable to us as
mathematics. That is, we needed to study people's everyday activities
that involved measuring, estimating, counting, calculating, and the
like, as the *precondition* for diagnosing indigenous mathematical understanding in relation to schooling. We also investigated the ways
in which Kpelle adults arranged for their children to acquire the
knowledge and skills needed to be competent Kpelle adults, as a
background against which to assess the schooling difficulties.

In our investigation we employed both tasks imported directly
from the United States and tasks chosen to model Kpelle ways of
doing things. The former included simple classification tasks, a jigsaw puzzle, and a vocabulary test of the sort often found in IQ tests.
These studies sometimes revealed the expected difficulties, and some-

times did not. For example, in one classification study we asked people to sort eight cards depicting large and small, black and white, triangles and squares into two categories, and then asked them to recategorize them. This task proved quite difficult. Adults often agonized before deciding (for example) to categorize the cards according to color. Very few were able to recategorize them in terms of form or size. The difficulties persisted when we replaced the geometric figures with stylized drawings of men and women. In one of the cases where we sought to model Kpelle ways of doing things, however, the results were dramatically different.

## Estimating Amounts of Rice

The Kpelle have traditionally been upland rice farmers who sell surplus rice as a way to supplement their (very low) incomes. Upland rice farming is a marginal agricultural enterprise, and most villages experience what was called a "hungry time" in the two months between the end of their supply of food from the previous year and the harvesting of the new crop.

As might be expected from the centrality of this single crop to their survival, the Kpelle have a rich vocabulary for talking about rice. Of particular concern to us was the way in which they talked about amounts of rice, because we had been told rather often that Kpelle "can't measure" and we wanted to test this in a domain of deep importance. John discovered that their standard minimal measure for rice was a *kopi*, a tin can that holds one dry pint. Rice was also stored in *boke* (buckets), *tins* (tin cans), and bags. The kopi acted as a common unit of measure. It was said that there were twenty-four kopi to a bucket and forty-four to a tin, and that two buckets were equivalent to one tin. People claimed that there were just short of a hundred kopi to a *boro* (bag), which contained about two tins. The relationships between cups, buckets, tins, and bags are not exact by our standards, but they are close, and they reflect the use of a common metric, the cup.

We also learned that the transactions of buying and selling rice by the cup were slightly different in a crucial way. When a local trader bought rice, he used a kopi with the bottom pounded out to increase the volume in the container; when he sold rice, he used a kopi with a flat bottom. We surmised that this small margin of difference would make a big difference to people who refer to two months of the year as hungry time, so we decided to experiment on people's ability to estimate amounts of rice in a bowl, using the local measuring tool, the kopi.

Using these materials, we conducted a "backward" cross-cultural experiment, that is, an experiment modeled on our notion of Kpelle practices. The subjects in this case were eighty American working-class adults, twenty American schoolchildren aged 10–13, twenty Kpelle adults, and twenty Kpelle schoolchildren. Each subject was presented with four mixing bowls of equal size holding different amounts of rice (1½, 3, 4½, and 6 kopi), shown the tin to be used as the unit of measurement, and asked to estimate the number of tin cans (kopi) of rice in each bowl. Kpelle adults were extremely accurate at this task, averaging only one or two percent error. American adults, on the other hand, overestimated the 1½-can amount by 30 percent and the 6-can amount by more than 100 percent. The American schoolchildren were similar to the American adults on the smallest amount and similar to the Kpelle schoolchildren for the other amounts.

These results supported our basic assumptions that people would develop cultural tools and associated cognitive skills in domains of life where such tools and skills were of central importance, as rice was central to Kpelle life. Whatever the cultural differences with respect to mathematics, a total lack of measurement concepts and skills was not one of them.

In the rice estimation task we were able to create an experiment which incorporated not only local knowledge concerning content, such as the Kpelle system of units for amounts of rice, but also local procedures under which such estimates would be relevant: at markets one often encountered women selling rice from large bowls containing various amounts. Consequently, our task provided Kpelle people with both relevant content and relevant procedures.

### Experimental Anthropology and Ethnographic Psychology

In our first foray into Kpelle mathematics in relation to schooling we discovered that young people who had attended school for a few years responded to many of our tasks quite differently from their un-schooled peers. Schooling was having an impact on their thinking, even if their achievement levels were low.

In 1966 we obtained a grant to continue and expand our research; instead of focusing on a particular content domain, we sought to study the impact of schooling on cognitive development, broadly conceived. The goal of improving school achievement remained, and so did our belief that such an investigation had to be grounded in people's everyday experience. But this round of research was decidedly more "basic" and less "applied" than our first efforts.[2]

We began the project with ethnographic observations of everyday activities with the intention of using them as models for follow-up experimental work. We hired a young anthropologist, Beryl Bellman, to live in a remote village where he could learn the language and advise us about appropriate activities to study (house building, arguing court cases, preparing to go to market, and so on).

We also used ethnographic observations of everyday activities as a standard of local people's intellectual capacities. If people used logical arguments in everyday discussions, we were loath to conclude that they could not argue logically on the basis of a psychological test.

Finally, we used our knowledge of local activities and modes of classification to determine the content of various experimental tasks. For example, John Gay carried out an extensive analysis of Kpelle classification systems as a precondition for designing memory studies such as those described in Chapter 2.

Starting from the psychological side, we conducted a number of studies using tasks borrowed from studies of cognitive development in the United States. But the standard procedures (informed by linguistic and ethnographic observation) were only the starting point for analysis. When we encountered markedly poor performance, we modified our procedures, seeking conditions under which presumably absent psychological processes would be manifested. The studies of free recall memory described in Chapter 2 illustrate this approach.

*Analyzing Indigenous Activities*

As an example of local activities where people's intellectual achievements can be observed and analyzed, we studied the strategies used in a traditional board game called *malang*, which is found widely in Africa and Southeast Asia under a variety of names. The game is played using a board with two rows of six holes. Four seeds are placed in each hole at the start and players seek to capture all of the seeds according to a set of rules. We held a tournament among sixteen adult players to observe the strategies used. We were able to identify several strategies: building a solid defense, luring opponents into premature moves, flexibility in redistributing one's seeds, and so on. Our observations convinced us that all the men studied engaged in such strategic intellectual behavior, some of it quite complex. But we did not succeed in using this game in experiments that would allow us to link such behavior with strategy use in tasks from the psychological literature. Nor did we compare schooled and unschooled people, because very few of the adult players had attended school.[3]

Similarly, we studied court cases for the use of strategies in rhetorical argumentation, and again we were able to come up with several likely candidates for cognitive skills: we identified people making logical arguments from evidence and seeking to avoid damaging judgments by presenting their evidence selectively. But we were unable to come up with a satisfactory experiment on verbal argumentation using court cases as a model.[4]

From our own experience in the field, as well as from the anthropological literature, we knew that when urban-educated Americans and Europeans go to rural Africa, they often have difficulty learning to distinguish various plants that are well known to the local population, even to the children. Beryl Bellman, the ethnographer who worked with our project, was interested in learning local medical practices, but was hampered by his inability to identify medicinal plants.

After discovering a local game in which children strung a number of leaves along a rope and challenged one another to move quickly down the row, naming each leaf in turn, we decided to investigate leaf naming and classification as part of our broader investigation of Kpelle categorizing and remembering. We arranged for a group of American and Canadian college students and Peace Corps volunteers and a group of nonliterate rice farmers to try their hand at identifying fourteen leaves from indigenous vines and trees.

Subjects from each group were assigned to one of three experimental conditions. Those in the first condition were told that the leaves came from trees or vines and asked which leaves came from which source. Those in the second condition were shown exactly the same set of leaves divided in the same way but were told that they belonged to fictional people named Sumo and Togba (two common local names) and were asked which person owned which leaves. In the third condition, the leaves were again said to belong to Sumo and Togba, but the leaves were assigned at random to names, so that the local categorization of leaves was irrelevant. In all cases, the correct names were provided trial by trial if the subject erred. The number of complete passes through the list needed before all leaves were correctly identified differed for the two population groups and for the three conditions, as follows:

|  | Tree-vine rule | Sumo-Togba rule | Sumo-Togba random |
|---|---|---|---|
| Liberians | 1.1 | 7.3 | 6.8 |
| Americans/ Canadians | 8.9 | 9.8 | 9.0 |

On the average, the American/Canadian students required about nine presentations to identify all of the leaves correctly, regardless of the conditions of learning. The local rice farmers generally learned more rapidly, but for them the conditions of learning made an enormous difference. If they were asked which leaves were from trees and which from vines, they identified almost all leaves correctly from the beginning. However, when asked which leaves belonged to Sumo and which to Togba, they performed no better in the case where all the tree leaves belonged to Sumo and all the vine leaves to Togba than when the leaves were assigned to the two categories at random (although in all cases they did better than the American/Canadian group). In the second condition they did not use a categorical distinction that they certainly knew.

In a follow-up to this study we found that in some cases American college students appeared so focused on discovering categories in paired associate lists (such as the one in which all vine leaves belonged to one man, all tree leaves to the other) that they had great trouble with lists with obvious category structures in which items were not paired (such as the condition in which leaves were assigned to the two men at random). The rice farmers, who were indifferent to latent category structure in these circumstances, learned such scrambled lists faster than the American students.

The leaves study was both interesting and perplexing. Local people clearly recognized the leaves and could classify them correctly according to appropriate categories. But when we created a fictitious and arbitrary classification (after all, why should Sumo own all the vine leaves while Togba owned all the tree leaves?), the known classification did not affect their behavior. These results meshed with those obtained in our studies of free recall memory (Chapter 2). Highly educated foreigners, by contrast, learned to identify the leaves very slowly and could not make use of the categorical distinctions at all, even though other studies had shown them to be highly attuned to looking for and using such information to structure their learning and memory.

When we stopped to take stock of our own second-generation research, we concluded that "cultural differences in cognition reside more in the situations to which particular cognitive processes are applied than in the existence of a process in one cultural group and its absence in another" (Cole, Gay, Glick, and Sharp, 1971, p. 233).

Note how neatly hedged this summary is. We did not deny the possibility that specific cognitive differences between cultural groups might arise from differences in specifiable experiences. Schooling is one such experience: experiments indicating that formal schooling induces people to organize disjointed information in order to remember it later, for example, pointed to one such cultural/cognitive difference. But we were *not* assuming that poor performance on our experimental tasks reflected deep and pervasive cognitive differences such as an inability to organize experience conceptually in memory; rather, when people performed poorly in one of our tasks we assumed that it was the task and our understanding of its relationship to locally organized activities, not the people's minds, that were deficient. Sometimes we were successful in devising tasks that did demonstrate the presence of the "missing ability"; sometimes we were not.

### Using Ethnographic Examples

When our ethnographically influenced modifications of experimental procedures did not lead to successful performance, we provided ex-

amples of the relevant cognitive abilities from ethnographic observations. For instance, we conducted a series of studies designed to
assess people's ability to communicate with others about objects
(Cole, Gay, and Glick, 1968). This task was modeled on research by
Robert Krauss and Sam Glucksberg (1969) conducted among children in the United States. Krauss and Glucksberg reported that until
the age of 10–11 years children performed poorly, presumably as a
consequence of pervasive egocentrism. Our version of the task required one person (the speaker) to tell another (the listener) which
of a set of objects to place in a line along the table top. The two
people sat facing each other but could not see each other because of
a screen placed between them.

Even when quite distinctive, locally meaningful stimuli were
used—sticks with various differentiating physical features—speakers
routinely gave listeners too little information. For example, when
communicating about a small, bent stick speakers would label it "the
stick" or "the small one" even though both its size and its shape were
needed to distinguish it from other possibilities. These difficulties
persisted when repeated opportunities were provided to practice the
task. We did not succeed in finding a variant of this task in which
subjects used subtler references. And yet it seemed absurd to conclude that normal Kpelle adults were subject to the same sorts of
egocentric limitations on thought as young children.

At this point we turned to observational work by ourselves and
others to illustrate that the cognitive ability absent in our experimental tasks was manifestly present in certain other cultural contexts. We had, for example, records of legal proceedings in which the
elders would begin to speak in "deep Kpelle," a metaphor-laden form
of speech designed to communicate within the group of elders about
the substance of the matter while communicating to others present
that they were not powerful enough to engage in such discussion.

Another example comes from E. E. Evans-Pritchard's (1963) discussion of a mode of discourse among the Azande of Kenya called
*Sanza*. Sanza is a genre of speech in which people exploit the ambiguity of language to control others and avoid retribution for the hostility they generate. As an illustration, Evans-Pritchard reports a conversation in which a man, in the presence of his wife, declares to a
friend: "friend, those swallows, how they do flit about there" (p. 211).

The friend and the wife both interpret this as criticism of the wife's behavior, and she gets angry. When she accuses her husband of being unfair, he claims she is being oversensitive. Evans-Pritchard characterizes the strategy of using Sanza as follows: "The great thing . . . is to keep under cover and to keep open a line of retreat should the sufferer of your malice take offense and try to make trouble" (p. 222).

Sanza seemed to be an example of communicative behavior subtle enough to simultaneously keep in mind the complexity of reference, several social norms, and other people's perspectives on events. Yet Kenyan native peoples, when tested using psychological tests, appeared no more competent in such areas than the Kpelle (Harkness and Super, 1977).

This kind of "appeal to ethnography" exercised for us what Mead (1978) called "the anthropological veto," in which counter-examples from other cultures are used to disprove claims about the universality, and hence "naturalness," of one's own cultural cosmos. However, no matter how convinced they may be that Evans-Pritchard is describing a real phenomenon and that the strategic perspective-taking involved is just what he says it is, psychologists cannot accept his account as data. There is no experimental method, there is no control group, and there is nothing to quantify for purposes of comparison. It would also be difficult, at the very least, to construct an experimental model of behavior that depends so heavily on bringing just the right level of ambiguity to bear in a situation of a specific character at just the right moment.

## Everyday Problem Solving and Schooling: Syllogisms in the Yucatán

During the 1970s we conducted another study of the developmental-cognitive consequences of schooling, replicating the Liberian research, among the Maya and Mestizo peoples of the Yucatán peninsula (Sharp, Cole, and Lave, 1979). The chief advantage of the Yucatán over Liberia for our purposes was that schooling had spread more broadly in the society over more decades but was still sufficiently unevenly distributed to make possible comparisons of people of widely differing ages and years of schooling. In the lingo of methodological behaviorism, we could separate age and education as independent variables, making possible an analysis of their causal contributions.

The basic pattern of results obtained in this work matched our findings among the Kpelle. Focused as we were on experimental tests of schooling effects, we relied rather heavily on the strategy of successively modifying experimental procedures. By and large, our data seemed to support the claim that schooling brings about a fundamental change in cognitive development. Repeatedly we found that for cognitive tasks involving deliberate remembering, the use of taxonomic categories to organize categorizing and remembering, and formal reasoning on logical syllogisms, performance improved as children grew older *only* to the extent that they entered and continued in school. By contrast, when tasks called upon people to categorize according to functional criteria, and tasks structured so as to make the organizing principles latent in the materials highly salient, performance increased with age, not with schooling.

A representative example involves responses to logical syllogisms. In our work among the Kpelle we had replicated Alexander Luria's studies of syllogistic reasoning, which found that nonschooled subjects are likely to draw upon their empirical knowledge while ignoring the logical implications of the terms. For example:

> If Juan and José drink a lot of beer, the mayor of the town gets angry.
> Juan and José are drinking a lot of beer now.
> Do you think the mayor is angry with them?

Instead of giving the apparently simple logical answer, people would often base their answers on knowledge of particular people, responding, for example, "No—so many men drink beer, why should the mayor get angry?"

Following the work of Luria and Sylvia Scribner (1975a), we categorized responses as theoretical (responding on the basis of the information given in the problem) or empirical (responding on the basis of everyday information about the world). Figure 3.1 shows the relative frequency of theoretical responses as a function of respondents' age and years of schooling. As the figure makes clear, the tendency to treat these verbal puzzles theoretically increased exclu-

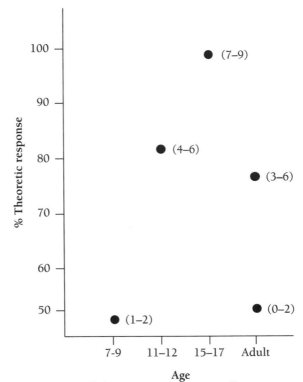

Figure 3.1.   Percentage of theoretic response to syllogistic reasoning problems as a function of age and years of education. Numbers in parentheses indicate years of education.

sively as a function of years of education; children and adults who had not attended school usually gave responses based on the empirical plausibility of the question posed.

   This pattern of results fits nicely not only with our own earlier studies but with the research of others showing attendance at school to be a stimulus to a broad range of cognitive abilities (Greenfield and Bruner, 1966; Stevenson, 1982).[5] Despite the apparent robustness of the findings, however, we emerged from this work with strong suspicions about the generalizability of our findings, because we began to see our investigatory procedures as covert models of schooling practices. We noted that virtually all of our experimental tasks resembled those used by Binet and Simon to predict children's success in school. Binet and Simon's tasks, derived largely from an examination of the school curriculum, use materials and forms of discourse characteristic of schools. The correlation between schooling and success-ful performance on the tasks was built into Binet and Simon's pro-cedures; as noted in Chapter 2, their test items were picked precisely because they discriminated among children at various levels of aca-demic achievement. In an analogous way, we argued, children who have attended school should be expected to do well on our cognitive tests because they receive massive practice in such tasks in the course of their schooling. The so-called cognitive effects of education, from this perspective, are a tautology or at best an illustration of the not-too-deep wisdom that practice makes perfect.

In more technical terms, we began to realize that far from being separate indices of performance, the tasks we had chosen as depen-dent variables were intimately, one might even say incestuously, cou-pled with the "independent" variable of schooling. We dramatized the point with the following thought experiment:

> Suppose . . . that we wanted to assess the consequences of learn-ing to be a carpenter. Sawing and hammering are instances of sensorimotor coordination; learning to measure, mitre corners, and build vertical walls requires mastery of a host of intellectual skills to produce a useful product . . . To be sure, we would be willing to certify a master carpenter as someone who had mas-tered carpentering skills, but how strong would be our claim for the generality of this outcome? Would the measurement of motor skills learned by the carpenter make him a skilled elec-trician or a ballet dancer, let alone a person with "more highly developed sensorimotor and measurement skills"? (Sharp, Cole, and Lave, 1979, p. 81)

Note that in doubting the evidence for a general cognitive transfor-mation associated with schooling we were not declaring that we had proved the converse.[6] Rather, we were distressed by the flaws in the evidence.

It would seem that all we had accomplished with several years of work was to rediscover century-old misgivings about the possibility of resolving questions of culture in mind within the paradigm of methodological behaviorism. Insofar as experiments, like the IQ tests designed by Binet, model the content and structure of school dis-course (see Chapter 2), and insofar as that content and structure differ from culturally organized experience outside of school, the experimental tasks cannot provide a common basis for drawing conclusions about general cognitive differences between schooled and nonschooled children.

Note that this conclusion fits quite well the context-specific approach to interpreting cultural differences in cognition. But its skeptical stance with respect to the interpretation of differences in performance associated with schooling and the efficacy of standardized procedures imported from the industrialized world did not sit well with cross-cultural researchers who based their work on the dominant developmental theories of the day (Dasen, Berry, and Witkin, 1979).

## Piagetian Approaches

The single largest body of cross-cultural research on the role of culture in cognitive development was inspired by work of Jean Piaget. Early in his career Piaget (1928/1995) argued for the existence of important cultural variations in thought processes. Citing the work of Lucien Levy-Bruhl (1910) and Emile Durkheim (1912), he distinguished between two kinds of societies, which Levy-Bruhl characterized as "primitive" and "civilized" and which today might be called "traditional" and "modern." He claimed that there is a distinct "mentality" corresponding to each type of social organization, "the mentality called primitive to the conformist or segmentary societies, the rational mentality to our differentiated societies" (1928/1995, p. 191). However, he disagreed with Levy-Bruhl's claim that there should be no developmental ordering of the two kinds of mentality; in Piaget's view at the time, primitive mentality is a precursor of civilized mentality much as child thought is a developmental precursor of adult thought.

Many of Piaget's early books contain references to the childlike thought of primitive adults. However, he did no research on this topic himself, and one of the few attempts to verify his ideas, by Margaret Mead (1932), failed to substantiate his claims about childhood animism.

It was not until the mid-1960s that Piaget returned to the issue of cultural variations in cognitive development. In a widely cited article, he divided potential influences on cognitive development into four main factors, each of which could be expected to influence the timing of developmental milestones:

1. *Biological factors.* Here Piaget mentions nutrition and general health, factors that influence the rate of physical maturation.
2. *Coordinations of individual actions.* This factor refers to equilibration, the active process of self-regulation resulting from the back-and-forth tug and pull of accommodation and assimilation. Equilibration is the proximal mechanism of development. All other factors operate through their influence on equilibration.
3. *The social factor of interpersonal coordination.* By this he meant the process by which children "ask questions, share information, work together, argue, object, etc." (Piaget, 1966/1974, p. 302).
4. *Educational and cultural transmission.* Piaget reasoned that children acquire specific skills and knowledge through interaction in culturally specific social institutions. Insofar as some societies provide more overall experience relevant to discovering the nature of the world, true developmental differences will be created in either the rate or the final level of development.

Piaget recognized that these four contributing factors are all tightly interconnected. This interconnection made it difficult to determine the sources of differences in developmental rate in those cases where they had been observed. He expressed the hope that future research would more carefully differentiate the four factors.

Piaget was skeptical of schooling's development-enhancing properties. He argued that the asymmetrical power relations of teacher and student created an imbalance because the pressure to accommodate to teachers' views far outweighed the pressure for assimilation of instruction to the child's already existing schemas. The result was learning of a superficial kind that was unlikely to create fundamental cognitive change. He believed that fundamental change was more likely to occur in informal actions where the asymmetry of power relations was reduced, allowing for a more equal balance between assimilation and accommodation. Evidence on this matter was too inconclusive in the mid 1960s to support more than speculation.

In general, the spate of Piagetian research begun in the 1960s found a good deal more variability among societies than Piaget had anticipated. In some cases, little or no difference in achieving Piagetian developmental milestones was observed (Price-Williams, 1961). In other cases, however, researchers reported that children from traditional, nonindustrialized societies achieved the stage of concrete operations one or more years later than children in Western industrialized societies (Dasen, 1972). There were also a few studies in which twelve- and thirteen-year-old children and even adults failed to demonstrate understanding of the principles underlying conservation in the Piagetian tasks (DeLemos, 1969; Goodnow, 1962; Greenfield, 1966). Reviewing the evidence available in the early 1970s, Pierre Dasen wrote, "It can no longer be assumed that adults of all societies reach the concrete operational stage" (1972, p. 31). Quite naturally there were competing interpretations of the apparent cultural variability in ages at which children achieved the Piagetian stage milestones (see Berry et al., 1992; Dasen, 1977a,b, 1984; Segall et al., 1990, for more detail on these discussions).

In 1972 Piaget confronted the evidence of cultural variation in performance on his operational tasks. Whereas the data concerning acquisition of concrete operations remained a source of contention (some found cultural differences, others did not), a consensus had formed that in many cultures, especially without formal schooling, formal operational thinking as manifested on Piagetian tasks does not develop (Jahoda, 1980; Neimark, 1975).

Piaget offered three possible reasons for the observed variability in the rates of change and degree of mastery in operational thinking. First, it might be that some cultures offer more intellectual stimulation overall than others. Second, it might be that formal operations are a kind of cognitive specialization in the manner of an individual difference in intelligence which allows certain individuals to penetrate particular domains of knowledge more deeply than others. The third possibility, which Piaget favored, was to assume that all individuals reach a universal stage of formal operational thinking, but that formal operations are attained first (and perhaps only) in fields of adult specialization (a view that Harris and Heelas, 1979, described as "local constructivism"). This view offers an obvious line of reconciliation of Piagetian theory with the facts about cultural variability.

During the 1970s, Dasen published a number of studies which provided support for some variant of the notion of local (cultural) constructivism (Dasen, 1974, 1975, 1977b). The basic idea was that performance within stages would vary as a function of the value a culture placed on the conceptual content of the particular task used. In a later paper Dasen (1984) contrasted performance of the Baoulé (Ivory Coast) with that of the Inuit (Canada) on conservation of liquid (quantity) and horizontality (assessed through judgments about the level of liquid in a jar tilted at various angles). The Baoulé, he reasoned, should tend to value and engage with quantitative concepts because they produce, store, and exchange vegetables and other foods in a market economy. By contrast, the Inuit are said to show little interest in precise quantitative comparisons, placing greater emphasis on spatial skills and associated concepts. Using the idea that "density of experience" grounded in everyday activities is the important factor pushing conceptual development, plus the notion that such densities vary from one activity to another within cultures, Dasen predicted that the hunters would perform better on the task grounded in spatial judgments than on quantitative tasks, while the Baoulé would show the opposite pattern. His predictions were borne out.

Dasen and his colleagues also undertook a series of training studies to determine if culturally linked differences in performance reflect differences in some relatively deep, underlying cognitive competence, or merely superficial performance factors associated with the language of experimentation or some surface aspect of the experimental procedures (Dasen, 1977b; Dasen, Lavallée, and Retschitzki, 1979; Dasen, Ngini, and Lavallée, 1979). They began by assessing children's spontaneous level of performance. Children who failed were trained to attend to relevant aspects of the problem. In many cases training quickly erased developmental lags, while in others the effects of training were slow, and in a few cases there were no effects of training at all.

Other researchers operating within a Piagetian framework sought to resolve questions about differences in performance by modifying the ways they presented the tasks or by using tasks of manifestly local content. With respect to content, Douglas Price-Williams, William Gordon, and Manuel Ramirez (1969) found that Mexican children growing up in a village where adults specialized in pottery making acquired conservation significantly faster than children from a comparison village where people did not make pottery.

An experiment on the effects of modifying testing procedures to match local cultural knowledge was conducted by Judith Irvine (1978), who studied conservation of liquid among the Wolof that followed up earlier research by Patricia Greenfield (1966). Greenfield had reported that children were much more likely to achieve conservation if they were allowed to pour the liquid themselves instead of watching the experimenter pour it. She speculated that this change in procedure reduced the Wolof children's tendency to interpret the experiment as something of a magic show, but she did not highlight these findings in her conclusions at the time (see Greenfield, 1976, for a discussion of her later thinking on these issues).

Irvine asked children to solve the conservation task and then to play the role of informants whose job it was to clarify, *for the experimenter,* the Wolof terms for resemblance and equivalence with respect to the task. When confronted with the critical test in which one beaker of water is poured into a narrower, taller beaker, the Wolof in the role of subject solving the problem gave the wrong response— they said that the beaker with water higher up its sides contained more liquid. But in their role as linguistic informants these same children explained that while the level of water was "more" the quantity was the same. Irvine's and Greenfield's results provide nice examples of the kinds of performance factors that can block the actualization of competence (to use Dasen's terminology).

The strategy of basing diagnosis of children's operational levels on tasks more nearly indigenous to the people being studied was pursued by Robert LeVine and Price-Williams (1974) and Patricia Greenfield and Carla Childs (1977) using the domain of kin relations. In studies carried out among the Hausa of Nigeria, among the Maya of Zinacantan, and in a remote fishing village in Hawaii, children's abilities to deal with the three levels of kinship relationship appear to fit well into a Piagetian sequence and timetable. Greenfield and Childs found in Zinacantan, for example, that most four-to-five-year-olds could answer ego-centered (Level 1) questions, but not more complex ones. Most eight-to-ten-year-olds could answer questions about relationships between two siblings, but not when the relationship involved themselves. And most thirteen-to-eighteen-year-olds could answer questions about both a sibling and themselves. As Greenfield and Childs note, these results fit rather well with Piagetian stage-theory notions, even to the extent of approximating the normative onset times of the operational substages.

The residual variability in outcomes from one study to the next produces some uncertainty about how this overall enterprise ought to be evaluated. I am sympathetic to the treatments of this issue in recent summary statements by Dasen and his colleagues (Berry et al., 1992; Dasen and de Ribaupierre, 1987; Segall et al., 1990), who offer the opinion that concrete operational thought is universal in the sense that most people in all societies display the accepted manifestations of concrete operational thinking in some version of some relevant task. But I am unable to interpret cases where proportions of people who perform the tasks are very low or where training does not bridge the gap. Such results, when obtained with children in Geneva or Minneapolis, are taken as evidence that children of "that age" have not attained the corresponding level of cognitive development within mainstream Piagetian psychology. Why shouldn't the same kind of evidence produce the same conclusion in cross-cultural comparisons?

The uncertainties that accompany the repeated appearance of developmental "lags" permit some to conclude that primitive peoples do in fact think like children from industrialized societies (e.g. Hallpike, 1979). I should note that these uncertainties in cross-cultural studies have their counterpart in Piagetian research in Europe and the United States. All during the period under review American and European researchers were reporting that children are capable of concrete operational thinking much earlier than previously estimated (Donaldson, 1978; Siegal, 1991).

At present there are a number of efforts to reformulate Piagetian theory to accommodate the evidence of within-subject, across-domain variability, as well as variability in the average age for mastery of various embodiments of operational thinking (Case, 1992; Fischer, Knight, and Van Parys, 1993). The overall trend, in both the cross-cultural and intra-cultural work, is to posit both a universal potential, perhaps linked with species-wide maturation of the nervous system in some sort of species-average "range of reaction," *and* domain-specific and context-specific variations resulting from differential density of experience driven by differing patterns of cultural practices and values.

By and large, research using Piagetian tasks provides negative conclusions with respect to the effects of education on cognitive development. Such effects, where they have been reported, appear to be related to familiarity with the testing procedures, and not indicative of deep differences in cognitive competence.

## Cognitive Style

Another major program of research on cultural differences in cognitive development is based on the idea that each culture engenders its own particular style of thought. This idea rose to prominence in the 1930s in the work of anthropologists interested in the mutual relationships between culture and personality (Bock, 1988).

In the 1960s this tradition of thinking about culture and personality was brought together with research on culture and cognition through the efforts of Herman Witkin (1967) and John Berry (1966). Witkin's prior research had been on the development of perception, particularly different styles of perceptual inference and analysis (Witkin et al., 1962).

Witkin believed that individual differences in perceptual style reflect differences in the degree of "psychological differentiation." He defined differentiation in relation to a system's structure. Although all systems exhibit some heterogeneity of structure, a differentiated system, according to Witkin and his colleagues, contains multiple subsystems related to specialization of function. When applied to psychological cognitive systems, differentiation implies separation of specific psychological functions such as perceiving, feeling, and acting as well as specific ways of functioning within domains.

The basic expectation of the cultural-style approach is that there should be a correspondence between levels of differentiation at the cultural and individual levels of analysis. Just as craft specialization or social stratification may be used as an indicator of sociocultural differentiation, so various behavioral indicators may be used to assess individual differentiation. In addition, there should be consistency in levels of differentiation from one psychological domain to another. Berry (1976, p. 26) summarized the expectation of individual consistency across domains of psychological functioning as follows: "[Differentiation] is considered to be a *characteristic of the organism,* and expectations are that tasks which sample differentiation of various kinds of behaviors should yield estimates of roughly similar levels of differentiation."

To implement these ideas, Berry and others have conducted cross-cultural studies among societies said to differ in degree of sociocultural differentiation. Their behavioral indicators are taken from Witkin's tradition of work on psychological differentiation. The basic procedure can be illustrated by two widely used tests of perceptual differentiation, the embedded-figures test (EFT) and the rod-in-frame test (RFT). In the EFT a distinctive figure is made part of a larger design and the subject must locate it; in the Rod-and-Frame Test the subject is required to adjust a rod to be vertical when the definition of vertical is ambiguous because the rod is presented in a frame that can be tilted at various angles with respect to the floor and the subject is seated on a platform that can also be tilted. The key question in the RFT is what frame of reference the subject chooses: Is vertical defined with respect to the frame, the room, or the subject's own body orientation?

Research conducted in the United States has identified two distinctive styles of responses to these tasks. Some people confronting the RFT attend less to the cues from the frame, defining vertical with respect to their own bodies, and are good at "disembedding" figures from their surroundings in the EFT. This pattern is identified as "field independent" because the person relies on internal cues for behavior, so appears autonomous. By contrast, "field dependent" people have difficulty disembedding figure from background and are oriented toward the environment in the RFT, so they define vertical with respect to the frame the rod is in.

Berry (1976) reported data on eighteen subsistence cultures, from West Africa to Northern Canada and Australia, in which he administered tests of cognitive style and questionnaires about socialization customs in subjects' families when they were children. The Human

Area Files were used to code information about ecological and cultural elements and socialization practices. Correlational techniques were then used to compare the relationships in the data to those expected from the ecocultural model. Berry summarized the results as follows:

> Cultural groups (and individuals) which are hunting and gathering in subsistence pattern, nomadic in settlement pattern, and loose in sociopolitical stratification emerge as clearly different in cognitive style from those which are agricultural, sedentary, and tight. And within this range of ecocultural adaptations, those which occupy intermediate positions ecoculturally also exhibit intermediate behavioral adaptations. . . . Taken at the level of a general overview, it is difficult to avoid the conclusion that the hypothesized relationships have been confirmed. (p. 200)

Despite Berry's confidence, a variety of questions were raised about his conclusions (see LCHC, 1983, pp. 650 ff for a more extended treatment of these issues and references). First, it was pointed out that while hypothesized first-order correlations among the variables showed significant relationships, one should not be under the illusion that a causal chain from ecology → economic activity → social organization → childrearing practices → cognitive outcome had been established or that one could talk about causality in these relationships at all. The problem is referred to as multi-colinearity, meaning that all the independent variables (causal factors) are correlated so that their independent contributions to one another and to the dependent variables are impossible to specify.[7]

Additional doubts about the theory focused on the assumption that styles of responding in one psychological domain should be the same as styles of responding in others. There should be self-consistency across cognitive domains. Psychologists raised two questions about the evidence for self-consistency. Some pointed to empirical studies that showed inconsistency in styles of responding among tasks within a single presumed psychological domain—for example, performance on rod-and-frame tests inconsistent with that on embedded-figures tests. Others pointed out that there was little evidence for stylistic consistency across domains—for example, results in the perceptual domain did not correlate in the expected way with those in the social-interactional domain (Jahoda, 1980; Serpell, 1976; Werner, 1979).

In a second large study conducted in the 1970s (but published later: Berry et al., 1986; Van de Koppel, 1983), the cognitive styles of Biaka pygmies of Central Africa were compared with those of an agriculturalist group living in the same geographical region on the edge of the Iturbi forest. The research team, composed of anthropologists as well as psychologists, sought a deep understanding of the local culture, engaged in extensive ethnographic documentation, and created special, culturally tailored forms of some of their tests (for example, using pictures of animals embedded in natural-looking environments or of a person shooting an arrow with a bow instead of geometric figures for the embedded-figures test). They also attempted to sample from many different domains of relevance to cultural style. For example, they created a measure of "social autonomy" designed to assess field independence in social interaction, which could then be correlated with their cognitive and perceptual tests to check for self-consistency.

Robert Serpell (1990) notes three major ways in which the results failed to meet the researchers' expectations:

1. The correlations among test scores indicating cognitive style were generally very low, and the measures of social behavior (crucial to establishing the notion of a "style" encompassing many different domains) did not correlate with the perceptual tests.

2. When the predictive power of two measures of acculturation was compared—a composite social index of prior contact with Western institutions and a psychological index of adaptability—it was adaptation to the test conditions themselves that best predicted performance. As Serpell notes, this result means that despite the painstaking effort to design culturally sensitive tests, the resulting procedures "remained essentially foreign to the indigenous cultures of the Biaka and the Bagandu" (p. 120).

3. Patterns of parental socialization (the independent variable) were not correlated with individual differences in cognitive style (dependent variables), leading the authors to conclude that "despite ethnographic and theoretical analyses, despite

careful scale construction and statistical refinement, both the socialization phenomena themselves, and their relationship to test performance, appear to have eluded our research efforts" (p. 212).

It is difficult to overemphasize how much care and work went into Berry's two large projects. The effort was enormous. My view, which is by no means universally held, is that at the end of all this effort the evidence does not present a compelling case for the presence of cultural differences in cognitive style. Correlational data are always suspect with respect to causal claims, but even if we accept the logic of Berry and colleagues' analysis, the resulting correlations are very modest. This does not mean that cognitive styles are a myth. I continue to find the idea an intuitively appealing one. But I come away from the research more impressed by the variability in behavior that is not explained than by the variability that is explained.

One additional point. In a number of cases Berry included educated as well as uneducated people in his samples. Although it covaried along with other population variables such as urbanization, education was generally associated with an increase in field dependence. It is difficult to know how to interpret this effect: it could result from the fact that educated people are more familiar with the stimulus materials and the ways in which they are generally used, or it could reflect a more pervasive change in cognitive style.

## A Summing Up

During the late 1970s and early 1980s the uncertainties generated by two decades of intense research on culture and cognitive development produced a good deal of stock-taking (Berry, 1981; Dasen and Heron, 1981; Eckensberger, Lonner, and Poortinga, 1979; LCHC, 1978, 1979; Marsella, Tharp, and Ciborowski, 1979; Munroe, Munroe, and Whiting, 1981; Rogoff, 1981; Serpell, 1982; Triandis and Lambert, 1980). What is most striking about these critical self-evaluations is how few substantive generalizations about culture in mind they contained. Despite more than a decade of effort at solving the methodological problems of the field, the only theme that seemed to unite different authors was the litany of now-familiar concerns:

(1) cross-cultural research is methodologically problematic; (2) the weakness of its theories stems from the ambiguous significance of its data.

On the surface, at least, research attempting to assess the impact of schooling on cognitive development would appear to be an exception to this dreary picture. If comparisons of schooled and nonschooled subjects produced a significant difference between the two groups, the schooled subjects always performed at higher levels.

Insofar as we take these results at face value, there is an irony in the apparent efficacy of schooling in promoting cognitive development. Most of the cross-cultural work on cognitive development was supported because of a widespread consensus that children from rural, poor, largely nonliterate populations achieve poorly in school. Psychologists involved in the research confirmed that there is a problem with the way "the natives" think. But according to their test procedures, schooling overcomes these cognitive problems. If schooling is so successful in bringing about cognitive change, shouldn't that be sufficient to bring about the economic and social changes hoped for by the architects of UNESCO policies?

Cross-cultural psychologists did not seem to recognize this discordance at the time. After all, we had helped to generate it by the ways in which we gathered data and interpreted our results. From my first visit to Liberia in 1964 I could see that schools were failing; John Gay and I often discussed them as part of a system of cultural disruption and social reorganization. What we did not have was a systematic way of thinking about the relation between the psychological reality we created through our research practices and the psychological reality of people in their everyday practices. Unfortunately, when given a second chance to address the issues, we were not up to the task of reconstructing psychology on the basis of people's everyday activities. Rather, our contribution (insofar as it was a contribution) was to reveal more and more clearly the shortcomings of the disciplinary division of labor within which we were working.

Cole's motivation

# 4 ⓖ

# From Cross-Cultural Psychology
# to the Second Psychology

If psychology must be changed in order to understand the
majority of mankind, then this is a fact of profound
importance.  *Harry Triandis*

WERE WILHELM WUNDT alive today to assess the attempt to use
the methods of experimental/quantitative psychology to found a culture-inclusive psychology, he would certainly have the right to declare "I told you so." After all, it was Wundt who warned us that it
is foolhardy to apply the methods of the natural sciences to any but
the most elementary, universal, and therefore *timeless* aspects of human behavior. It was Wundt who pointed out that individual human
psychological processes are conditioned by an earlier history of the
community to which they have no direct access. And it was Wundt
who asserted that genetic (historical, developmental) methods are
needed to deal with culturally mediated, historically contingent,
"higher" psychological processes. It seems that Wundt correctly diagnosed modern objections to cross-cultural research before the first
such study was even conducted.

In seeking for a better way to include culture within a single psychological enterprise, I do not want to discard the results of the last
hundred years of research in the first psychology, including cross-

cultural experimental studies. Cross-cultural studies, especially when they are sensitive to the local organization of activity, can serve to refute ethnocentric conclusions that "those people" suffer from general cognitive deficits as a consequence of cultural inadequacies. From time to time they may even induce adherents of the first psychology to rethink their conclusions and their experimental methods. I believe this has happened, for example, with respect to the increasing attention being paid to issues of context by scholars working within the first psychology's paradigm, especially those concerned with cognitive development (Siegal and Cohen, 1991; Wozniak and Fischer, 1993).

However, as I have tried to demonstrate in earlier chapters, cross-cultural research within the first psychology is limited in its power to provide a *positive* explanation for the role of culture in mental life. It has also proven a weak guide to practice. What is needed is an alternative form of psychological inquiry. It is time to elaborate a second psychology, the goal being to be able, eventually, to supersede that ancient set of dichotomies to which both the first and second psychologies belong.

## Rethinking the Two Psychologies

As a first step toward formulating a more adequate approach to the relations between mind and culture, we need to recognize that psychology (like all of the social sciences) is a sharply divided discipline (Koch and Leary, 1985).

The 1960s and 1970s, the high-water mark of experimental cross-cultural psychology, were also the decades in which the "cognitive revolution" swept the discipline. It once again became possible and fashionable to include theoretical mental entities or processes occurring between stimulus and response as a focal concern of psychology. The dominant metaphor of cognitive psychology was that of the person as an information-processing system thought of in terms of modern computers. The dominant methodologies remained well within the framework of methodological behaviorism; what changed was the complexity of the transformations attributed to the structures mediating the interval between input and output.

The 1970s saw a new organization of academic resources for addressing the nature of mind: cognitive science. The dominant voices in cognitive science, like those in cognitive psychology, remained firmly in the tradition of the first psychology. In bringing the neurosciences together with the social-behavioral sciences around the use of modern computer sciences and artificial intelligence, cognitive science brings about a quite understandable extension of Wundt's idea of physiological psychology.

Lacking from this picture, of course, is the role played in this development by the second psychology. Jerome Bruner (1990), a leading figure in the cognitive revolution, has argued that at its inception that revolution was intended to be more than a way of improving on behaviorism. It was to bring into being a psychology focused on the process of making meaning.

By Bruner's account, the original intentions of the cognitive revolution were hijacked by those who reduced minds to machines. He sides with those who worry that the change from cognitive psychology to cognitive science and the increased focus on reduction of the cognitive to the physiological dehumanizes the concept of mind that the fathers of the revolution had set out to rescue.

During these same decades, the other social-behavioral sciences were undergoing their own transformations. In sociology and anthropology, to which psychology had ceded the study of social groups and culture, one encountered renewed criticism of the division of labor that had formed these disciplines around the turn of the century. This criticism was accompanied by a search for new frameworks for the study of human nature.

For some, cognitive science, with its emphasis on interdisciplinary cooperation and the reintegration of philosophy and linguistics into the social sciences, provided a promising starting point for reintegrating culture into the study of mind (Hutchins, 1995). For others, like Bruner, cognitive science represented only the latest form of human fascination with technology and techno-rationalism and the delusion that machines provide the measure of humanity. Consequently, new academic forums would need to be discovered or created. Many argued in support of the "interpretive turn" which would reintegrate the social sciences with the humanities and arts, thereby undoing a century of mischief engendered by runaway positivism (Edwards,

1995; Gergen, 1994; Ortner, 1984; Rabinow and Sullivan, 1987). Communication, my current disciplinary home, is one new discipline in which these issues are of central concern.

I do not have the scholarly range and depth to provide a comprehensive account of these events. I mention them here simply to alert the reader to the fact that neither psychology nor its sister disciplines are intellectual monoliths whose structures are uniformly agreed upon. Quite the contrary, we seem to be living in a period when orthodoxies no longer retain their holding power and new possibilities abound. One such possibility is particularly relevant to the present inquiry: the possibility of going back to the early decades of psychology and starting out on the road not taken, the road along which culture is placed on a level with biology and society in shaping individual human natures. The name currently given to that enterprise is *cultural psychology,* a major late-twentieth-century manifestation of the second psychology.

## Visions of Cultural Psychology

Given the current burst of interest in the topic, I find it interesting to note that statements promoting the formation of a cultural psychology are to be found throughout the psychological literature of the twentieth century. Although the early formulations differed in various ways, they all emphasized points that have appeared often in earlier chapters of this book: the insights to be gained from fixed-task psychological experiments are limited, and sociocultural context is an integral part of mental functioning (Stern, 1920/1990; Krewer, 1990, reviews several such proposals).

For the better part of this century, a second psychology according a central role to culture failed to win a significant following. In recent decades, however, stimulated in part by the difficulties of cross-cultural approaches and in part by a more general dissatisfaction with the progress of psychology or the social sciences (Koch and Leary, 1985), proposals employing the term "cultural psychology" have begun to appear in great profusion.

Stephen Toulmin (1980) urged psychologists to reconsider Wundt's proposal for a *Völkerpsychologie,* which he translated as "cultural psychology." At almost the same time, Douglass Price-Williams (1979, 1980) recommended that cross-cultural psychology be broadened into a *cultural* psychology, which he defined as "that branch of inquiry that delves into the contextual behavior of psychological processes" (1979, p. 14). He suggested that this new approach should draw on semiotics, the study of pragmatics in language, and cultural studies more broadly conceived.

Lutz Eckensberger, Berndt Krewer, and their colleagues in Saarbrücken began to argue for a cultural psychology based on the ideas of Ernst Boesch, whose psychological theories combine the German historical tradition that led Wundt to claim the need for a *Völkerpsychologie* with a form of action theory and Piagetian constructivism (Boesch, 1990; Eckensberger, 1990; Krewer, 1990). Boesch confirmed the intellectual problem at the core of cultural psychology when he wrote: "It is the dilemma of psychology to deal as a natural science with an object that creates history" (quoted in Cole, 1990, p. 279).

The Saarbrücken group underscored the theme that cultural psychology requires a developmental approach to the study of human nature. They believed their action theory approach to cultural psychology offered, at least theoretically, "the possibility of interrelating the three main levels of the concept of development within the same theoretical language: the actual genesis (process), the ontogeny, and the historio-genesis; that is it allows linking historical change to individual change substantially" (Eckensberger, Krewer, and Kasper, 1984, p. 97).

In addition to Boesch's form of action theory, this group drew on the ecological psychology movement as represented in the work of Roger Barker and his students (Barker, 1968), on certain strains of German and American critical social sciences (e.g. Habermas, 1971; Ortner, 1984), as well as on a variety of European and American anthropological sources.

Richard Shweder, whose ideas about cultural psychology I discussed briefly in the Introduction, focused both on the context and content-specificity of human thought and on the centrality of mediation by meaningful symbols. He declared a key idea of cultural psychology to be that "no sociocultural environment exists or has identity independent of the way human beings seize meanings and resources from it, while every human being has her or his subjectivity and mental life altered through the process of seizing meanings and resources from some sociocultural environment and using them" (1984, p. 2). The dual process of shaping and being shaped through culture implies that humans inhabit "intentional" (constituted) worlds within which the traditional dichotomies of subject and object, person and environment, and so on, cannot be analytically separated and temporally ordered into independent and dependent variables. All disciplines that take semiotic mediation to be a core principle for the analysis of human nature are relevant to the new discipline envisioned by Shweder.

Jerome Bruner's (1990) vision of cultural psychology also emphasizes the premise that human experience and action are shaped by our intentional states. It locates the emergence and functioning of psychological processes within the social-symbolically mediated everyday encounters of people in the lived events of their everyday lives. These events are organized in large part, Bruner argues, by a "folk psychology," which provides "a system by which people organize their experience in, knowledge about, and transactions with the social world" (p. 35). Central to this folk psychology are a theory of how minds work and canonical narrative structures, or event representations, that "organize up" people's meaning-making processes in their everyday activities. This approach leads Bruner and his colleagues into such varied paths as discourse analysis of spontaneous and elicited narratives, comparative studies of normal and autistic children's developing theories of mind, case studies of children and even of families (Bruner, 1990; Feldman, 1994; Lucariello, 1995). His cultural psychology synthesizes these data using theoretical constructs drawn from across the humane sciences.

I do not want to minimize the differences among these prescriptions. Bruner and Shweder, for example, place a greater emphasis on the centrality of interpretation and methods of analysis derived from the humanities than do Price-Williams or the German action theorists. They also differ in the particular historical roots of cultural psychology they draw upon and the kinds of data that provide their core empirical foundations. For example, Shweder comes to the problematic of cultural psychology as a psychological anthropologist, while Bruner comes to it as a developmental psychologist. Shweder draws heavily on Western European and American sociocultural the-

ories of culture and rarely mentions German or Russian work. Bruner's initial frame was provided by Vygotsky.

I will return to consider current discussions about cultural psychology in the final chapter. At this juncture I am primarily concerned to highlight their points of agreement. If we combine the
attributes of cultural psychology suggested by those who view themselves as cultural psychologists, without insisting on total agreement,
the union of their characteristics provides a promising starting point
for my own formulation.

I take the main characteristics of cultural psychology to be as follows:

It emphasizes mediated action in a context.

It insists on the importance of the "genetic method" understood
   broadly to include historical, ontogenetic, and microgenetic levels of analysis.

It seeks to ground its analysis in everyday life events.

It assumes that mind emerges in the *joint* mediated activity of people. Mind, then, is in an important sense, "co-constructed" and
   distributed.

It assumes that individuals are active agents in their own development but do not act in settings entirely of their own choosing.

It rejects cause-effect, stimulus-response, explanatory science in
   favor of a science that emphasizes the emergent nature of mind
   in activity and that acknowledges a central role for interpretation
   in its explanatory framework.

It draws upon methodologies from the humanities as well as from
   the social and biological sciences.

## A Cultural-Historical Approach

It should be clear that I have a great deal of sympathy for the sort of
scientific enterprise proposed by contemporary adherents of cultural
psychology. Any of their proposals could serve as a useful starting
point for the elaboration of a second psychology from the core ideas
they share. However, as I indicated earlier, I came to adopt a "cultural-
historical" approach to cultural psychology. The notion of cultural-
historical psychology applies to the thinkers of many national
traditions, but it is commonly associated with the Russian scholars
Alexei Leontiev, Alexander Luria, and Lev Vygotsky. It was in terms

of their ideas that I came to formulate a cultural psychology. The resultant approach, which I have taken to calling cultural-historical activity theory, provides one productive way to overcome the dichotomy of Wundt's two psychologies while incorporating culture in mind.

### Attractions of This Approach

My first encounter with the ideas of the cultural-historical school came when I was a postdoctoral fellow studying with Alexander Luria in Moscow. As I have indicated elsewhere (Cole, 1979), I was not well prepared by my education to appreciate Luria's approach to psychology. It was more than a decade following my work in Moscow before I began to take his ideas to heart as a possible framework for my own thinking.

Initially I interpreted cultural-historical psychology as the rough equivalent to American neobehaviorism of the 1960s. Vygotsky diagrammed the "cultural habit of behavior" using a "mediated stimulus-response" formulation (S-x-R) that looked uncannily like the diagrams drawn by the students of well-known learning theorists such as Clark Hull and Kenneth Spence, who had great influence on the way general psychology approached the study of cognitive development (Hilgard, 1956). In that part of Luria's work with which I was then familiar, the cultural habit of behavior was spoken of in terms of the "second signaling system," a concept applied by Pavlov and his followers to language. I was familiar with Pavlov's work, which was an accepted part of the history of American learning theories, but I was not a developmental psychologist, so I interpreted talk about the second system as another way to talk about mediated stimulus-response learning, an idea that had won wide favor at the time (for example, Kendler and Kendler, 1962). I didn't pay this discussion much mind; I was working with rats and adults to discover universal laws of learning, not with children in cultural contexts.

I first began using cultural-historical psychology when I went to Africa and found myself wondering what sorts of experiments I might conduct to determine the sources of children's difficulties with learning in school. I knew that Vygotsky attached great importance to the acquisition of literacy and that Luria had done some cross-cultural studies of reasoning with results that had never been fully published. To learn what this work was about, I spent the summer of 1966 in Moscow, where Luria and I went systematically through his files of data from Central Asia (which he subsequently published: Luria, 1971, 1976). As noted in the previous chapter, in later years my colleagues and I replicated and extended a number of his experimental techniques, and we began to use ideas borrowed from cultural-historical writings to explain some of our results (Cole et al., 1971; Sharp, Cole, and Lave, 1979; Scribner, 1977).

A crucial next step in my education in cultural-historical thinking came from editing four texts, the first by Vygotsky, the others by Luria. Coming back to Vygotsky's ideas after a decade of research on culture and cognitive development, I still found him very difficult to read. I could no longer mistake him for an American learning theorist clothed in Russian terminology. But I did not understand his focus on early-twentieth-century psychologists. I did not know their work well enough to appreciate the arguments Vygotsky made, and I could not see their relevance to my current concerns. After all, hadn't they been superseded by the theorists I had studied in graduate school?

Nonetheless, I had allowed Luria to talk me into taking responsibility for publishing a book by Vygotsky, so I had to learn to understand Vygotsky's ideas well enough to make a case that they were worth reading. My first move was to seek help from colleagues who had a deeper background in the relevant issues than I, Vera John-Steiner, Sylvia Scribner, and Ellen Souberman, with whom I eventually coedited a volume of Vygotsky's essays called *Mind in Society* (1978). Over several years we exchanged texts and met to argue over points of interpretation. We found agreement so difficult on some points that we wrote two separate commentaries on the text.[1] To the surprise of everyone involved, this book sparked a very broad interest in Vygotsky's works.

Editing Luria's autobiography, *The Making of Mind* (1979), was a simpler task because most of the text had begun as the script for a documentary film, which contained summaries of easily understood empirical research. Still, I found myself mystified by many of Luria's references to nineteenth- and early-twentieth-century psychologists of whom I had never heard.

In an attempt to understand why such "old-fashioned" ideas were so important to Vygotsky and Luria, I spent a good deal of effort learning more about the history of psychology. Editing Luria's two longitudinal case studies (*Mind of a Mnemonist* and *Man with a Shattered World*) gave me insight into how the theory applies to adults as well as children, and stimulated me to rethink my methods for collecting and interpreting data.

Luria's account of his fifty-year career made clear an overall plan, the "paradigmatic foundation" of cultural-historical psychology. It explained the many connections among the apparently separate lines of research he and his colleagues had pursued: cross-cultural variations in thought, language and thought in mentally retarded children, the neuropsychology of brain damage, the development of memory and attention, comparisons among identical and fraternal twins, and so on. Eventually I came to believe that the Russian cultural-historical psychologists were proposing the kind of total reorganization of psychological theory that Harry Triandis had said might result when culture was made central to the discipline. Unlike most contemporary scholars who are proposing a cultural psychology, the Russians were neither proposing a new discipline of cultural psychology nor a subdiscipline of psychology devoted to cultural studies. Instead, if their view were to prevail, all psychology would treat culture, along with biology and social interaction, as central.

In arguing for the total reorganization of the discipline, Vygotsky and his colleagues traced the existing incompatibility between different schools of psychology back to the divide between natural and cultural sciences which split the discipline at its birth. They believed the cultural-historical approach could, in principle, bring about a resolution of the problem of "two psychologies."[2]

This analysis appealed to me because it explained so clearly the origins of the many contradictions I had encountered as I tried to work through the methodological quagmire of cross-cultural psychology. It also offered a systematic way to think about a solution that could help make greater sense of the issues. But I could not simply embrace the form of cultural psychology that the Russians offered. On the basis of my own research, I was critical of their methodology in cross-cultural research. I rejected their inferences about cultural differences and was skeptical of their broad conclusions concerning the cognitive impact of writing and schooling.

Over time, however, I began to see ways to combine key insights

and methods of the cultural-historical approach with equally important insights and methods from American approaches. Before beginning to describe the synthetic approach that has emerged during the
past decade, I shall discuss the benefits and difficulties of building a
cultural psychology starting from the ideas of the Russian cultural-
historical psychology.

## Basic Principles of Cultural-Historical Psychology

The central thesis of the Russian cultural-historical school is that the
structure and development of human psychological processes emerge
through culturally mediated, historically developing, practical activity. Each term in this formulation is tightly interconnected with, and
in some sense implies, the others. At the risk of unproductive simplification, I summarize the key concepts in serial order.[3]

   1. *Mediation through artifacts.* The initial premise of the cultural-
historical school is that human psychological processes emerged simultaneously with a new form of behavior in which humans modified material objects as a means of regulating their interactions with
the world and one another. (It was common at the time to refer to
such mediational devices as tools, but I prefer to use the generic
concept involved, *artifact,* for reasons that will become clear.)

   Luria (1928), in the first publication of the ideas of cultural-
historical psychology in English, begins with the assertion: "Man differs from animals in that he can make and use tools." These tools
"not only radically change his conditions of existence, they even react
on him in that they effect a change in him and his psychic condition"
(p. 493).

   When Luria and others wrote about "tool" mediation they did not
have in mind only such artifacts as hoes and plates. They considered
language to be an integral part of the overall process of cultural mediation, the "tool of tools," and they had a decidedly two-sided notion
of how such tool mediation operates. The consequence of tool cre-
ating/using for the basic structure of behavior is that "instead of applying directly its natural function to the solution of a particular task,
the child *puts between that function and the task a certain auxiliary
means* . . . by the medium of which the child manages to perform the
task" (Luria, 1928, p. 495).[4]

This idea of tool mediation is not original to the early Russian cultural-historical psychologists. It is also central to the ideas of John Dewey, whose work was well known among Russian educators and psychologists. Tools and works of art, he wrote, "are simply prior natural things reshaped for the sake of entering effectively into some type of behavior" (Dewey, 1916, p. 92, quoted in Hickman, 1990, p. 13). In Henri Bergson's words:

> If we could rid ourselves of all pride, if, to define our species, we kept strictly to what the historic and prehistoric periods show us to be the constant characteristic of man and of intelligence, we should say not *Homo Sapiens* but *Homo Faber.* In short, *intelligence, considered in what seems to be its original feature, is the faculty of manufacturing artificial objects, especially tools for making tools, and of indefinitely varying the manufacture.* (1911/1983, p. 139)

A very similar formulation was put forward by the American psychologist C. H. Judd (1926), who had studied with Wundt:

> The tools which man has invented are powerful influences in determining the course of civilized life. Through the long ages while man has been inventing tools and learning to use them, his mode of individual reaction has been undergoing a change. He is no longer absorbed in direct attack on prey which furnishes him his food. He does not develop more skill in the use of claws and teeth in order that he may cope with his environment. He has adopted an indirect mode of action. He uses instruments which he has devised or borrowed from his forefathers or from his neighbor. (pp. 3–4)

*2. Historical development.* In addition to using and making tools, human beings arrange for the rediscovery of the already-created tools in each succeeding generation. Becoming a cultural being and arranging for others to become cultural beings are intimately linked parts of a single process called enculturation. As a consequence of this form of activity,

> we live from birth to death in a world of persons and things which is in large measure what it is because of what has been

done and transmitted from previous human activities. When this fact is ignored, experience is treated as if it were something which goes on exclusively inside an individual's body and mind. It ought not to be necessary to say that experience does not occur in a vacuum. There are sources outside an individual which give rise to experience. (Dewey, 1938/1963, p. 39)

Culture, according to this perspective, can be understood as the entire pool of artifacts accumulated by the social group in the course of its historical experience. In the aggregate, the accumulated artifacts of a group—culture—is then seen as the species-specific *medium* of human development.[5] It is "history in the present." The capacity to develop within that medium and to arrange for its reproduction in succeeding generations is *the* distinctive characteristic of our species.

3. *Practical activity.* The third basic premise of the cultural-historical approach, adopted from Hegel by way of Marx, is that the analysis of human psychological functions must be grounded in humans' everyday activities. It was only through such an approach, Marx claimed, that the duality of materialism versus idealism could be superseded, because it is in activity that people experience the ideal/material residue of the activity of prior generations.

ⓖ A number of additional key principles of cultural psychology follow from the three already mentioned. Perhaps most important is that the historical accumulation of artifacts and their infusion in activity implicate *social origins* of human thought processes. As Vygotsky (1929) argued, all means of cultural behavior (artifacts in my terminology) are social in their essence. They are social, too, in the dynamics of their origin and change, as expressed in what Vygotsky called "the general law of cultural development":

Any function in children's cultural development appears twice, or on two planes. First it appears on the social plane and then on the psychological plane. First it appears between people as an interpsychological category and then within the individual child as an intrapsychological category . . . but it goes without saying that internalization transforms the process itself and changes its structure and function. Social relations or relations among people genetically underlie all higher functions and their relationships. (1981, p.163)

This view of social origins requires paying special attention to adults' power to arrange children's environments so as to optimize their development according to existing norms. It generates the idea of a "zone of proximal development" which affords the proximal, relevant environment of experience for development. It is the foundation upon which, in an ideal world, the education of children would be organized.

## The Grand Scheme

The theoretical framework uniting these different principles is exceedingly broad from the perspective of the first psychology. It requires that psychologists study not only the moment-to-moment changes marking the process of developmental change and ontogenetic change, but phylogenctic and historical change as well. In addition, these domains must be considered in relationship to one another. A commitment to the study of the process of human development is ineluctably also an inquiry into human origins.

Statements about origins of cultural mediation in relation to phylogeny and cultural history can be found in several of the key publications written by Vygotsky and his colleagues in the 1920s and early 1930s, notably in Vygotsky's *Genesis of Higher Psychological Functions* (1930/1956), *Tool and Symbol in Child Development* (1930/1994), and *Studies on the History of Behavior* (1930/1993), which was coauthored by Luria.[6]

Vygotsky and Luria (1930/1993, p. 36) declare it their aim to "schematically present the path of psychological evolution from the ape to cultural man." Their schema assumes inclusion of the now-familiar "main lines" of development, the evolutionary, the historical, and the ontogenetic. Each has its own "turning point": "Every critical turning point is viewed primarily from the standpoint of *something new* introduced by this stage into the process of development. Thus we treated each stage as a starting point for further processes of evolution" (p. 37). The turning point in phylogeny is the appearance of tool use in apes. The turning point in human history is the appearance of labor and symbolic mediation (and perhaps, later, the emergence of writing). The major turning point in ontogeny is the coming together of cultural history and phylogeny with the acquisition of language.

The overall story went something like this: With the higher apes one reaches a point of anthropoid evolution where tool use is observed (Vygotsky and Luria based much of this on Kohler's work), bespeaking the phylogenetic development of practical intelligence. But there is more to the specifically human form of development than tool use:

> All the factors separating the behavior of ape and man could be summed up and expressed in one general statement to this effect: in spite of the fact that the ape displays an ability to invent and use tools—the prerequisite for all human cultural development—the activity of labor, founded on this ability, has still not even minimally developed in the ape . . . this form of behavior does not constitute the main form of adaptation for them. We cannot say that the ape adapts itself to its environment with the help of tools.
>
> Quite the opposite is true of tool use among humans: The entire existence of an Australian aborigine depends upon his boomerang just as the entire existence of England depends upon her machines. Take the boomerang away from the aborigine, make him a farmer, then out of necessity he will have to completely change his life style, his habits, his entire style of thinking, his entire nature. (p. 74)

In characterizing the turning point from ape to human, Vygotsky and Luria draw heavily upon Engels's *Dialectics of Nature* (1925). Engels postulated a process of anthropogenesis in which a form of activity called labor plays the central role.[7] Labor involves more than tool use to overcome barriers to a goal: "In short, the animal merely *uses* external nature, and brings about changes in it simply by his presence; man by his changes makes it serve his ends, *masters it*. This is the final, essential distinction between man and other animals, and once again it is labor that brings about this distinction" (quoted in Vygotsky and Luria, p. 76).

The final ingredients that must be added to the ape's ability to use tools are language and symbolic mediation, "tools for the mastery of behavior." The product of this new combination is a qualitatively new form of mediation, one in which tools and language unite in the artifact. At this point "primitive man" emerges.

Vygotsky and Luria note that in speaking of "primitive man" they are talking about an abstraction, "the starting point of historical development." Yet, they argue, data about prehistoric humans ("the lowest rung of cultural development") and about people from different contemporary cultures can all provide evidence about the psychology of primitive man.

Historical change from "ur-humans" to modern adult humans occurs along two dimensions. First, there is an increasing use of cultural/mediated/higher functions in place of natural/unmediated/lower functions. Second, there is development in the use of the mediational means themselves. The development of memory provided one of Vygotsky and Luria's favorite examples of this process. In primitive cultures natural remembering holds sway. One kind of natural memory is eidetic imagery, "picture memory," which was believed to be common in such societies. But incidental rememberings for participation in events, what we might call "everyday memory," also qualify as natural remembering. It is conceived of as a process by which humans passively record the world but do not actively use their memories to transform the world or their own behavior.

This sort of "natural" (to humans) form of everyday memory does not undergo historical change. It is built upon elementary psychological processes and will be universal across cultures and historical periods. "Cultural" memory develops, instead, through the elaboration of more complex "tools of remembering" associated with historically new forms of artifact-mediated experience, and is accompanied by a change in the role that natural processes play in the overall functional system created with more complex mediational systems. Historical development of memory is not a change in "ability to remember." The evolution of memory now changes to perfection of the "mediational means" by which memory is accomplished. The tying of knots to control one's memory from the outside and the Inca *quipu* provided clear examples of what Vygotsky and his colleagues meant by the "cultural form of behavior."

With respect to the memory function, the act of writing plays an important role in cultural-historical thinking because writing is an early, persistent, and highly visible new form of mediation that permits new forms of human interaction by reorganizing human mnemonic activity. With writing one gets systematic knowledge, scientific concepts, and schools as enculturating institutions where the young acquire the ability to mediate their interactions in the world through codified, reified speech structured in the appropriate fashion by scientific knowledge. Thus one arrives at the current historical state of *Homo sapiens,* represented by those among us who are highly educated and lead lives for which our education was designed to prepare us.

In short, according to this view, culture undergoes both quantitative change in terms of the number and variety of artifacts, and qualitative change in terms of the mediational potentials that they embody. And as a consequence, both culture and human thinking develop.

Such was the cultural-historical story circa 1930. Nor was this view restricted to Russia. One can find very similar views among leading German, French, British, and American scholars of the day (Dewey, Stern, Levy-Bruhl, and so on). The story of Man the Toolmaker provided an account of how "Man makes himself" through the conversion of nature into culture. It was one of the ways in which the nineteenth-century evolutionary ideas about culture in mind, which I described in Chapter 1, were taken up in the formation of new scientific disciplines in the twentieth century. Moreover, many elements of this story continue to live in various contemporary reconstructions of human anthropogenesis and sociocultural evolution (such as Donald, 1991).

⑥ Systems of ideas, as René Van der Veer and Jan Valsiner (1991) note, undergo significant transformations when they are imported across national traditions of thought. American psychologists (myself included) have selectively attended to and borrowed from the ideas of Vygotsky and his followers. How much of what we have borrowed

really is in the original? How is the original transformed in the process of translation and appropriation in new cultural-historical circumstances?[8]

As more originals become available in full and meticulous translation, we should be able to get a richer notion of the Russian sources
of our ideas and become subtler thinkers as a result. I, certainly, have
benefited enormously from the retranslations of *Thinking and Speech*
(1987) and the publications of heretofore unpublished articles and
books, such as *Studies on the History of Behavior* (1993) and *The
Vygotsky Reader* (Van der Veer and Valsiner, 1994). But a fuller corpus
of materials will not end controversies of interpretation. Nor shall we
trace full correspondence between (say), Russian and American versions of cultural-historical psychology, no matter how complete the
translations. Consequently, in the chapters to follow, my focus will
be on an attempt to formulate an approach to psychology that draws
upon both national traditions.

I begin my reconstruction in Chapter 5 by elaborating a conception
of culture and mediation that retains the key elements of the Russian
approach and at the same time fits in with a large body of theorizing
in contemporary cultural anthropology and cognitive psychology.
Chapter 6 provides a critical updating of the narrative about psychological development in the phylogenetic and cultural-historical domains. In Chapter 7 I sketch out several cultural mechanisms of ontogenetic development highlighted by a cultural-historical perspective.
Chapter 8 returns to questions of methodology and addresses the crucial issue of a proper unit of analysis for a cultural-historical psychology. In Chapters 9 and 10 I describe concrete research projects motivated by the principles developed in the earlier chapters. With these
materials in hand, in Chapter 11 we can return to consider the paradigm that links them.

# 5 ⑥

# Putting Culture in the Middle

IN THIS CHAPTER I begin the process of reconstructing the cultural-historical approach to development by elaborating on the notion of tool mediation, and by retaining some features of the Russian approach while changing others. I initially found the Russian cultural-historical psychologists' ideas about culture attractive because they seemed to offer a natural way to build up a theory of culture in mind that begins from the organization of mediated actions in everyday practice. This was the same point to which our cross-cultural research had brought my colleagues and me, so it was an obvious point of convergence. But our cross-cultural experience had also induced a profound skepticism about concluding, on the basis of interactional procedures treated as if they were free of their own cultural history, that nonliterate, "nonmodern" people think at a lower level than their modern, literate counterparts. In their belief in historical and mental progress, the Russians were led into many of the same methodological traps we had fallen into in our own cross-cultural work (Cole, 1976).

In light of these considerations, I shall begin my attempt to create a conception of culture adequate to the theories and practices of a second, cultural psychology with the phenomenon of mediation.

Rather than start with the concept of a tool, as did the Russians, I shall treat the concept of a tool as a subcategory of the more general conception of an artifact.

## Artifacts

Ordinarily one thinks of an artifact as a material object—something manufactured by a human being. In anthropology, the study of artifacts is sometimes considered part of the study of material culture, which is somehow distinct from the study of human behavior and knowledge. According to this "artifact as object" interpretation, it is easy to assimilate the concept of artifact into the category of tool— but from this nothing much is to be gained.

According to the view presented here, which bears a close affinity to the ideas of John Dewey and also traces its genealogy back to Hegel and Marx, an artifact is an aspect of the material world that has been modified over the history of its incorporation into goal-directed human action. By virtue of the changes wrought in the process of their creation and use, artifacts are simultaneously *ideal* (conceptual) and *material*. They are ideal in that their material form has been shaped by their participation in the interactions of which they were previously a part and which they mediate in the present.

Defined in this manner, the properties of artifacts apply with equal force whether one is considering language or the more usually noted forms of artifacts such as tables and knives which constitute material culture.[1] What differentiates the word "table" from an actual table is the relative prominence of their material and ideal aspects and the kinds of coordinations they afford. No word exists apart from its material instantiation (as a configuration of sound waves, hand movements, writing, or neuronal activity), whereas every table embodies an order imposed by thinking human beings.[2]

The dual material-conceptual nature of artifacts was discussed by the Russian philosopher Evald Ilyenkov (1977, 1979), who based his approach on that of Marx and Hegel. In Ilyenkov's system, ideality results from "the transforming, form-creating, activity of social beings, their aim-mediated, sensuously objective activity" (quoted in Bakhurst, 1990, p. 182). From this perspective, the form of an artifact is more than a purely physical form. "Rather, in being created as an embodiment of purpose and incorporated into life activity in a certain way—being manufactured for a *reason* and put into *use*—the natural object acquires a significance. This significance is the 'ideal form' of the object, a form that includes not a single atom of the tangible physical substance that possesses it" (Bakhurst, 1990, p. 182).

Note that in this way of thinking mediation through artifacts applies equally to objects and people. What differs in the two cases is the ways in which ideality and materiality are fused among members of these two categories of being, and the kinds of interactivity into which they can enter.

⑥ This view also asserts the primal unity of the material and the symbolic in human cognition. This starting point is important because it provides a way of dealing with the longstanding debate in anthropology and allied disciplines: Should culture be located external to the individual, as the products of prior human activity, or should it be located internally, as a pool of knowledge and beliefs? Both views have a long history in anthropology (D'Andrade, 1995; Harkness, 1992). However, over the past twenty years or so, coincident with the cognitive revolution in psychology and the advent of Chomskian linguistics, the study of culture as patterns of behavior and material products appears to have given way to the tradition that considers culture to be composed entirely of learned symbols and shared systems of meaning—the ideal aspect of culture—that are located in the head.

The concept of artifacts as products of human history that are simultaneously ideal and material offers a way out of this debate. At the same time, as I hope to demonstrate, it provides a useful point of contact between cultural-historical psychology and contemporary anthropological conceptions of culture in mind.[3]

## The Special Structure of Artifact-Mediated Action

The Russian cultural-historical psychologists used a triangle to picture the structural relation of the individual to environment that arises *pari parsu* with artifact mediation (see Figure 5.1). Simplifying their view for purposes of explication, the functions termed "natural"

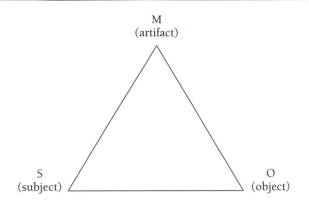

M
(artifact)

S
(subject)

O
(object)

Figure 5.1. The basic mediational triangle in which subject and object are seen not only as "directly" connected but simultaneously as "indirectly" connected through a medium constituted of artifacts (culture).

(or "unmediated") are those along the base of the triangle; the "cultural" ("mediated") functions are those where the relation between subject and environment (subject and object, response and stimulus, and so on) are linked through the vertex of the triangle (artifacts).

There is some temptation when viewing this triangle to think that when cognition is mediated, thought follows a path through the top line of the triangle that "runs through" the mediator. However, the emergence of mediated action does not mean that the mediated path replaces the natural one, just as the appearance of culture in phylogeny does not mean that culture replaces phylogeny. One does not cease to stand on the ground and look at the tree when one picks up an axe to chop the tree down; rather, the incorporation of tools into the activity creates a new structural relation in which the cultural (mediated) and natural (unmediated) routes operate synergistically; through active attempts to appropriate their surroundings to their own goals, people incorporate auxiliary means (including, very significantly, other people) into their actions, giving rise to the distinctive, triadic relationship of subject-medium-object.

In this and later chapters I will expand upon this basic structural diagram to develop an appropriately complex approach to the cultural mediation of thought. But even this basic notion that human thought is the emergent consequence of intermingling of "direct, natural, phylogenetic" and "indirect, cultural" aspects of experience is sufficient to bring to the fore the special quality of human thought referred to as the duality of human consciousness. Many expressions of this idea can be found in both the Russian and the Western European/American traditions (Durkheim, 1912). For example, the American anthropologist Leslie White wrote: "An axe has a subjective component; it would be meaningless without a concept and an attitude. On the other hand, a concept or attitude would be meaningless without overt expression, in behavior or speech (which is a form of behavior). Every cultural element, every cultural trait, therefore, has a subjective and an objective aspect" (1959, p. 236).[4]

True to the spirit of cultural-historical approaches, White emphasized the temporal aspect of cultural mediation and its psychological implications: "With words man creates a new world, a world of ideas and philosophies. In this world man lives just as truly as in the physical world of his senses . . . This world comes to have a continuity and a permanence that the external world of the senses can never have. It is not made up of present only but of a past and a future as well. Temporally, it is not a succession of disconnected episodes, but a continuum extending to infinity in both directions, from eternity to eternity" (White, 1942, p. 372).

Luria described this double world in the following way:

> The enormous advantage is that their world doubles. In the absence of words, human beings would have to deal only with those things which they could perceive and manipulate directly. With the help of language, they can deal with things that they have not perceived even indirectly and with things which were part of the experience of earlier generations. Thus, the word adds another dimension to the world of humans . . . Animals have only one world, the world of objects and situations. Humans have a double world. (1981, p. 35)

A great deal more can and will be said about this basic mediational conception and the peculiar form of consciousness to which it gives rise. Artifacts and artifact-mediated individual human action are only a starting point for developing the needed conceptual tools. Neither artifacts nor actions exist in isolation. Rather, they are interwoven with each other and with the social worlds of the human beings they mediate to form vast networks of interconnections (Latour, 1994).

Some way is needed to talk about structure in the resulting cultural medium.

The minimal mediational structure given in Figure 5.1 cannot stand alone as a representation of mediated action in its social context. In order to elaborate a cultural-historical psychology to guide our research in complex, everyday settings, we need to be able to talk about aggregations of artifacts appropriate to the events they mediate and to include the mediation of interpersonal relationships along with mediation of action on the nonhuman world.

## Three Levels of Artifacts

One useful suggestion for how to elaborate on the notion of artifact was made by Marx Wartofsky, who proposed a three-level hierarchy. Wartofsky described artifacts (including tools and language) as "objectifications of human needs and intentions *already* invested with cognitive and affective content" (1973, p. 204).

The first level of Wartofsky's framework consists of *primary artifacts*, those directly used in production. As examples, he gives "axes, clubs, needles, bowls"; my examples will include words, writing instruments, telecommunications networks, and mythical cultural personages. Primary artifacts correspond closely to the concept of artifact as matter transformed by prior human activity that I provided earlier, although I do not distinguish for current purposes between production of material goods and production of social life in general.

*Secondary artifacts* consist of representations of primary artifacts and of modes of action using primary artifacts. Secondary artifacts play a central role in preserving and transmitting modes of action and belief. They include recipes, traditional beliefs, norms, constitutions, and the like.

The third level is a class of artifacts "which can come to constitute a relatively autonomous 'world,' in which the rules, conventions and outcomes no longer appear directly practical, or which, indeed, seem to constitute an arena of non-practical, or 'free' play or game activity" (p. 208). Wartofsky calls these imagined worlds *tertiary artifacts*. Such imaginative artifacts, he suggests, can come to color the way we see the "actual" world, providing a tool for changing current praxis. In modern psychological jargon, modes of behavior acquired when interacting with tertiary artifacts can transfer beyond the immediate contexts of their use. Wartofsky applies his conception of tertiary artifacts to works of art and processes, of perception; I want to generalize his conception by linking the notion of artifact on the one hand to notions of schemas and scripts and on the other hand to notions of context, mediation, and activity found in contemporary cognitive psychology, anthropology, and allied parts of the cognitive sciences.

If one accepts this characterization of artifacts as the linchpin of cultural mediation along the lines suggested by Wartofsky, one next step is to look at ways in which artifacts of the three different kinds are woven together in the process of joint human activity. How patterned are the artifacts constituting human culture?

## The Cohesion and Coherence of Culture

Contemporary anthropologists are divided with respect to the closely linked issues of how different parts of culture are interconnected and how coherent culture is across situations. In a wide-ranging discussion of this issue a few years ago, Paul Kay suggested "semi-seriously" that the supposed coherence of culture is a coherence imposed on the anthropologist by the need to publish a coherent story. It is an illusion: "if I go out and study the 'whoevers,' I've got to come back and tell a consistent and entertaining story about what the 'whoevers' are like—and everything they do better fit into this one story" (in Shweder and LeVine, 1984, p. 17).

Kay was immediately challenged by Clifford Geertz, whose work was almost certainly one of the sources of Kay's provocative remark. Geertz is justly famous for developing the notion that different parts of culture cohere such that, for example, one could use a Balinese cockfight or puppet theater (tertiary artifacts in Wartofsky's scheme of things) as an organizing metaphor for all of Balinese society (Geertz, 1973). In the early 1970s Geertz cited with approval Max Weber's image of humankind as "an animal suspended in webs of significance he himself has spun," and declared: "I take culture to be those webs" (1973, p. 5). Later in the same work, Geertz suggested that culture should be conceived of by analogy with a recipe or a computer program, which he referred to as "control mechanisms."

Geertz's work is pivotal in my efforts to reconcile the ideas of the Russian cultural-historical psychologists with those of contemporary cultural anthropologists. Geertz is often read as an anthropologist who adopts the conception of culture as inside-the-head knowledge. While this is certainly an aspect of his thinking that has become more dominant over time (Geertz, 1983), I find it significant that he explicitly rejects the strictly idealist notion of culture in favor of a view that links up neatly with the notion of artifact mediation:

> The "control mechanism" view of culture begins with the assumption that human thought is basically both social and public—that its natural habitat is the house yard, the marketplace, and the town square. Thinking consists not of "happenings in the head" (though happenings there and elsewhere are necessary for it to occur) but of traffic in what have been called, by G. H. Mead and others, significant symbols—words for the most part but also gestures, drawings, musical sounds, mechanical devices like clocks. (1973, p. 45)

I hope it is clear that there is a close affinity between this notion of culture as control mechanism and the mediation of action through artifacts.

Geertz's use of Weber's metaphor of "webs of significance" evokes images of the beautiful patterning of a spider's web, while the recipe metaphor suggests that the patterning is quite local and specific to particular ingredients, the rules for combining them, and the circumstances in which they are cooked. Diversity and uniformity, no less than the internal versus external interpretations of culture, were warring in Geertz's definition.

When responding to Kay's suggestion that the coherence of culture may be entirely in the eye of the outside observer, Geertz sought a new metaphor to describe his sense that human beings' cultural medium is neither made up of unconnected bits and pieces nor a perfect configuration: "the elements of culture are not like a pile of sand and not like a spider's web. It's more like an octopus, a rather badly integrated creature—what passes for a brain keeps it together, more or less, in one ungainly whole" (quoted in Shweder, 1984, p. 19).

The Geertz-Kay discussion suggests two extremes to be avoided in anthropologists' efforts to characterize the overall degree of cultural cohesion: (1) human life would be impossible if every event was experienced *sui generis,* as an isolated instance, and (2) it is no more helpful to believe that a single, uniform configuration of cultural constraints is constitutive of all events within a culture. Rather, it is essential to take into account the fact that human activity involves elaborate and shifting divisions of labor and experience within cultures, so that no two members of a cultural group can be expected to have internalized the same parts of whatever "whole" might be said to exist (D'Andrade, 1989; Schwartz, 1978, 1990).

As a consequence of these difficulties, it is not possible to say, in general, how much cultural coherence and integration exists between the two extremes of uniqueness and chaos; in order to say anything useful, it is necessary to specify sources of coherence and patterning as a part of the ongoing activities that the inquirer wants to analyze. In fact, when one considers simultaneously the heterogeneous sources of structure in the cultural medium and the necessarily partial knowledge of the people who use it, the wonder is that human beings are capable of coordinating with one another at all (a point made many decades ago by Durkheim, 1912).

The "internal" and "external" approaches to culture, applied to how to locate structure in the cultural medium, veer in predictably different directions. As external sources of coordination one can point to the many material manifestations of human action, the intricate "webs of significance" in its outer aspect. These are clearly visible as embodied symbols, routines, and rituals for coordinating artifacts. The opposite, internal line of explanation posits internal psychological structures or cultural knowledge as the sources of intersubjectivity and coordinated action and seeks to understand the processes of interpretation.

The version of a cultural-historical approach that I am proposing identifies the point of articulation of these two sides of culture in the dual nature of artifacts. The challenge is to show that this formulation supersedes the "inner" and "outer" approaches to culture and mind that dominate contemporary discourse.

## Cultural Models, Schemas, and Scripts

It was my good fortune that when I began formulating the ideas described in this chapter I was a member of an informal interdisciplinary discussion group associated with the Center for Human Information Processing at the University of California at San Diego. Our topic was our differing approaches to human thought processes, and possible ways to bridge the differences between them.[5]

Several members of this group had pioneered the idea that human experience is mediated by cognitive schemas which channel individual thinking by structuring the selection, retention, and use of information. In psychology *schema* is a term used to refer to knowledge structures in which the parts relate to one another and the whole in a patterned fashion (Mandler, 1985). According to David Rumelhart, "a schema contains, as part of its specification, the network of interrelations that is believed normally to hold among constituents that are instances of the schema" (1978, p. 3). There are schemas representing our knowledge of objects, situations, events, sequences of events, actions, and sequences of action (Rumelhart and Norman, 1980).

Schemas are selection mechanisms. They specify how certain essential elements relate to one another while leaving other, less essential elements to be filled in as needed according to the circumstances. Some elements, so-called default values, may not be specified at all. For example, if I hear my cat mewing outside the door, the elements, "breathes," and "warm blooded" are plausible default values. I know they are true without having to think about them. Under some circumstances, such as when I see the cat lying under the car and it is not clear if it is dead or alive, those elements of the schema may be crucial to my reasoning.

One appealing characteristic of the kind of schema theory my colleagues were developing is that it implies the context-specificity of thinking. Rumelhart made this point with respect to adult reasoning, arguing that while schemas play a central role in reasoning, "most of the reasoning we do apparently *does not* involve the application of general-purpose reasoning skills. Rather it seems that most of our reasoning ability is tied to particular schemata related to particular bodies of knowledge" (1978, p. 39). Jean Mandler pointed out an implication of this view that seemed to describe both the cultural differences in thinking and the difficulties engendered by the use of standardized psychological testing in cross-cultural research when she remarked that behavior will differ in familiar and unfamiliar situations because "familiar situations are those for which schemata have already been formed and in which top-down processes play a larger role" (1980, p. 27).

Roy D'Andrade (1984, 1990, 1995) has generalized the notion of schemas for objects and events in order to link these concepts from psychology with the concepts and phenomena of psychological anthropology. He introduced the idea of *cultural* schemas, patterns of elementary schemas that make up the meaning system characteristic of any cultural group. In D'Andrade's terms, "Typically such schemas portray simplified worlds, making the appropriateness of the terms that are based on them dependent on the degree to which these schemas fit the actual worlds of the objects being categorized. Such schemas portray not only the world of physical objects and events, but also more abstract worlds of social interaction, discourse, and even word meaning" (1990, p. 93).

D'Andrade (1990, p. 108) refers to intersubjectively shared cultural schemas as *cultural models*. Cultural models function to interpret experience and to guide action in a wide variety of domains, "including events, institutions, and physical and mental objects." A monograph edited by Naomi Quinn and Dorothy Holland (1987) contains studies which illustrate how adults use cultural models to reason about objects (such as cats), social institutions (such as marriage), and general properties of human beings (such as how the mind works).

An especially important kind of schema for purposes of grounding a cultural-psychological theory in people's everyday activities is event schemas, often referred to as *scripts* (Schank and Ableson, 1977). A script is an event schema that specifies the people who appropriately participate in an event, the social roles they play, the objects they use, and the sequence of actions and causal relations that applies.

Both Jerome Bruner (1990) and Katherine Nelson (1981, 1986) base their analysis of cognitive development on such event representations. Nelson refers to scripts as "generalized event schemas." Scripts, she writes, provide "a basic level of knowledge representation in a hierarchy of relations that reaches upward through plans to goals and themes" (1981, p. 101). Nelson illustrates the development of script-mediated thinking using the following examples, the first from

a three-year-old, the second from a child a little under five, responding to a request to "tell me about going to a restaurant." Here is the
three-year-old:

Well, you eat and then go somewhere.

The five-year-old has more to say:

Okay. Now first we go to restaurants at night-time and we, um,
we and we go and wait for a while, and then the waiter comes
and gives us the little stuff with the dinners on it, and then we
wait for a little bit, a half and hours or a few minutes or something, and um, then our pizza comes or anything, and um [in-
terruption] . . . [The adult says, "So then the food comes . . ."]
Then we eat it, and um, then when we're finished eating the
salad that we order we got to eat our pizza when its done, because we get the salad before the pizza's ready. So then when
we're finished with all the pizza and all our salad, we just leave.
(Nelson, 1981, p. 103)

Several points about these children's formulations stand out. First,
they are indeed generalized, although grounded in particulars; the
children are talking about a habitual event ("You eat," "We go"). Second, the descriptions are dominated by the temporal sequencing of
actions. Third, the causal logic of the event inheres in the temporal
ordering of actions (pizza is eaten after salad because it takes longer
to prepare). Finally, there is a good deal left unsaid, in part because
it is taken for granted—we open the door and enter the restaurant,
we pick up our forks and use them to eat the salad, and so on—and
in part because the child is not involved and most likely does not
understand (for example, that one pays for the food and leaves a tip).

In her work on children's acquisition of event representations, Nelson highlights other important properties of scripts that mark their
nature as mediators. First, she suggests that scripts, like the cultural
schemas discussed by D'Andrade, serve as guides to action. When
people participate in a novel event, they must seek out an answer to
the question, "What's going on here?" Once a person has even a crude
idea of the appropriate actions associated with going to a restaurant,
he or she can enter the flow of the particular event with partial knowledge, which gets enriched in the course of the event itself, facilitating

later coordination. "Without shared scripts," Nelson writes, "every social act would need to be negotiated afresh" (p. 109).

Nelson also points out that children grow up within contexts controlled by adults and hence within adult scripts. By and large, adults direct the children's action and set the goals, rather than engage in direct teaching. In effect, they use their notion of the appropriate script to provide constraints on the child's actions and allow the child to fill in the expected role activity. In this sense, "the acquisition of scripts is central to the acquisition of culture" (p. 110). I will return to this point in Chapter 7.

According to Bruner (1990), scripts are best considered elements of a narrative, which play a role in his theorizing similar to that of cultural models in D'Andrade's approach. For Bruner, it is narrative, the linking of events over time, that lies at the heart of human thought. The representation of experience in narratives provides a frame ("folk psychology") which enables humans to interpret their experiences and one another. If it were not for such narrativized framing, "we would be lost in a murk of chaotic experience and probably would not have survived as a species in any case" (p. 56).

## Schemas and Artifacts

Since schema theory started to gain wide acceptance among cognitive psychologists and anthropologists somewhat over a decade ago, schemas have generally been interpreted as mental structures inside the head. Interpreted in this way, schemas and scripts fit comfortably with the internal notion of culture as meanings, which come unmoored from their material instantiation. Interpreted in this light, the notion of schema is incompatible with the notion of artifact-mediation I have been seeking to develop. The solution, of course, is to say that scripts are not uniquely inside-the-head phenomena but, like all artifacts, participate on both sides of the "skin line."

Interestingly, F. C. Bartlett, whose ideas have inspired several modern schema theorists, provided an alternative interpretation of schema when the term came into psychology in the 1920s (Bartlett, 1932). Bartlett wrote about schemas as conventions, social practices which were both inside and outside the head; they are both materialized practices and mental structures (Edwards and Middleton,

1986). This notion of schema obviously coincides nicely with the notion of artifact mediation I am proposing.

Recent developments indicate that something akin to Bartlett's approach is finding favor in cognitive anthropology. For example, D'Andrade (1995), who once adhered to the "inside" view of culture, has recently argued for a definition of culture that harks all the way back to E. B. Tylor: culture as the entire content of a group's heritage, including both its cultural schemas and models and its material artifacts and cultural practices. Still, the two sides of culture remain separate in D'Andrade's approach. He posits two kinds of cognitive structures, schemas and symbols. *Schemas* are the ideal side of artifacts as conceived of here; they are abstract mental objects. *Symbols* are physical things: words, phrases, pictures, and other material representations. The meaning of the symbol is taken to be the schema which the symbol signifies.

D'Andrade summarizes the relationship of symbols, schemas, and the world as follows: "The schema which represents the sound of a word and the schema which represents the thing in the world referred to by that word are entirely different, although tightly connected in that the schema which represents the sound of a word signifies (has as its meaning) the schema which represents the thing in the world" (1995, p. 179). While differences remain, it is clear that there is agreement of a tight connection between symbol/schema and artifacts.

Edwin Hutchins (1995), another anthropologist who has sought to integrate the internal and external conceptions of culture, proposes a different way to think of the intimate three-way connection of culture, cognition, and the world. Culture, according to Hutchins, should be thought of as a process, not as "any collection of things, whether tangible or abstract." Culture "is a process and the 'things' that appear on list-like definitions of culture are residua of the process. Culture is an adaptive process that accumulates the partial solutions to frequently encountered problems . . . Culture is a human cognitive process that takes place both inside and outside the minds of people. It is the process in which our everyday cultural practices are enacted" (p. 354).

In more recent work, Bruner (1996) and Nelson (1986) also treat scripts as dual entities, one side of which is a mental representation, the other side of which is embodied in talk and action. For example,

Bruner writes that "learning and thinking are always *situated* in a cultural setting and always dependent upon the utilization of cultural resources" (1996, p. 4).

Whether one draws on D'Andrade, Hutchins, or other like-minded anthropologists (see the volumes edited by D'Andrade and Strauss, 1992, and Holland and Quinn, 1987) or on Nelson and Bruner, I find encouraging the compatibility of their ideas with the notion of schemas as conventions (in Bartlett's terms) or artifacts (in mine). Nor am I alone in making this connection.[6]

## The Need for More Inclusive Analysis

Secondary artifacts such as cultural schemas and scripts are essential components of the "cultural tool kit." They partake of both the ideal and the material; they are materialized and idealized (reified) in the artifacts that mediate peoples' joint activities. By that very fact of reification they are present as resources both for the idiosyncratic interpretation that each person will have of their joint activity and for the constant reproduction of the coordination necessary to reproduce that activity.

However, it requires little reflection to realize that even when conceived of as secondary artifacts, scripts and schemas are insufficient to account for thought and action. Even under the most generous assumptions about mechanisms that link object schemas together into hierarchies or event schemas into sequentially ordered sets, such knowledge structures drastically underdetermine what one should think or how one should behave on any given occasion *even assuming that one has acquired the cultural model or script in question.*[7]

Every schema "leaves out an enormous amount and is a great simplification of the potential visual, acoustic, sensory, and propositional information that could be experienced" (D'Andrade, 1990, p. 98). Consequently, while culture is a source of tools for action, the individual must still engage in a good deal of interpretation in figuring out which schemas apply in what circumstances and how to implement them effectively. For example, a large, orange, striped, furry leg with a cat-like paw dangling from the shelf in our child's closet is likely to evoke a different schema, different emotions, and different actions from those evoked by a similar object glimpsed under our hammock in a lean-to in the middle of a Brazilian rain forest. Such considerations lead to the unavoidable conclusion that in order to give an account of culturally mediated thinking it is necessary to specify not only the artifacts through which behavior is mediated but also the circumstances in which the thinking occurs.

These considerations lead us back to the essential point that all human behavior must be understood relationally, in relation to "its context" as the expression goes. But implementation of this insight has been a source of continuing disagreement and confusion. These difficulties are indexed by the varied vocabulary used to speak about the "something more" that must be added to artifact mediation if one is to give an account of the relationship between culture and mind. In the previous paragraph I used the term *circumstances* as a commonsense gloss on what that something more might be. When we turn to technical discussions of this issue, the relevant terms include *environment, situation, context, practice, activity,* and many more. At issue here is a problem very similar to the one we encountered in thinking about the relation of the material and the ideal in artifacts. In that case argument swirled around which comes first in shaping artifacts, materiality or ideality. In this case the argument turns on which comes first in human thought, the object (text) or its surround (context).

As Kenneth Burke remarked several decades ago, considerations of action and context create inescapable ambiguity because the very notion of a *substance* (sub stance) must include a reference to the thing's context "since that which supports or underlies a thing would be a part of the thing's context. And a thing's context, being outside or beyond the thing, would be something the thing is *not*" (1945, p. 22). Faced with these complexities that have defeated so many others, I will not aspire to a definitive treatment of context in this book. But I will aspire to distinguishing between two principal conceptions of context that divide social scientists and to accumulating some necessary conceptual tools to act as heuristics in guiding research on culture and development.

## Situations and Contexts

Many years ago John Dewey (1938) proposed a relational theory of cognition in which he used the term *situation* in a manner that leads naturally into a discussion of context: "What is designated by the word 'situation' is *not* a single object or event or set of objects and events. For we never experience nor form judgments about objects and events in isolation, but only in connection with a contextual whole. This latter is what is called a 'situation' " (p. 66). Dewey goes on to comment that psychologists are likely to treat situations in a reductive fashion: "by the very nature of the case the psychological treatment [of experience] takes a *singular* object or event for the subject-matter of its analysis" (p. 67). But: "In actual experience, there is never any such isolated singular object or event; *an* object or event is always a special part, phase, or aspect, of an environing ex-perienced world—a situation" (p. 67).

Isolating what is cognized from life circumstances is often fatally obstructive to understanding cognition. It is such isolation (typical of experimental procedures in psychological studies of cognition), Dewey argued, that gives rise to the illusion that our knowledge of any object, be it "an orange, a rock, piece of gold, or whatever," is knowledge of the object in isolation from the situation in which it is encountered.

Dewey's equation of situation with a contextual whole provides a proper relational orientation for the concept of *context,* perhaps the most prevalent term used to index the circumstances of behavior. Despite Dewey's prescient comments half a century ago, psycholog-ical analysis of context has all too often fallen into the difficulties about which he warned us.

## Context as That Which Surrounds

When we retreat to Webster's dictionary as a starting point for ex-amining the concept of context, we find crucial ambiguities that serve to obscure the errors to which Dewey pointed. Context is defined as "the whole situation, background, or environment relevant to a par-ticular event," and "environment" is defined as "something that sur-rounds." "The whole situation" and "that which surrounds" are mixed together in the same definition.

The notion of context as "that which surrounds" is often repre-sented as a set of concentric circles representing different "levels of context" (see Figure 5.2). The psychologist's focus is ordinarily on

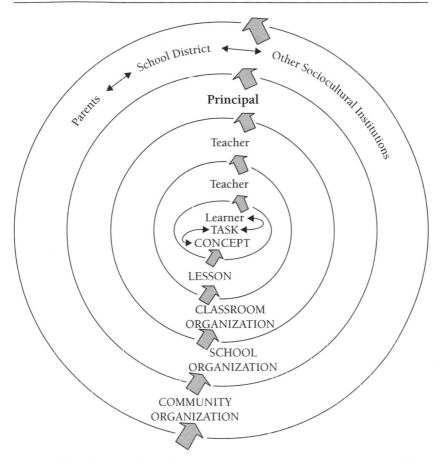

Figure 5.2.  Concentric circles representing the notion of context as "that which surrounds," with a child at its center. The context here is the one surrounding children's performance in a classroom lesson.

the unit "in the middle," which may be referred to as a task or activity engaged in by individuals. When using the "surrounds" interpretation of context, the psychologist seeks to understand how this task is shaped by the broader levels of context.

This image is probably best known in connection with Urie Bronfenbrenner's (1979) book on the ecology of human development. He describes embedded systems, starting with the microsystem at the core and proceeding outward through mesosystems and exosystems, to the macrosystem. In applying the notion of context to issues of education, Peg Griffin and I took as the "unit in the middle" a teacher-pupil exchange that was part of a lesson that was part of a classroom that was part of a school that was part of a community (Cole, Griffin, and LCHC, 1987).

The study of language is an important domain in which the promise and problems of the idea of "layers of context" has been usefully applied (Bateson, 1972; Jakobson and Halle, 1956). A fundamental property of language is that its levels of organization are mutually constituted; a phoneme exists as such only in combination with other phonemes which make up a word. The word is the context of the phoneme. But the word exists as such—"has meaning"—only in the larger context of the utterance, which again "has meaning" only in a relationship to a large unit of discourse. Gregory Bateson summarized this way of thinking: "This hierarchy of contexts within contexts is universal for the communicational . . . aspect of phenomena and drives the scientist always to seek explanation in the ever larger units" (1972, p. 402).

Note that in this description there is no simple, temporal ordering. "That which surrounds" occurs before, after, and simultaneously with the "act/event." We cannot say sentences before we say words, nor words before we synthesize phonemes in an appropriate way; rather, there is a complex temporal interdependence among levels of context which motivates the notion that levels of context constitute one another. To take our example of the teacher-child exchange, it is easy to see such events as "caused" by higher levels of context: a teacher gives a lesson, which is shaped by the classroom it is a part of, which in turn is shaped by the kind of school it is in, which in turn is shaped by the community, and so on.

While more inclusive levels of context may constrain lower levels, they do not cause them in a unilinear fashion. For the event "a lesson" to occur, the participants must actively engage in a consensual process of "lesson making." Teachers often vary considerably in the way they interpret the conventions of the school, and school communities participate in the selection of the board of education. Without forgetting for a moment that the power relations among participants "at different levels of context" are often unequal, it is no less important when using the nested-contexts approach to take into account the fact that context creation is an actively achieved, two-sided process. (See Duranti and Goodwin, 1992; Lave, 1993; and McDermott, 1993, for trenchant criticisms of context treated as the container of objects and behaviors.)

## Context as That Which Weaves Together

In seeking uses of the term *context* which avoid the pitfalls of context as that which surrounds, I have found it useful to return to the Latin root of the term, *contexere,* which means "to weave together." A similar sense is given by the *Oxford English Dictionary,* which refers to context as "the connected whole that gives coherence to its parts."

The frequency with which metaphors of weaving, threads, ropes, and the like appear in conjunction with contextual approaches to human thinking is quite striking. For example, the microsociologist Ray Birdwhistell described context this way:

> I'll tell you what I like to think about: sometimes I like to think of a rope. The fibers that make up the rope are discontinuous; when you twist them together, you don't make them continuous, you make the thread continuous . . . even though it may look in a thread as though each of those particles are going all through it, that isn't the case. That's essentially the descriptive model . . . Obviously, I am not talking about the environment. I am not talking about inside and outside. I am talking about the conditions of the system. (quoted in McDermott, 1980, pp. 14–15)

When context is thought of in this way, it cannot be reduced to that which surrounds. It is, rather, a qualitative relation between a minimum of two analytical entities (threads), which are two moments in a single process. The boundaries between "task and its context" are not clear-cut and static but ambiguous and dynamic. As a general rule, that which is taken as object and that which is taken as that-which-surrounds-the-object are constituted by the very act of naming them.[8]

In light of my goal of studying artifacts and situations/contexts in terms of people's concrete activities, I was gratified to discover that there is an intimate connection between context, interpreted as a process of weaving together, and the notion of an event. This connection is provided by Stephen Pepper in his analysis of contextualism as a world view (what might currently be called a scientific paradigm).

Pepper (1942) suggests that the root metaphor underlying a contextualist world view is the "historic event." By this, he says,

> the contextualist does not mean primarily a past event, one that is, so to speak, dead and has to be exhumed. He means the event alive in its present. What we ordinarily mean by history, he says, is an attempt to *re-present* events, to make them in some way alive again . . . We may call [the event] an "act," if we like, and if we take care of our use of the term. But it is not an act conceived as alone or cut off that we mean; it is an act in and with its setting, an act in its context. (p. 232)

An "act in its context" understood in terms of the weaving metaphor requires a *relational* interpretation of mind; objects and contexts arise together as part of a single bio-social-cultural process of development.

Bateson (1972), in a way very reminiscent of Pepper's writing, discusses mind as constituted through human activity involving cycles of transformations between "inside" and "outside." "Obviously," he writes, "there are lots of message pathways outside the skin, and these and the messages which they carry must be included as a part of the mental system *whenever they are relevant*" (p. 458, emphasis added). He then proposes a thought experiment: "Suppose I am a blind man, and I use a stick. I go tap, tap, tap. Where do I start? Is my mental system bounded at the handle of the stick? Is it bounded by my skin? Does it start halfway up the stick? Does it start at the tip of the stick?" (p. 459).

Bateson argues that such questions are nonsensical unless one is committed to including in one's analysis not only the man and his stick but his purposes and the environment in which he finds himself. When the man sits down to eat his lunch, "the context changes," and with it the stick's relation to mind is changed. Now it is forks and knives that become relevant. In short, because what we call mind works through artifacts, it cannot be unconditionally bounded by the head or even by the body, but must be seen as distributed in the artifacts which are *woven together* and which weave together individual human actions in concert with and as a part of the permeable, changing, events of life.

The relevant order of context will depend crucially upon the tools through which one interacts with the world, and these in turn depend upon one's goals and other constraints on action. Similarly, relevant interpretation of context for the analyst of behavior will depend upon the goals of the analysis. According to this view of context, the combination of goals, tools, and setting (including other people and what Lave, 1988, terms "arena") constitutes simultaneously the context of behavior and ways in which cognition can be said to be related to that context.[9]

## Activity and Practice

While *context* and *situation* continue to appear in discussions of culture in mind, in recent years there has been increasing use of the terms *activity* and *practice* in their place. In part this shift has resulted from dissatisfaction with the concept of context in the reduced form of an environment or cause (Lave, 1988; Zuckerman, 1993). In part it has been brought about by the infusion of ideas from social and cultural theory which trace their roots back to Karl Marx and to post-Marxist debates about human agency and social determination.

In contemporary discussions, the terms activity and practice are sometimes taken as synonyms and sometimes treated as if they index different kinds of social structuration. This terminological confusion can be traced back to the formulations of Marx. In the first of his *Theses on Feuerbach* (1845), Marx wrote: "The chief defect of all materialism . . . is that the thing, reality, sensuousness, is conceived only in the form of the *object* or of *contemplation,* but not as *sensuous human activity, practice,* not subjectively."

This passage leads us to understand that Marx meant to rearrange the ontological separation among humans and artifacts as a way of superseding the dichotomy between the material and the ideal. His formulation of the interpenetration of activity and practice and materiality/ideality is based on the assumption that "The object or product produced is *not* something 'merely' external to and indifferent to the nature of the producer. It is his activity in an objectified or congealed form" (Bernstein, 1971, p. 44). It is this duality that gives activity "the power to endow the material world with a new class of properties that, though they owe their origin to us, acquire an enduring presence in objective reality, coming to exist independently of human individuals" (Bakhurst, 1991, pp. 179–180).

Activity/practice emerges in this account as medium, outcome, and precondition for human thinking. It is in the territory of activity/practice that artifacts are created and used.

### Following the Thread of Practice

A great many contemporary scholars in anthropology, sociology, and cultural studies currently invoke the notion of practice in their discussions of human thought. Central to all of these accounts, despite differences among them, is the attempt to achieve something akin to a combination of the notion of context as that-which-surrounds and the weaving conception of context.

Charles Taylor (1987) suggests that humans' baseline, taken-for-granted social reality is composed of social practices, which provide the intersubjective medium of mind. The ensemble of a society's practices provides the foundation for community and discourse. Meanings and norms (secondary artifacts in my scheme of things) are "not just in the minds of the actors but are out there in the practices themselves; practices which cannot be conceived as a set of individual actions, but which are essentially modes of social relations" (p. 53).

Anthony Giddens (1979) adopts the unit of practices in order to create a theory of socialization which assumes neither that the subject is determined by the environment ("nurture") nor by its "inherent characteristics" ("nature"). The first view, he writes, "reduces subjectivity to the determined outcome of social forces, while the second assumes that the subjective is not open to any kind of social analysis" (p. 120).

According to Giddens, practices (rather than roles, for example) are the basic constituents of the social system. They are also a unit of analysis that overcomes such dualisms as "individual versus social," which re-create one-sided accounts of development. The resolution of such dualisms, he claims (following Marx) is to be found at the level of practices: "In place of each of these dualisms, as a single conceptual move, the theory of structuration substitutes the central notion of *duality of structure*. By the duality of structure, I mean the essential recursiveness of social life, as constituted in social practices: structure is both medium and outcome of the reproduction of practices, and 'exists' in the generating moments of this constitution" (1979, p. 5).

The French anthropologist-sociologist Pierre Bourdieu (1977) also seeks to block simplified notions of context as cause and to overcome dualistic theories of cognition and social life. Bourdieu warns against theories that "treat practice as a mechanical reaction, directly determined by the antecedent conditions" (p. 73). At the same time, he warns against "bestowing free will and agency on practices."

Central to Bourdieu's strategy for balancing these two unacceptable extremes is the notion of *habitus*, "a system of lasting, transposable dispositions which, integrating past experiences, functions at every moment as a *matrix of perceptions, appreciations, and actions* and makes possible the achievement of infinitely diversified tasks" (pp. 82–83). In Bourdieu's approach, *habitus* is the product of the material conditions of existence and the set of principles for generating and structuring practices. Habitus, as its name implies, is assumed to take shape as an implicit aspect of habitual life experiences. It constitutes the (usually) unexamined, background set of assumptions about the world. It is, Bourdieu remarks, "history made nature" (p. 78). "The habitus is the universalizing mediation which causes an individual agent's practices, without either explicit reason or signifying intent, to be none the less 'sensible' and 'reasonable' " (p. 79).

### Following the Thread of Activity

Activity theory is anything but a monolithic enterprise. Within Russia there are at least two schools of thought about how best to formulate Marx's ideas in psychological terms (Brushlinskii, 1968; Zinchenko, 1995). There is a long German tradition of research on activity theory (Raeithel, 1994), a Scandinavian/Nordic tradition (Hydén, 1984; Engeström, 1993), and now, perhaps, an American tradition (Goodwin, 1994; Nardi, 1996; Scribner, 1984). A good statement of general tenets of this approach is provided by Engeström, who writes that an activity system

> integrates the subject, the object, and the instruments (material tools as well as signs and symbols) into a unified whole.

An activity system incorporates both the object-oriented productive aspect and the person-oriented communicative aspect
of human conduct. Production and communication are inseparable (Rossi-Landi, 1983). Actually a human activity system
always contains the subsystems of production, distribution, exchange, and consumption. (p. 67)

The attractiveness of this formulation in light of the discussion of
artifact mediation at the beginning of this chapter should be apparent:
Engeström's formulation promises a way to incorporate ideas about
the duality of artifacts but does not privilege production over social
cohesion.

Engeström represents his conception of activity in a manner that
both includes and enlarges upon the early cultural-historical psychologists' notions of mediation as individual action. Once again we
see a triangle, but now it is a set of interconnected triangles (Figure
5.3). At the top of the figure is the basic subject-mediator-object
relationship depicted in Figure 5.1. This is the level of mediated action through which the subject transforms the object in the process
of acting upon it. But action exists "as such" only in relation to the
components at the bottom of the triangle. The *community* refers to

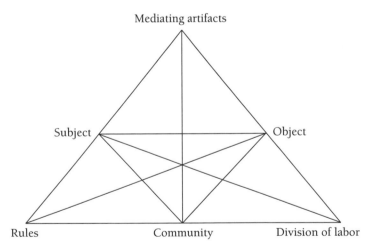

Figure 5.3.   The basic mediational triangle expanded (after Engeström,
1987) to include other people (community), social rules (rules), and the
division of labor between the subject and others.

those who share the same general object; the *rules* refer to explicit norms and conventions that constrain actions within the activity system; the *division of labor* refers to the division of object-oriented actions among members of the community. The various components of an activity system do not exist in isolation from one another; rather, they are constantly being constructed, renewed, and transformed as outcome and cause of human life.

In activity theory, as summarized in Figure 5.3, contexts are activity systems. The subsystem associated with the subject-mediator-object relationships exists as such only in relationship to the other elements of the system. This is a thoroughly relational view of context.

Jean Lave (1993) provides a succinct summary of several themes uniting scholars interested in activity and practice theory:

1. An emphasis on the dialectical character of the fundamental relations constituting human experience (in Lave's terms, human agency is "partially determined, partially determining").
2. A focus on experience in the world that rejects the structure and dynamics of psychological test procedures as a universally appropriate template.
3. A shift in the boundaries of cognition and the environment such that, in Lave's phrasing, cognition "is stretched across mind, body, activity and setting" (a perspective sometimes referred to as "distributed cognition": Hutchins, 1995; Norman, 1991; Salomon, 1993).

## Context/Practice/Activity and Ecological World Views

There are important affinities between the various views about a supra-individual unit of analysis associated with the notions of context, practice, activity, and so on, and the views of those who identify themselves as ecological psychologists (Altman and Rogoff, 1987). These affinities grow out of a common starting point, the ecology of everyday human activities, and are evident in the proclivity of researchers of both views to conduct their research in naturally occurring social settings rather than experimental laboratories.

These affinities can also be seen in the appearance of the metaphor of weaving in the writings of both groups. The following example is taken from the work of the pioneer ecological-developmental psychologists Roger Barker and Herbert Wright, who were attempting to characterize the relation of ecological setting to psychological processes. On the basis of their detailed records of children's activities, Barker and Wright were impressed that children's behavior appeared to be very strongly controlled by the settings they inhabited. They also noted the wide range of different behavioral settings children participated in daily:

> The number of things a child did in a day, according to our criteria of episodes, varied approximately from 500 to 1,300 . . . Most of the episodes did not occur in isolation. Behavior was more often like the interwoven strands of a cord than like a row of blocks in that the molar units often overlapped . . . The behavior continuum was cord-like, too, in the sense that overlapping episodes often did not terminate at the same time but formed an interwoven merging continuum. (1951, p. 464)

This metaphorical invocation of threads and cords echoes Birdwhistell's description of context in interpersonal interaction, although the contents of their descriptions are markedly different. What makes such metaphorical correspondences possible across levels of behavioral analysis is their grounding in a unit of analysis corresponding to events and activities.

Although their vocabularies are somewhat different, I believe the same points of agreement can be attributed to Dewey in his discussions of situation and to those context theorists, such as Bateson, who held firmly to the conviction that it is essential to see an "action as *part* of the ecological subsystem called context and not as the product or effect of what remains of the context after the piece which we want to explain has been cut out from it" (1972, p. 338).

William Wentworth (1980) brings several threads of this discussion together. Context, he writes, is the "unifying link between the analytic categories of macrosociological and microsociological events": "The context is the world as realized through interaction and the most immediate frame of reference for mutually engaged actors. *The context may be thought of as a situation and time bounded arena for human activity. It is a unit of culture*" (p. 92).

This notion of context recognizes the power of social institutions relative to individuals and the potential of individuals to change the environments that condition their lives. On the one hand, aspects of the "macro" level serve as constraints/resources in constituting context (and hence local activity tends to reproduce the relations in society). On the other hand, each situation is idiosyncratic in the mix of resources/constraints brought to bear and hence there is no strict determination of the consequences of action that result.[10]

## Culture as Helping Things Grow

The discussion thus far has characterized culture as a system of artifacts and mind as the process of mediating behavior through artifacts in relation to a supra-individual "envelope" with respect to which object/environment, text/context are defined. This approach allows me to make use of the notion of culture as medium and of context as both that which surrounds and that which weaves together. It also provides me with a basic unit of analysis that has natural linkages to the macro pole of society and its institutions and the micro level of individual human thoughts and actions.

The final set of comments I invoke here for thinking about culture brings many of the conceptual tools discussed thus far together in a manner that I see as especially useful for developmentally oriented research on culture and cognition. "Culture," wrote Raymond Williams, "in all of its early uses, was a noun of process: the tending *of* something, basically crops or animals" (1973, p. 87). From earliest times, the notion of culture has included a general theory for how to promote development: create an artificial environment where young organisms could be provided with optimal conditions for growth. Such tending required tools, perfected over generations and designed for the special tasks to which they were put. So close were the concepts of growing things and tools that the word for culture once referred to ploughshares.

In common parlance, we speak of an artificial environment for growing crops as a "garden," a conception encoded in the idea of a kindergarten (children's garden) where children are protected from the harsher aspects of their environment. A garden constitutes the linkages between the "microworld" of the individual plant and the "macroworld" of the external environment. A garden, in this sense, brings together the notion of culture and that of context, providing a concrete model for thinking about culture and human development.

In addition, the garden metaphor naturally links us to ecological thinking by reminding us that we must be concerned not only with the system of interactions within a particular setting, but also with the way the internal system is related to the "next higher level of context." While it is possible, given sufficient knowledge and resources, to induce a radish to grow in Antarctica or outer space, it is not nearly so easy to sustain the conditions that enable that growth. For the work of developmental psychologists to be widely applicable, they must be concerned not only with a theory of how to create the conditions for development *in vitro* (in artificially constructed environments such as a kindergarten) but with a theory of how to create conditions for development which will survive when the child moves out of the children's garden into the world at large *in vivo*.

⑥ We can summarize the view of culture given here in the following terms:

1. Artifacts are the fundamental constituents of culture.
2. Artifacts are simultaneously ideal and material. They coordinate human beings with the world and one another in a way that combines the properties of tools and symbols.
3. Artifacts do not exist in isolation as elements of culture. Rather, they can be conceived of in terms of a heterarchy of levels that include cultural models and specially constructed "alternative worlds."
4. There are close affinities between the conception of artifacts developed here and the notions of cultural models, scripts, and the like. Exploitation of these affinities requires conceiving of schemas and scripts as having a double reality in the process of mediation.
5. Artifacts and systems of artifacts exist as such only in relation to "something else" variously referred to as a situation, context, activity, and so on.
6. Mediated activity has multidirectional consequences; it simultaneously modifies the subject in relation to others and the

subject/other nexus in relation to the situation as a whole, as well as the medium in which self and other interact.

7. Cultural mediation implies a mode of developmental change in which the activities of prior generations are cumulated in the present as the specifically human part of the environment. This form of development, in turn, implies the special importance of the social world in human development, since only other human beings can create the special conditions needed for that development to occur.

A number of methodological prescriptions follow from this shift in culture's status vis-à-vis mind and behavior. Central is the need to study culturally mediated behavior developmentally to reveal the dynamic interactions uniting different parts of the overall life system. Equally important is the need to conduct research at several developmental/historical (genetic) levels in order to analyze the ways in which they intertwine and fuse in human life over time.

This catalog of concepts could easily be extended. But it is time now to apply and elaborate the properties of culture discussed here to longstanding controversies in psychological theory and to empirical research with children. I will come back to draw upon the concepts introduced here and will introduce additional concepts along the way as I attempt to account for the empirical phenomena of interest to cultural psychology.

# 6 ⑥

# Phylogeny and Cultural History

Neither tool-use nor social cognition can be considered in isolation as prime evolutionary movers. Rather the two are parts of an interdependent behavioral complex. Nor do discrete behaviors such as tool-making, the use of a tool to make a tool, imitation, or sharing distinguish apes and humans. Rather humans reach higher levels of performance in each domain and exhibit greater interdependence of social and technological skills.   *Kathleen Gibson*

Tools, hunting, fire, complex social life, speech, the human way and the brain evolved together to produce ancient man of the genus *Homo*.   *Sherwood Washburn*

AS WE LEARNED in Chapter 5, cultural-historical psychology treats human cognition as the emergent outcome of transformations within and among several developmental domains: phylogenetic history, cultural history, ontogeny, and microgenesis. The requisite methodology for studying such a process is developmental-historical. In this chapter I focus on the phylogenetic and cultural-historical domains.

## Phylogenetic Precursors

Historical reconstructions of the process of change are fraught with the possibility of a false teleology.[1] In the case of human origins, the paucity of paleoanthropological data, together with the high levels of inference which a coherent story requires, make consensus impossible to achieve. Comparative research on the relationship of the cognitive and linguistic behavior of apes with that of humans suffers

*impossible to agree @ human origins*

from a different set of problems, but important gaps in evidence about human origins have a similar effect.

This problem is certainly less severe today than it was fifty years ago when cultural-historical psychology was being formulated. The intervening decades have brought an enormous increase in our knowledge, in large part as a result of technologies that permit dating of fossil specimens and audio-visual recordings of primate behaviors. But the underdetermination of theory by data remains an acute problem.

Bruno Latour and Shirley Strum note the inevitable ego- and ethnocentrism that result: "Each story tells who is ancestral and who is noble and who is commoner, what comes from nature and what comes from culture, what is rooted in tradition and what can be modified . . . Every item in an account of society will be scrutinized closely by each audience if their status, rank, role or past is modified by the account" (1986, p. 172).

Traditionally, reconstructions of anthropogenesis seek to wed two sources of evidence: paleontology and the fossil record, and studies of living primate species, anthropoid apes in particular. The evidence from living primates provides an estimate of the cultural/mental capacities of the creatures from which *Homo sapiens* evolved. The fossil record provides evidence concerning the process of successive transformations of species. Both are topics of unresolved debate. The weight of evidence, however, suggests that both the story of *Homo faber* and the claims for human uniqueness need to be modified.

## Tools and Bodily Change

Three decades ago consensus concerning the origins of culture and emergence of *Homo sapiens* fit well with the notion that tool making and tool use play the central role:

> It would now appear . . . that the large size of the brain of certain hominids was a relatively late development and that the brain evolved due to new selection pressures *after* bipedalism and consequent upon the use of tools. The tool-using, ground-living hunting way of life created the large human brain rather than a large-brained man discovering certain new ways of life . . . The uniqueness of modern man is seen as the result of a technical-

social life which tripled the size of the brain, reduced the face, and modified many structures of the body. (Washburn and Howell, 1960, p. 49)

Since that time, the picture has become more complicated.

Accounts of human origins generally begin approximately 4 million years ago with the earliest hominids, australopithecines, the creatures made famous by the Leakeys' studies in the Olduvai Gorge of what is now Tanzania (Leakey, 1981). These first hominids walked upright and had a more complex social structure than their forerunners. There is no evidence that tool use was present in the early australopithecines, but the simplest stone tools are found in sites that they inhabited toward the end of their existence, around 2.5 to 1.5 million years ago, along with their successors, *Homo habilis* (Toth and Schick, 1993).

Most accounts I have read credit *Homo habilis* as the earliest documented tool makers and users.[2] The brain size of *Homo habilis* relative to their body size (the "encephalization quotient" suggested by Harry Jerison, 1981) was larger than that of australopithecines, providing the earliest evidence of a link between tool making and brain capacity. However, the tools they used were so simple and the skeletal remains that have been found are so few that not much can be made of this link.

The first largely agreed upon change in brain capacity associated with a marked increase in the complexity of tool manufacture and use occurred with *Homo erectus,* which emerged approximately 1.5 million years ago and survived for over a million years. During that time, brain size and complexity increased (judging from the properties of the skulls found); expansion of Broca's area (associated with speech comprehension) suggests increased vocal abilities. Evidence from the sites where *Homo erectus* skeletons have been found also indicates the use of sharp-edged stone tools, control over fire, and increasingly complex social organization.

This picture of a connection between changes in tool complexity and changes in brain complexity is significantly blurred in the transition from *Homo erectus* to early *Homo sapiens* some 200,000–250,000 years ago. While there is accepted evidence of a marked increase in relative brain size and changes in the vocal tract that make it close to that of modern humans, the main evidence for changes in tool manufacture was the refinement of the set of tools. Among *Homo sapiens* one observes the appearance of distinctive styles of tool making, suggesting the existence of cultural norms which became more pronounced with time (Toth and Schick, 1993).

The final marked change from archaic *Homo sapiens* to *Homo sapiens sapiens*—anatomically modern human beings—occurred some 40,000 years ago. At this point there emerges the kind of life that has left its traces in the caves at Lascaux, which included complex tools made of several components, tools made of materials like bone that require other tools for their manufacture, and representational art.[3] Changes in the shape of the frontal, parietal, and occipital lobes occurred at this time, but their precise significance is uncertain.

Although the connection between complex tool use and larger, more complex brains is generally accepted, there is a substantial, and perhaps growing, body of opinion that tool use is less important than previously thought—that differences in social organization are a leading cause of changes in the brain associated with human evolution (Humphrey, 1976; Dunbar, 1993):

> Since intentional action is frequently co-operative and socially regulated in non-human primates, it makes more sense to derive co-operation from social interactions where it already exists than from object-using programs where it does not. Consequently, a theory of the evolution of human technology should place less emphasis on the differences in the tool-using capacities between humans and apes (important as they are) but ask instead how emergent tool-using capacities become integrated into the domain of intentional social action. (Reynolds, 1982, p. 382)

Robin Dunbar (1993), a leading proponent of this view, has demonstrated a correlation between relative brain size and the size of the primary social group in primates in the hominid line. However, essential data linking brain size and social organization for prehuman hominid forms are unavailable, so I shall return to this argument when I examine the data on our contemporary primate relatives.

## Changes in Language and Thought

Inferences about anthropogenesis based on evidence concerning tool use and brain development are fragmentary, (but at least there are material objects to work with.) When we consider questions about how the development of the brain and the use of tools are related to changes in thought and language, already uncertain and disputable stories become even more problematic, for the obvious reason that language and thought do not materially inscribe themselves in nature. Physical data exist concerning the anatomical foundations of oral language-producing capacity (Liberman, 1991), but the main explanation given for the evolution of language and advanced forms of thought is that increases in the complexity of tool use and social organization require them.

A plausible reconstruction of cognitive evolution based on tool manufacture and social organization associates the major transition points (the emergence of *Homo erectus, Homo sapiens,* and *Homo sapiens sapiens*) with the corresponding emergence of new cognitive and communicative capacities which, in turn, are associated with new forms of cultural organization (Donald, 1991; Raeithel, 1994). In Merlin Donald's account, the starting point for cognitive evolution is what he refers to as "episodic culture," based upon an ability to represent the concrete, perceptual nature of lived events. Three fundamental transformations are worked upon the foundation that episodic culture/representation provides:

1. *Mimesis.* This is the ability to represent events in a new way by translating event perceptions into motoric action. This stage coincides with the emergence of *Homo erectus.* Whether language is absent at this time, or present in the form of a "proto-language" involving one- and two-word utterances, is hotly debated (Bickerton, 1990; Liberman, 1991; Dunbar, 1993).

2. *Spoken language associated with mythic culture.* This stage is associated with the emergence of *Homo sapiens.* The evidence of what Donald calls mythic culture includes burial customs in which various objects of apparent symbolic significance are included with the body (for example, burial of a boy with a finely wrought hand axe and the bones of wild cattle "as though meat had been included to sustain him in his journey"). The strong-

est evidence for the presence of spoken language is that *Homo sapiens* possesses a physical apparatus for the production of oral language comparable to that of modern humans.[4] The emergence of language enables (à la Dunbar) far more complex forms of knowledge accumulation, more efficient enculturation, and more complex social organization.

3. *External symbols.* These are associated with the appearance of *Homo sapiens sapiens* and manifested in the symbolic art and other representational artifacts found in the Upper Paleolithic period and subsequently.

Arne Raeithel offers a similar three-stage theory. He emphasizes the process of "co-mimesis" in which one individual imitates another with a slight variation so that the other may reciprocally imitate. Co-mimesis is emphasized for its importance in the evolution of teaching, which propagated and stabilized new cultural innovations in society as well as new modes of learning. A mechanism of this kind seems necessary to explain how complicated tool manufacturing processes could be reliably transmitted from one generation to the next.[5] Raeithel links this form of mimesis to what he calls dramatic communication, in which one dramatizes one's own experiences so that watchers replicate this experience and later engage in their own dramatization. This process, he suggests, provides for ritual recreation and elaboration of shared experience, creating a form of collective memory and the possibility of collective anticipation of future events.

*dramatic comm.*

In one respect, Donald's and Raeithel's accounts are diametrically opposed to each other. Donald begins with the cognitive properties of individuals and seeks to determine how changes in individual capacities influence changes in culture and social life. (He writes, for example, of the "social consequences of mimetic representation.") Raeithel (see also Dunbar, 1993) starts from properties of the social group and seeks to explain how mimetic representation and co-mimesis arose as means of reproducing the social order.

*Donald — start w/ ind*
*Raeithel — start w/ grp*

As commentaries on both Donald's and Raeithel's work make abundantly clear (*Behavioral and Brain Sciences*, December 1993; *Mind, Culture, and Activity*, Winter/Spring 1994), such reconstructions are subject to conflicting empirical claims and interpretations at virtually every turn. However, they have the virtue of integrating a large part of what is known with what is plausible in light of current theories of language and thought. For my current purposes, what is important is that both accounts assume that a complex interplay of ecological constraints, changes in artifacts, and changes in social organization are reciprocally bound up in the process of human evolution.

## Apes and Humans

The different story lines about the transformations that produced modern *Homo sapiens* have their counterparts in alternative accounts of the cognitive, linguistic, and tool-using capacities of contemporary primates. Here too, arguments over basic questions of fact and crucial interpretations are common and fundamental.

Typically this discussion is framed in terms of human uniqueness. The Russian cultural-historical psychologists made strong claims for a principled discontinuity between humans and other species. For example, L. S. Vygotsky wrote that "culture creates special forms of behavior, changes the functioning of the mind, constructs new stories in the developing system of human behavior . . . In the course of historical development, social humans change the ways and the means of their behavior, transform their natural premises and functions, elaborate and create new, specifically cultural forms of behavior" (1983, pp. 29–30).

The contrary view was championed by Charles Darwin. Although he acknowledged a giant gap between the mental powers of other animals and human beings, he also denied discontinuity in the mechanisms underlying human and animal behavior. He wrote that one must recognize large quantitative differences between species even "if we compare the mind of one of the lowest savages, who has no words to express any number higher than four, and who uses hardly any abstract terms for common objects or the affections, with that of the most highly organized ape" (1859, p. 287). However, he disputed the existence of species-specific qualitative differences in the nature of mind and the mechanisms of change. He summarized his argument in the following famous passage:

The difference in mind between man and the higher animals, great as it is, is certainly one of degree and not of kind . . . If it be maintained that certain powers, such as self-consciousness, abstraction, etc., are peculiar to man, it may well be that these are the incidental results of other highly-advanced intellectual faculties; and these again are mainly the result of the continued use of a highly developed language. (p. 105)

Earlier in this century, before the structure of genes was known and before the development of modern techniques for the analysis of genetic material, it was easy to believe (on the basis of physical similarities alone) that there was a major gap between chimpanzees and humans. In fact, to believe otherwise was to invite ridicule, as reactions to Darwin clearly revealed.

However, current studies of the genetic composition of chimpanzees and human beings are converging on the conclusion that perhaps as little as one percent of the genomes differentiate them. Even this one percent is so distributed that it is probably inappropriate to speak of "human genes versus chimpanzee genes." This same conclusion appears to be more than a little relevant to comparisons of the behavior of chimpanzees and humans.

## Tool Using, Problem Solving, and Culture

Wolfgang Köhler (1925), whose studies of problem solving among chimps served as the main source of evidence for Vygotsky and his colleagues, believed there to be a qualitative gap between chimpanzee and human thought associated with language and culture: "The lack of an invaluable technical aid (speech) and a great limitation to those very important components of thought, so-called 'images,' would thus constitute the causes that prevent the chimpanzee from attaining even the smallest beginnings of cultural development" (p. 267).

Research in recent decades has cast doubt on this conclusion. At present it is common to encounter the claim that all of the characteristics traditionally used to differentiate humans and other animals (such as tool use, symbolic communication, cultural transmission, pedagogy) are present in some individuals of one or more species of monkeys or apes (see Wrangham et al., 1994, for a representative sampling of opinion).

Thanks to the pioneering work of Köhler, followed by decades of research by others (summarized in Heltne and Marquardt, 1989; Gib-

son and Ingold, 1993; Parker and Gibson, 1990), the evidence of
deliberate problem solving in apes is beyond question. In recent years
investigators using Piagetian-style tasks have found that various species of monkeys and apes achieve sub-stage 5 of the sensory motor
stage (trial-and-error discovery of instrumental means, imitation of
novel behaviors). It is also claimed that great apes complete sub-stage
6 (insightful discovery of instrumental means, deferred imitation),
which Piaget takes to be the hallmark of the appearance of representation, but the evidence on this point is disputed (Parker, 1990).

There is growing evidence that apes (and in some cases monkeys)
engage in behavior that has many of the earmarks of deliberate deception (Whitten and Byrne, 1988; Cheney and Sayfarth, 1990; Povinelli, 1994). The following observation gives a flavor of the phenomenon:

> Leslie, a high-ranking vervet female, had just chased Escoffier
> away from a grooming bout with Leslie's mother, Borgia. After
> grooming Borgia briefly, Leslie approached Escoffier, who cow-
> ered. Leslie lipsmacked—a sign of appeasement—and began to
> groom Escoffier. After a few minutes, Escoffier relaxed visibly
> and stretched out to allow Leslie to groom her on the back. At
> this point, Leslie picked up Escoffier's tail and bit it, holding it
> in her teeth while Escoffier screamed. (Cheney and Sayfarth,
> 1990, p. 184)

Goodall (1986) offers similar observations of chimpanzees.

There is broad evidence for the ability to use tools. The most extensive tool users and tool makers among primates are chimpanzees,
which appear to be the only primate species other than *Homo sapiens
sapiens* that uses material artifacts as a significant part of life in the
wild. The major tools used are for subsistence (fishing out termites
with a stick, using a chewed leaf to sponge up water, using a stone
to crack nuts). However, sticks and stones have been used as weapons
and for self-stimulation (tickling).

It has also become common for primatologists to claim the presence of culture among chimpanzees in the wild (McGrew, 1992;
Wrangham et al., 1994). Goodall (1986), for example, argues for the
existence of cultural traditions on the basis of observations of stable
differences among different troops in the way that they fish out ter-

mites or use leaves to get water. By her account, "young chimpanzees learn the tool-using patterns of the community during infancy, through a mixture of social facilitation, observation, imitation, and practice —with a good deal of trial and error thrown in" (p. 561). Although chimpanzees are known to make tools by modifying natural objects (for example breaking off blades of grass to fish for termites), there are few reports of chimpanzees using a sequence of tools (for example, different kinds of sticks held and manipulated in different ways) to obtain honey (Brewer and McGrew, 1989; Matsuzawa, 1994).

Christophe Boesch has claimed evidence for the active teaching of tool use among chimpanzees. In one case, a young chimp positioned a nut on an anvil incorrectly and its mother intervened to position the nut correctly. In another case a mother chimp (Ricci) sat by for a while as her daughter (Nina) unsuccessfully tried to crack open some nuts, then joined the daughter, who gave her the stone used as a hammer. Then, with the daughter watching, the mother,

> in a very deliberate manner, slowly rotated the hammer into its best position for efficiently pounding the nut. As if to emphasize the meaning of this movement, it took her a full minute to perform this simple rotation. With Nina watching her, she then proceeded to use the hammer to crack ten nuts (of which Nina received six entire kernels and portions of four others). Then, Ricci left and Nina resumed cracking. Thereafter, she succeeded in opening four nuts in 15 minutes. (1993, p. 177)

Boesch concludes: "The mother, seeing the difficulties of her daughter, corrected the error in her daughter's behavior in a very conspicuous way and then proceeded to demonstrate to her how it works with the proper grip. She stopped before having cracked all the nuts so that Nina could immediately try by herself, and her daughter seemingly understood the lesson perfectly" (p. 177). Observations like these would certainly appear to erode, if not erase, the border between chimps and humans with respect to tool use and culture.

Evidence for symbolic behavior and language is, if anything, more impressive than evidence for tool use and culture. Early research by Kellogg and Kellogg (1933) and Hayes and Hayes (1951) with a chimp raised at home by humans demonstrated comprehension of dozens of words and phrases, as well as various kinds of tool use. But oral language production was either minimal or nonexistent, depending upon who does the interpreting. Subsequent work using manual signs instead of spoken words produced clear evidence of the use of words to request and refer, but claims for the presence of syntax (flexible, rule-bound variation in word order to produce meaningful phrases) became bogged down in technical disputes over the criteria for the evidence (e.g., Premack, 1971; Terrace, 1979).

The work of Sue Savage-Rumbaugh and Duane Rumbaugh has contributed greatly to the current belief in symbolic communication among chimpanzees (Rumbaugh, Savage-Rumbaugh, and Sevcik, 1994; Savage-Rumbaugh, 1986, Savage-Rumbaugh et al., 1993). The Rumbaughs combined several strategies that had been developed by others and added some of their own. For example, instead of insisting on oral production or signing they provided chimps with a lexical keyboard. They arranged for the chimps to live in a colony so they could find out if chimps who learned to use the keyboard communicated with others. They used standard, discrete trial-reinforcement techniques to train the chimps in a basic vocabulary, but rather than attempting specific training of oral comprehension, they emphasized natural use of oral language by the humans who worked with the chimps in everyday, routine activities.

Their most successful student has been Kanzi, a pygmy chimpanzee. Although he himself had not been trained to use the lexical keyboard but had only been present during his mother's training, Kanzi was able to use lexigrams to request things, to comment on his activities, to comprehend the meaning of lexigrams used by others, and even to understand spoken English words and phrases (Savage-Rumbaugh et al., 1993).

Kanzi's comprehension of a wide variety of unusual sentences was comparable to the performance of a two-year-old child. For example, Kanzi responded correctly to the request "Feed your ball some tomato." He also responded correctly to "Give the shot (syringe) to Liz" and "Give Liz a shot" by handing the syringe to Liz in the first case and touching the syringe to her arm in the second case.

Kanzi's productive abilities are also impressive, but less so than in the case of comprehension. Most of his "utterances" (indicated using his lexical keyboard) are single words that are closely linked to his ongoing actions and are most often used to make requests. However, he also uses two-word utterances in many different combinations and occasionally makes non-instrumental observations. For example, he produced the combination "car trailer" on an occasion when he was in the car and wanted (so his caretakers believed) to be taken to the trailer by car rather than walk. He created such phrases as "playyard Austin" when he wanted to visit a chimp named Austin in the play-yard and "potato oil" when a researcher put oil on him while he was eating a potato.

Savage-Rumbaugh and her colleagues do not claim that Kanzi or any nonhuman primate is capable of full-blown human language, tool use, or culture. However, the evidence concerning tool use and culture gathered by other researchers, together with their own data on symbolic communication, leads them to conclude "Language in its basic dimensions may no longer rationally be held as the characteristic that separates human beings from animals" (Rumbaugh, Savage-Rumbaugh, and Sevcik, 1994, p. 332).

## Alternative Interpretations

Despite the evidence presented above, important reservations central to the question of tool use, language, and culture among nonhuman primates have been raised that speak directly to the concerns of cultural-historical psychologists. Michael Tomasello and his colleagues (Tomasello, 1990, 1994; Tomasello, Kruger, and Ratner, 1993) have examined the evidence of tool use and cultural mediation among chimpanzees and concluded that if we want to claim that chimpanzees "have culture," it must be in a different sense than our attribution of culture to human beings. There are several reasons for their caution.

Although there is some elementary tool use by chimpanzees in their natural habitat (such as stripping leaves from a branch and then using the branch to probe for termites), such tool use is rudimentary by human standards and there is considerably less in other, allied species. In fact, tool use directed at objects, which appears early in children's play, is relatively rare among primates in the wild; it is more common to encounter the instrumental use of other members of their species, such as that involved in begging (Bard, 1990). There are only a few reported cases of using one kind of tool to manufacture an entirely different kind (using a stone axe to make a bone instrument), and primates do not use materials that stick together, tie knots, or heat things. Gibson summarizes these limitations as follows: "In general, tool-using schemes lacking in apes are those which develop relatively late in human children and which demand keeping several spatial relationships or objects in mind simultaneously" (1993, p. 255).

It is also unclear how much faith should be placed on evidence that nonhuman primates engage in deliberate instruction. The two examples offered by Boesch are widely cited, but both depend heavily on interpretation of chimp motives and therefore are open to alternative interpretations. For example, Goodall (1986) offers as an example of teaching the taking away of a poison plant from a youngster.

It might be argued that cultural transmission is possible without deliberate arrangement of the experiences of subsequent generations if the novices are skilled in imitation, and the folklore about apes is that they are masters at learning by imitation. But the evidence on this issue diverges from folk wisdom in important ways.

Tomasello (1994) points out that there are very few reports of apes imitating in the wild and that experimental attempts to induce imitation by apes raised in captivity have failed (Tomasello, Savage-Rumbaugh, and Kruger, 1993; Whitten and Ham, 1992). Even in cases where it might seem that tool use has been learned by observation, other, simpler processes appear to account for the results.

For example, Tomasello and colleagues (1987) trained a chimpanzee to rake in food items with a metal T-bar; on some trials the food was placed so that the chimp had to go through a two-step procedure to get it. Other chimps were allowed to observe this behavior and then were tested themselves. Most of the observer chimps learned to use the T-bar as a rake after a few trials, but they did so in a wide variety of ways they had not observed and none of them learned the two-step procedure. On the basis of this and other evidence from similar studies, Tomasello argues that the chimps had indeed learned about the relevance of the T-bar to food getting, but that they were not copying the behavioral methods of the demonstrator (imitation) but instead sought only to produce the end result (a process Tomasello refers to as emulation). Analysis of presumed imitation of gestures by chimps produced an analogous finding.

In effect, this work suggests that chimps attend to the behavior of others, which puts them in a position to learn through imitation, but that their learning is not the result of imitation. According to Tomasello, their observation of others merely orients them to the task. Once so oriented, they learn on their own, not through imitation of the behavioral processes of others. If this line of reasoning is correct, the continuity of tool use across generations depends entirely upon individuals' rediscovering the innovations of prior generations because they inhabit the same ecological niche. By contrast, humans engage in deliberate instruction and are skilled at imitation of underlying behavioral process in a wide variety of niches.

This difference in process would explain one of the major characterstics that all observers agree differentiates human cultures from their possible counterparts in nonhuman primates: among humans, accumulation of artifacts over generations is a hallmark of culture, while among nonhuman primates social traditions involving gestures and material artifacts diffuse but do not accumulate, and continue to occupy only a small part of the overall social ecology of the group.

Similar doubts are raised with respect to the question of language in nonhuman primates. Greenfield and Savage-Rumbaugh (1990, p. 572) declare that the capacity for grammatical rules displayed by a pygmy chimpanzee "shows grammar as an area of evolutionary continuity" because the rules produced and learned by the chimp are very similar to those produced by normal two-year-old children. The problem is that there is no clear agreement that such utterances by human children constitute human language. Greenfield and Savage-Rumbaugh acknowledge this issue, suggesting that such utterances be considered "protolanguage" in both chimps and humans.

Bickerton (1990) also urges that we consider such utterances to be a protolanguage, not language, but he draws a quite different conclusion about continuity. A protolanguage, he writes, has only a limited number of topics about which information can be exchanged while human language has an infinite number. He concludes that fundamentally different principles must underlie the two kinds of communicative systems: "the differences between language and the most sophisticated systems of animal communication that we are so far aware of are qualitative rather than quantitative" (p. 8).

Tomasello and his colleagues emphasize an additional contrast between humans and chimps concerning an ability that is central to human communication and cultural accumulation—the ability to direct another's attention to an object. In normal human development, children begin to direct the attention of others to objects shortly before one year of age. Joint attention to objects (shared attention), which appears shortly thereafter, is believed to be important to language acquisition and to children's developing theories of mind (Bruner, 1983; Butterworth, 1991; Wellman, 1990). Tomasello, Kruger, and Ratner (1993) propose that underlying these developments is children's increasing understanding that other people are intentional agents whose behavior should be interpreted in terms of their goals. It is for this reason that Tomasello and colleagues interpret the failure of chimps raised by other chimps to imitate others' intentional behaviors as symptomatic of an important difference from humans.

Field studies of chimps and other apes indicate that they do not use pointing as a means of recruiting joint attention, suggesting the absence of an appreciation of intentionality. But enculturated chimps—as Tomasello calls those raised and trained by human beings—and other apes (for example orangutans: Call and Tomasello, 1996) do engage in joint attention with humans and other enculturated conspecifics.

In his recent work, Tomasello has sought to focus attention on an important regularity of the pattern of findings concerning tool use, culture, cognition, and communication among apes: virtually all of the well-documented examples of complicated tool use, teaching, learning by imitation, pointing to recruit attention to objects, and symbolic communication involve enculturated apes. Citing many studies showing that enculturated chimps are the ones which display human-like capacities, Tomasello concludes: "A humanlike social-cognitive environment is essential to the development of human-like social-cognitive and imitative learning skills . . . More specifically, for a learner to understand intentions of another individual requires that the learner be treated as an intentional agent" (1994, pp. 310–311). According to this hypothesis, the learning skills that apes acquire in the wild are sufficient to create and maintain behavioral traditions of a limited sort, but not to create the kind of environmental transformation that is characteristic of human culture.)

Although he does not mention Vygotsky in this context, Tomasello's suggestion is the equivalent of an interspecies "zone of proximal development" where the less able partner is supported in behavior that has not developed sufficiently to be sustained independently. In these terms, chimpanzees display the "buds of development" that flower to their full extent only within human culture.

⑥ Kathleen Gibson, who has spent many years studying problem-solving behaviors in nonhuman primates and considering their implications for human evolution, offers what seems to me a fair judgment of current controversies over human uniqueness: "The demolition of one behavioral discontinuity after another brings us no closer to charting the evolution of human cognition than did the discontinuity theories of earlier decades" (1993, p. 7). However, the enormous scientific labor devoted to this problem in recent decades does permit us to reevaluate and where necessary amend the ideas about the relation between phylogeny and cultural history proposed by early-twentieth-century cultural historical psychologists.

## Temporal Succession

One early-twentieth-century misconception that the Russian cultural-historical psychologists shared with their anthropological colleagues in the United States was that there is a strict temporal succession: first comes phylogeny, then cultural history. They summarized their notion of how the different developmental domains interact as follows: "One process of development dialectically prepares for the next one, transforming and changing into a new type of development. We do not think that all three processes fall into a straight-line sequence. Instead, we believe that each higher type of development starts precisely at the point where the previous one comes to an end and serves as its continuation in a new direction" (Vygotsky and Luria, 1930/1993, p. 38).

The first sentence in this passage appears a straightforward statement of the reasonable idea that phylogeny constitutes the context for cultural-history and that cultural history forms the proximal context of ontogeny. Each time two streams of history come together, a context is created in which new processes, a new type of development, emerges. This idea needs to be held on to and elaborated.

But, as James Wertsch (1985) has pointed out, the idea that each "higher" level starts precisely at the point where the previous one comes to an end is a real problem. This idea reflects a "critical point" theory of cultural origins of the kind proposed by Alfred Kroeber (1917) when he introduced the idea of culture as a superorganic reality separate from phylogeny. As seen in Figure 6.1, Kroeber depicts cultural history "lifting off" from phylogeny. The evidence presented earlier that mediation through artifacts makes its appearance in the hominid line millions of years before the appearance of *Homo sapiens* argues against a critical point theory and for a process of dialectical interaction between phylogenetic and cultural history.[6]

A second problematic assumption in the passage is that there is a genetic hierarchy within and among domains. I am uncertain about what it could mean to say that ontogeny was a "higher level" than phylogeny or cultural history, except insofar as ontogenies are always constituted of the most recent developments in phylogeny and cultural history. This sort of interpretation of evolution-as-progress, a pervasive notion in the nineteenth and twentieth centuries, is subject to a plethora of criticisms, and not only by post-modernists (Toulmin, 1990).

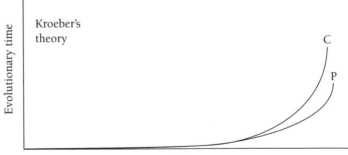

Figure 6.1.   Alfred Kroeber's conception of culture as a superorganic level of development. At some point in evolution, culture begins to accumulate independently of the phylogenetic substrate.

With respect to understanding the dialectical interaction among genetic domains, Vygotsky himself offered a more promising description in a statement written at almost the same period concerning the course of ontogenesis:

> The growth of the normal child into civilization usually involves a fusion with the processes of organic maturation. Both planes of development—the natural and the cultural—coincide and mingle with one another. The two lines of change interpenetrate one another and form what is essentially a single line of socio-biological formation of the child's personality. To the extent that development occurs in the cultural medium, it becomes transformed into an historically conditioned biological process. (1930/1960, p. 47)

This statement retains the idea that a qualitative reorganization of the developing entity is brought about when different genetic domains fuse. But instead of the principles of one domain replacing those of the other, the two become intermingled into a single life system in which new, synthetic, principles of development operate.

## The Coevolution of Phylogeny and Cultural History

It would be foolish of me to attempt *the* definitive account of human evolution prior to the appearance of *Homo sapiens* 140,000–290,000 years ago or of the cognitive and linguistic capacities of primates today. I will settle for noting that evidence of tool use exists from the appearance of *Homo habilis* about 2 million years ago. With the emergence of *Homo sapiens sapiens* some 40,000 years ago the range of artifacts expanded markedly to include not only a variety of tools but stone figurines, lunar calendars, and cave paintings, that is, a range of artifacts bespeaking the presence of human culture.

Perhaps earlier, but certainly with the advent of *Homo sapiens*, a new principle of development, cultural evolution (what Tomasello, 1994, refers to as the ratchet effect) begins to interact with the principles of evolution governing other species. Bickerton (1990), following in the tradition of virtually all who accord culture a central role in human nature, asserts that the key feature of this change was that modifications in artifacts rather than modifications in morphological

characteristics such as jaws, teeth, or hands became the major form
of adaptive mechanism. He credits language and the capacity for artifact creation as the catalyst for the qualitatively new form of interaction between species and environment characteristic of *Homo
sapiens sapiens,* a position in obvious agreement with the cultural-
historical perspective.

Weston La Barre summarizes the idea of a new form of inheritance
and change as follows:

> With human hands the old-style evolution by body adaptation
> is obsolete. All previous animals had been subject to the *auto-
> plastic* evolution of their self-substance, committing their bodies
> to experimental adaptations in a blind genetic gamble for sur-
> vival. The stakes in this game were high: life or death. Man's
> evolution, on the other hand, is through *alloplastic* experiments
> with objects outside his own body and is concerned only with
> the products of his hands, brains, and eyes—and not with the
> body itself. (1954, p. 90)

A key fact about this new form of activity mediated by language/
culture is that it accumulates "successful" interactions with the past
environment extrasomatically. Consequently, whereas genetic change
is primarily Darwinian (that is, it occurs via natural selection acting
on undirected variation), cultural evolution is Lamarckian in the
sense that the useful discoveries of one generation are passed directly
to the next (Gould, 1987). D. P. Barash (1986) elaborates on this
point in a useful way:

> Culture can spread independently of our genes and in response
> to conscious decisions . . . Natural selection does not involve
> any conscious choice on the part of those genes and gene com-
> binations that experience maximum reproductive success. By
> contrast, culture often proceeds by the intentional selection of
> specific practices from among a large array of those available.
> In this sense, then, it is "teleological" or goal directed in a way
> that biological evolution never is. (p. 47)

Although I am persuaded by these kinds of arguments of significant discontinuity in the life process separating humans from nonhuman primates, two provisos should be added. First, it is possible

to consider an artifact to be the cause of a fitness-increasing outcome, when it is in fact fitness-decreasing. Such errors can come about because artifact-mediated cultural practices that are initially fitness-increasing may have long-term negative consequences (the use of pesticides may be a current example), or because people's theories about a practice rely on superficial features rather than causal ones (see Barkow, 1989; Durham, 1991; Shweder, 1977). Examples of the latter include the prohibition in many cultures against children nursing shortly after birth when colostrum is flowing but before milk flows, as well as various uses of magic around the world.

Second, I believe it an error to assume that the fact of cultural mediation implies the total independence of human development from phylogenetic constraints. The problem is how best to characterize the relationship of phylogenetic and cultural mechanisms of change. At a general level, Theodozius Dobzhansky was correct when he wrote:

> The history of the human species has been brought about by interactions of biological and cultural variables; it is just as futile to attempt to understand human biology if one disregards cultural influences as it is to understand the origin and rise of culture if one disregards human biological nature. Human biology and culture are parts of a single system, unique and unprecedented in the history of the living world. (1951, p. 385)

In sorting out the complex relation between human biology and culture, it is important to realize that Dobzhansky's statement is more than a characterization of the *current* relationship that appeared at some specific moment in phylogenetic history with the appearance of *Homo sapiens*. Rather, over millions of years of phylogenetic history, creatures in the line to *Homo sapiens* elaborated their artifact-mediated interactions with the physical and social environment even as the biological properties of these artifact-using creatures were undergoing organic evolution.

When Clifford Geertz (1973) examined the mounting evidence that the human body, and most especially the human brain, underwent a long (perhaps 3 million year) coevolution with the basic ability to create and use artifacts, he was led to conclude:

Man's nervous system does not merely enable him to acquire culture, it positively demands that he do so if it is going to function at all. Rather than culture acting only to supplement, develop, and extend organically based capacities logically and genetically prior to it, it would seem to be ingredient to those capacities themselves. A cultureless human being would probably turn out to be not an intrinsically talented, though unfulfilled ape, but a wholly mindless and consequently unworkable monstrosity. (p. 68)

Hence, instead of Kroeber's picture of culture "lifting off" into the realm of the superorganic, we get a picture of the organic and the artifactual mutually constituting each other over the course of human evolution (Figure 6.2). That is, while it is correct, as Arnold Gesell (1945) insisted, that the glove does not determine the shape of the hand in the short run (phylogenetically speaking), Gesell is wrong in the long run. Phylogeny and cultural history are mutually constituting a single system in our species.

However, because of the temporal limits of cultural modifications

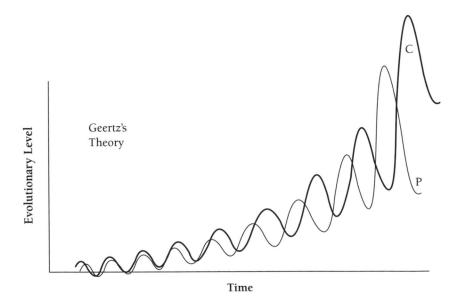

Figure 6.2.   Clifford Geertz's view of phylogeny-culture relations, which assumes a constant interaction through human phylogeny.

vis-à-vis phylogenetic time, it is mere illusion to think that *Homo sapiens* can transcend nature. La Barre provides the most plausible overall description of the relationship between phylogeny and cultural history when he cautions that "cultural man proposes, but (unknown) reality disposes, for man is only another kind of animal" (1970, p. 61). (In sum, a teleological, Lamarckian system is embedded in a blind, Darwinian one.

A slightly different idea is conveyed by Charles Lumsden and Edward Wilson's (1983, p. 60) notion that phylogeny and culture are held together by an unbreakable but elastic leash: "As culture surges forward by means of innovation and the introduction of new ideas and artifacts from the outside, it is constrained and directed to some extent by the genes. At the same time, the pressure of cultural innovation affects the survival of the genes and ultimately alters the strength and torque of the genetic leash." This metaphor is useful because it allows for the possibility that the cultural "dog" will lead its phylogenetic "master" into dangerous and potentially life-extinguishing circumstances (thermonuclear holocaust, for example) as well as into more inclusive ecological niches (outer space, for example). At the same time, such metaphors have the negative property of disguising real theoretical differences. Lumsden and Wilson assume that it is possible to translate directly between culture and genes, denying culture any special properties that cannot be translated back to the level of the genome. (I believe that culture must be treated as a level of organization that is not directly mappable onto the human genome but instead fuses the Lamarckian principle with the Darwinian one.)

In the last analysis, I arrive at a mixed answer to the uniqueness of our species. Either position taken to the extreme is clearly false: there is evidence of tool use in the pre–*Homo sapiens* fossil record and evidence of limited forms of tool use, linguistic communication, and social intelligence in living nonhuman primates. At the same time, all this evidence points to significant restrictions on the complexity of these accomplishments when compared to those of human beings over at least the past 40,000–50,000 years. Most significant in my opinion is the extreme paucity of evidence that cultural mediation is a central feature of any species along the phylogenetic line from which *Homo sapiens* emerged. While other creatures show evidence of bits and pieces of the fabric of human culture, the essential pattern is missing.

## The Cultural-Historical Level: Heterogeneity and Hierarchy

As I noted in Chapter 5, the Russian cultural-historical psychologists believed that historical change in human thought arises in two interrelated ways. First, there is a shift from natural, unmediated, to cultural, mediated thought. Second, there is development in the complexity and sophistication of mediational means that entails a corresponding development of thinking.

In the basic writings outlining the principles of their new psychology, they substantiated this view largely by referring to the ideas and data of late-nineteenth and early-twentieth-century sociology and anthropology, especially the work of Lucien Levy-Bruhl (1910) and Richard Thurnwald (1922). For example, they found evidence for a shift from unmediated to mediated thinking in Levy-Bruhl's account of the absence of generic categories in primitive languages, his claims that primitive people do not think in terms of concepts but rather in terms of concrete situations and that they use their memories instead of engaging in logical problem solving. They drew upon Thurnwald's writings for data concerning cultural variations in the use of historically pivotal mediational systems such as counting systems and writing. Thurnwald's pictures of Inca knotted strings as mnemonic devices became one of the iconic examples of what they meant by mediated remembering, and the sequential development of writing systems from pictographic to ideographic systems was incorporated into their research on writing in children (Luria, 1928/1978; Vygotsky, 1978).[7]

Significantly, this picture of cognitive advance accompanying socioeconomic-cultural advance was complicated by the fact that the Russians, like Levy-Bruhl, argued for the heterogeneity of levels of cognitive functioning depending upon the kind of activity that people habitually engaged in. I noted in Chapter 1 that Levy-Bruhl insisted that the phenomena he was talking about did not apply to practical, everyday events where a kind of commonsense thinking was called for. The qualitatively distinctive, primitive form of thinking was restricted to occasions, as he put it, when people are guided by their collective representations (see also Levy-Bruhl, 1910/1966). Moreover, he readily agreed that the advent of logical thinking did not uniformly replace pre-logical thinking: "For these traces [of pre-logical thinking] to disappear, all concepts that we use, for example, in everyday living, would have to express exclusively objective properties and relations of beings and phenomena. Actually this occurs with respect to only a very small number of our concepts, specifically those used in scientific thinking" (1930, quoted in Tulviste, 1991, p. 24).

Vygotsky and Luria (1930/1993) make the same points with respect to the ethnographic record, and Vygotsky (1934/1987) applied the same mode of thought in seeking to account for the developmental heterogeneity of thinking among the well-educated members of societies with advanced industrial modes of life. The analogous set of changes is from everyday (spontaneous) to scientific (true) conceptual processes. Vygotsky's account of this transition includes clear statements that the higher-order form of conception totally transforms the everyday thinking, the thinking in terms of spontaneous concepts (pp. 216–217). Yet elsewhere he cautions that "in adult thinking, transitions from thinking in concepts to concrete, complexive, thinking occur continually . . . In our everyday lives, our thinking frequently occurs in pseudoconcepts" (p. 155).

During the period when the cultural-historical psychologists were publishing these views, a massive collectivization campaign was transforming the lives of peasant peoples throughout the USSR. In the Soviet Republics of Central Asia, the cultural-historical psychologists saw a great natural experiment. The combination of collectivization (which radically altered modes of economic activity and social organization) and the expansion of formal education (which was presumed to bring about a transformation in mind) promised a way to study the interplay between cultural and individual development in a single community over a short period of time.

In 1929 an expedition was sent to parts of Siberia north of Lake Baikal to observe children's everyday activities and attempt to assess their mental development using, among other things, the Stanford-Binet test (for an excellent summary, see Valsiner, 1987). The main lessons carried away from this work were the need to study children's everyday lives to discover the areas where their knowledge is dense and a thoroughgoing rejection of the use of IQ tests in nonliterate

*Ch. in remote Siberian villages solved probs diff*

cultures. Not only did tests standardized in Paris produce results that fell in the mentally retarded range, but it was clear that the children tested in remote Siberian villages were going about solving problems using different processes from those encountered in European cities.

These initial forays were followed up in an ambitious cross-cultural research program headed by A. R. Luria, who journeyed with teams of psychologists to Central Asia in the summers of 1931 and 1932 (see Luria, 1976). In announcing his plans in the American journal *Science,* Luria declared that the aim of the expedition was to record changes in thought and other psychological processes brought about by "the introduction of higher and more complex forms of economic life and the raising of the general cultural level" (1931, p. 383).

His conclusion when this work was terminated in 1932 was that the introduction of schooling and new modes of socioeconomic life (the two were intertwined in his sample) brings about a qualitative shift in the processes of perceiving, categorizing, reasoning, imagination, and self-analysis. In experiments in each of these traditional psychological categories, Luria found that the more educated/modernized peasants produced more analytical, self-conscious, and abstract forms of reasoning.

When he wrote up this work in the early 1970s, Luria was aware of subsequent cross-cultural research up to the mid-1960s, which gave him no reason to change his views.[8] He summarized the difference between the traditional groups he had studied and those who had become enmeshed in schooling and new forms of economic activity as follows:

> Closely associated with this assimilation of new spheres of social experience, there are dramatic shifts in the nature of cognitive activity and the structure of mental processes. The basic forms of cognitive activity begin to go beyond fixation and reproduction of individual practical activity and cease to be purely concrete and situational. Human cognitive activity becomes a part of the more extensive system of general human experience as it has become established in the process of social history, coded in language. (Luria, 1976, p. 162)

All spheres of human cognition undergo such changes. Perception based on "graphic, object-oriented experience" gives way to "more complex processes which combine what is perceived into a system of abstract, linguistic categories." Thought processes grounded in "practical, situational" thinking give way to more abstract theory-driven modes of thinking. Luria called the general tendency in all the domains he studied the "transition from the sensory to the rational."

In the context of both the time in which he collected his data and the time, forty years later, when he wrote them up for publication, there is nothing particularly unusual about these conclusions. They were, in fact, being echoed, if not quoted, by United Nations personnel continuing the UN's push for increased economic well-being through the promotion of literacy, schooling, and "modern thinking." To me however, they posed a significant problem. My experience of cross-cultural differences in thinking had led me to emphasize the context-specificity of cognitive functioning and the inappropriateness of using Western psychological tasks as general indicators of cognition among people from a different culture; thus Luria's conclusions did not sit well.

## Context Specificity

The crux of my concerns follows from my critique of similar cross-cultural studies earlier in this book. Rather than sample the activities of native people to understand their intellectual organization, Luria was making judgments about how people think in general from tests that are samples of the common experience of Muskovites (and Berliners, Parisians, or New Yorkers). I could understand how Western European and American psychologists had come to adopt such practices; I had been trained in that mode of thinking. But it was difficult for me see how a Soviet psychologist, for whom the grounding of psychological analysis in everyday activity was a postulate, could proceed in such a manner.

During the 1980s my colleagues and I made our first forays into a serious reconciliation of our context-specific learning theory approach with the ideas of the cultural-historical psychologists (Cole, 1985, 1988; LCHC, 1983; Scribner, 1985; Scribner and Cole, 1981). We sought to combine the Russian tradition, which emphasized the mediated structure of higher psychological functions and broad historical changes in the nature of mind, with the American tradition, which emphasized the synchronic variability of thinking within historical periods owing to differences in the functional structure of different activities (the context-specific approach). The key to this combination was the contention that tool use implies both mediation and context specificity, while context dependence implies the historical contingency of mental processes.

The argument ran as follows: The Russian cultural-historical psychologists were correct in their insistence on the mediated nature of mind and the instrumental aspect of mediators, but when making pronouncements about broad cultural differences in thinking they neglected to take seriously their own and Levy-Bruhl's contention that the processes, as well as the contents, of thought differ according to particular circumstances. A commitment to tool mediation as the fulcrum of thought logically requires the inclusion of context-level constraints on thinking: all tools must simultaneously conform to constraints arising from the activity they mediate and from the physical and mental characteristics of the human beings who use them. There is no universal, context-free tool, independent of task and agent, as critics of such dreams in the study of artificial intelligence have repeatedly pointed out (e.g. Dreyfus and Dreyfus, 1986; Zinchenko and Nazarov, 1990).

At the same time, our ahistorical, context-specific approach failed to take into account the historical origins of the context in question. The agricultural practices of the Kpelle of Liberia or the animal husbandry of the Uzbeki peasant are by no means universal forms of activity, nor is print-mediated formal education. If a context-specific theory was to overcome its psychological particularism to account for generalities in behavior across contexts, and for obvious cultural differences in the structure of people's everyday activities, it had to take into account not only the internal organization of different activities but the historically conditioned connections between them as constituents of social life.

James Wertsch (1991) discusses two major ways in which cultural-historical psychologists have incorporated the idea of heterogeneity of modes of thinking into theories of developmental change. The first view assumes a genetic hierarchy, such that later forms of activity/thinking are more advanced than earlier ones. According to this perspective, when already-completed stages of development reappear they are considered regressions.

Perhaps the best-known example of this viewpoint is the discussion of the heterogeneity of human consciousness in Freud's *Civilization and Its Discontents* (1930). Regarding what he called the "problem of preservation," Freud rejected the idea that old knowledge is obliterated, preferring instead the hypothesis that in mental life nothing which has once been formed can perish, that everything is somehow preserved. Freud likens the layering of knowledge in the mind to the layers of history in Rome where traces of the most remote epochs are mixed with the remnants of the metropolis of the last few centuries and decades. He goes on to examine the applicability of this archaeological metaphor to human mental life. After probing various problems with the metaphor, he concludes: "We can only hold fast to the fact that it is rather the rule than the exception for the past to be preserved in mental life" (1930, p. 19).

Writing at approximately the same time as Freud, Vygotsky used a geological metaphor, which he attributed to Ernst Kretschmer, a German psychiatrist. Vygotsky applied this "law of stratification" in the history of development both to the ontogenesis and regression of behavior resulting from brain insults and to the ontogeny of concepts. With respect to research focusing on the brain he wrote: "Research has established the presence of genetically differentiated layers in human behavior. In this sense the geology of human behavior is undoubtedly a reflection of 'geological' descent and brain development" (1930/1971, p. 155). With respect to his well-known studies of concept formation he wrote: "Forms of behavior that have emerged very recently in human history dwell amongst the most ancient. The same can be said of the development of children's thinking" (1934/1987, p. 160).

Vygotsky also cited Heinz Werner, who quite explicitly drew the parallel between ontogeny and cultural history. Declaring that human beings may vary in the genetic level of their thinking from one moment to the next, Werner suggested: "In this demonstrable fact that there is a plurality of mental levels lies the solution of the mystery of how the European mind can understand primitive types of mentality" (Werner, 1926/1948, p. 39).

A second line of interpretation retains the idea that different forms of thinking arise in a sequential fashion, but denies that later forms are more powerful or effective than early ones in any general sense— rather, in this interpretation, power and efficacy depend crucially on the activities that different forms of thinking mediate. Sylvia Scribner (1985) attributes this view to Vygotsky who, she argues, "does not represent higher systems as general modes of thought or as general structures of intelligence in a Piagetian sense. Vygotsky addressed the question of general processes of formation of particular functional systems, a project quite at variance from one aimed at delineating a particular sequence of general functional systems" (p. 132). This view, which Wertsch refers to as "heterogeneity despite genetic hierarchy," is appropriate to the kind of contextual, cultural-historical approach we began advocating in the mid-1980s.

This same argument has been made by Luria's student Peeter Tulviste, who replicated and extended some of the early cross-cultural studies during the 1970s (Tulviste, 1991).

> There is an obvious connection between various forms of activity and the heterogeneity of thinking. This is true between and within cultures. The reason for the heterogeneity of verbal thinking must not be sought in the accidental preservation in society or in the individual of "old," "lower," or "previous" sociohistorical or ontogenetic stages of thinking. Instead, it must be sought in the multiplicity of activities that are distributed in society and carried out by the individual. Heterogeneity developed through social history such that with the development of material and mental production new forms of activity appeared. These new forms of activity required new types of thinking and gave rise to them. At the same time, to the degree that earlier forms of activity, which fulfill some role in the society, are preserved, the "old" types of thinking that correspond to them are preserved and continue to function. (1986, pp. 24–25)

Wertsch points out that this view bears a strong affinity to William James's view of the relation of modes of thinking to forms of activity. James (1916) referred to three kinds of thinking that he labeled common sense, science, and critical philosophy. He argued that although these types emerged in an historical sequence, it is inappropriate to

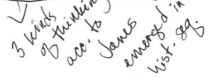

consider one type better than another. All thinking is instrumental. Hence the question of which kind of thinking is better depends crucially on the sphere of activity within which it occurs.

## Conditional Relativism

I come around in this discussion to points made in earlier chapters. Insofar as there are differences in the kinds of problems recognized and embodied in the cultural practices of different societies, one must logically adopt the position of cultural relativism—no universal notion of a single, general, psychological characteristic called "level of thinking," or some surrogate, is universally appropriate.

However, this radical relativist position does not represent the full position of the kind of cultural-historical, activity-based theory my colleagues and I have been developing, because it neglects to consider the fact that cultural groups interact. When groups interact, they are generally in competition for resources. That competition has sometimes been friendly, but more often the ability of one group to dominate the other has been crucial to shaping the nature of subsequent culturally organized activities in both groups, and particularly among the dominated.

Key resources in such struggles have been culturally elaborated tools (ranging from the bow and arrow to intercontinental ballistic missiles and from rudimentary record-keeping systems to digital computers). It has been tempting in recent centuries to assume that mastery of those technologies associated with "the modern world" provides an index of the extent to which the users of those technologies have developed further than others in the *common* problem of sustaining life on the planet earth. With respect to *that* problem, the superiority of modern industrialized societies must be considered with deep suspicion.

The general proposition is as follows:

If one wishes to abstract a particular kind of activity from its cultural context and assert (a) that it is a universal kind of activity that differing people have mastered to differing degrees, and (b) that one has a true theory of developmental stages in that domain, then it is possible to do a kind of *conditional comparison* in which we can see how different cultures have organized experience to deal with that domain of activity. When this conditionality is forgotten, the door is left open to severe abuses of the scientific method in favor of ethnocentric claims about the true nature of reality. (LCHC, 1983, p. 710) )

Even this kind of conclusion rests upon the assumption that when one abstracts activities from their cultural context there is a meaningful sense in which they can be considered the same activity. To make such an assumption is to adhere to the notion that cognitive tasks can be specified independently of their contexts, an assumption upon which cross-cultural work casts grave doubt and to which I will return in Chapter 8.

*no specification of tasks ind of context*

⑥ As I remarked early in this chapter, global claims about the phylogeny and cultural history of mind are not likely to receive definitive confirmation or rejection on the basis of evidence now at our disposal, if ever. The fields of inquiry are so vast and there are so many gaps in our data that many accounts can "satisfice" in providing a coherent narrative.

My less ambitious goal was to determine what modifications would have to be made in the theory proposed by cultural-historical psychologists two-thirds of a century ago to bring it into line with contemporary data and modes of interpretation. By and large I have been surprised that so little of the basic theoretical apparatus has had to be abandoned: rather, the changes have consisted of returning to the basic principles to redress imbalances that fit with earlier times but are no longer acceptable.)

*Changes*

The first change was to emphasize the necessary duality of mediation vis-à-vis other human beings and the nonhuman world in order to ensure a balanced treatment of production and consumption on the one hand and social coordination on the other. The second change was to reject the idea that "first comes" one or another of the factors that contribute to human evolution, after which a new factor takes over. In like manner, we must reject the idea that a single factor accounts for whatever is distinctive about our species. In both cases, it is the fusion of different principles that gives rise to new life formations. Third, at the cultural-historical level of analysis we have reaffirmed the need to ground cultural differences in cognitive performance to activities within societies in order to capture the necessary degree of heterogeneity of cognitive processes within persons across activities. Textual evidence that the early cultural-historical psychologists entertained both of these ideas might be used as justification for arguing their current viability. But resort to citation-mongering is not necessary. The original principles, interpreted in the light of contemporary data, can do the job.

# 7 ⑥

# A Cultural Approach
# to Ontogeny

WITH A MODIFIED cultural-historical approach to questions of phylogeny and cultural history in hand, we can now turn to the topic that has been the main focus of my own research: ontogeny in its cultural-historical contexts. When we take ontogenetic development as our central concern, we arrive at a level of analysis that corresponds to our everyday experience. But we do so within a theoretical frame in which the developing individual represents a third stream of history, a third strand that becomes interwoven with the phylogenetic and cultural-historical strands. Important principles from our analysis of the processes of change in those genetic domains carry over when ontogeny is approached in this way.

1. Development involves the commingling of different historical strains that follow different processes of change: Darwinian and Lamarckian evolution.
2. Phylogenetic (Darwinian) change and cultural-historical (Lamarckian) change occur at different rates; the historical sources of change relate to each other heterochronously.
3. "Levels of development" are internally heterogeneous.
4. Strict cause-effect relationships do not explain development which entails the emergence of novel forms and functions of interaction among people and their worlds.

5. An appropriate unit of analysis for studying the interanimation of ontogeny and cultural history is a cultural practice, or activity system, which serves as the proximal environment of developmental change.

Patricia Miller provides a useful summary of the general process of ontogenetic development proposed by Russian and American cultural-historical psychologists:

> As children engage in activities with others, intermental activities, particularly dialogue, become intramental. In this way individual mental functioning has sociocultural origins. Language between people eventually becomes spoken speech for self (egocentric speech), then silent, mental, speech-like inner speech. Children internalize (Vygotsky) or appropriate (Rogoff) information and ways of thinking from their activities with parents, teachers, other adults, more capable peers.
>
> Technical and psychological tools provided by the culture mediate intellectual functioning. Language, in particular, helps children to direct their own thinking efficiently; they plan, think logically, and so on. (1993, p. 421)

I read straight through this passage nodding my head, saying to myself "good summary." But there are hidden problems with the view presented. Miller notes one of them: the summary is insufficiently developmental. One can see what she means by looking back at the previous passage and asking oneself how the process of change itself changes in the course of ontogeny. Miller summarizes general principles of mediation and the acquisition of mind, but the conditionality of their embodiment in the experience of children at different ages is left out.

When filling in the needed additional considerations, we might want to note another feature of this description. It is benign and conflict free. We are told that language "helps" children, and this is true. But, as is true of all mediational systems, language simultaneously constrains and assists children, it is simultaneously enabling and constraining. The tug and pull of actual human relationships, as experienced by people enduring the difficulties of everyday life, is absent. This feature bespeaks an idealized representation of the sociocultural role of children in mediating adult experience of the world. Children are not always compliant and adults are not always well intentioned (Goodnow, 1990; Litowitz, 1993; Smolka, De Goes, and Pino, 1995).

This limitation is exacerbated by the absence of methodologies for dealing with the rich variety of activities that serve as the contexts of development. I postpone the methodological discussion until Chapter 8. In this chapter I will examine a variety of ways in which culture enters into the process of ontogenetic development. This treatment will differ from the earlier discussion (Chapter 3) organized around cross-cultural experimental data. While not ignoring those data, my account will be about universal processes of cultural mediation as they play themselves out from birth onward.

## The Newborn Encounters the Group

John Dollard, one of the ancestors of current social learning theorists, offered a compelling way of thinking about the encounter of a new human being with the postnatal environment and the eventual impact of culture on its behavior:

> Accept two units for our consideration: first, the group which exists before the individual; and second, a new organism envisioned as approaching this functioning collectivity. The organism is seen at this moment as clean of cultural influence and the group is seen as functioning without the aid of the organism in question . . . Let us ask ourselves at this point what we can say systematically about what this organism will be like when it comes of age, sex granted. All of the facts we can predict about it, granted the continuity of the group, will define the culture into which it comes. Such facts can include the kind of clothes it will wear, the language it will speak, its theoretical ideas, its characteristic occupation, in some cases who its husband or wife is bound to be, how it can be insulted, what it will regard as wealth, what its theory of personality growth will be, etc. (1935, pp. 14–15)

This thought experiment graphically describes some obvious ways in which culture affects children's development. Moreover, Dollard is correct that over time new members of the community will come to feel that the culture "belongs to them" in such a powerful sense "that they act as if they had thought up for themselves what had been prescribed by tradition." There is a fundamental structural change during ontogeny such that an organism that lives in a cultural medium but cannot make use of it becomes one for which mediation of action through culture has become "second nature." The challenge is to explain how "over time" this transformation came about.

I will highlight four characteristics of culture discussed in Chapter 5 to explicate the distinct nature of a cultural-historical approach to ontogenic development. First is the basic unit of analysis within which life processes are organized—people's everyday, culturally organized activities (Bruner, 1982; Rogoff, 1990; Super and Harkness, 1986). The representation of context as concentric circles and the garden metaphor of culture both have at their core such everyday activities as the proximal environment of development.

Second is the central importance of artifacts, the ideal/material mediators of human experience that act as tools for, and constraints on, human action. Primary, secondary, and tertiary artifacts all enter into this account. Children are not born able to mediate their activity through artifacts, but they are born into a world where the adults who care for them do have this ability. In fact, as we shall see, children are themselves, in an important sense, cultural objects as they enter the world. The changing means by which they appropriate the cultural tool kit of their society in the process of becoming adult members is central to the process of ontogenetic change.

A third important feature of the way culture enters into ontogenetic development concerns temporality. As a rule, cultural change proceeds more rapidly than phylogenetic change; the biological characteristics of our species have changed relatively little. And cultural change is generally slower than ontogenetic change.[1] This heterochrony among genetic domains provides essential, but little-recognized, resources for human mental functioning and development.

The final property of culture I plan to discuss is connected with the metaphor of weaving together. A favorite theme in Vygotsky's writings was the way that qualitatively new characteristics of the organism emerge when hitherto separate lines of development intersect. Nevertheless, a significant shortcoming of cultural-historical research at present is the failure to give an adequate account of how the natural and the cultural lines of development, phylogeny and cultural history, coincide and mingle during ontogeny.

Each of these aspects of culture is always present as a potential conditioner of, and resource for, interaction and thought, but they are not equally prominent in particular instances. My goal here is not to provide a comprehensive account of how each aspect influences development in all circumstances or at all ages, but rather to illustrate the ways in which each operates in cases where it plays a prominent role.

## Past, Present, and Future

I begin my discussion of culture and ontogeny with the temporal properties of culture, in part because this topic has been widely neglected and in part because its operation is visible in a particularly clear way at the moment a newborn child emerges into the world.

With respect to embryogenesis, we have a pretty good idea of the way the past is related to the future and the present. The genetic code assembled from the past when sperm and egg unite at conception provides current and future biological constraints within which the biological process of development can take place. As cells proliferate, distinctive new structures come into being. For example, about five weeks after conception the hands begin to emerge as limb buds. Cells proliferate very rapidly, and soon the limb buds elongate into the shape of a paddle. Then five protrusions appear on the edge of the paddle, which will become a five fingered hand, with muscles, bone, tendons, nerve cells situated in a pattern appropriate to a human hand. None of this could happen if the genetic code had not provided the necessary constraints ahead of time. It is in this sense that the past enters the future in order that the end can be in the beginning. Note that the genes cannot be said to "cause" development. It is only the combination of the constraints they provide and the interactions of the proliferating cells with their environment (including one another) that permit the emergence of successive physical forms and patterns of interaction between the developing organism and its environment. Developmental change of this kind is called epigenesis, a vague term which identifies local processes of interaction as the locus of change. Of course, the "final cause" or "telos" coded in the pattern of genetic constraints is only an "if all other things equal" final cause. The actual process of development is one of probabilistic, not predetermined epigenesis (Gottlieb, 1992). If the right sorts of interactions between the organism and its environment do not happen at an appropriate time (for example, if thalidomide disrupts cell division five weeks after conception), distortions in development of a potentially life-destroying type will occur.[2]

There appears to be an analogous set of temporal relationships with respect to cultural constraints and development in Dollard's thought experiment, where the cultural past greets the newborn as its cultural future. But to explain how the palpable constraints in place in adulthood are transformed into palpable constraints at birth we must show how that "future structure from the past" is transformed into constraints on the interaction of organism and environment in the present, starting at birth, if not before. The name of the cultural mechanism that brings "the end into the beginning" is *prolepsis*, meaning, according to Webster's dictionary, "the representation of a future act or development as being presently existing."

Recently there have been several suggestions about the role of prolepsis in the organization of human psychological functions. Ragnar Rommetveit (1974) pointed out that human discourse is proleptic "in the sense that the temporarily shared social world is in part based upon premises tacitly induced by the speaker" (p. 87). Through prolepsis "What is said serves . . . to induce presuppositions and trigger anticipatory comprehension, and what is made known will hence necessarily transcend what is said" (p. 88).

Addison Stone and his colleagues (Stone, 1993; Stone and Wertsch, 1984) use prolepsis to characterize the way teachers seek to induce children's understanding of how to complete difficult cognitive tasks; in effect, the teachers presuppose that the children understand what it is they are trying to teach as a precondition for creating that understanding.

## Prolepsis in the First Face-to-Face Meeting

A basic fact about human nature stemming from the symbolic character of cultural mediation is that when neonates enter the world they are already the objects of adult, culturally conditioned interpretation. To paraphrase Leslie White's comment about water, they come bathed in the concepts their community holds about babies just as surely as they come bathed in amniotic fluid.

In the 1970s the pediatrician Aidan Macfarlane recorded conversations between obstetricians and parents at their children's birth. He found that the parents almost immediately start to talk about and to the child. The things they say arise in part from phylogenetically determined features (the anatomical differences between males and females) and in part from cultural features they have encountered in their own lives (including what they know to be typical of boys and girls). A typical comment about a newborn girl might be "I shall be worried to death when she's eighteen" or "It can't play rugby." Putting aside our negative response to the sexism in these remarks, we see that the adults interpret the phylogenetic-biological characteristics of the child in terms of their own past (cultural) experience. In the experience of English men and women living in the 1950s, it could be considered "common knowledge" that girls do not play rugby and that when they enter adolescence they will be the object of boys' sexual attention, putting them at various kinds of risk. Using this information derived from their cultural past and assuming cultural continuity (that the world will be very much for their daughter as it has been for them), parents project a probable future for the child. This process is depicted in Figure 7.1 by following the arrows (1) from the mother to the (remembered) cultural past of the mother (2) to the (imagined) cultural future of the baby (3) back to the present adult treatment of the baby.

Two features of this system of transformations are essential to understanding the contribution of culture in constituting development. First, and most obviously, we see an example of prolepsis. The parents represent the future in the present. Second, if less obviously, the parents' (purely *ideal*) recall of their past and imagination of their child's future become a fundamental *materialized constraint* on the child's life experiences in the present. This rather abstract, nonlinear process of transformation is what gives rise to the well-known phenomenon that even adults totally ignorant of the real gender of a newborn will treat the baby quite differently depending upon its symbolic/cultural "gender." For example, they bounce infants wearing blue diapers and

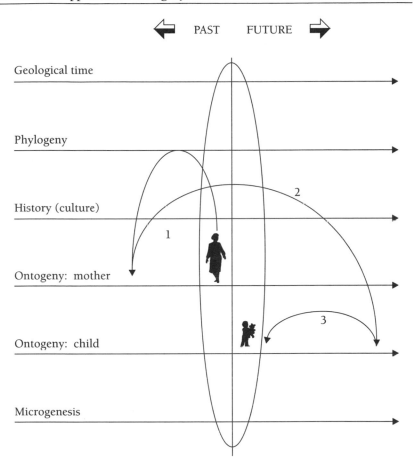

Looking backward, looking forward

Figure 7.1.    The horizontal lines represent time scales corresponding to the history of the physical universe, the history of life on earth (phylogeny), the history of human beings on earth (cultural-historical time), the life of the individual (ontogeny), and the history of moment-to-moment lived experience (microgenesis). The vertical ellipse represents the event of a child's birth. The distribution of cognition in time is traced sequentially into (1) the mother's memory of her past, (2) the mother's imagination of the future of the child, and (3) the mother's subsequent behavior. In this sequence, the ideal aspect of culture is transformed into its material form as the mother and other adults structure the child's experience to be consistent with what they imagine to be the child's future identity.

attribute "manly" virtues to them while they treat infants wearing pink diapers gently and attribute beauty and sweet temperaments to them (Rubin, Provezano, and Luria, 1974). In other words, adults literally create different material forms of interaction based on conceptions of the world provided by their cultural experience.

Note how this situation differs from that embodied in the learning-theory view of development. The adults are not building upon the child's existing repertoire of behavior and modifying it bit by bit. The baby is, for them, a cultural being, and it is in those terms that they treat it.

Macfarlane's example also demonstrates an important distinction between the social and the cultural, which are often conflated in theories of development based upon such dichotomies as environment versus organism or nature versus nurture. "Culture" in this case refers to remembered forms of activity deemed appropriate, while "social" refers to the people whose behavior is conforming to, and implementing, the given cultural pattern. This example motivates the special emphasis placed on the *social* origins of higher psychological functions by cultural-historical psychologists (Cole, 1988; Rogoff, 1990, Valsiner, 1987; Vygotsky, 1981; Wertsch, 1985). Humans are social in a sense that is different from the sociability of other species. Only a culture-using human being can "reach into" the cultural past, project it into the future, and then "carry" that conceptual future "back" into the present to create the sociocultural environment of the newcomer.

Finally, this analysis of parental comments upon first seeing their child helps us to understand ways in which culture contributes to both continuity and discontinuity in individual development. In thinking about their babies' futures, these parents are assuming that the way things have always been is the way things will always be. This assumption of stability calls to mind White's telling image that temporally, the culturally constituted mind is "a continuum extending to infinity in both directions" (1942, p. 120). In this manner, the medium of culture allows people to "project" the past into the future, thereby creating a stable interpretive frame which is then read back into the present as one of the important elements of psychological continuity.

The assumption of cultural stability is wrong, of course, whenever there are conditions of cultural change following the birth of the child. The invention of new ways to exploit energy or new media of representation, or simple changes in custom, may sufficiently disrupt the existing cultural order to be a source of significant developmental discontinuity. As but a single example, in the 1950s American parents who assumed that their daughter would not be a soccer player at the age of sixteen would probably have been correct, but in the 1990s most girls in my home town play soccer.[3]

I know of no recordings equivalent to Macfarlane's from other cultures, but an interesting account of birthing among the Zinacanteco of south-central Mexico appears to show the same processes at work. In their summary of developmental research among the Zinacanteco, Greenfield, Brazelton, and Childs (1989) report a man's account of his son's birth at which the son "was given three chilies to hold so that it would . . . know to buy chili when it grew up. It was given a billhook, a digging stick, an axe, and a [strip of] palm so that it would learn to weave palm" (p. 177). Baby girls are given an equivalent set of objects associated with adult female status. The future orientation of differential treatment of the babies is not only present in ritual; it is coded in a Zinacantecan saying: "For in the newborn baby is the future of our world."

Although I do not pursue the issue here, I take prolepsis to be a ubiquitous feature of culturally mediated thought. Elsewhere (Cole, 1992) I present examples of prolepsis from later infancy and childhood. Chapters 8 and 9 of this book include further discussion of prolepsis.[4]

## Routine Activities as Proximal Environments for Development

The earliest, essential condition for continued development once a neonate has been "precipitated into the group" is that the newcomer be incorporated into the daily life of the group. This incorporation requires that children and those who care for them become coordinated in such a manner that the adults are able to accumulate enough resources to accommodate the newcomer while the newcomer gets enough food, care, and warmth to continue developing. Adults must make room for the child, for one more mouth to feed. The child must fill that space by "making itself welcome." Many ways of conceptualizing the effective unit of analysis linking children to their sociocultural environment and the process of developmental change have been proposed over the years.

Charles Super and Sara Harkness (1972, 1986), elaborating the tradition of eco-cultural theory proposed by J. W. M. Whiting (1977), refer to the child's "developmental niche" within the everyday practices of the community. They conceive of the developmental niche as a system composed of the physical and social settings within which children live, culturally regulated customs of child care, and the parents' theories about children.

My colleagues and I identified cultural practices as the proximal units of children's experience (LCHC, 1983). We defined cultural practices as activities for which there are normative expectations for repeated or customary actions. Within cultural practices, all objects are social objects—they are socially constituted. Cultural practices are functionally and structurally similar to what Super and Harkness refer to as developmental niches, and what others refer to as contexts or activities (see Chapter 5).

Jaan Valsiner (1987) distinguishes niches with respect to the role of adult involvement in a manner that complements the positions sketched out so far. The innermost level of the developmental niche is called the Zone of Free Movement (ZFM); it structures the child's access to different parts of the environment, exposure to different objects and events, and ways of acting. Within the ZFM, adults promote children's actions in various ways, creating the Zone of Promoted Action (ZPA). According to this scheme, Vygotsky's idea of a Zone of Proximal Development (ZPD) is treated as a ZPA so matched to the child's present developmental state that it guides the child's further development. Each way of structuring interactions provides essential constraints enabling development.

An important feature of all of these approaches needs to be emphasized: while adults may initiate the creation of developmental niches and by virtue of their power provide constraints on the organization of behavior within them, the events that transpire within culturally organized activities are *joint* accomplishments. Both the child and the sociocultural environment are active agents in the developmental process.

Barbara Rogoff makes the cautionary point quite clearly: "Even when we focus attention separately on the roles of the individual and the social milieu, these roles are defined in terms that take each other into account" (1990, p. 28).

Citations emphasizing this point could be drawn from any of the authors cited above, but an excellent summary comes from Sue Savage-Rumbaugh's work on language development in chimpanzees, discussed in Chapter 6. A central part of Savage-Rumbaugh's strategy of inducing language (whether dealing with chimps or children) is to focus on what she and her co-workers refer to as "interindividual routines," defined as "a more or less regularly sequenced set of interindividual interactions that occur in a relatively similar manner on different occasions" (Savage-Rumbaugh et al., 1993, p. 25). Savage-Rumbaugh links interindividual routines to scripted events of which they are a part. Such routines are highly repetitive and rhythmic, while subject to variation within a conventional range. They coordinate the organized patterns of interplay between child and caretakers(s) and synchronize their behavioral-emotional states.

Diaper changing is given as an early prototype of an interindividual routine. Children must cooperate to the extent of lying still enough to keep a pin from being stuck through their skin instead of the diaper. If a caretaker lifts the child in an unfamiliar way the child may wriggle away because she is uncertain of what is to follow. The routine is disrupted if either participant fails to follow it, because it depends upon their joining their behaviors in a smooth manner. As Savage-Rumbaugh and her colleagues put it, "Each sort of interindividual routine is something like a delicate dance with many different scores, the selection of which is being constantly negotiated while the dance is in progress, rather than in advance. Experienced partners know what turns the dance may take, and, more important, they have developed subroutines for negotiating what to do when one or both partners falter in the routine" (p. 27).

Of course, even experienced partners do not always accomplish diapering seamlessly and smoothly. My children, at least, were perfectly capable of resisting being diapered, and I can attest that even highly skilled parents stick pins in even compliant babies. These nonideal episodes have a way of being selectively forgotten, and along with them the constant possibility of friction in the enactment of adult scripts.

## Interactions in Early Developmental Niches

Examples of early developmental niches illustrate how children are integrated into the social group in a way that simultaneously sustains their development and allows the group to readjust and go on about its business.

Hilliard Kaplan and Heather Dove (1987) report that among the Ache, a hunter-gatherer people of eastern Paraguay, children under three years of age spend 80–100 percent of their time in direct physical contact with their mothers and are almost never seen more than three feet away. A major reason for this situation is that the Ache do not create clearings in the forest when they stop to make camp. Rather, they remove just enough ground cover to sit down upon, leaving roots, trees, and bushes more or less where they find them. In consequence, mothers either carry their infants or keep them within arm's reach.

Quechua mothers also keep their infants close to them, but in a different way and for different reasons. The Quechua inhabit the highlands of Peru, an area approximately 12,000 feet above sea level, where the partial pressure of oxygen is 62 percent of its value at sea level, humidity is extremely low, and the temperature reaches freezing an average of 340 days a year (Tronick et al., 1994). Quechua newborns spend almost all of their time in a *manta pouch,* constructed of at least four layers of cloth, the outer layer being a rectangular wool blanket placed inside a carrying cloth. The blankets are folded to seal off the child from the outside so that no part of the child's body is exposed except when being changed. The environment within the manta pouch is warmer, more humid, and more stable than the outside conditions. Tronick and his colleagues propose that this environment helps the infant to conserve energy, reducing the number of calories needed for growth in an environment poor in nutritional resources. As children grow older and stronger, the wrappings are loosened and exposure to the environment is increased.

The way culturally regulated childcare practices are designed to coordinate infant-caretaker interactions can be highlighted by contrasting the ways American urban-dwelling and rural Kenyan (Kipsigis) parents organize their children's sleeping patterns (Super and Harkness, 1972). Among children in the United States, there is a marked shift toward the adult day/night cycle a few weeks after birth; by the end of the second week, they are averaging about 8½ hours of sleep between the hours of 7 P.M. and 7 A.M. Between four and eight months the longest sleep episode increases from about four to eight hours a night. The pressures toward sleeping through the night are not difficult to identify. American urban dwellers live by the clock. A large proportion of mothers and fathers must leave the house at a specified time to get to work, and the child must be ready at that time. As a consequence of the child's need for sleep, the adults' need to get to work, and the adults' desire for some leisure time while the child is asleep, American adults are likely to push hard for the child to eat and sleep when it is convenient for them.

The course of getting on a schedule is very different for Kipsigis infants. At night they sleep with their mothers and are permitted to nurse on demand. During the day they are strapped to their mothers' backs, accompanying them on their daily rounds of farming, household chores, and social activities. They do a lot of napping while their mothers go about their work. At one month, the longest period of sleep reported for Kipsigis babies is three hours; and their longest sleep episode increases little during the first eight months. Kipsigis children gradually increase the length of their sleeping as their patterns of participation in community activities broaden. As adults, they will be more flexible in their sleeping patterns than their American counterparts.[5]

## Reciprocal Action within Developmental Niches

A shortcoming of the examples I have presented thus far is that they fail to display the co-constructed nature of the process. In every case, they imply that agency rests exclusively with the (more powerful) parents and other older kin. However, there is also evidence indicating the reciprocal nature of the interactions between children and their caretakers, even in the early days of postnatal life.

Kenneth Kaye and his colleagues (Kaye, 1982) have provided a

variety of illustrations of this point. One series of studies was devoted
to the development of nursing, a form of behavior that Piaget had
studied in terms of the gradual modification of reflexes into primary,
secondary, and tertiary schemas as a result of assimilation and accommodation. Piaget's account does not consider the active role of the
mother in arranging the conditions of the child's behavior. Kaye
found that even during the very first feeding mothers occasionally
jiggle their baby (or the bottle). These jiggles do not come at random
intervals; rather, they are most likely to occur during pauses in the
infant's sucking. The jiggles increase the probability of sucking and
prolong the feeding session, thereby increasing the amount of milk
the neonate receives.

Sucking in response to jiggling is not a reflex in the sense that
rooting is a reflex. Rooting is an automatic, involuntary response to
being touched on the side of the mouth. There are no known neural
connections that make sucking inevitable when a baby is jiggled. Yet
it happens, it is to some extent automatic, and it has clear adaptive
value. Kaye speculates that the mother's jiggles between her infant's
bursts of sucking are her way of intuitively "conversing" with her
baby by filling in her "turn" during the pauses in the baby's rhythmic
sucking. Mothers' reports support Kaye's view. Although they are not
aware that they are jiggling their babies in a systematic way, mothers
report that they actively try to help their babies nurse. They notice
and disapprove of the pauses between bursts of sucking. When mothers are asked about their jiggling behavior, a typical response is that
the baby "gets lazy," or "dozes off," "so I jiggle her to get her to pay
attention."

The interactions observed by Kaye are easily overlooked. His research indicates that when we examine the earliest mother-child interactions carefully enough, reciprocity of behavior as part of childrearing routines is seen to be there from the beginning, though the
form of this reciprocity may vary from one cultural setting to another.

By the middle of the first year of life, infants' ability to initiate and
share control of interactions, and even to wrest control from adults,
is well documented. Barbara Rogoff provides an example in which
an adult is trying to initiate a turn-taking routine:

When the adult tried to take the ring, the baby firmly held onto
it and looked away. When the adult forcibly removed the ring

from the baby's grasp, the baby stared at him with a look of indignation, and then, with her eyes fixed on him, her face melted into a pout. The adult immediately exclaimed, "Oh, don't cry, I'll give it back to you!" and extended the ring to the baby, who was by then shrieking . . . The adult tried four more times to play give-and-take, but each time he took the ring away and handed it back, the baby turned away or looked down, apparently displeased, but eventually grasped the ring when it came in contact with her hand. Finally, the baby pushed the adult's hand away from the ring, and the adult left the ring in the baby's possession. (1990, pp. 91–92)

Rogoff comments that the child provided ample evidence of understanding the adult's give-and-take game script, but an equally strong disinclination to engage in it.

⑥ As children's physical abilities and accumulating experience increase, the developmental niche organized for them by adults changes. Beatrice Whiting and Carolyn Edwards (1988), following Margaret Mead (1935), provide a normative developmental sequence of the niches that children are allowed to inhabit. The *lap* or *back* child (0–2.5 years) lives in "a bounded space centered on the emotional and physical presence" of caretakers (p. 35). The *knee* child (2.6–3.5) moves around on its own but in a circumscribed area where it is closely monitored by its caretakers. The *yard* child (3.6–5.5) is allowed access to the entire area in and immediately surrounding the home and begins to come under the control of adults outside the immediate family. *Community* or *school* children engage in activities that take them far from home and also outside of immediate supervision by adults.[6]

## Intersubjectivity and Joint Mediated Activity

At the same time that babies and their caretakers are becoming coordinated with each other through joint participation in caretaking routines, they are also establishing the foundations for sharing experiences (Cole and Cole, 1996). Contemporary research demonstrates that immediately after birth infants visually track a schematic face as it moves in front of them (Morton and Johnson, 1991). At about 2½ months changes in brain functioning owing to maturation are accompanied by increased visual acuity and the appearance of a new form of reciprocal behavior called social smiling. For the first time, children's smiles are reliably connected with events originating in the social environment, and this calls forth stronger feelings of connectedness on the part of caretakers.

The new pattern of interactions provides the potential for the sharing of emotional states that Colwyn Trevarthen (1980) refers to as *primary intersubjectivity.* The following episode of emotional sharing between a three-month-old infant and its mother, described by Daniel Stern, indicates this form of connectedness:

> His eyes locked on to hers, and together they held motionless . . . This silent and almost motionless instant continued to hang until the mother suddenly shattered it by saying "Hey!" and simultaneously opening her eyes wider, raising her eyebrows further, and throwing her head up and toward the infant. Almost simultaneously the baby's eyes widened. His head tilted up . . ., his smile broadened . . . Now she said, "Well hello! . . . heello, . . . heeelloooo!," so that her pitch rose and the "hellos" became longer and more stressed on each successive repetition. With each phrase the baby expressed more pleasure, and his body resonated almost like a balloon being pumped up. (Stern, 1977, p. 3)

At about eight months of age, babies exhibit a variety of behaviors indicating a second marked increase in their level of connectivity with their surroundings. It is at this time that children first begin to search actively for hidden objects, to imitate actions seen several hours earlier, to display overt wariness of novelty, to fear strangers, and to become upset when left by their parents. Changes in EEG patterns indicating increased power and coherence of this measure of brain activity coincide with these behavioral changes (Dawson and Fischer, 1994).

With respect to the capacity for joint activity the most important development in this period is the ability to pay attention to people and objects as part of the same action. Trevarthen uses the term *secondary intersubjectivity* to refer to the new pattern of interpersonal relations that illustrates this ability. The essence of secondary intersubjectivity is that the infant and the caregiver can now share understandings and emotions that refer beyond themselves to objects and other people. For example, if a mother and five-month-old baby are looking at each other and the mother suddenly looks to one side, the infant will not follow the mother's gaze and look in the direction she is looking. At about eight months, babies follow the line of their mother's gaze and engage in joint visual attention with her (Butterworth and Jarrett, 1991).

A striking example of secondary intersubjectivity between infants and their caretakers is called *social referencing*. Babies use social referencing when they come upon something unfamiliar and look back to their caretakers for some indication of what they are supposed to do. It comes into prominence as a means of communication as soon as babies begin to move about on their own (Campos and Stenberg, 1981). When babies notice that their caretaker is looking at the same thing they are looking at and appear to be concerned, they will hesitate and become wary. If their caretaker smiles and looks pleased about the new situation, they will be more relaxed and accepting (Walden and Baxter, 1989).

A parallel, and presumably linked, change in children's problem solving is equally important to the development of culturally mediated action. Ever since the pioneering work of Piaget it has been known that during this same period one observes the earliest forms of tool use in which children are able to coordinate two schemas (for example, "drop object in tin box" and "make an interesting sound"). In Piaget's words, the first schema "serves as a means whereas the second assigns an end to the action" (Piaget, 1952, p. 55).

A series of behavioral changes which converge in the months surrounding the child's first birthday initiate a totally new level of ability to mediate actions through artifacts and other people. An example of this is pointing as a means of recruiting a caretaker's attention. Around one year of age babies begin pointing at objects (Bruner, 1983; Franco and Butterworth, 1991). When twelve-month-olds see a remote-controlled car roll past, first they point at it and then they look to see how their mothers react to it (social referencing).

⑥ "Verbal pointing" (using nonconventional sounds) also makes its appearance early in the second year. For example, Elizabeth Bates made the following observation of a thirteen-month-old girl: "C. is seated in a corridor in front of the kitchen door. She looks toward her mother and calls with an acute sound *ha*. Mother comes over to her, and C. looks toward the kitchen, twisting her shoulders and upper body to do so. Mother carries her to the kitchen, and C. points toward the sink. Mother gives her a glass of water, and C. drinks it eagerly" (1976, p. 55).

Michael Tomasello and his colleagues argue that the ways in which infants begin to coordinate attention to objects and people as part of the same act indicate their awareness that persons are intentional agents, unlike inanimate objects: "Infants do not attempt to look where their doll is looking, they do not attempt to use a chair as a social reference point, and they do not request actions from their bottle. They do these things only when they are interacting with another person, and this is because they understand the behavior of other persons in terms of underlying perceptions and intentions" (Tomasello et al., 1993, p. 498). According to Tomasello and his colleagues, this emerging ability to treat others as intentional agents is critical in making possible the forms of imitation children will need to acquire their group's store of cultural knowledge.

Conventional developmental psychological wisdom marks 18–24 months as the period when converging changes in the social, biological, and psychological spheres result in a qualitatively new stage of development, marking the end of infancy. This is the period that Piaget marks as the advent of representational thought. It is the period when, according to Vygotsky, cultural history and phylogeny begin to merge, bringing about a qualitative transformation in human thought. Important markers of these changes include the following:

1. At 18 months the function of pointing becomes communicative in a more complex way. As noted earlier, if a self-propelled toy car rolls across the floor unexpectedly, 12-month-olds are likely to point to the car and then look to see if their mothers are looking too. Around 18 months of age, the children are more likely first to look at their mothers to see if they are looking at the car and *then* to point to it. If infants this age are alone in the room when the electric car appears, they do not point *until the adult walks back into the room,* clearly demonstrating that

their pointing is instrumental and meant to communicate (Butterworth, 1991).

2. Problem solving mediated by symbolic combinations of possible solutions makes its appearance. Piaget's (1952) description of his daughter Lucienne's ability to get a stick through the bars of her crib is a classic illustration. Instead of going through the slow process of trial and error the child seems to picture a series of events in her mind before she acts. Piaget singled out the baby's ability to infer that she could pull the stick through the bars if she reoriented it without making any overt attempts as the key evidence for the existence of a new form of thought separate from immediate action.

3. From about 12 to 18 months, babies use objects in play much as adults would use them in earnest; that is, they put spoons in their mouths and bang with hammers. But as they near their second birthdays, babies begin to treat one thing as if it were another. They "stir their coffee" with a twig and "comb the doll's hair" with a toy rake or pretend that the edge of a sandbox is a roadway. This kind of behavior is called symbolic play—play in which one object *represents* another, as the rake stands for a comb. For the next several years, play will be an important cultural context within which children can simulate the cultural practices they observe and participate in, including the roles they will be expected subsequently to carry out in earnest. Play is proleptic.

4. There is a rapid blossoming of language. Children begin to put together complicated sentences and their vocabulary increases at an accelerated rate.

There are a variety of other indicators that children are beginning to mediate their understandings of the world through symbols. Adult standards begin to guide their behavior. When confronted with their image in a mirror, they recognize themselves. They begin to use words in a way that indicates they are referring to themselves (for example, when a block tower crashes, the child will say "Uh-oh, I did it"). They experience more complex emotions and begin to learn how to navigate a social world that has become more complex and less tied to adults (Cole and Cole, 1996, ch. 6).

## Modularity and Context

The preceding examples have illustrated cultural contributions to development and more or less ignored the crucial contributions of phylogenetic constraints. To redress the balance I shall turn to a line of modern work on phylogenetic ("innate") contributions to children's intellectual development captured by the notion of "modularity." According to the version of cultural-historical psychology I am advocating, modularity and cultural context contribute jointly to the development of mind.

I am not certain of the origins of the concept of modularity, but my own knowledge of it stems from the debate between Piaget and Chomsky (and various commentators) edited by Massimo Piatelli-Palmerini (1980). In controverting Piaget's claim that language is constructed on the basis of previously developed sensorimotor schemata, Chomsky argued for the existence of what has come to be called a language module:

> If we really look into the details of the development [of a particular linguistic structure] . . . I would expect to find exactly the same thing in the study of any physical organ. The way in which an organ develops is going to depend on all sorts of factors in the environment, but I think that what we would expect to find, and do find over and over again, is that the fundamental organizing properties, the general features, simply are not up for grabs but rather are fixed. (1980, p. 176)

In the course of the debate, Jerry Fodor applied the logic of Chomsky's theory of language to cognitive development in general, an argument for which he provided an extended treatment in his book *The Modularity of Mind* (1983). Simplifying greatly, Fodor claimed that:

1. Psychological processes are domain-specific. Environmental information passes through a system of special input systems or modules (special-purpose sensory transducers) that output data in a common format where it is processed by a "central processor."
2. The psychological principles that organize each domain are innately specified, in a sense similar to that intended by Gesell

or Chomsky. They have a fixed neural architecture, they operate automatically and rapidly, and they are "triggered" by relevant environmental input and not constructed in the manner suggested by Piagetian theory.[7]
3. Different domains do not interact directly; each is a separate mental module. Knowledge provided by modules is coordinated through a "central processor" which operates on their outputs.
4. Modules cannot be influenced by other parts of the mind, which have no access to their internal workings.

Fodor proposed a number of candidate modules in addition to language. These include the perception of color, shape, three-dimensional relations, and recognition of voices and faces. Subsequently, others have suggested a wide variety of possible modules including ones for mechanical causality, intentional movement, number, animacy, and music (Hirschfeld and Gelman, 1994).

The modularity hypothesis comes in both a weak and a strong version. According to the weak version, the behavioral dispositions that are built into the genome are richer and more complex than traditional theories of cognitive development have recognized. These genetically specified characteristics provide the starting point, the initial structure, upon which later cognitive abilities are constructed. They set constraints upon the way the developing organism attends to and hypothesizes about experience, channeling development along species-typical lines. The strong version of the modularity hypothesis goes on to propose that behavioral characteristics within these domains do not really develop at all; they are innate, requiring only the right environmental triggering to realize them (see Fischer and Bidell, 1991; Karmiloff-Smith, 1992; Hirschfeld and Gelman, 1994, for representative discussions).

My own view is that the weaker form of modularity—as skeletal principles and starting points—can be usefully combined with notions of cultural mediation. Such a combination offers an attractive way to account for the intertwining of "natural" and "cultural" lines of development as part of a single process.

The process of language acquisition can serve as a paradigm case. How does the interweaving of genetic and cultural constraints give rise to language?

*Language Acquisition*

No area of culture and human development has attracted more scholarly attention than the question of the role of cultural experience in the acquisition of language. Must language be acquired through a process of culturally mediated learning or constructive interaction like any other human cognitive capacity? Or is language a specialized, bounded domain (module) which needs only to be triggered to spring into action? (See Bruner, 1983; Piatelli-Palmerini, 1980; and Pinker, 1994, for discussions of the contending viewpoints.)

No one believes that language can be acquired in isolation. Still, the modularity position with respect to language assumes that its development proceeds akin to the development of any bodily organ: any environment adequate to sustain the life of the social group is adequate to produce the development of language without the need for any special attention.

Since the environment that sustains life is one transformed by culture, it is necessary to specify more carefully what minimum conditions of culturally mediated interaction between children and adults are sufficient to support development of the "language organ." It is also necessary, as in the case of the biological study of organogenesis, to specify the nature of the interactions from which the "language organ" emerges.

I find the garden metaphor useful as an aid to thinking about these issues. Consider, for example, an ordinary bean seed of the sort commonly used in kindergarten classrooms to illustrate the process of growth. Imagine placing it in some damp earth in a jar and then placing the jar in a toolshed. After an allotted period of time, say two or three weeks, the seed will begin to sprout. A stem will appear and then leaves, the yellow-green waxy leaves of early spring. However, for further development to occur, the seedling now *must* interact with sunlight. If you do not take it out of the dark toolshed, it will wither and die. But if you place it in the sunshine, it can grow and flower.

I want to draw an analogy between the contrasting conditions of the seed in the shed and in the sunshine and the situation facing human children in their environments. Like a seed in soil, the human child must be provided with sufficient support to maintain life; it must be kept warm enough and fed or it will die.

Several features of the "seeds" of language have been shown to be present at birth or acquired so shortly after birth as to deny the importance of extended experience. These features include the ability to distinguish a very broad set of phonemic distinctions, the ability to distinguish syllables from nonsyllables, a preference for speech sounds over nonspeech sounds, and a preference for speech sounds which adhere to natural clause boundaries, vowel duration, linguistic stress, and rhythm. In short, children are born with a rich supply of linguistically relevant aspects, or seeds of language (for overviews see Adamson, 1995; Karmiloff-Smith, 1992). What then are the conditions under which these seeds will sprout and flower?

## Evidence from Children Deprived of Language Experience

Cases of children reared in conditions that reduce their immersion in culture help to specify the universal lower limits of cultural support needed to sustain language development. One is the well-known case of Genie, studied by Susan Curtiss (1977). Genie was locked in a room by herself sometime before her second birthday. For the next eleven years she lived chained to a potty by day and trussed up in a sleeping bag at night. During this time she had virtually no normal linguistic input and only a minimum of social interaction that could be considered normal in any culture. No one was allowed to speak to her, and her father, when he fed her, made only animal noises.

When she was liberated from these horrible circumstances at the age of thirteen, Genie was in pitiful shape: She was emaciated and very short. She could not walk normally, rarely made a sound, and was not toilet trained. Although upon testing she showed remarkable skills for spatial analysis, she had failed to acquire language. Nor did she recover from her many years of severely deprived existence: she acquired a small vocabulary and some forms of appropriate social interaction, but her behavior remained abnormal despite attempts at therapeutic intervention.

There are several intermediate cases between this extreme deprivation and the situation of the vast majority of children. One particularly instructive situation arises among children born deaf to hearing parents who do not believe that it is useful for their children to sign, insisting instead that they learn to interact through oral language (Goldin-Meadow, 1985; Goldin-Meadow and Mylander, 1990). These children are reared in an environment which is rich in culturally mediated social interactions (including linguistic mediation among other household members) that include the child and proceed very much as they would if the child could hear: people eat meals together, the children are given baths and put to bed, they go to the store, they are toilet trained. Thus they live in a world suffused with meaning, although they lack access to the specifically linguistic behavior that fills the gaps between actions. These children bring to their interactions an active mind that certainly contains event representations and schemas. In many face-to-face situations, these resources suffice both to get the children through the interaction and to develop their underlying schemas to a degree necessary to participate with others.

Under these circumstances, children are known spontaneously to begin to employ "home sign," a kind of communication through pantomime. Goldin-Meadow showed that home sign exhibits a number of properties also found in the early stages of natural language acquisition. Deaf children in these circumstances begin to make two, three, and longer sign sequences around their second birthdays, at about the same time that hearing children create multiword sentences. Most significantly, Goldin-Meadow reported that these deaf children were able to embed brief sign phrases within others ("You/ Susan give me/Abe cookie round") even though none of the gestures used by parents had this property. This kind of behavior reveals that the children could engage in an elementary form of recursion, a form of communicative behavior that is characteristic of all human languages. Interestingly, this level of language development appears quite similar to that claimed for Kanzi by Greenfield and Savage-Rumbaugh (1990).

However, their language development comes to a halt at this point. The cultural medium is simply too thin to support the development of fully mature language. It is as if one tried to grow a bean from a seed in deep shade. It appears that unless such children have access to some form of language as a part of their culturally organized environments they will not develop its subtler features, upon which sustainable cultural formations depend. However, if such children are subsequently taught a sign language such as ASL, they appear capable of developing extensive linguistic abilities, even when their exposure to a full language system occurs in adolescence, well after the critical period usually associated with first-language acquisition (Morford and Goldin-Meadow, 1994; Emmorey, Grant, and Ewan, 1994).[8]

It is important to add that at the other extreme, where children have access to language but not to culturally organized activity, language development also fails to take place. Children who have been left alone for long time with a television set broadcasting in a foreign language do not acquire that language (Snow et al., 1976).

## *The Normal Environment of Language Acquisition*

It seems an inescapable conclusion from this kind of evidence that in order for children to acquire more than the barest rudiments of language they must not only hear (or see) language but also participate in the activities which that language is helping to create. In everyday activity, language is the essential means for establishing and maintaining coordination, for filling in the gaps between gestures and other actions, and for making possible the fine-tuning of expectations and interpretations. Note that I am not saying that adults must deliberately teach language; rather, they must arrange/allow children to participate in culturally organized activities mediated by language.

In attempting to specify the environmental circumstances necessary for language acquisition, Jerome Bruner (1982) refers to the social interactional constraints provided by everyday activities as *formats*. The format, according to Bruner, "is a rule-bound microcosm in which the adult and child *do* things to and with each other. In its most general sense, it is the instrument of patterned human interaction. Since formats pattern communicative interaction between infant and caretaker before lexico-grammatical speech begins, they are crucial vehicles in the passage from communication to language." Bruner later adds that once formats become conventionalized they seem to have a kind of "exteriority" that allows them to act as constraints on the actions that occur within them.

In this respect, Bruner's notion of format is very similar to the way in which Katherine Nelson (1981, 1986) talks of the generalized event schemas called *scripts,* "sequentially organized structures of causally and temporally linked acts with the actors and objects specified in the most general way." In effect, formats or scripts are event-level cultural artifacts, which are embodied in the vocabulary and habitual actions of adults, and which act as structured media within which children can experience the covariation of language and action while remaining coordinated in a general way with culturally organized forms of behavior. In the process of negotiating such events with enculturated caregivers, children discover the vast range of meanings encoded in their language at the same time as they find new ways to carry out their own intentions.[9]

Bruner nicely captured the cultural view of language development when he wrote that language acquisition cannot be reduced to "either the virtuoso cracking of a linguistic code, or the spinoff of ordinary cognitive development, or the gradual takeover of adult speech by the child through some impossible inductive *tour de force*. It is rather, a subtle process by which adults artificially arrange the world so that the child can succeed culturally by doing what comes naturally, and with others similarly inclined" (1982, p. 15).

Arguments over the importance of the environment in language acquisition gave rise to a large literature on parents' ways of structuring children's activities (see, for example, de Villiers and de Villiers, 1978). Parents in many societies adopt something akin to "baby talk" when speaking to their children, before and while the children are acquiring language. Ferguson (1977) speculated that a special "baby talk register" (using higher pitch and intonation, simplified vocabulary, grammatically less complex sentences, and utterances designed to highlight important aspects of the situation) is a universal, acquisition-enhancing form of adult language-socialization behavior. Cross-cultural data have shown, however, that while adults everywhere speak to young children in ways different from their talk with older children and adults, the particular form of baby talk involving simplified grammar and vocabulary characteristic of middle-class American parents is not universal. There is some evidence that other features of baby talk such as the use of distinctive pitch and intonation may be universal, but the data on cultural variation remain sparse (Fernald, 1991).

In many societies, adults deliberately teach vocabulary, styles of address, and other linguistic features. The Kaluli of Papua New

Guinea, for example, are reported to hold their small infants facing away from them and toward other people while the mother speaks *for* them rather than *to* them. There are also subcultures within the United States (working-class people in Baltimore; Miller, 1982) in which it is firmly believed that children must be explicitly taught vocabulary, using quite rigid frames of the sort "How do you call this?" (see Schieffelin and Ochs, 1986, for a wide range of examples). However, while the adults involved in such practices may believe that such special tailoring helps their children acquire language, the data indicate that significant benefits associated with variations in cultural patterns of mother-infant interactions involving language are found rather rarely and in restricted domains (Snow and Ferguson, 1977).

It is also a mistake to believe that the kinds of formats that serve as proximal environments for language acquisition are tightly knit with language acquisition as a major adult goal. An example from the work of Richard Shweder provides a more representative example of the contexts of language acquisition:

> *"Mara heici. Chhu na! Chhu na!"* is what a menstruating Oriya mother explains when her young child approaches her lap. It means, "I am polluted. Don't touch me! Don't touch me!" If the child continues to approach, the woman will stand up and walk away from her child. Of course, young Oriya children have no concept of menstruation or menstrual blood; the first menstruation arrives as a total surprise to adolescent girls. Mothers typically "explain" their own monthly "pollution" to their children by telling them that they stepped in dog excrement or touched garbage, or they evade the issue. Nevertheless, Oriya children quickly learn that there is something called *"Mara"* (the term *chhuan* may also be used) and when *"Mara"* is there, as it regularly is, their mother avoids them, sleeps alone on a mat on the floor, is prohibited from entering the kitchen . . . eats alone, does not groom herself and is, for several days, kept at a distance from anything of value. Children notice that everything their mother touches is washed. (Shweder, Mahapatra, and Miller, 1987, p. 74)

Despite the ambiguity of the term *Mara,* children begin to attach meanings to it that are consistent with adult usage, if incomplete.

Most six-year-olds think it is wrong for a *"Mara"* woman to cook food or sleep in the same bed with her husband, and by nine years of age most children think that *Mara* is an objective force of nature that makes it immoral for women the world over to touch or cook for other people when they are in that state.

In addition to illustrating the range of activities within which children come to acquire language, this example illustrates Vygotsky's insistence that word meanings develop over time. Oriya children can use the term *Mara* in appropriate ways to interact with adults long before they come to share adult meanings of the term.

Culturally organized joint activity that incorporates the child into the scene as a novice participant is one necessary ingredient in language acquisition. As children in such activities struggle to understand objects and social relations in order to gain control over their environment and themselves, they re-create the culture into which they have been born, even as they reinvent the language of their forebears.

## Modular Contributions to the Development of Thought

When we move from the domain of language to that of cognitive development, the weak form of the modularity hypothesis is most frequently invoked using the concept of constraints. The key argument is made by Rochel Gelman (1990).

> It is necessary to grant infants and/or young children domain-specific organizing structures that direct attention to the data that bear on the concepts and facts relevant to a particular cognitive domain. The thesis is that the mind brings domain-specific organizing principles to bear on the assimilation and structuring of facts and concepts, that learners can narrow the range of possible interpretations of the environment because they have implicit assumptions that guide their search for relevant data. (p. 4)

Gelman refers to these constraints as "skeletal principles" because they provide the core structure that supports the growth of knowledge.

Much of the current evidence that modular-like constraints affect development comes from studies with young infants (some as young as a few hours, but more often two to four months of age) indicating the existence of an impressive array of innately specified, "skeletal" cognitive structures. These include "proto-knowledge" in such widely dispersed domains as basic physical properties of objects (Baillargeon, 1987; Spelke, 1990) intentionality (Bruner, 1990; Premack, 1990), arithmetic (Gelman, 1990), the animate-inanimate distinction (Gelman, 1990), and physical causality (Leslie, 1994).

## Relating Modular Constraints to Cultural Constraints

Theorizing about modular, biologically constrained, psychological processes became fashionable in psychology at almost the same time that the idea of contextually, cultural-historically constrained processes came into fashion. Many reasons can be offered for this "specificity Zeitgeist," but perhaps most relevant to the present discussion was a growing dissatisfaction with the Piagetian research program, especially Piaget's claims that the thinking abilities of three-to-five-year-olds are severely limited and that human infants are born with only a few reflexes and three poorly specified mechanisms for producing change (assimilation, accommodation, and equilibration), on the basis of which all later knowledge is constructed (Gelman, 1978; Gelman and Baillargeon, 1983; LCHC, 1983).

Those who emphasized factors of cultural context sought, in the spirit of the cross-cultural work discussed in Chapter 3, to determine if preschoolers' failure to manifest various cognitive abilities in researchers' tests resulted from the researchers' unwitting use of unfamiliar problem content and procedures. They focused on tasks that make sense to small children in everyday terms (Donaldson, 1978). Concepts such as "context" or "domain" were used loosely in this work to refer either to culturally identifiable forms of activity or to psychological tasks presumed to assemble cognitive processes applicable to a wide variety of domains or contexts, such as perspective taking, various kinds of reasoning, and remembering (see Cole and Cole, 1996, ch. 9, for a review of this literature).

Those emphasizing modularity focused primarily on young infants or on exceptional children who demonstrated apparently wide discrepancies in development across conceptual domains (child chess whizzes, mathematicians, musicians, and, on the negative side, children with autism or Williams' syndrome: Frith, 1989; Bellugi et al., 1990; Feldman, 1994). While researchers pursuing these topics also employ procedures that minimize extraneous features of the tasks presented (for example, relying on demonstrations of surprise rather than requiring a motor response such as grasping or a linguistic response), their choice of tasks has been motivated by the idea that children's intellectual development is organized around a few (presumably key) ontological domains which specify the kinds of objects that are relevant and the ways in which those objects act upon one another.

Annette Karmiloff-Smith (1991) sums up the implications of this research: "Piaget's view of the initial state of the neonate mind was wrong. It is clear that at the outset some aspects of human mind are innately specified, and often in some detail. Knowledge is initially domain-specific and constrains subsequent learning in complex interaction with the environment. It is not based solely on the outcome of domain-general sensori-motor action. Subsequent development can be viewed within a constructivist framework" (p. 192). Karmiloff-Smith's conclusion sets the terms for the following discussion: to be successful, a cultural theory of development must incorporate the findings of research on early, phylogenetically constrained cognitive processes, and must show how culturally mediated social interaction contributes to the development of more complex thought.

### Mathematics

The literature on modularity has been extensively reviewed in recent years (Carey and Gelman, 1991; Karmiloff-Smith, 1992; Hirschfeld and Gellman, 1994). As a concrete and representative example of how cultural-historical psychology can incorporate the findings of modularity theorists, I have chosen to focus on the domain of mathematics because there is sufficient evidence about the phylogeny, ontogeny, and cultural organization of thinking in this domain to provide an integrated picture of development and culture's role in it.

*Phylogenetic precursors.* Research has demonstrated that some birds and nonhuman primates possess some rudimentary knowledge of number (Klein and Starkey, 1987). Hicks (1956) reported that rhesus monkeys could be trained to choose collections of precisely three items when presented with stimuli in groups of one to five. This learning required thousands of trials, but once the monkey could reliably pick the array with three objects it generalized this learning to entirely new kinds of stimuli.

Sarah, a chimpanzee who starred in David Premack's work on language acquisition, was able to match stimuli with one to four elements by selecting an appropriate, numerically matching response object (Premack, 1986). Sarah also learned to construct arrays of objects in one-to-one correspondence with one another. But when Sarah was tested on new stimuli she failed; the ability was locked into the context of training.

More recently, Sarah Boysen (1993) has demonstrated that when training in number-related skills is integrated into a way of life that is rich in what Savage-Rumbaugh refers to as interpersonal routines, and when training grows out of a preestablished relationship based upon play, a chimpanzee not only is capable of understanding one-to-one correspondence but can learn to count, to add, and even to solve arithmetic problems similar to those achieved by three-year-old children.

I interpret these data on the phylogeny of arithmetic to indicate that elements of the form of activity we call mathematical thinking can be achieved by nonhuman primates raised in a cultural environment that includes them in a human-like way. These results fully accord with evidence concerning language in chimpanzees. What then of human ontogeny?

*Early ontogeny.* Under the influence of Piaget, developmental psychologists spent a great many years assuming that mathematical abilities make their earliest appearance late in infancy as infants become capable of mentally representing an absent object.

Current research leaves no doubt that by the middle of the first year of life, more than a year before they will be able to engage in a simple conversation, babies are able to respond to numerosity and to count small arrays of objects (Gallistel and Gelman, 1992; Klein and Starkey, 1987; Wynn, 1992). A few examples illustrate the conditions under which this knowledge is tapped.

Infants six months old or younger were habituated to visual displays containing two to six dots (the number differing for each group) and then shown a different dot pattern. The patterns were so arranged that they controlled for such potentially correlated cues as array length, density, and configuration. The babies dishabituated to a new number of dots if the number was four or fewer (Antell and Keating, 1983). Infants are also capable of recognizing that the number of drumbeats corresponds to a visual display with the same number of visual objects; that is, a primitive, amodal, numerical matching mechanism operates for small numbers (Starkey, Spelke, and Gelman, 1990).

Karen Wynn (1992) showed four-month-old babies the events depicted in Figure 7.2. First a mouse doll was placed on an empty stage while the baby watched. Then a screen was raised to hide the doll from the baby's view. Next a hand carrying an identical doll moved behind the screen and withdrew without the doll. The screen was then lowered. When the screen was raised again, in half the cases there were two dolls behind the screen (the expected outcome). In the other half there was only one doll (the unexpected outcome). The babies looked longer at the unexpected outcome. Additional experiments showed that the babies expected two minus one to be one and three minus one to be two.

There is some controversy about how number is processed by preverbal infants. Klein and Starkey (1988) lean toward the explanation that a special perceptual process, called subitizing, is the basis for infant numeration. This primitive process is then supplemented by a more elaborate counting procedure. Gallistel and Gelman (1992) believe that infants in fact have a preverbal enumeration system, identical in its basic properties to elementary enumeration abilities in nonhuman primates, which serves as the species' general foundation, or initial set of constraints, upon which various counting systems are imposed.

The details of this dispute are not important here, but evidence of very early enumeration abilities is relevant because this system provides the initial, module-like crude structure upon which a more elaborate, cultural system of mathematics can be constructed. The question then becomes, under what conditions will the primitive abilities of the young infant be realized in appropriate behaviors that are a part of its everyday life?

**Sequence of events 1 + 1 = 1 or 2**

1. Object placed in case

2. Screen comes up

3. Second object added

4. Hand leaves empty

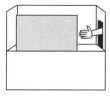

**Then either:**
**possible outcome**

5. Screen drops...

**or:**
**impossible outcome**

5. Screen drops...

revealing 2 objects

revealing 1 object

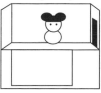

Figure 7.2.   Sequence of events presented to infants to assess their sensitivity to number. While a single mouse is out of sight, a second mouse is placed behind the screen. Infants indicate surprise if only one mouse is revealed when the screen is lowered, suggesting that they mentally calculate 1 + 1 = 2.

Although there is only spotty evidence of early number-related knowledge in children growing up in societies where mathematical knowledge is not highly elaborated, what little evidence we have indicates that the density of mathematical knowledge in a culture begins to affect development of mathematical thinking very early. Jill Posner (1982) compared the development of the ability to identify relative quantity and carry out elementary arithmetic operations among children from two West African tribal groups. Children from the group which engaged in commercial trading for a living out-performed those from a subsistence agricultural group.

Geoffrey Saxe (1981, 1982) studied the development of counting and elementary arithmetic operations (comparison of relative quantity, simple addition) among Oksapmin children of New Guinea. The Oksapmin use their body parts as a counting device, and children learn to use this device at an early age. However, according to Saxe, the Oksapmin have little need to engage in computations with numbers. When they trade goods within the traditional cultural frame-work, they use various one-for-one or one-for-many exchanges that involve counting but no need for the use of calculational procedures. Children's ability to use counting to mediate comparisons of the number of objects in two arrays or to carry out simple addition is slow to develop. Saxe observed actual arithmetic calculations, of the sort studied by Klein and Starkey among American children, only among children who began attending school and adults who became in-volved with the money economy of New Guinea.

While these studies fit nicely with the idea that culture builds upon universal mathematical knowledge based upon skeletal principles specific to this cognitive domain, they do not tell us much about the process by which children come to acquire the knowledge embodied in the cultural system used by adults (cf. Saxe, 1994). Granted the points made earlier in this chapter about the process of ontogenetic change—that cognitive development occurs within scripted events and that children must actively appropriate the cultural tools of their society in the process of development—how does one make available for analysis the ways in which modular knowledge and cultural prac-tices combine in development?

Research by Saxe and his colleagues on the development of arith-metic knowledge among American children aged 2½–4 illustrates how these dynamics work in a manner that links up nicely with the notion of a zone of proximal development from the Russian cultural-historical tradition (Saxe, Guberman, and Gearhart, 1987). From work on early arithmetic understanding such as that described above, they identified four kinds of numerical tasks (Saxe refers to these tasks as cognitive *functions*) that children are capable of achieving in early childhood: naming, counting and cardinality (using last count name as the name of the set), comparing and reproducing sets, and using arithmetical operations to transform numerical values. They also expected to see various cognitive *forms* (such as strategies for achieving an accurate count of a set or for adding two sets together).

The research began with interviews of mothers about the everyday practices in which issues bearing on number and arithmetic arose. Maternal responses were analyzed according to the numerical functions involved (for example, identifying and pushing elevator buttons, counting coins, comparing amounts of two sets of numbered buttons on an elevator, counting pennies, comparing two piles of coins, adding checkers to find their sum) and how these functions were carried out. The data revealed regular age-related changes in the level of tasks which children encountered and accomplished.

Next the investigators sought to observe the dynamics of change. They videotaped mothers and children engaging in tasks that required either a low-level function (determining the total number of objects in an array) or a higher-level function (reproducing the total number in one array with a new array). Analyses of the videotapes showed the development of more complex functions and how mothers and children adjusted to each other as subgoals of the task emerged.

For example, in the number-reproduction task, mothers were given an array containing three or nine pictures of the *Sesame Street* Cookie Monster and asked to instruct their child to put as many pennies in a cup as there were Cookie Monsters in the array. Mothers of older (or more competent) children tried to structure the task in terms of its highest-level goals, while mothers of younger (or less competent) children provided instructions focused on simpler goals.

The highest-level instructions simply repeated the overall goal, "Get just the same number of pennies as there are Cookie Monsters." If the child had difficulty, the mother might say "Get nine pennies for the Cookie Monster." If that failed, the mother might ask "How many Cookie Monsters are there?" or "Count the Cookie Monsters." When all else failed, the instruction might be "Get nine pennies." Saxe (1994) summarizes the pattern of results concerning the way new functions arise in the course of this activity: "Mothers were adjusting their goal-related directives to their children's understandings and task-related accomplishments and . . . children were adjusting their goal-directed activities to their mother's efforts to organize the task. Further, as children's ability to produce numerical goals of different complexity levels changed with development, they were afforded new opportunities for creating more complex numerical environments" (p. 147). Research focused on many different activities in different societies indicates that the principles found in this example operate quite broadly (Saxe, 1994).


## The Intertwining of the Natural
## and Cultural Lines Reconsidered

In Chapter 6 we encountered the problems caused by "critical point" theories that assume a discrete break between phylogenetic and cultural change. I argued there that the evidence urges upon us the idea that phylogenetic and cultural change are intertwined and fused in the process of anthropogenesis, creating the qualitatively distinct nature of *Homo sapiens* as a species.[10]

When considering processes of ontogenetic and microgenetic change a similar set of issues arises. Just as the cultural-historical theorists assumed a critical point theory of anthropogenesis, they identified the fusing of ontogeny and cultural history that occurs with the acquisition of language as the critical point in the acquisition of higher psychological functions and the "cultural habit of thinking." An analogous critical point is to be found in Gelman and Greeno's (1989) modification of Fodor's ideas about modules and cognition; first come modular filters, then cultural constraints, which the central processor then works on. *With respect to human ontogeny, one cannot say that first comes the phylogenetic part and then comes the cultural part and the individual part. All are there from the outset.*

I can illustrate contrasting views of how cultural mediation and modular processes might combine by referring to the graphic representations in Figure 7.3. At the top left is a visualization of Fodor's modularity position. Input transducers feed a central processor which reconciles their inputs in the service of action. The drawing at top right includes cultural mediation but retains a "critical point" perspective in that the modular outputs come first and are then filtered by a set of cultural models, which the central processor then works on. At the bottom is the kind of cultural-historical approach suggested by contemporary research. Cultural "threads" are interwoven with modules, arranging and rearranging their contexts of existence. The active organism must of course do its part, using the cultural tool kit and its phylogenetic resources to promote its own development.

I am encouraged that during the time I have been working on this book other scholars who have been puzzling about the relationship of domain-specific biological constraints and sociocultural contexts have begun to argue for a similar view of the role of biological and cultural constraints in the process of developmental change. Gelman and Greeno (1989) point out that not only do children start life with "skeletal principles" to constrain and enable them to acquire knowledge in various essential cognitive domains; also, the sociocultural environment comes packaged in ways that have developed to take account of that prepackaged structure; the two levels complement each other. Giyoo Hatano (1995) makes a similar argument.

Karmiloff-Smith (1992) has proposed that knowledge develops through iterative transformation in which "skeletal modules" are modified by a process that she calls "redescription." Her claim is that "a specifically human way to gain knowledge is for the mind to exploit internally the information that it has already stored (both innate and acquired), by redescribing its representations or, more precisely, by iteratively re-presenting in different representational formats what its internal representations represent" (p. 15). The process she describes is referred to within the cultural-historical framework as re-mediation—a new, differently mediated form of interaction between individuals and their environments.

Karmiloff-Smith's study of children's increasingly complex representations of a maze illustrates the process of redescription. The maze

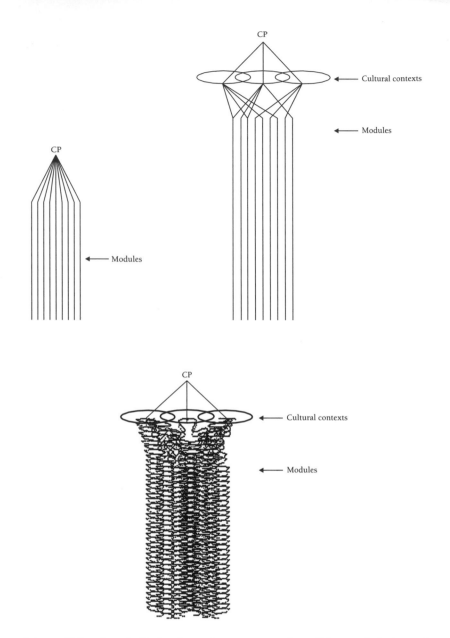

Figure 7.3. (top left) A schematic representation of the modularity point of view put forward by Fodor (1983). (top right) Intervention of constraints arising from the cultural context between input and the central processor (CP), as suggested by Gelman and Greeno (1989). (bottom) A preliminary attempt to represent the interweaving of modular and contextual constraints which denies temporal priority to either and which provides for "leakage" between modules in microgenetic time.

consisted of a series of branching choice points laid out on a long piece of rolled-up butcher paper. Each new choice point was exposed as the paper was unrolled and it was the child's task to learn the entire sequence. The child was given a pencil to record the sequence. At first the recordings were iconic, consisting merely of redrawings of the maze. But as children gained more experience traversing such mazes, they began to develop symbolic shortcuts to the iconic map. At first this might be a long list of L's and R's for left and right turns, but eventually, without any feedback or correction from the experimenter, children invented the maximally compact and abstract sequence of letters and numbers (for example, 2R, 3L, R, 2L . . .). From a cultural-historical perspective Karmiloff-Smith's work provides evidence of the intimate interconnection between the overall system through which the child achieves a new level and the mediational means that afford that new achievement.

Lauren Resnick (1994) offers what she calls a "situated rationalist" synthesis of the cultural-historical and modularity points of view. By situated Resnick means a loose collection of theories and perspectives that propose a contextualized and social view of the nature of thinking and learning. By rationalist she means the theories that claim a priori biological constraints on the development of domain-specific knowledge (Carey and Gelman, 1991).

Resnick unites the ideas of sociocultural and biological constraints in the concept of a "prepared structure." According to this view, individuals develop their abilities in a domain-specific manner, in each situation, on the basis of their prepared structures. These prepared structures are both biological and sociocultural in origin. What changes with development is their relative contributions.

According to Resnick, the biological roots of development predominate in infancy and early childhood, while the sociocultural roots take "increasing control . . . as each individual's personal history of situations grows and initial biologically prepared structures are successively modified" (p. 479). As a coda she notes that there are good reasons to believe that the earlier, biologically based schemas do not wholly disappear in adulthood.

Howard Gardner adopts a similar view in his discussion of the cognitive abilities of young children as they reach the threshold of formal schooling:

The category of "natural development" is a fiction; social and cultural factors intervene from the first and become increasingly powerful well before any formal matriculation at school . . . Once the child reaches the age of six or seven, however, the influence of the culture—whether or not it is manifested in a school setting—has become so pervasive that one has difficulty envisioning what development could be like in the absence of cultural supports and constraints. (1991, p. 105)

I hope it is clear from the foregoing discussion that Vygotsky was perfectly justified in claiming that the process of development undergoes a qualitative change with the acquisition of language. However, in my view he misjudged the nature of that change in two basic ways. First, he repeated Kroeber's error by placing phylogenetic influences ahead of cultural ones temporally without taking into account the coevolution of culture and the human body. Second, he failed to understand that even very young infants incorporate cultural constraints as basic constituents of their developing selves because they are "inside adult scripts" and adults embody their (ideal) cultural futures in the ideal/material current contexts of their everyday lives. As a consequence, he underestimated the extent to which the cultural and natural lines of development—cultural history and phylogeny, in my rendering—have interpenetrated each other well before the acquisition of language. The metaphor of the intermingling of two multistranded ropes, rather than two (implicitly homogeneous) lines, would have more accurately embodied his basic insights.

⑥ It is clearly impossible in a single chapter to encompass all of cognitive development as seen from a cultural-historical perspective. Consequently, my presentation has been highly selective and there are many issues I have not covered.

Elsewhere I have sought to provide a broad reconciliation of cultural-historical ideas with the traditional paradigms of psychology (Cole and Cole, 1996). I believe it is an attainable goal, although how changed a cultural-historical theory will be when such a synthesis is achieved remains difficult to say. But I do not want to belabor that issue here. Whether it is achieved or not, further understanding will depend upon a good deal of mucky empirical work. It is to empirical projects designed to provide the methodological foundations for a cultural-historical psychology that I turn in succeeding chapters. Each of these projects is aimed at providing methodologies that would allow cultural-historical psychologists to follow their principles by grounding their theories in people's everyday activities.

# The Cognitive Analysis of Behavior in Context

In the constant talk about extrapolating from the
experiment to the "real" or the "social" world, we must not
forget that the experiment is itself a part of that real and
that social world.  *Neil Friedman*

A RECURRING THEME in earlier chapters, whether dealing with
cultural differences in remembering or the development of mathematical knowledge and problem solving within a cultural group, has
been the need to ground theoretical statements and empirical claims
in a unit of psychological analysis that corresponds to the lived events
of everyday life. Such units are variously referred to as activities,
contexts, situations, practices, and so on. However, while adoption
of a cultural-historical approach provides added reasons for making
everyday activity the starting point of analysis, it in no way solves
the problem of how to carry out such analyses in a methodologically
acceptable way. So, for example, I was critical of Luria's failure to
include an analysis of everyday activities in his cross-cultural research
as a foundation for conclusions about the sources and nature of cognitive change.

how to
carry out
analysis?

More generally, I have pointed to reliance on face-to-face, two-
person interactions as a major shortcoming in the empirical foundation of a cultural-historical activity theory. But I have not offered
evidence that this shortcoming can be overcome. In this chapter I
directly address the issue of describing and analyzing what I have
been glossing as everyday life. Until and unless the problems in such

settings can be brought into the same scientific arena as adult-child instructional interactions and therapeutic interventions organized on a one-to-one basis, neither the exhortation to start one's analysis of psychological processes with everyday practices nor the ensuing story is going to be adequate.

What was needed, and what my colleagues and I sought, was a new way of thinking about experimental procedures and the process of comparing cognitive performances across tasks and settings. Each of the three empirical research projects to be described in this chapter represents a different line of attack.

Recall from Chapter 3 that by the time my colleagues and I had replicated the basic findings of our work in Liberia among Mayan peasants in rural Yucatán we had become profoundly suspicious of the adequacy of our methods. The strategy of the first project to be described below, among the Vai of Liberia, was one response to those suspicions. In that research we collected data at four different levels of abstraction: tests of presumably generalized cognitive abilities, tests of metalinguistic knowledge, experiments modeling actions at the level of everyday activities mediated by print, and ethnographic observations of target activities themselves. Our hope was to find converging evidence for the cognitive consequences of literacy.

The strategy we employed in two other studies, both carried out in New York City, was to contrast the behavior of the same children in their classrooms, when they were being tested, and in an activity outside the school. The first of these projects was inspired by the work of William Labov and Clarence Robbins demonstrating situational variability in African-American children's manifestation of linguistic competence (Labov, 1972). Their approach was subsequently used to argue against the idea that African-American children routinely enter school without having acquired a normal grasp of their native language (English, or African-American English).

The final project was a head-on attack on the major shortcoming we saw in prior studies of the cognitive consequences of schooling, namely the use of experimental tasks and tests as if they were models of everyday practices in both the school and the wider community. Taken together, the two studies sought to determine if behavior manifested in one setting could be compared meaningfully with manifestations of the same behavior in a different setting. Does children's use

of language outside of school reveal complexity hidden by test procedures? Is it legitimate to conclude that someone who exhibits difficulty remembering or solving problems on one occasion has a
"memory problem" or a "cognitive deficit" that will pop up whenever
such mnemonic tasks arise?

Little reflection is needed to conclude that such questions are fundamentally unanswerable *unless* it is possible to show that the same
cognitive task actually occurs in the two settings. Claims that IQ tests
sample the kinds of activities that children are expected to carry out
in school rest on the assumption that it is possible to find problem
isomorphs of the testing procedures in classroom lessons. Similarly,
claims that tests of various kinds are indicative of general abilities
presuppose that the tasks arise in a broad variety of activities.

## The Problem of Ecological Validity

Before turning to the studies themselves, I shall summarize important
contributions by psychologists to the understanding of the problem
of ecological validity—the extent to which behavior sampled in one
setting can be taken as characteristic of an individual's cognitive processes in a range of other settings. Concerns about ecological validity
speak to the heart of the question of how to analyze behavior-in-
context and how to compare behaviors across activity systems, but
these concerns are seldom the direct objects of psychological discussion or analysis.[1]

A 1943 symposium on psychology and the scientific method featured the work of Kurt Lewin and Egon Brunswik, two German scholars who emigrated to the United States in the 1930s to escape Fascism
in Germany. Although each developed his own distinctive approach
to psychology, both placed at the center of their conceptions of mind
a supra-individual level of environmental structuration with respect
to which all psychological processes occurred. Their ideas are especially relevant to cultural-historical psychologists because German
thought was one of the sources of the Russian cultural-historical psychologists' ideas (see Van der Veer and Valsiner, 1991; Luria, 1932,
for discussions of these connections).

Brunswik envisioned "ecological psychology" as a discipline in
which psychological observations would be made through wide sam-

pling of the environments within which particular tasks are embedded. The purpose of such sampling is to determine the effects of different environments on the organism's responses. Lewin's contribution to this symposium was his formulation of the "psychological ecology," a way of "discovering what part of the physical or social world will determine, during a given period, the 'boundary zone' of the life space of an individual" (1943, p. 309). By life space Lewin meant "the person and the psychological environment as it exists for him" (p. 306). This kind of unit corresponds more or less faithfully to the various person-in-context formulations of a unit of analysis for cultural-historical psychology discussed in Chapter 5.

An examination of Brunswik's procedures will clarify what Brunswik and Lewin meant by the psychological ecology and how their ideas are related.[2] Brunswik's overall goal was to prevent psychology from being restricted to "narrow-spanning problems of artificially isolated proximal or peripheral technicalities . . . which are not representative of the larger patterns of life" (1943, p. 262). In order to avoid this problem, he suggested that situations, or tasks, rather than people, should be considered the basic units of analysis. In addition, these situations or tasks should be "carefully drawn from the universe of the requirements a person happens to face in his commerce with the physical and social environment" (p. 263). As an example of such an approach, he made repeated observations on size constancy by an individual who was "interrupted frequently during her normal daily activities and asked to estimate the size of the object she just happened to be looking at" (p. 264). This person's estimates of size correlated highly with actual measurements of the objects and not with their retinal image size. This result, Brunswik tells us, "possesses a certain generality with regard to normal life conditions" (p. 265).

To make Brunswik's idea concrete, consider the procedures he offered for evaluating the ecological validity of size constancy in an everyday environment. First, he posed a problem for the subject (asked a question) such as "How big is that chair?" which would elicit a circumscribed response based upon limited aspects of the physical environment. Second, he had available a physical model of the stimulus elements that were critical to his analysis (a model of measurement which allowed him to scale size of object, distance from subject, and, hence, physical size of the image on the retina). Third, he had a strong hypothesis which specified relations between the physical stimulus and the subject's response—that either physical stimulus size (the "distal" stimulus) or stimulus size projected on the retina (the "proximal" stimulus) would govern the subject's size-estimation response. Fourth, he obtained a very clear-cut result: correlation between reported size and physical size was essentially perfect, whereas the correlation with retinal size was poor.

In my colleagues' and my opinion, Brunswik's success was not accidentally related to the fact that the examples he worked out came from the area of visual perception, which represented (and represents) one of the most sophisticated areas of psychological theory. This subject matter gave him several advantages. First, because he could draw on the theory of physical measurement, he could confidently use a ruler to measure the dimensions of the objects, the distance from the subject to the object, and the size of the retinal image. In short, he could describe exactly the relevant aspects of the task environment and disregard such irrelevant aspects as the heat in the room, the color of the objects, and so on.

Second, Brunswik was confident about what the subject would do when asked "How big is that_____?" He had strong reason to believe that the question would focus the subject's attention on exactly those aspects of the environment that he thought relevant and that he could measure.[3]

In addition, Brunswik could rely on competing hypotheses, derived from the laboratory, about how the theoretically relevant aspects of the environment mapped onto two aspects of the subject's response; that is, he could specify the meaning of correlations between retinal and object size. Finally, he obtained essentially perfect prediction for one of the alternative hypotheses. All of these constraints on the task and its interpretation were important resources for his analysis.

While Lewin agreed in part with Brunswik's ideas, certain of the principles he put forth at the 1943 symposium led him to question Brunswik's conclusions. Lewin argued his well-known position that behavior at time $t$ is a function of the situation at time $t$ only, and hence we must find ways to determine the properties of the lifespace "at a given time." This requirement amounts to what ethnographers refer to as "taking the subject's point of view." It seeks to unite the subjective and the objective.

If one agrees that understanding psychological processes in terms of the lifespace of the subject is important, following the logic of Lewin's argument, Brunswik's questions may not have been appropriate because they did not fit the lifespace of his subjects. Instead of observing someone making a size estimation in a real-life environment, Brunswik had made a size-estimation experiment happen in a nonlaboratory environment. He had, in Lewin's terminology, changed the subject's lifespace to fit the requirements of his predefined set of observation conditions.

Ulric Neisser (1976a) emphasized that ecological validity is an important goal of cognitive research because it reminds psychologists that the artificiality of laboratory tasks may render the results irrelevant to the phenomena that we really want to explain (implicitly, phenomena found outside the laboratory). He pointed to the "spatial, temporal, and intermodal continuities of real objects and events" as important aspects of normal environments which are generally ignored in laboratory research (1976a, p. 34).

Especially relevant to discussion of quandaries involving research on the cognitive consequences of schooling is Neisser's discussion of the difference between "academic" and "general" intelligence:

> Intelligent behavior in real settings often involves actions that satisfy a variety of motives at once—practical and interpersonal ones, for example—because opportunities to satisfy them appear simultaneously. It is often accompanied by emotions and feelings, as is appropriate in situations that involve other people. Moreover, it provides continual opportunities for cognitive growth of many kinds, because most situations turn out to have facets of which we were formerly unaware. (1976b, pp. 136–137)

By contrast, in school we are expected to "solve problems that other people have set. Notice also that problems on school tests are supposed to be 'fair'—that is, all the information needed to solve them is typically given from the beginning. The pupil does not find out anything as he goes along that might have been otherwise" (p. 137).

Urie Bronfenbrenner (1979, 1986) is an especially influential advocate of ecologically valid research, and his ideas have influenced
my own thinking. His specification of the characteristics of ecological
validity combines the perspectives of Lewin and Brunswik. Ecologically valid research, he writes, must fulfill three conditions: (1) maintain the integrity of the real-life situations it is designed to investigate;
(2) be faithful to the larger social and cultural contexts from which
the subjects come; (3) be consistent with the participants' definition
of the situation, by which he means that the experimental manipulations and outcomes must be "perceived by the participants in a
manner consistent with the conceptual definitions explicit and implicit in the research design" (1977, p. 35).

Note that there is a crucial difference between Bronfenbrenner's
and Neisser's interpretations of how to conduct ecologically valid
research and Brunswik's procedures. Neisser, Bronfenbrenner, and
others do not propose that we carry around our laboratory task and
make it happen in a lot of settings. They propose that we discover
and directly observe the ways tasks occur (or do not occur) in nonlaboratory settings. Moreover, in Bronfenbrenner's version of this enterprise we must also discover the equivalent of Lewin's "lifespace,"
that is, how the task and all it involves appear to the subject.

The idea that such discovery procedures are possible was quite
widespread at the time, and I suspect it is not noticeably less so
to this day. No less an authority than Herbert Simon asserted that
there is

> a general experimental paradigm that can be used to test the
> commonality of cognitive processes over a wide range of task
> domains. The paradigm is simple. We find two tasks that have
> the same formal structure (e.g., they are both tasks of multi-
> dimensional judgment), one of which is drawn from a social
> situation and the other is not. If common processes are impli-
> cated in both tasks, then we should be able to produce in each
> task environment phenomena that give evidence of workings of
> the same basic cognitive mechanisms that appear in the other.
> (1976, p. 258)

However, there also were plenty of reasons to believe that the requirements for establishing ecological validity would place an enor-

mous analytical burden on psychologists. As decades of experience
have shown, once we move beyond the laboratory in search of rep-
resentativeness, our ability to identify tasks is weakened. Failure to
define the parameters of the analyst's task or to ensure that the task-
as-discovered is the subject's task vitiates the enterprise.[4]

## Modeling Local Practices: Literacy among the Vai

I begin with the work my colleagues and I did on literacy, for it is
the last of my cross-cultural efforts. At first blush, a choice as broad
as literacy would appear to be an inauspicious topic for applying the
kind of "experiment as model of activity" approach that had been
evolving in our efforts to account for culture and development.

Literacy has typically been seen as *the* great mental transforming
invention underpinning the accumulation of systematic knowledge,
the transformation of human thought, and the development of civilization (Goody, 1977; Havelock, 1963; Olson, 1994). Institutionalized in schools and government programs, literacy has been seen as
the engine of the machinery that produces the cognitive and social
consequences of involvement in schooling (Lerner, 1958; Greenfield
and Bruner, 1966). Since, as we have seen, experimental psychology
encounters severe difficulty in assessing the psychological consequences of schooling, what advantage could there be to focusing on
literacy?

Paradoxically, since in earlier chapters I emphasized the limitations
of cross-cultural research, the first answer to this question is that
literacy is not equivalent to schooling. Although rare, cases where
literacy is acquired independent of schooling do exist, offering an
opportunity to unpackage these oft-confounded forms of activity
(Berry and Bennett, 1989; Scribner and Cole, 1981). Equally important, the exercise of analyzing various kinds of literacy practices not
only motivates a reconceptualization of the question of schooling's
impact on cognition but demonstrates rather clearly the possibility
of modeling local cultural practices in experiments.

Second, early cultural-historical theorists were among those proposing literacy as a major new mediational means with far-reaching
cognitive consequences. Luria (1928/1978) made a special study of
the "prehistory" of writing in young children, emphasizing the way

the incorporation of writing changed the structure of important psychological processes such as remembering. Vygotsky (1934/1987, 1978), following Janet and many other contemporary psychological thinkers in Western Europe and the United States, proposed that the acquisition of literacy or schooling made possible a higher, more logical mode of thinking owing to the way writing changes a person's resources for systematic thought. Written speech, he wrote, "forces the child to act more intellectually."

In the 1970s Sylvia Scribner and I received support to study literacy and schooling among the Vai, a tribal group residing along the northwest coast of Liberia bordering on Sierra Leone.[5] The Vai had first come to my attention while I was working among the Kpelle, and we reported one pilot study on literacy and memory in *The Cultural Context of Learning and Thinking*. Sylvia had written about theories of literacy as a graduate student and was excited about Vygotsky's ideas. She rightly saw Vai literacy as an opportunity to test competing theories.

Although standard ethnographies of the Vai made them appear to be similar in most respects to their neighbors, they were remarkable because they had been using a writing system of their own invention for more than one hundred years. Most important, their literacy was acquired without any formal schooling.

Our research, which is described in detail in Scribner and Cole (1981), was carried out in three overlapping phases. In order to understand the local organization of literacy, we conducted a survey of the social correlates of literacy and schooling that spanned all of Vai country and the Vai section of the capital, Monrovia, and an ethnography of daily life in a single Vai village.[6] We added to the survey a battery of psychological tests that had previously produced evidence of schooling effects to answer the most straightforward question one might pose: does Vai literacy substitute for schooling in producing improved cognitive performance on learning, classification, and problem-solving tasks?

From this preparatory research we learned that three kinds of literacy were to be found among the Vai: about 20 percent were literate in Vai, 16 percent had some degree of literacy in Arabic (mostly, but not entirely, to read from the Qur'an), and about 6 percent were literate in English, which they had acquired in school. (Very few women were literate in Vai or Arabic, so our experimental analyses were restricted primarily to men.)

Our survey and ethnographic observations taught us that unlike literacy acquired in school, Vai literacy involves no mastery of esoteric knowledge or new forms of institutionalized social interaction. Nor does it prepare the learner for a variety of new kinds of economic and social activity in which mediation of action through print is essential. Learning is almost always a personal affair carried out in the course of daily activities (most often, when a friend or relative agrees to teach the learner to read and write letters).

Vai literacy skills play a useful role in traditional occupations primarily as a means of keeping records and writing letters, which are carried by the ubiquitous taxicabs that ply the Liberian countryside. Although we collected several examples of Vai "books" that contained stories and aphorisms, they were all handwritten copies; there is no tradition of text production for mass distribution, and no traditional occupations require that one be literate.

Our psychological test data produced a straightforward answer to our question about the cognitive impact of Vai literacy: neither Vai nor Qur'anic literacy substituted for schooling with respect to performance on psychological tests; in general those who had been to school performed better on the test battery, especially when asked to explain the basis of their performance.

In a second round of experimental research, we narrowed our focus. Instead of chasing after "cognitive change in general" we sought to test the widespread notion that practice in reading and writing changes a person's knowledge of the properties of language. Our tasks in this "metalinguistic survey" included the ability to define words, to engage in syllogistic reasoning, to distinguish between an object and its name, to make judgments about the grammaticality of various utterances, and to explain what was wrong in the case of ungrammatical utterances.

The grammaticality task was the only one that consistently yielded a positive influence of Vai literacy. This result is disappointing with respect to the notion that literacy promotes metacognitive awareness in general, but promising because it points to a close link between cognitive task and everyday activity as the locus of the effects of Vai literacy.

From our observations of Vai literates engaged in their daily activities, we knew that discussions of whether or not a phrase contained in a letter was in "proper Vai" were common, so it seemed most plausible to attribute Vai literates' skill in this area to their practices when writing and reading letters. This result was promising, but we wanted to study a broad variety of everyday tasks involving mediation of activity through text.

During both rounds one and two we were on the lookout for forms of literacy involvement that might serve as models for experimental analysis. For example, an analysis of a large corpus of letters revealed that while the contents were often routine, and hence easy to interpret, they nonetheless included various context-setting devices to take account of the fact that the reader was not in face-to-face contact with the writer. We reasoned that extensive practice in writing letters to people in other locales ought to promote a tendency to provide fuller descriptions of local events.

In the third round of this research, we tested this notion by creating a simple board game that was similar to games common in the area but different enough to require rather explicit instructions. We asked Vai literate and nonliterate people to learn the game and then describe it, either to another person face to face or by dictating a letter to someone in another village in enough detail for that person to be able to play the game on the basis of the instructions alone. Consistent with our expectations, Vai literates were better at this task than nonliterates, and among Vai literates, amount of experience in reading and writing was positively associated with performance.

In a series of studies on reading and writing based on other ethnographic observations, Sylvia constructed a variety of rebus-like tasks in which pictures of common objects had to be combined to make meaningful sentences (see Figure 8.1). Pronunciation of words in a sentence differs from that of the words considered in isolation; for example, the words for chicken *(tiye)* and paddle *(laa)*, when combined without change of pronunciation, yield the word for waterside *(tiyelaa)*. The bottom half of Figure 8.1 displays an entire "sentence" made up of such pictures. In order to "read" the sentence, a person had to be able to integrate the pictures and transform their sounds appropriately (seven such changes are needed in this example). We evaluated people's reading both by correctness of pronun-

tiye                          laa

Kai            laa            tiye           ba             ta

Figure 8.1.   (top) Pictures of a chicken *(tiye)* and a paddle *(laa)* which combined yield the word for waterside. (bottom) A series of pictures corresponding to the sentence "The man cooked a big chicken."

ciation and by their ability to answer simple comprehension questions (such as "Is the chicken dead?" "What happened to it?" for the sentence in the figure).

Perhaps surprisingly, given the unfamiliarity of the materials and task, after a brief training session even nonliterate Vai people were able to read and comprehend roughly 50 percent of the sentences. But literates were considerably more skillful, performing correctly about 80 percent of the time. Vai literates were especially good at interpreting sentences (like the one in the figure) which required several sound transformations, whereas these sentences were very difficult for nonliterates. Similar results were obtained when people were given a set of pictures and asked to "write" a sentence.

The Vai writing system represents spoken language at the level of syllables, not phonemes; it is a syllabary, not an alphabet. In writing, no spaces are placed between words, which complicates the job of parsing the written text to reconstruct its linguistic constituents. When reading, people often sound out a word in various ways, piecing the syllables together. We speculated that, as a consequence, Vai literates might be especially skilled at analyzing language at the level of syllables.

To test this speculation we used a task in which a "sentence" was presented and people were asked to repeat what they had heard. The "sentences" were of three kinds. In the "syllable" condition, a meaningful sentence was read with a two-second delay after each syllable. For example, the sentence *Anu ma ta kunumu mutina* (They didn't visit us yesterday) was read in a monotone voice as *a nu ma ta ku nu mu ti na*. In the "word" condition, each sentence was read in a monotone with two-second delays between words. Finally, in a "word scrambled" condition, the words were read in a nonsensical, random order. There were no differences at all between Vai literates and nonliterates when scrambled words were presented. When the words were presented in standard order, the Vai literates slightly outperformed the nonliterates. But when the syllables were pronounced separately, the Vai literates far outperformed the nonliterates.

A summary of results from a variety of tasks used in this work is provided in Table 8.1, where the check marks indicate that a group performed better than a group of nonliterate controls. This table highlights certain important results that were passed over in focusing exclusively on the Vai literates, but that are helpful in drawing the major lessons from this work.

Note that the entry labeled "incremental recall" is the only case where neither schooling nor Vai literacy improved performance but where study of the Qur'an did. We tested incremental recall using a procedure proposed by Mandler and Dean (1969) in which lists of words are built up by starting with a list length of one item and adding one item per trial. We included this procedure because it seemed to model teaching practices we had seen in Qur'anic classes, where people learned to memorize passages in just such an incremental fashion. By contrast, when the order of the items changed from trial to trial (free recall), school literacy was the only one that affected performance.

Midway down the table are the results from the rebus and sentence-repetition tasks. Note that integration of syllables is the only case in

Table 8.1

| Category of effect | Type of Literacy | | | |
|---|---|---|---|---|
| | English/ school | Vai script | Qur'anic | Arabic language |
| Categorizing | | | | |
| Form/number sort | ✓ | ✓ | | ✓ |
| Memory | | | | |
| Incremental recall | | | ✓ | ✓ |
| Free recall | ✓ | | | |
| Logical reasoning | | | | |
| Syllogisms | ✓ | | | |
| Encoding and decoding | | | | |
| Rebus reading | ✓ | ✓ | | |
| Rebus writing | ✓ | ✓ | | ✓ |
| Semantic integration | | | | |
| Integrating words | ✓ | ✓ | ✓ | ✓ |
| Integrating syllables | | ✓ | | |
| Verbal explanation | | | | |
| Communication game | ✓ | ✓ | | |
| Grammatical rules | ✓ | ✓ | | |
| Sorting geometric figures | ✓ | | | |
| Logical syllogisms | ✓ | | | |
| Sun-moon name-switching | ✓ | | | |
| (Because of ambiguities in this task, only those literacy effects appearing in more than one administration are included.) | | | | |

which Vai literacy is the only factor that promotes performance, while integration of words is improved by any of the literacy practices. At the bottom of the table, we see that while schooling generally increases the ability to give a verbal explanation of one's cognitive performance, literacy in Arabic does not, and Vai literacy does so only in cases that are closely linked to Vai literacy practices (writing and reading letters).

What are we to say about the fact that for the wide variety of cognitive tasks sampled in this study, schooling is most likely to improve performance? Were this yet another study of the effects of schooling we could do little more than repeat earlier positions. Either schooling does indeed have a transforming effect on cognitive performance (especially the ability to talk about one's own classification, memory, and problem-solving processes) or the pattern of results is an artifact because the form and content of the testing are very similar to the form and content of schooling.

Because this research included experimental procedures modeled on alternative literacy practices and schooled people performed more poorly than Vai literates in certain key cases, a richer alternative explanation offers itself. Formal schooling is constituted as a set of practices no less than Vai literacy or Vai forms of Qur'anic literacy. There is no more reason to attribute cases where schooled people excelled at our tasks to their ability to read and write, *per se,* than there is in the cases where Vai or Qur'anic literates excel. For example, the fact that schooling promotes skill in the verbal explanation of problem-solving processes seems most naturally explained by noting that such skills are demanded by typical teacher-pupil dialogue in classrooms (Griffin and Mehan, 1981; Mehan, 1979). Teachers often require students to respond to questions such as "Why did you give that answer?" or "Go to the blackboard and explain what you did."

By locating cognitive change in cultural practices and applying this principle to the practices of schooling no less than those of letter writing and record keeping, and by treating cognitive experiments as models of the associated practices, we achieve that symmetry between experimental methods and everyday practices whose possibility I questioned at the beginning of this chapter. This cultural-practice approach also suggests a way to readdress the issue of "general" versus "specific" changes in cognition associated with changes in the cultural organization of behavior. And it accounts for the apparent asymmetry in cognitive performance when schooling is compared with other forms of literacy as in Table 8.1.

Our survey and ethnographic data indicated that the range of literacy practices among the Vai is restricted relative to the range of practice we associate with literacy in technologically advanced societies. The reasons for this restricted range are many: absence of a technology of mass production, legal restrictions on the use of Vai script in civil affairs, adherence to a religion that uses a completely different writing system and a foreign language, and so on. Our activity-based, cultural-practice approach emphasized that if the uses of writing are few, the skill development they foster will also be limited to a narrow range of tasks in a correspondingly narrow range of activities and content domains.

By the same token, when technological, social, and economic conditions create many activities where reading and writing are instrumental, the range of literacy skills can be expected to broaden and increase in complexity. Under these conditions, the "context specific" and "general ability" interpretations of literacy's consequences converge. In any society where literacy practices are ubiquitous and complexly interrelated, the associated cognitive skills will also become more widespread and complexly related, giving the *appearance* of a general transformation in modes of thought.

Here we see one of the powerful effects of wedding the diachronic, historically based view of the Russian cultural-historical psychologists with the synchronic view of the American context/activity-based scholars. The combination provides a systematic way to recover the real diversity that characterizes how sociocultural change occurs. The Russians saw literacy as a transformer of human experience and promoted its potential to transform mind and society. My colleagues and I, while sharing the idea of literacy as a cognitive and social tool, were focused on the context-specificities of literacy effects and its role in amplifying the social inequalities it was being used to overcome. How the resulting heterogeneity should be sorted out remains a matter of dispute, but the grounds have shifted away from the "literacy as general transformer" view to one which takes the social organization of activity as a problematic to be worked out case by case (Goody, 1987; Olson, 1994; Wagner, 1993).

## Preschoolers' Talk

My next example is based on the common observation that children appear to talk in a more sophisticated way and to accomplish more complex intellectual tasks in the course of spontaneous interactions than when they are being interrogated by adults. This issue is of special interest when it comes to evaluating the psycholinguistic abilities of minority-group children for purposes of academic placement and instruction. In a famous demonstration of situational variability in the sophistication of children's language use, Labov (1972) claimed that the failure of children who speak nonstandard (black) English to score well on standardized tests of language competence arises from inadequacies of the testing, not inadequacies of the children. To demonstrate his point that sociolinguistic factors control speech, Labov arranged for a comparison of the language used by an eight-year-old boy, Leon, in three settings.

In the formal test setting, Leon is brought into a room where a large, friendly, white interviewer puts a toy on the table in front of him and says "Tell me everything you can about this." There ensues a painful sequence of verbal prods from the interviewer and minimal verbal productions from the child, with pauses of up to twenty seconds between questions and monosyllabic answers. The standard interpretation of this behavior is that the child has failed to acquire grammatical competence; Labov's interpretation is that the child is actively attempting to avoid saying anything in a situation where "anything he says can literally be held against him" (pp. 205–206).

In a test of his belief that appropriate changes in the social circumstances and content of the talk would reveal Leon's competence, Labov arranged for a black interviewer, Clarence Robbins, a native of Harlem, to interview Leon at home. The topic this time was street fighting. Although the changes in interviewer, setting, and topic were designed to be more evocative, the results were similar to those obtained in the test situation: the adult asked questions and when Leon responded at all, he did so in one-word answers.

In the third situation, Robbins brought along a supply of potato chips and Leon's best friend, eight-year-old Gregory. He sat down on the floor with the boys and introduced taboo words and topics; cumulatively, these changes created a more informal, almost party-like situation in which the power relations between adult and children were changed. The effect of these changes on Leon's speech was dramatic. Not only did he go beyond one-word replies to questions, but he actively competed for the floor, talking excitedly with both his friend and Robbins about street fighting, among other things. On the basis of these observations, Labov concludes that Leon had no difficulty using the English language and displayed a rich variety of grammatical forms typical of black English vernacular.

Labov drew two major conclusions from these observations. First, he asserted that what applied to his test-like situation (derived from the Illinois Test of Psycholinguistic Abilities) applied to IQ and reading tests as well: they would underestimate such children's verbal abilities. Second, he insisted that the social situation is the most important determinant of verbal behavior, and that adults who want to assess children's capacities must enter into the right kind of social relation in order to find out what the child is capable of.

There is no doubt that Labov succeeded in weakening claims on the basis of standardized testing that poor, black children are retarded with respect to linguistic and intellectual development. However, the implication that formal one-to-one testing and the informal three-way conversation about taboo topics are equivalent or that Leon's poor performance in the one-on-one interaction resulted from his defensiveness were not well grounded. To sustain such conclusions, it would be necessary to show that in some formal sense, the task confronting Leon in the test-like and party-like situations were equivalent with respect to their structure, function, and cognitive demands.

A number of investigators have pointed out that test situations present special difficulties for those being tested even if they are interested in the topic, are unafraid, and speak the same language as the tester (Blank, 1973; Cicourel et al., 1974; Mehan, 1979). These difficulties boil down to the fact that acceptable responses to test questions or to teachers' questions in a class are highly constrained; one knows that the questioner knows the answer to the question, which must be answered on the questioner's terms, which are not made explicit. Conversations among peers or among people of different statuses in other settings, by contrast, are more likely to allow shared control of topic, the criteria for evaluating an acceptable reply, and so on.

The relative difficulty of responding to questions in test-like circumstances is supported by observations with very young children who were unable to repeat a sentence spoken by an adult even when they themselves had spoken that same sentence ten minutes earlier (Slobin and Welch, 1973). Such failures to display *already manifested competence* suggest that spontaneous speech encodes an "intention to say such and such," whereas elicited speech requires the child to process and produce sentences in linguistic terms alone, robbing speech of its intentional and contextual supports (Bloom, Rocissano, and Hood, 1976).

In the 1970s my colleagues and I attempted to replicate Labov and Robbins's basic result. We conducted an experiment in which twenty-four children between the ages of three years, two months and four years, ten months were taken to the supermarket in pairs by a researcher who had spent several weeks in the classroom as a teacher's aide (see Cole et al., 1978). Their talk in the supermarket was then compared with their talk in the classroom. The children rode from school to the supermarket in a shopping basket that also carried a tape recorder. They were allowed to handle merchandise but not to abuse it, and each child was allowed to purchase a piece of bubble gum. Upon their return to school, their teacher asked them about what they had seen and done at the market. This conversation was also recorded.

Trips to the supermarket lasted between thirty and forty-five minutes. Discussions with the teacher upon return lasted about ten minutes. As speech samples, we picked three-minute sections from the middle of each conversation for comparative analysis.

In some instances we obtained dramatic confirmation of the phenomenon reported by Labov: children who spoke rarely and mostly in monosyllables in the classroom spoke more often and at greater length in the supermarket. One child who was relatively talkative in the supermarket was observed to say only 15 words for the rest of the morning at the preschool. Those 15 words were in response to 9 of the 63 questions directed at him; he was silent in response to the remaining 54.

Our initial analyses were focused on such categories of behavior as the number of spontaneous utterances per minute, the mean length of utterances, and the number of grammatical structures children used in the two settings. In every case, the conversations in the supermarket yielded higher scores than those in the classroom (for example, 5.8 vs. 2.4 utterances per minute, 6.9 vs. 3.8 different grammatical structures, and 3.4 vs. 2.9 words per utterance). The differences were especially marked for the younger children.

While these results provide an interesting confirmation of Labov's pioneering work under more constrained and quantifiable conditions, our scoring scheme suffers from the same shortcomings as

Labov's: we have not shown that the constraints on talk in the two settings are equivalent so that the children are, in effect, confronting the same task in the supermarket and the classroom. By the same token, we have no analytic apparatus to identify how the constraints on talk differ in the two settings.

To overcome these shortcomings, and to provide a principled test of the influence of social context on the complexity of children's speech, my colleagues and I took advantage of the formalism provided by a theory of communicative acts developed by Dore (1978) which elaborated on prior work by Austin (1962) and Searle (1975). Dore's descriptive system categorized adult and child utterances into categories based on propositional content, grammatical structure, and function in conversation. The following categories proved helpful in comparing children's talk in school and a nonschool setting:

RQ: Requests (soliciting information).
RS: Responses (providing information directly complementing prior requests). Responses are subdivided into RSWH (responses to Wh questions), RSYN (responses to yes-no questions) and RS (responses to all other kinds of questions).
DES: Descriptions and statements (of events, properties, locations, facts, beliefs, attitudes, etc.), e.g., "The cat climbed onto the table" or "You have to share your toys with others."
ID: Identifications.
Q: Questions.
QUAL: Qualifications (supplying unsolicited information in relation to a question), e.g., "I didn't do it."
ST: Statements.

A pair of example transcripts, the first from the supermarket, the second from a conversation after return to the preschool, give the flavor of how we scored and categorized the conversational patterns:

*Supermarket*

*Child:* Uh, do elephants eat, uh, do elephants eat spaghetti? (RQ)
*Adult:* Do elephants eat spaghetti? (RQ) No. (RS) You know what they eat?(RQ)
*Child:* Yeah. (RS) What? (RQ)
*Adult:* Peanuts. (RS)

*Child:* An el . . . an el, and spaghetti? (RQ)

*Adult:* No, they, elephants don't eat spaghetti. (RS)

*Child:* I saw an elephant in the zoo eat spaghetti and he ate a popcorn and some a dese. (DES)

*Classroom*

*Adult:* Come here! (RQ) I want to ask you something. (ST) Sit down. (RQ) Let me ask you something. (RQ) Where did you go? (RQ)

*Child:* Store. (RS)

*Adult:* You went to where? (RQ)

*Child:* To da store. (RS)

   Table 8.2 displays the results of grouping the younger children's talk according to conversational acts. Such tabular presentations are a little unwieldy, but they reward careful examination. The first striking difference between the two settings is that there are many more turns at talking in the supermarket (282 vs. 161 total utterances in the three-minute sample, representing 23.5 vs. 13.4 utterances per child). Second, when one looks at the relative frequency of the different kinds of conversational acts, it is evident that in the classroom the children are most likely to be engaged in responding to questions from teachers. Children also occupy the "responding slot" in supermarket conversations, but they are far more likely to be initiators (as indicated by the relatively high frequency of questions, requests, identifications, and descriptions). Third, and most telling of all with

Table 8.2

| C-Act | Supermarket | | Classroom | |
|---|---|---|---|---|
|  | Frequency | MLU | Frequency | MLU |
| RSWH | 28 | 1.92 | 72 | 2.57 |
| RSYN | 32 | 1.68 | 41 | 1.45 |
| Other RS (responses) | 37 | 1.98 | 11 | 2.12 |
| Qualifications | 11 | 2.46 | 6 | 5.25 |
| Questions | 24 | 3.37 | 4 | 2.66 |
| Requests | 36 | 2.87 | 16 | 2.21 |
| Identifications | 31 | 1.90 | — | — |
| Descriptions | 83 | 4.30 | 11 | 5.75 |
| Average MLU | | 2.82 | | 2.14 |

respect to the issue of using linguistic formalisms for purposes of comparing behavior across settings, the mean lengths of utterance *within categories of conversational acts* are very similar: in fact, there are several cases where mean length of utterance for a given category of talk is greater in the classroom than the supermarket (although the numbers of cases are sufficiently small to make statistical treatment ineffective).

These results suggest that it is indeed productive to use the formalism provided by Dore's theory of speech acts to categorize children's talk. Insofar as the constraints on talk indexed by different speech acts are associated with particular cognitive demands, these data provide evidence of *similarity* in behavior in different settings because there are *no differences* associated with engaging in particular tasks such as responding to questions or offering descriptions. Rather, the influence of social context is to change the relative frequency of different speech acts, each of which produces utterances of characteristic length for the two social contexts compared in this study.

## Tests, School, and Club

We had realized, during our work in the Yucatán, that we needed to find some way to identify cognitive tasks in everyday life in terms that meshed with the concepts of cognitive psychology. We decided to undertake a direct analysis of the relationship between cognitive psychological tasks, classroom lessons, and more neighborhood-based forms of activity. Our idea was to select nonschool, nontest activities which might, a priori, be expected to yield many occasions for observing cognitive behaviors that also occur in school and in tests. We could then answer the essential question about cognitive consequences of schooling: Can cognitive difference be seen to operate in everyday settings that are not controlled by a researcher or a teacher?

Begun in the fall of 1976, this research involved seventeen children, eight to ten years old, from a variety of ethnic and social class backgrounds who attended a small private school in New York City.[7] Our approach was direct to the point of being simpleminded. We reasoned that if psychological tasks organized by psychologists actually measure the sorts of things that go on outside of experimental interactions, then we should be able to see people engaging in such tasks and to say something about how they are doing it.

We wanted to conduct this work in such a way that we could record in detail what happened in each of three kinds of environments: psychological tests, schoolrooms, and afterschool activities. We reasoned that if psychological tests model school practices we should be able to "see" psychological processes at work in both a test and a classroom, and then determine if the child performs equally well in both settings. By the same token, if we engaged the children in activities such as "Nature Club" and "Cooking Club" we ought to see school-like, and thus test-like, tasks occurring in the clubs and broaden the range of settings in which we saw the same children engaging in specified cognitive tasks.

In collaboration with George Miller (and with generous support from the Grant Foundation), we created a large playroom where children of various ages could be observed while we video- and audio-recorded their activities.[8] We also recorded hour-long testing sessions during which each child was presented a variety of laboratory-derived cognitive tasks by a professional educational tester. Finally, we recorded in these same children's classrooms while children and teachers went about their daily routines. We were fully aware that we were sampling a limited set of situations, but we hoped that our observations would allow us to talk about how particular cognitive tasks and performances change as a function of the settings in which they occur.

The cognitive tests we selected were meant to be representative of tests used to predict and evaluate scholastic aptitude or cognitive development. We also sought, insofar as possible, test instruments that made visible what the child was doing, and we tried to sample widely from the spectrum of task demands that we imagined might be encountered in school and in our nonschool environments.

Our test battery included modified versions of the word-similarities subtest of the Wechsler Intelligence Scale for Children (WISC), a mediated memory test first developed by Alexei Leontiev (1931), a figure-matching task of the sort used to assess impulsivity, a syllogistic reasoning task, and a classification task employing common household objects. We suffered from no illusion that this set of tasks exhausted the possible list of intellectual demands that children encounter daily. But we were confident that they were relevant to the classroom and club settings.

We began observing in the children's classroom to see if (a) we could specify the ways in which the children responded to intellectual tasks there, and (b) we could observe the occurrence of any task that could be administered in a later test session. We videotaped samples of many kinds of classroom activities: directed lessons (such as an exercise in division or classification of the animal kingdom), individual study time (during which the teacher passed from student to student, checking on and assisting in a variety of assignments), group discussion of social interactional problems that arise in the classroom, and individual "free time" (during which children could elect to engage in any one of a number of activities such as drawing, playing board games, reading, keeping a diary).

Initially we were encouraged because we seemed to be able to identify the occurrence of various cognitive tasks in the course of our classroom observations. Tasks resembling classification, free recall, paired associate learning, and a number of other well-studied experimental tasks could be found as a natural part of the children's activities, particularly during formally organized lessons.

To be sure, the tasks as encountered in the classroom were not isomorphic with the laboratory tasks. Nor were they constantly occurring; a good deal of the time it appeared that nothing was happening. But our initial results suggested that something like laboratory tasks did occur in actual school settings, so we had a starting point for making intersituational comparisons.

A few weeks later we also began to observe these same children in afterschool clubs. Half the children attended a club that emphasized nature activities, while the remainder constituted a cooking club. These club sessions, which lasted one and one-half to two hours, were conducted in the specially prepared playroom at the Rockefeller University. The children's activities included preparing various dishes (cakes, breads, entire meals), training animals, growing plants, experimenting with electricity, and a variety of similar "constructing" tasks. The children's behavior was not rigidly controlled, but we did attempt to structure the activities by varying the extent to which successful completion depended on information available from written instructions, the club leader, and other children.

The most striking feature of these club sessions was the extreme rarity of identifiable cognitive tasks. If the classroom could be characterized as an environment where cognitive tasks were observable with intervals of "doing nothing" interspersed, the club sessions could be characterized as an environment of chaotic activity with identifiable tasks interspersed at rare intervals. It was certainly not the case that the children were sitting quietly, lost in thought. They were active, argumentative, and constantly busy. But classification, inference, and other tasks we had hoped to discover were not easily detectible, even after several viewings of our videotaped record. We found ourselves in a somewhat absurd situation: activities that clearly required the cognitive processes we were interested in studying must have been operating (the recipes got read, the cakes baked, the animals trained), but we could not identify how these goals were accomplished in a way that was directly related to those intellectual tasks that are the backbone of process-oriented cognitive psychology.

We had originally set out to answer a number of questions: How often are the cognitive tasks that have been studied in the laboratory actually encountered in various classroom and club settings? Could we show similarities and differences in the behavior of individual children for tasks encountered in the different settings? Granting that the exact form of a given task would differ according to the context in which it occurred, could we specify how the context influenced the particular form of the task and the child's response to it? Our initial assumption that we could identify cognitive tasks outside the laboratory and classroom and answer these questions was clearly wrongheaded. But the solution to the problem of how to identify and analyze cognitive behavior across settings was not at all obvious.

A few examples taken from transcriptions of our videotapes will indicate the seriousness of the analytical problem. The first example comes from an argument over how many rooms the children have in their apartments. Dolores initiates the task of remembering by asking Jackie how many rooms she has and then asserting that she thinks that the correct number is thirteen:

1. *Dolores:* (pointing to Jackie) Well she has thirteen (rooms). No you don't.

2. *Jackie:* Uhhuh, I just made, I, we just made a bathroom.
3. *Mike:* They cut one (room).
4. *Dolores:* (to Jackie) Count them all (Dolores holds up pinky).
5. *Jackie:* Three bathrooms (holds up three fingers).
6. *Dolores:* That's not a room.
7. *Reggie:* They're rooms. Bath rooms.
8. *Jackie:* No, I'm counting bathrooms. For my (holds out arms) whole house we got thirteen rooms. There are two (inaudible).
9. *Dolores:* (holds up 3 fingers) Three, two (adds 2 more fingers).
10. *Jackie:* Five (holds up 5 fingers also; Dolores adds one more). O.K. (Jackie holds up six too).
11. *Dolores:* No five (holds up five).
12. *Jackie:* O.K. (holds up 5 too). My um mother's and father's room. Six (both hold up six). Then we have (Pause) um.
13. *Dolores:* Your room.
14. *Jackie:* My room and my brother's room (both hold up eight) and then we have um.
15. *Dolores:* The living room (9 fingers).
16. *Jackie:* The living room (9 fingers).
17. *Dolores:* The kitchen (10 fingers).
18. *Jackie:* The kitchen (10 fingers). And the place where we eat. The place where we eat. 11. And then we have, then when you walk (moves hands indicating direction) (inaudible) and you walk here. You know (pause) well we made a new room.
19. *Dolores:* Oh, well you counted that already.
20. *Jackie:* No, I didn't count the new room.
21. *Dolores:* Yes, you did.
22. *Reggie:* Yes, you did count the livingroom.
23. *Dolores:* No, the new room. You counted the new room. (Discussion continues.)

Here remembering is called for, and the items are counted, but the information can come from anywhere just so long as it is relevant to the task before the group. For example, we can see Dolores storing part of the information for Jackie (with her fingers), actively joining in the recall process, supplying the necessary information (line 13, line 1), contributing by acting as a mnemonic cue for Jackie (line 15).

A quite different example occurred when we attempted to create a natural excuse for children to engage in free recall by arranging for each child to go with an adult to a different interesting locale in the city and then meet the others for lunch. I remained behind and took care of meal preparations. Consequently, when I asked children where they had been and what they had seen, it was a genuine question in the sense that I could not know the answer. By prearrangement, we agreed that adults would avoid, insofar as possible, filling in information for the children.

The first child I asked said that she had been to the museum of natural history and had seen the dinosaurs. "What else did you see?" I asked. She paused a minute, looked at the adult who had accompanied her, and asked him "What else?" He said, "Gee I don't know, don't you remember anything else?" That question brought the interaction to an abrupt halt. The child immediately sensed the artificial nature of the interaction and refused to answer any more questions about her visit to the museum. Moreover, it was difficult to get any of the children to engage in systematic remembering about their morning's activities.

We were able to collect a number of such examples from our many hours of recording, although a great deal of the time, as I noted before, it was virtually impossible to say that particular children were confronting "a task" and to specify how they dealt with it. The children's rule of interaction seemed to be, insofar as possible, *not* to confront intellectual obstacles, but to ask someone else, change the topic, or simply wait for the problem to go away.

An interesting exception to this phenomenon of "invisibility of cognitive tasks" concerned a child who had been diagnosed as learning disabled (see Cole and Traupmann, 1981). Our initial interest in Archie arose because we did not find out until well into the first year of observations that he was said to be learning disabled and we did not discover it from our interactions with him or our analyses of videotape. Rather, we learned it from a teacher who asked me if Archie was proving a problem in the clubs. I was surprised at the idea. Archie's companion, Reggie, kept getting into interpersonal difficulties that tended to spill into the hallways and thereby disturb my colleagues. But Archie was generally helpful and compliant.

Once alerted to the notion that Archie had difficulty with processing text, we began to notice that he would sometimes mispronounce words ("paschetti" instead of "spaghetti," for example) and that he often depended on others to get information from the written text. Archie experienced some distinctive difficulties in the formal testing procedure, and we noticed from tapings in class that he was a master at avoiding being called on to answer questions. He also had a lot of trouble when we held an "IQ Bee" during a special club session. However, the most interesting observations came from two occasions when Archie worked with Reggie. These sessions came late in the year when we had begun to realize that a major reason we could not "see cognitive tasks happen" was that adults and children all filled in for each other in a noisy, but tightly woven, division of labor that minimized disruptions in the activity. Consequently, we began to manipulate possible divisions of labor by making up excuses for the adult to be less available to the children in the hopes of bringing about discoordinations in activity that would make the cognitive tasks they were engaged in more visible.

Reggie was a very able reader, but he had trouble keeping his mind on the task at hand and cooperating with Archie. On one occasion, a week after an episode in which Archie had joined another boy in excluding Reggie from their group, Reggie and Archie were grouped together and the other boy was absent. The tape reveals the pathos of Archie's situation and his remarkable skills in dealing with it. At the beginning of the session, Reggie very deliberately refuses to help Archie get the information they need to bake a banana cake. Archie attempts to get the information from the adult present, but the adult both has made up an excuse for not helping and is annoyed with Archie for failing to listen to the preliminary instructions. After helping Archie decode instructions for a few items, the adult loses patience and tells him to figure it out by himself. Other kids are no more helpful, and after several confusions and refusals of help, Archie begins to cry.

No sooner does Reggie see Archie start to cry than he agrees to be helpful. From that moment forward a remarkable division of labor springs into being. Reggie, who can read but not pay attention, has the text stuck under his nose when Archie needs information, and Archie actively organizes Reggie to attend to the process of baking so that the banana bread eventually gets made. The following week Reggie begins by telling Archie that he will be cooperative, and the cognitive division of labor seen previously is replicated.

## Ecological Validity Reconsidered

In struggling with the findings from our comparisons of tests, classrooms, and clubs, we were influenced by our reading of F. C. Bartlett's (1958) book on thinking. Bartlett distinguished three kinds of thinking which can be roughly related to three classes of contexts for problem solving. First he discussed the properties of closed systems which have a fixed goal, a fixed structure, and known elements. These are exemplified by anagram problems, extrapolation of numerical sequences, or calculations of combination and permutations.

Bartlett contrasts closed systems where the task elements and allowable responses are known ahead of time with two kinds of open systems. First, people involved in *experimental* thinking are in the position of explorers rather than spectators. They have a notion of the goal, but the set of appropriate responses is unspecified, as are other constraints on attempts to reach the goal. They must use whatever tools are available for adding to the structure that is not yet finished. "The materials that he must use have properties of their own, many of which he cannot know until he uses them, and some of which in all likelihood are actually generated in the course of their use" (p. 137). A biologist seeking a cure for cancer in a virology laboratory would be an example of a person working in an open, experimental system. Bartlett points out that in a closed system, the answer is *the* answer; in an open system, *an* answer is but the specification of a new step in the larger domain of interest.

Second, Bartlett discusses a class of open systems which he says characterizes everyday thinking, "by which I mean those activities by which most people . . . try to fill up gaps in information available to them in which, for some reason, they are especially interested" (p. 164). This gap filling does not obey the constraints of either closed-system or experimental thinking, and consequently it is often very difficult to determine what processes are involved.

Our conclusion at the end of this work was that by and large, the use of standardized cognitive-psychological experimental procedures implies that a closed analytic system is being successfully imposed upon a more open behavioral system. To the degree that behavior conforms to the pre-scripted analytic categories, one achieves ecological validity in Brunswik's sense. Yet our work, as well as studies by Cicourel and his colleagues (1974) and others, had shown that even psychological tests and other presumably closed-system cognitive tasks are permeable and negotiable. Insofar as the psychologist's closed system does not capture veridically the elements of the open system it is presumed to model, experimental results systematically misrepresent the life process from which they are derived. The issue of ecological validity then becomes a question of the violence done to the phenomenon of interest owing to the analytic procedures employed.[9] In this sense, we argued, ecological *in*validity is built directly into the standardized test procedures themselves.

## A Mid-course Assessment: Cognitive Analysis in Activity

The three studies summarized here demonstrate that it is indeed possible to carry out analyses of behavior in relatively complex, multi-party activities that make contact with the methods favored by cognitive psychologists. In the case of Vai literacy practices we were able, in some cases, to build experimental models that engaged the cognitive skills and knowledge that such practices entail. This work strongly reinforces the "activity relative" perspective I offered in Chapter 5. In the case of preschoolers' language use, we found that starting with a theoretically motivated scheme for categorizing speech acts, we were able to pinpoint differences in kinds of language used during an informal visit to the supermarket and a discussion of the same content in a subsequent classroom show-and-tell session. In the studies directed at the issue of ecological validity we found that by videotaping a group of children and adults during tests, in a classroom, and in an afterschool club, we were able to make visible for analysis the social-interactional constraints on talking and thinking that are characteristic in the three kinds of activity. Although such occasions were relatively rare, we demonstrated that from time to time the division of labor characterizing the joint activities in the club made it possible to see people engaging in recognizable (to psychologists) cognitive tasks. The ability of people to arrange and rearrange the circumstances under which they carried out the activity emerged as an important feature distinguishing tests from school lessons and school lessons from afterschool club activities.

Our three studies were not, of course, the only ones to illuminate the nature of cognitive psychological experimentation in relation to everyday practices. Over the past two decades many scholars who agree with our critiques of standard cross-cultural research have been developing their own strategies for overcoming the inadequacies of research and theory they found there.

## Locating Experiments

Sylvia Scribner (1975b) coined the term "locating the experiment" to address the relations between experiments and indigenously organized activities. Her point was that experimental tasks themselves always occur as constituents of a context (note that she was operating with the "context as prior constraint" version of context here), so the objective of research should be to design experiments that can be "naturally located" with respect to the activity being analyzed. The Vai project is one illustration of this strategy.

Douglas Price-Williams (1975), one of the first cross-cultural psychologists to call for a cultural psychology focused on context and meaning, proposed a "graduated steps" design to bridge between naturally occurring events (that is, events constructed for reasons other than the psychologists' convenience) and traditional experimentation. He divided events into three elements: the task the person is asked to complete, the materials, and the social context. As one or more of these elements is changed from its habitual state, the experiment becomes more and more like the standardized format.

Two studies conducted in the mid-1970s illustrate this approach. Carla Childs and Patricia Greenfield (1980) conducted a study of pattern-representation and pattern-completion among Zinacantecan weavers in southern Mexico. The "familiar" task was to copy a traditional red-and-white pattern using sticks to represent stripes of the target pattern. Childs and Greenfield found that girls (who begin weaving some time after the age of eight) copied the patterns precisely as they were woven, but they experienced difficulty completing an unfamiliar pattern.

A second implementation of this approach can be found in research by Jean Lave (1977a, b), who visited Liberia not long after we undertook the Vai research and decided to initiate a project of her own. She was seeking to compare the extent to which mathematics skills acquired by tailors in the course of their everyday practices were used when tackling unfamiliar problems. She was also interested in the extent to which formal educational experience affected tailors' mathematical problem-solving abilities. Her interests had much in common with ours.

After a period spent observing tailors and conducting pilot studies, Lave came up with a set of tasks ranging from very familiar in the tailor shop to very unfamiliar. A number of the unfamiliar problems were in fact similar to word problems used in school instruction, while others were not likely to be taught in either setting (for example, a task that required the subject to match proportions of two figures printed on a card).

Multiple regression analyses of performance scores were used to determine the relative influence of years of schooling versus years of tailoring on problems of the various kinds. When the problem was unfamiliar on the basis of either schooling or tailoring experience, neither variable affected performance. For the problems modeled on school exercises, years of schooling was more important than tailoring in predicting performance, while for the problems modeled on tailoring practice, years of tailoring was more important than years of schooling. This pattern of results pointed to the "compartmentalization of problem solving skills that have been learned in different contexts" (1977b, p. 179).

An important ingredient that this work brought to the discussion was its emphasis on the importance of maintaining analytic symmetry between experiments and mundane situations. Lave criticized as "experiment-centric" the idea that cognitive psychologists possess specially privileged tools when they seek to model properties of the system being analyzed.

## The Advantages of a Well-specified Domain

An important characteristic of the previous examples is that the primary data were drawn from artificially constructed tasks, albeit tasks designed to model aspects of various cultural practices. Other efforts have focused more directly on the analysis of cognitive activity in situ.

H. J. Reed and J. Lave (1979) made an important contribution to understanding the conditions affording *in situ* cognitive analyses in their discussion of the ways Vai tailors deployed Vai and English number systems in arithmetic problem solving. They argued that "the systemic properties of the arithmetic domain make possible powerful inferences about the problem solving processes that are taking place when particular problems elicit particular responses. Few domains of human activity (language being a notable exception) are formal enough to offer this opportunity" (p. 568).[10]

Lave first exploited this insight in her studies of the cognitive consequences of apprenticeship training and formal schooling. Later she used it in a study contrasting supermarket and weight watchers' mathematics with the mathematics taught in school. Analysis of the much discussed example of someone figuring out three-quarters of two-thirds of a cup of cottage cheese by first estimating three-quarters of a cup and then two-thirds of the remainder, instead of immediately taking a half cup, provides a clear case in which the structure of mathematics provides a tool both for the participants to solve their tasks and for the analyst to say something systematic about their problem-solving activities (Lave, 1988; Lave, Murtaugh, and de la Rocha, 1984).

Tenezhina Carraher, David Carraher, and Analucia Schliemann (1985) and their colleagues in Recife, Brazil, provide several examples of the cognitive analysis of activity associated with social practices using mathematics. Their work was conducted among child street vendors. One of their methods was to approach children in the marketplace and pose questions about potential purchases, as in the following case of a twelve-year-old coconut vendor, M., a third grader (the interviewer is referred to as the customer):

*Customer:* How much is one coconut?
*M:* Thirty-five
*Customer:* I'd like ten. How much is that?
*M:* (Pause) Three will be 105; with three more, that will be 210. (Pause) I need four more. That is . . . (pause) 315 . . . I think it is 350.

The researchers plausibly suggest that the child solves the problem in the form $105 + 105 + 105 + 35$. How the child arrived at the original 105 is less certain, whether as $35 + 35 + 35$ or as $3 \times 35$. This procedure was, they are sure, *not* learned in school, where the procedure $10 \times 35$ is taught.

This example perfectly "locates" the experiment within an "everyday interaction." This is possible because in this case the task the psychologist is interested in (arithmetic) is rather tightly constrained by cultural convention. The child answers the adult's question just as if it is "real," which it is from the child's point of view. Here we get virtually perfect ecological validity, a correspondence between the "natural" task and the psychologist-imposed task.[11]

The Recife group and other researchers extended their examples to a variety of domains of everyday practice, including the building trades and various kinds of crafts, as well as schooling and formal experiments (Bremmer, 1985; Carraher, 1986; Saxe, 1982, 1985, 1991). Several of these studies have shown that schooled people will use the algorithms and procedures learned in school in a variety of out-of-school settings. The opposite also occurs. For example, the Vai children studied by Betsy Bremmer (1985) used strategies found among tailors and carpenters (such as reducing multiplication to successive addition) as well as school-based strategies. Furthermore, those who were observed to use the most different strategies tested highest. Geoffrey Saxe (1982) also observed Oksapmin children using the Oksapmin body-counting system to come up with answers in their school lessons.

A striking finding in this literature is that when the same arithmetic problem is encountered both in school and in everyday practices (measuring cloth, selling coconuts or candy), the solution rate is higher in the everyday practice (Carraher, Carraher, and Schliemann, 1985; Lave, 1977a,b; Scribner, 1984). Careful studies of problem-solving processes reveal (as in the case of the coconut seller described above) that people have developed a variety of specialized strategies to deal with routinely encountered problems (decomposing the problem, regrouping numbers, and a variety of other rules of thumb that simplify their calculations).

In addition to acquiring simplifying strategies, experienced workers are also sensitive to errors that lead to unreasonable answers, so they can take corrective measures. Experienced practitioners virtually never come up with absurd answers, whereas children who have learned all their arithmetic in school often do.

The substantive findings of this research bear upon how we think about the organization of curriculum, although there is little consensus on what, precisely, the lessons for organization of classroom instruction are (see the recent controversy over interpreting the general significance of everyday math for school instruction: Brown, Collins, and Duguid, 1989; Palincsar, 1989). What most interests me in the present context is the demonstration that analysis of joint activity is facilitated when a logically closed set of cultural conventions is a prominent part of the activity.

## Experimenting within the Structure of the Cultural Practice

While activity mediated by the formalisms of mathematics has proven to be one of the most fruitful realms in which to conduct cognitive research on everyday thinking, analysts have also shown that it is possible to take advantage of other sources of structure provided by cultural practices. For example, Joy Stevens (1990) studied waitresses in a short-order restaurant. Through participant observation in this work setting, Stevens established that waitresses (who serve up to ten customers at a time) develop a complex set of strategies for keeping track of orders, calling orders into the kitchen, and timing their movements between kitchen and customers. They use a variety of external memory aids (the order slip/receipt; the sight of sandwich, drink, or dessert in front of the customer; the customer's location) to keep track of who needs what at what time. Stevens intervened slightly in the setting: she arranged for five confederates to come in for a meal to create a strategically balanced list of items being ordered, and she induced waitresses to wear wireless microphones so that the sequence in which they called in orders could be tracked. This bit of added structure allowed her to analyze the way the waitresses grouped to-be-remembered items; it was not the customers, but the kinds of meal items and the customers' locations that were grouped together as part of the complex job of remembering who got what and when.

Additional studies by Beach (1993, 1995), Hutchins (1995), Kawatoko (1995), Ueno (1995), Scribner (1984), Goodwin (1994), Suchman (1987), and many others drive home the essential point: sufficiently well informed knowledge of local practices can provide a strong basis for cognitive analysis in situations not set up with cognitive assessment as a goal.

## Displaying the Dynamics of Development

Commenting on cross-cultural research carried out in the activity-based tradition, Geoffrey Saxe (1994) notes that it rarely reveals much about the actual mechanisms of developmental change. Using the power of mathematics to analyze everyday practices available in the domain of mathematics, Saxe has been able to study the socio-cultural dynamics of developmental change among candy-selling Brazilian children (Saxe, 1991).

Working with children between the ages of six and fifteen years, Saxe was able to study the development of more complicated forms of mathematics including the manipulation of ratios. Complexity of the materials was increased by the high inflation in Brazil, which created a situation where children needed to manipulate large sums.

Saxe (building on the work of Nunes, Schliemann, and Carraher, 1993) started with an analysis of everyday practices. He discovered that candy selling is carried out in a cycle consisting of four phases (purchasing candy wholesale, pricing the candy to sell, selling, and selecting new candies to purchase for the next cycle). Each phase evokes its own set of mathematical goals.

Saxe demonstrated that the actual goals that arise depend upon the children's prior knowledge and the kinds of social interactions of which they are a part: very often younger, less capable children were helped by older children and adults in a manner that calls to mind Vygotsky's notion of a zone of proximal development. Cultural artifacts also play an important role in the goals children seek to achieve. An example is the convention for pricing candy in ratio form (for example, three packages for 500 cruzeiros or five packages for 1000 cruzeiros). These conventions both simplify and complicate children's transactions, depending upon which phase of the activity one considers (it makes selling easy, for example, but complicates calculations of markup when preparing to sell).

As children's age and experience increased, Saxe observed shifts in cultural forms to accomplish emerging mathematical goals. These shifts, in turn, depended upon the child's social position and existing skills: younger sellers had an advantage in the selling phase of the activity because they were cute, but older sellers were more adept at the various mathematical calculations. Consequently older sellers helped younger ones with difficult calculations until the younger ones could fend for themselves. As sellers took on more responsibility they also began to take on more difficult cognitive tasks; they began to use price ratios not only when selling their candy, for example, but when calculating their markup.

⑥ The evidence presented in this chapter demonstrates that it is possible to create experimental tasks modeled on everyday practices and to carry out effective analysis of cognitive processes outside of formal experimental tasks when everyday practices are subject to sufficient constraints or when an appropriate formalism can be applied. In some cases (when video- or audiotaped data are involved) the procedures required to carry out such analyses may be quite arduous, and there remain a great many situations and many interesting psychological questions for which cognitive analyses of the kind presented here do not exist. However, with respect to a number of cognitive domains of central concern to developmentalists (in particular, domains that are the content of modern educational practices), it has proven possible to carry out the kinds of cognitive analysis demanded by the expanded cultural-historical theory I began developing in Chapter 5.

The next challenge is to demonstrate that in addition to providing a plausible story of human development that begins from the analysis of culturally organized everyday activities, cultural-historical theory can be a useful tool for addressing practical problems of concern to contemporary society. It is to this task that I now turn.

# 9 ⑥

# Creating Model Activity Systems

THE RESEARCH discussed in Chapter 8 featured two basic strategies for dealing with the kinds of complex, multiperson interactions that characterize activity in what psychologists refer to as everyday life. The first was to use everyday events as the inspiration for experimental models (for example, the work on Vai literacy or Stevens's study of waitresses' remembering); the second was to observe behavior in the settings of interest and analyze it in terms of an appropriate formalism (for example, speech act theory or the rules of arithmetic, or a formal-psychological recall task).

Despite differences among them, those studies can be considered "basic research" in that they did not involve deliberate application of theoretical principles to change the lives of the people who participated in them. To be sure, the rationale in each case included social concerns: the work on Vai literacy followed a long tradition of interest in promoting economic and educational development in rural Africa; the comparison of children in classrooms and supermarkets addressed concerns over language and cognitive development among inner-city children; the work on ecological validity was directly tied to questions about education and testing.

The studies to be described in this and the next chapter take the additional step of using theoretical principles to guide the construction of activities deliberately designed for educational purposes. Consequently, within the traditional paradigms used by psychologists, each can be considered an example of "applied cultural psychology." However, the standard division of psychological research into applied and basic branches does not apply in the case of cultural-historical psychology. As noted in Chapter 4, the Russian cultural-historical psychologists contended that the ability to apply their principles in practical settings provided essential validation for their theoretical analysis.

The two studies I discuss in this chapter bring my work much closer to a theory-and-practice methodology. The first involved collaboration with a teacher team to create curricula-as-cognitive-tasks. It can be considered a transitional approach in that responsibility for implementing our ideas rested with the teachers. The second study led us back into afterschool time and an interest in the remediation of learning disabilities. In this case, we took full responsibility for implementing the activities we designed and for the welfare of the children who participated.

## Same Tasks in Different Settings

Our work with afterschool clubs impressed upon us the close connection between psychologists' ability to specify cognitive processes through experiments and the social arrangements of formal schooling. Cognitive tasks do not "just happen"; they are made to happen in joint activity among people. They are made to happen in particular ways in places called schools where children answer teachers' questions and take tests. Under such conditions, the definition of a task is relatively straightforward because classroom interactions conform, more or less, to the constraints that characterize cognitive psychological experiments.

This line of reasoning suggested that our search for cognitive tasks had gone about matters the wrong way. Instead of seeking to discover cognitive tasks it would have been more sensible for us to make the same task happen in different settings and then observe how it was reassembled, transformed, dispersed, or destroyed in the course of the activity of which it was a part. That way we would have a better chance of specifying the social work that had gone into creating the task in the first place.

The strategy we adopted at the outset was to work collaboratively with teachers to create curricular units that embodied cognitive tasks.[1] During the course of two years we constructed and implemented experimental curriculum units in science (electricity, animals, household chemicals), mathematics (long division), and social studies (Native Americans). Within each unit we arranged for "the same tasks" to occur in a variety of social circumstances: large-group lessons, small-group activities, tutorials, and an afterschool club-like activity. The contents of each unit implemented a part of the state-mandated educational objectives for third and fourth graders. For example, the household chemicals unit was chosen as a way to meet a natural sciences requirement. It was suggested by a teacher who was concerned about spontaneous fires from mixing cleaning solvents and other health hazards in the home. We were delighted with the idea because it mapped directly onto a well-known Piagetian task.

We conceived of the common logical schemas shared by implementations of the curriculum in different instructional contexts (small groups, one-on-one tutorials, and so on) as "problem isomorphs" (Gick and Holyoak, 1980). Ordinarily the study of such isomorphs is restricted to a single social context, the experimenter-subject relationship, and interest is focused on variations in problem content. In our case, variation across social structuring of the task for problems of the same logical structure was of paramount interest, although we also varied the content of tasks in some cases.

Our analysis of the Piagetian combination-of-variables task illustrates the procedures and the kinds of results that this strategy yielded. In the one-on-one, adult-child version of the task, the children were presented with stacks of little cards. The cards in each stack contained the picture of a different movie or TV star. Starting with four stacks, the child was asked to find all the ways that pairs of movie stars could be combined (to find all possible pairs of cards). When the child had completed as many pairs as possible, the adult instituted a bit of training by asking the child to check to see if any pairs were missing, and modeled a systematic checking procedure ("Do you have all the pairs with Mork?" "Do you have all the pairs with Elvis?" and so on). When the checking was completed, the stacks of cards were put back together and a fifth stack was added. Again the child was first asked to make all the possible pairings and then coached in the checking procedure if such coaching was needed. When the child completed the task with five stacks of cards, a sixth stack was added and the procedure repeated.

We scored performance to give credit for any instance of a child going through part or all of the pairings involving a particular card, such as 1&2, 1&3, 1&4; or 2&3, 2&4. The more complete the answer, the higher the score. As would be expected for third and fourth graders, few used a systematic logical procedure without help, although a majority began to display systematic strategies for pairing cards after they had been through the checking procedure.

These same children also participated in a small-group activity where three to four children went to a work area at the back of the room and were asked to find combinations of chemicals in beakers. Each group was given four beakers containing colorless solutions numbered to make them easily identifiable. They were also given a rack of tubes, and a sheet of paper with two columns marked "Chemicals" and "What happened?" on which they were urged to record their results. The chemicals were chosen so that each combination would produce a distinctive result. The teacher got one of the children to read the instructions aloud, then told them to investigate all the possible pairs without duplicates and busied herself with paperwork to make it clear that the children should proceed on their own.

Because the children who completed the movie star tutorial also completed the chemical combinations task, we could compare their performances across settings. But here the different social contexts of the tasks made themselves clearly felt.

In the two-person tutorial, the procedures divided the cognitive labor relatively neatly between the child and adult so that for each move in the problem it was possible to say either that the child did it on her own or that she was helped in varying degrees by the experimenter. But in the multichild chemical-pouring task matters were considerably more complicated. Since there was no imposed division of labor, it was often impossible to determine how much each child contributed to, or understood about, the solution of the task.

For example, if one child was in charge of pouring and one child was in charge of recording, their interactions may not have revealed the understandings of the recorder. This difficulty follows directly from the additional freedoms allowed the children by the teacher, and it confirms the difficulty of drawing conclusions about "same task in different settings" even when we make certain that the same task is there at the outset of the interaction. The normative constraints of the activity overwhelm the constraints of the task.

However, we also discovered that embedding the combination-of-variables task in a multiperson activity revealed an important aspect of the task that the standard procedure routinely obscured—the children's discovery of the task goal. When finding all combinations of chemicals the children began by addressing a problem that does not arise in the standard version of the task: how to make sure everyone gets a fair turn to combine chemicals. Only after a turn-taking procedure and division of labor were worked out did the children turn their attention to the question of which chemicals to combine.

There is no evidence that the children were initially oriented to the task of discovering all possible combinations of chemicals. Disputes were more likely to concern fair turn taking than chemical combinations. Once the children solved the problem of social equity and succeeded in testing several of the possible combinations, the task we were interested in (finding all possible combinations) arose as a result of the need to know if there were any more turns to be taken. In these circumstances the children spontaneously articulated their involvement in the task of finding all possible combinations because they needed to communicate with their partners about the ongoing social order.

By contrast, in the one-on-one sessions using combinations of cards, where we had excellent evidence about what parts of the adult-defined task the child fulfilled, we *never* obtained evidence that the child actually formed the goal intended by the adult. Children conformed to already-formulated (by the adult) goals by making pairs, but because it was (implicitly) the adult who was responsible for seeing that the child reached the goal, the goal-formation part of the task did not arise as a social issue, and hence was not assessable.

An additional event in this unit affirms again the fragility of "same tasks" even when they make an appearance in a particular setting. Bud Mehan and Margaret Riel conducted an out-of-school version of the combination-of-variables task. The activity was called The Back

Pack Bears, and on the occasion in question the children were engaged in the task of choosing meals for a hypothetical hike of several
days duration. Each meal was to be a stew made up of two out of a
possible five ingredients (carrots, beans, peas, and so on). The children started out to make different stews with different ingredients,
and for an instant the task of finding all combinations emerged. But
soon the children picked the ingredients they liked best and ignored
the rest of the task. This result came as no surprise given our experience in the cooking club, but it did serve as a reminder that the
presence of "the task" in an activity must be jointly achieved and
maintained.

Another part of the household chemicals unit provided an important lesson about the conditions under which teachers assess children's knowledge as part of classroom lessons. The lesson in question
was designed to prepare the children for the chemical mixing task
just described. In this lesson, given to four to six children at a time,
the teachers intended to provide the children with hands-on experience in mixing chemicals and keeping records. Initially the teachers
expected the lesson to have a wrap-up phase in which they would
discuss the range of chemical reactions the children had created by
the different combinations. They also knew they were preparing the
kids for the full-blown experiment in mixing chemicals, where the
subskills of mixing and recording would be necessary.

As a consequence, when the lesson began, the goals of the teachers
and the children were very different. The teachers were attempting
to prepare the children for upcoming tasks. The children, of course,
knew nothing of this future. They were simply excited to get their
hands on real chemicals after hours of talking about them.

The lesson was structured so that the children first mixed two
assigned chemicals and then wrote down what happened on the record sheet. They did this twice, for two different pairs of chemicals.
The teacher oversaw and coached the work of each group as she
deemed necessary.

We coded instances of teachers helping children in terms of two
sub-tasks: mixing the contents of the two beakers, and recording the
results on the record sheet. Within each sub-task, we distinguished
between low-level help focused on local operations and a higher form
that provided an overall view of the task. For each sub-task we scored

the help children got into two categories: "needed help" and "cannot tell if needed help," because in many cases the teachers gave help when the child had not asked for it, but in circumstances where it might have been needed. For example, teachers would give help in response to a request about mixing the content of two beakers and then tell the children to record it before we could assess if the children needed a reminder to record or not. Results are shown in Figure 9.1.

Several aspects of the results are worth highlighting. First of all, note that a large proportion of the help in almost all cases is ambiguous in the sense that the child gives no discernible sign of a need for help. Second, the amount of higher-level help decreased from the first to the second problem, indicating that children were learning the task. Third, the amount of help the teacher offered remained high even when the children didn't ask for it.

To get a better understanding of these interactions, we interviewed the teacher. With respect to the overall high level of help, she said that this lesson was designed to prepare the students for the next lesson. She was particularly worried about the recording step because she had said less about it in her introductory instructions and because recording was going to be essential in the next lesson. With respect to the situations where she gave help that was not asked for, she said that she was reinforcing actions she assumed the students could carry out themselves to make sure they would do them right in the next lesson. Here we see the principle of prolepsis, which I discussed in Chapter 7. The teacher's actions (and hence the children's experiences) are guided by contingencies not of the moment but of anticipated requirements for action in the future.

Of the many other interesting results from this project, I will mention only a case which elaborates directly on the central roles of ambiguity and prolepsis as systemic features of culturally mediated joint activity and cognitive change. This curriculum unit was designed and implemented by Marilyn Quinsaat as teacher and Andrea Pettito as researcher (see Petitto, 1985; Newman, Griffin, and Cole, 1989, ch. 6).

The cycle was designed to teach the process of long division to fourth graders who were encountering it for the first time. The lesson consisted of two phases, a demonstration in which the teacher carried out several problems on the board while individual children supplied

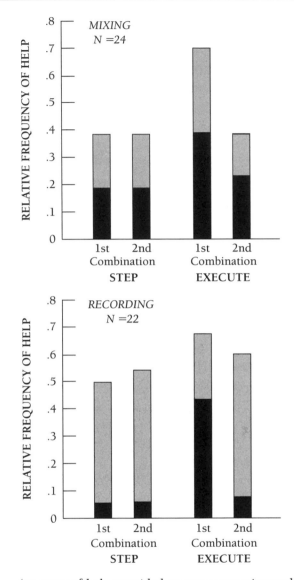

Figure 9.1.   Amounts of help provided on two successive problems in
which children were asked to mix chemicals (top) and to record the outcome (bottom). The darker portion of each bar reflects help given that
was clearly needed; the lighter portion reflects occasions in which help
was given without indication that it was needed.

parts of the solution, and a worksheet phase during which children solved problems on their own with assistance from the teacher when she thought it needed. The children were expected to know their "multiplication facts" ("7 times 6 equals 42") and simple division as reverse multiplication ("What times 7 is 42? 6"). In this lesson the teacher introduced a new goal for cases where there was a remainder, so simple division using multiplication facts would not work ("7 goes into 46 how many times?"). In such cases, she told the children, the "7 goes into 46" problem is solved "in the same way" as simple division: by finding a number which, when multiplied by 7, produces a number "close to 46 except it doesn't go over" and then subtracting to find the remainder.

Even for people who know how to do long division, such an explanation can be confusing. For children who are encountering the problem for the first time, even children who know their multiplication tables and simple division and who have some prior experience with the idea of remainders, the procedure poses difficult challenges.

The difficulty for the uninitiated child was brought home to me during a conference attended by several colleagues from Japan, at which Andrea presented her analysis. She introduced her talk by saying that fourth graders seem to have trouble grasping the "gazzinta" relation, and then launched into an analysis of how teachers and children negotiated the instructional interactions around division problems which were supposed to result in children understanding and using "gazzinta." Her explanation made perfect sense to me, since members of the research team had been discussing the work for some time, but the Japanese were baffled. Eventually, one of them raised his hand to ask for an explanation of this new concept, "gazzinta." Andrea was nonplussed. "Goes in to" she said, slowly and with exaggerated intonation, and then demonstrated the entire procedure for determining how many times 7 gazzinta 46. Even then several of the Japanese remained confused. A conversation in a mixture of English and Japanese ensued. At the end it appeared that everyone understood the implications of their confusion for understanding the situation of schoolchildren encountering new concepts more rapidly than they can assimilate them.

The fourth grader encountering long division for the first time faces a far more difficult task than our Japanese colleagues, who knew the concepts involved in division as well as the process of estimating the probable quotient. The child hears the word, gazzinta, and seeks, like the Japanese visitors, to figure out its meaning. But teachers do not say what gazzinta means. In fact, it probably is not possible to give an unambiguous explanation of gazzinta for someone who does not already understand the concept. Gazzinta involves an iterative estimation procedure that is a combination of multiplication and subtraction carried out on the number line.

Faced with the difficulty of explaining the concept of gazzinta, the teacher created a "sure-fire" procedure that children could use to produce the correct answer. Suppose that the problem was $17 \div 3$. If a child did not figure out that 6 was a likely quotient with some prompting, the teacher told him to go through the multiplication table for the divisor: $1 \times 3 = 3$, $2 \times 3 = 6$, and so on. Often she put the requisite times table on the blackboard next to the problem the children were supposed to solve. As she walked the children through several problems, they began to find shortcuts to the cumbersome, but certain, trip through the multiplication table. With practice, some began to do what skilled adults do—use their knowledge of the multiplication facts in a flexible manner to make rapid estimates and then fine-tune their answers. However, few children exhibited such fluency during the experiment.

When the children began to catch on to what was being requested of them and no longer needed to resort to the written-out times tables, we noticed a strange phenomenon. The teacher and a child might be talking about different parts of the same problem (for example, the teacher saying something about the quotient, the child something about the dividend), but without noticeable disruption in the conversation the child would arrive at the correct answer. It was as if teacher and child were in close enough coordination, despite discrepancies in the precise part of the problem they were referring to, to permit the action to unfold.

These and similar observations in the other curriculum models led us to reconceptualize the notion of cognitive task. Our initial conception of a cognitive task—a goal and the conditions for achieving it—now seemed inadequate to the diversity of interactions we observed. Not only do the conditions for achieving the goal change from situation to situation and from moment to moment, but the goal itself may disappear, reappear, and change.

Moreover, it became clearly problematic to talk about "the" task, given the different perspectives of different participants. Even standardized psychological experimental tasks are interpreted differently by different participants; it is just that the interactions are set up so that only one "official" interpretation is accepted. Within this framework, there is no category of "doing a different task." There is only doing more or less well on "the" task.

We concluded that cognitive tasks are best thought of not as fixed entities but as strategic fictions that participants use as a means of negotiating a common interpretation of the situation. In this sense, a cognitive task plays the role that Katherine Nelson ascribed to scripts; it is an interpersonal, public resource for coordinated action. There is no necessary one-to-one correspondence between the script considered as an interpersonal artifact and the script considered as internal cognitive representation.

At the end of our work with children in afterschool clubs described in Chapter 8, we had come away believing that ecological invalidity was built into the standard procedures of cognitive psychology. At the end of this follow-up project we arrived at a similar conclusion, now applied to the relation of basic psychological research to teaching practice. Psychologists who conduct diagnostic tests or learning experiments and teachers engaged in classroom instruction participate in markedly different forms of activity. Psychological-educational cognitive research has as its goal differential diagnosis of children's abilities and evaluation of teaching procedures that assume a one-to-one interaction between adult and child. If the child becomes unhappy, she can leave the experiment and return to her classroom, where no negative sanctions await.

Teachers must deal with twenty-five or thirty children at a time. While teachers also need to diagnose children's current levels of knowledge and skill, they must simultaneously create the conditions for increasing those skills. An issue like "giving too much help" during instruction is not likely to be important to a teacher. However, if the child gets discouraged and gives up, or becomes upset and leaves the classroom, it will certainly be a source of problems for the teacher as well as the child. From this perspective, it is little wonder that teachers so routinely find the output of educational-psychological research to be invalid in the working conditions of their everyday lives.

## A Re-medial Approach to Reading Instruction

Our work in the cooking clubs described in Chapter 8 left us impressed with how much Archie was capable of learning, despite the difficulty he experienced in reading. Inspired by his abilities as much as by his problems, we proposed a full-blown project focused on children labeled learning disabled using a version of our "same task, different setting" strategy.[2] In place of a single child labeled learning disabled (LD) we decided to study a classroom of children labeled in this manner and to treat the children as a set of unique cases to be studied in depth for at least a year. Each child would be observed in the regular classroom, during special education training by the school's learning disability specialist, on the playground during recess, in the neighborhood after school, and at home. Each child would also be given a battery of standard tests consisting of tasks widely used to make judgments about learning disabilities, and would undergo extensive cognitive skills training. Those were the plans.

The research got off to an encouraging start. We found two schools with diverse populations of children in terms of their demographic makeup, active programs for children who were identified by the school as poor readers, and sympathetic remedial learning specialists. We planned to use one school as the locus of the cognitive training interventions and the other for comparison purposes. Beginning with the first school, we made baseline observations of the children in the various settings and administered a standardized test for purposes of identifying the range of profiles that the children presented. We discovered that if we judged by the test scores, the children were a diverse group indeed, including a few who fit classic profiles of LD children and many who did not.

Before long, however, the teachers began to express discomfort at our presence in their classrooms. We were a nuisance, tolerated but not welcomed by busy teachers who could see no immediate payoff for their work in what we were doing. Despite support from the resource room teacher and the principal, classroom teachers wanted to restrict our access to the children in ways that would have rendered the research useless from our perspective. Since we had begun standardized testing at the second school, we decided to move the focus of our work there. Much to our dismay, there too the teachers wanted to restrict our access to children.

We had a great deal of sympathy for the teachers' point of view. They were under heavy pressure to raise the reading scores of their children *now*. A new curriculum mandated by the school district specified precise amounts of time they should be spending on each topic at each part of the day. They might have been more sympathetic if we could have assured them that our research would improve the educational performance of the poor readers more than their own efforts would, but of course we were in no position to offer such a guarantee.

Faced with this crisis, Peg Griffin and Bud Mehan met with the teachers and the principal as a group to see what could be done. The teachers agreed, reluctantly, to our presence in their classrooms. But they imposed further restrictions that would have thoroughly undermined the research.

At this point, the project almost folded. Unwilling to give up and unwilling to continue under the constraints that were being imposed on us, we proposed moving the entire operation from the school day to after school. Instead of observing the children's educational activities during the school day, we would create our own lessons with our own curriculum content and then contrast behavior in those settings with the others outlined in our original proposal.

The principal allowed us to use the school library. We invited all of the children who had previously been identified for our study to participate. On December 7, 1981, we opened "Field College" to twenty-four children, about half of whom fit the clinical definition of learning disabled.

The early history of this effort, which continued for another two years, is summarized in a report completed the summer after we began to take responsibility for teaching children to read as a fundamental aspect of our research (LCHC, 1982). In brief, led by Peg Griffin, we created four different curriculum modules, each of which drew upon extant research on reading acquisition.[3] The children were divided into two groups of twelve, and came on Monday and Wednesday or Tuesday and Thursday. Each module was implemented with a group of about six children.

One of the first lessons this effort brought home to us was the enormous amount of work that goes into designing and implementing a curriculum. Were it not for Peg Griffin's expertise and tireless efforts, the research would have proven a fiasco. Instead, each curriculum module produced evidence that the children were learning and each provided us with interesting data about their difficulties.

Perhaps the other major lesson was that in moving reading instruction from the school day to after school, we were moving from an institutional setting backed by legal sanctions to one that was voluntary. The same was true in the case of the afterschool clubs we had conducted at Rockefeller University, but we felt it less there because the club sessions were held only once a week and they had no mandatory pedagogical component—they were designed to be fun and by and large the children treated them as fun. But how does one make reading instruction fun for a group of children who have been failing to learn to read for two to four years in their classrooms, most recently earlier the same day?

We tried to make the curriculum models interesting by making them small-group activities that kept the children actively involved. We also arranged for the children who were not involved in reading to play computer games. When disciplinary problems arose we dealt with them in a variety of ways. The major strategy was to respond to disruptive behavior indirectly in an attempt to subvert it, creating elaborations of the instructional scripts that appropriated activities favored by the children (such as drawing or crumpling paper into wads to throw). We resorted to direct control only when physical damage was threatened. In such cases, we reminded the children that participation was voluntary, and said we would be happy to escort them home. In only one case did we exclude a child from participation—because he threatened severe harm to a staff member and himself. In a few other cases, we did escort children home. But in general the children preferred to stay and engage in the activities with us.

## Traditional Theories of Reading Acquisition

The study I report on in this section was carried out during the second year of Field College, after we had established relatively stable and workable routines. It focused on the diagnosis and re-mediation of children's reading difficulties as part of a single system of activity.

There is broad agreement that reading is a complex skill requiring the coordination of several related subprocesses and sources of information, and a great deal is known about the processes involved for those who have acquired some degree of skill (Crowder and Wagner, 1992). But despite intensive research throughout this century, and especially over the past two decades, the process of acquisition remains disputed (see Adams, 1990, for a juxtaposition of conflicting views). The problem is an important one because at present a great many children of normal intelligence fail to acquire reading skills deemed adequate for productive participation in modern societies (Miller, 1988).

Modern approaches to reading have distinguished two, presumably distinct, major components of reading: decoding (the process by which letters of the alphabet are associated with corresponding acoustic patterns) and comprehension (the process by which meaning is assigned to resulting visual/acoustic representation). Within this seemingly obvious dichotomy, theorists differ on the questions of how to sequence instruction (whether to emphasize code or meaning first) and how best to help children "break the code" (by teaching phonetic analysis or by teaching whole words).

An example of a "code first" approach can be found in the work of Jean Chall (1983) who proposes the following stage theory of reading development (I concentrate here on the early stages that apply to the children with whom we worked):

Stage 0: Prereading. Children at this stage may pretend to read and know some letter names.

Stage 1: Decoding. The basic task of Stage 1 is to learn the arbitrary set of letters in the alphabet and to decode their correspondence to the sounds of spoken language.

Stage 2: Confirmation, fluency, ungluing from print. New readers confirm and solidify the gains of the previous stage. To avoid confusion, they are given familiar texts which do not demand much mental effort to comprehend.

Stage 3: Reading for learning something new. Instead of relating print to speech, children now are asked to relate print to ideas. It is only at this stage, writes Chall, that "reading begins to compete with other means of knowing."

In the two remaining stages, children elaborate their comprehension skills, learning to juxtapose facts and theories and to construct complex ideas with the help of print.

Critics of this approach to instruction (Goodman and Goodman, 1990) start from the assumption that children living in a literate society arrive at school with the rudiments of reading-as-comprehending-the-world-through-print already in their repertoires; for example, children can read various road signs, pick out the McDonald's logo, and perhaps recognize their own names in print. Unlike Chall's approach, the Goodmans' model of acquisition is nondevelopmental in the sense that acquisition does not entail the emergence of any new process or the reorganization of old ones. All children need from the beginning of formal instruction is to expand the repertoire of functions they can accomplish with the aid of print. This expansion occurs naturally with the accretion of experience in comprehending the world through print. Consequently, mastery of the code goes hand in hand with expanding the functions to which reading is put.

## A Cultural-Mediational Model

Like Chall, my colleagues and I believe that reading is a developmental process and that the goal of reading instruction is to provide means for children to reorganize their interpretive activity using print. Like the Goodmans, we believe that reading text is an elaboration of the preexisting ability to "read the world" using signs of various kinds.

The approach we developed is distinctive in its simultaneous emphasis on three interrelated points. First, we believe that reading instruction must emphasize both decoding and comprehension in a single, integrated activity (an assumption that can be interpreted in terms of the idea that reading requires the coordination of "bottom up" (feature → letter → word → phrase → . . .) and "top down" (knowledge-based, comprehension-driven) processes out of which new schemas emerge (McClelland and Rumelhart, 1981).

Second, we believe that under ordinary circumstances, adults play an essential role in coordinating children's activity such that the development of reading becomes possible. Put differently, reading acquisition is a joint activity, and needs to be treated as such.

Third, we believe that successful adult efforts depend crucially on their organizing a "cultural medium for reading" which has the properties of culture that I have been emphasizing here: it must use artifacts (most notably, but not only, the text), it must be proleptic, and it must orchestrate social relations to coordinate the child with the to-be-acquired system of mediation in an effective way.

Figure 9.2, which repeats the structure of Figure 5.1, but with Text substituted for Artifact, reminds us that reading, in the broadest sense, requires the coordination of information from two routes. Any reader must "see" the world as refracted through a text; but in order for this to be possible, the reader's more direct access to the world, topicalized by the text, must be simultaneously engaged. As in the general discussion of mediation in Chapter 5, the mediational process depicted in Figure 9.2 is a timeless ideal. Even among skilled readers, the act of coordinating the two routes often requires adjustments in the representation of the "worlds" arrived at by either route to permit a new representation (expanded understanding) to emerge. The slight discoordination depicted in Figure 9.3 more accurately reflects the dynamic process that I have in mind. Here comprehension is depicted as the emergent outcome of information coming from the "two routes," and time is explicitly excluded.

With this minimal structural apparatus in hand, we can now turn to the crucial question: Assuming that children do not enter school

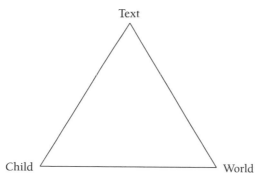

Figure 9.2.   The basic mediational triangle with text replacing the generic subject-medium-object representation.

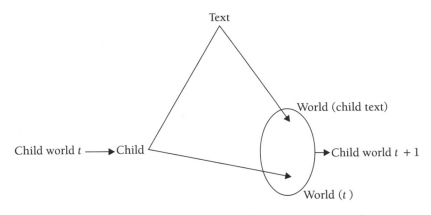

Figure 9.3.   The closed system in Figure 9.2 represented as a dynamic system of coordination in which the child's understanding at time *t* must be coordinated with the changes wrought by mediation through the text to arrive at a new interpretation at time *t* + 1.

able to expand their ability to comprehend their experience by reading alphabetic text, how can we arrange for them to develop this new system of mediated action? In attempting to answer this question, we are simultaneously tackling the crucial question of how it is possible to acquire a more powerful cognitive structure unless, in some sense, it is already present to begin with. This question, called the paradox of development by Fodor (1983) and the learning paradox by Bereiter (1985), calls into doubt any developmental account of reading that fails to specify the preexisting constraints that make development possible. Bringing the endpoint "forward" to the beginning is not less relevant in developing the ability to read than in any other developmental process.

Developmental theories of reading such as Chall's are vulnerable to the learning paradox. Since we share her belief that the acquisition of reading is a developmental process requiring a qualitative reorganization of behavior (a process we refer to as "re-mediation," that is, mediating in a new way), we must begin by showing in what sense the endpoint of development, the ability to mediate one's comprehension of the world through print, could be present in embryonic form at the outset of instruction.

A solution to this problem is to invoke Vygotsky's (1978) "general genetic law of cultural development": functions that initially appear

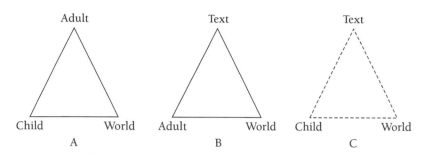

Figure 9.4. The to-be-coordinated systems of mediation that exist when a novice begins to learn to read from an expert. (A) The child can mediate interactions with the world via an adult. (B) The adult can mediate interactions with the world via text. (C) The child-text-adult relationship is the goal of instruction.

on the interpsychological plane shared between people can then become intrapsychological functions of the individual. In this case, what we seek is the structural endpoint of mature reading in the interaction between child and adult as a *precondition* for this new structure of activity to appear as an individual psychological function in the child.

Figure 9.4 displays in graphic form the fact that at the beginning of instruction there are two preexisting mediational systems which can be used as resources for creating the necessary structural constraints to permit the development of reading in the child. At the far left of the figure we represent the commonsense fact that children enter reading instruction with years of experience mediating their interactions with the world via adults. In the center we represent the equally commonsense fact that literate adults routinely mediate their interactions through text. Finally, on the far right of the figure is the to-be-developed system of mediation for the child that is our target.

Figure 9.5 shows the next stage in the analytic/ instructional strategy: the given and to-be-developed systems of child mediation are juxtaposed and the given adult system is then superimposed, to reveal the skeletal structure of an "interpsychological" system of mediation that, *indirectly*, establishes a dual system for the child, which permits the coordination of text-based and prior-world-knowledge-based information of the kind involved in the whole act of reading.

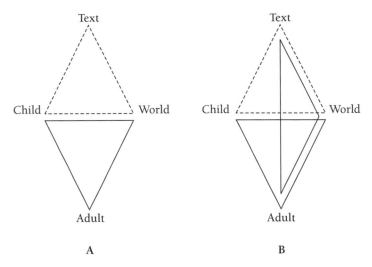

Figure 9.5.   The juxtaposition of existing and to-be-formed systems of mediation that have to be coordinated. (A) The two existing systems. (B) The two existing systems plus the to-be-formed system.


### Creating the Activity: Question-Asking-Reading

The instructional/developmental task is now better specified: we must somehow create a system of interpersonal interaction such that the combined child-adult system at the right of Figure 9.5 can co-ordinate the child's act of reading before she can accomplish this activity for herself. Our strategy for accomplishing this goal was a modification of the reciprocal teaching procedure of Ann Brown and Ann-Marie Palinscar (1982), in which teacher and student silently read a passage of text and then engage in a dialogue about it. Together they summarize the text, clarify comprehension problems that arise, ask a question about the main idea, and predict the next part of the text. In part because the children we were dealing with still had dif-ficulty decoding text, and in part because we wanted to make the activity as interesting as possible, we expanded the number of roles and chose texts that we thought would be of interest to the children (see LCHC, 1982, for additional details). In so doing, we both ma-nipulated the division of labor and provided as attractive a goal as possible.

The core of the procedure is a set of roles or division of labor.

Each role corresponds to a different hypothetical part of the whole act of reading. The roles are printed on index cards. Every participant is responsible for fulfilling at least one role in the full activity of Question-Asking-Reading. The cards specify the following roles:

The person who asks about words that are hard to say.
The person who asks about words that are hard to understand.
The person who asks a question about the main idea of the passage.
The person who picks the person to answer questions asked by others.
The person who asks about what is going to happen next.

All participants including the instructor have a copy of the text to read, paper and pencil to jot down words, phrases, or notes (in order to answer questions implicit in the roles), and their card to remind them of their role. The steps in the scripted procedure are written on the blackboard where answers are recorded. All these artifacts represent tools to be used by the adults to create a structured medium for the development of reading and by the children to support their participation, even before they know how to read.

In order to move from the script and other artifacts to the process of reading instruction, we embedded the procedural script in a complex activity designed to make salient both the short-term and long-term goals of reading and to provide a means of coordinating around the script. It is in this embedding process that we make the transition from a focus on the structural model of reading depicted in Figures 9.2–9.5 to a focus on reading acquisition as a joint activity.

Recognizing the need to create a medium rich in goals that could be resources for organizing the transition from reading as a guided activity to independent, voluntary reading, we saturated the environment with talk and activities about growing up and the role of reading in a grown-up's life. This entire activity was conducted in the global activity structure we called Field Growing-Up College (it took place in the auditorium of the Field Elementary School). As part of their application to participate in Field College, of which Question-Asking-Reading was a major activity, the children filled out applications that emphasized the relationship between reading and growing up. They got involved with us in discussions about the difference between growing older and growing up as well as how our reading activities related to their goal of growing up.

As shown in Figure 9.6, Question-Asking-Reading began each session with such "goal talk," discussion about the various reasons that children might have for wanting to learn to read. These included such poorly understood reasons (from the children's point of view) as the need to read in order to obtain an attractive job such as becoming an

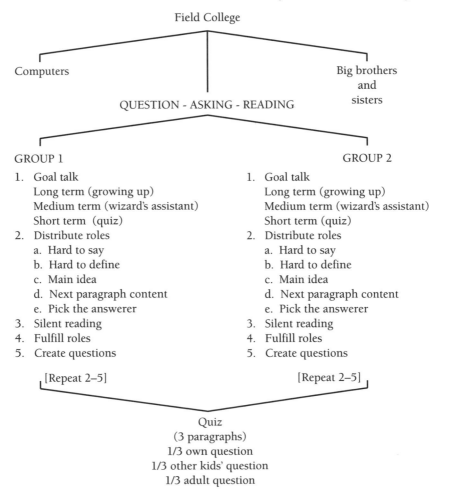

Figure 9.6.  The overall structure of Question-Asking-Reading at Field College.

astronaut, intermediate-level goals such as graduating from Question-Asking-Reading to assisting adults with computer-based instruction, to quite proximate goals—such as getting correct answers on the quiz at the end of each reading session.

We began with a group discussion of the title or headline of the story to be read that day. Following the script outline shown in Figure 9.6, which was written on the blackboard, the role-bearing cards were passed around. A good deal of talk usually ensued about who had gotten what roles; "pick the answerer" was an obvious favorite, while the card implicating the main idea was avoided like the plague. Once the cards were distributed, the text for the day (usually taken from local newspapers with content that related to matters of potential interest to the children) was distributed, one paragraph at a time. The participants (including the instructor and one competent reader, usually an undergraduate, as well as the children) then bent over their passages to engage in silent reading.

This system of instruction, which we referred to by its initials (QAR), is an example of a design experiment for creating reading with meaning (Brown, 1992). It was designed to be a zone of proximal development working at the level of small groups, and it has the proleptic property that Courtney Cazden (1981) attributes to zones of proximal development, providing for "performance before competence." Children were not required to do the "whole act of reading" in order to participate in QAR. They were asked to fulfill partial roles which, as an ensemble, constituted many overlapping moments of reading for meaning. QAR allows the children to participate in the whole act of reading-as-comprehending, where initially the adults and the artifacts bear a large part of the load, but where children come to be fuller participants (that is, competent readers) over time.

Initially QAR was strange to everyone, even the adult researchers, who were inventing it as they went along. But after a few sessions a microculture had grown up around QAR. Rituals emerged, such as having a snack to begin the session and a period to run around outside while the adults quickly made up the day's quiz. Everyone got to play all of the roles. The adults had no less role-playing to do than the kids, dividing their attention between being a member of the group and being the group leader. These and other procedural arrangements constituted our attempt to organize a medium which would repeatedly create moments when the three mediational triangles depicted in Figure 9.3 would be coordinated to create the conditions for *re*-mediating the children's entering systems of mediation.

## The Data

Our evidence for the way this procedure worked is derived from several sources: videotaped recordings of the instructional sessions, the children's written work on the quizzes, and various test results. Although we gathered data from the beginning of the first session, the crucial evidence for our analysis came after several sessions when the children had mastered the overall script so that the group was working as a coordinated structure of interaction.

Our strategy was greatly influenced by Alexander Luria's monograph *The Nature of Human Conflicts* (1932), devoted largely to an experimental procedure designed to reveal "hidden psychological processes," such as thoughts and feelings. The basic idea of Luria's procedure, which he called "the combined motor method," was to create a scripted situation where a subject had simultaneously to carry out a motor response (squeeze a bulb) and a verbal response (give the first word that comes to mind) when presented with a stimulus word.

In the most dramatic form of this procedure, which has subsequently been incorporated into lie-detector systems, Luria interrogated suspected criminals. He began by presenting either simple tones or neutral words until the subject could respond rapidly and smoothly. Then, among the neutral words, he would present a word that had special significance in the crime (handkerchief, for example, if a handkerchief had been used to gag a victim). He argued that *selective* disruption of the smoothly coordinated baseline system of behavior revealed the subject's special state of knowledge.

In place of a bulb to squeeze and deliberate deception, our concern was with texts, role cards, and the selective disruption of the smoothly running script of Question-Asking-Reading. Hence, it was of paramount importance that we create the conditions for a smoothly coordinated joint activity mediated by the roles, special artifacts, and text.

The first few sessions, while the children were learning to perform the scripted activity, were anything but smooth. We were assisted by undergraduates who participated in Field College as "older siblings." The presence of at least two adults, the researcher and the undergraduate, meant that at a minimum two participants were coordinated through the script and engaged in the full act of reading. Eventually the children got the hang of how to participate in Question-Asking-Reading *even if they had severe difficulties reading*, thereby creating the conditions for diagnosing the "hidden psychological processes" that interfered with their reading.

⑥ Here I will concentrate on the *in situ* process of coordination and discoordination around the scripted activity as a key source of evidence about individual children's ability to internalize the scripted roles. It is at this microgenetic level that we can observe the points where internalization *fails*, resulting in selective discoordinations of the ongoing activity structure. In the example to follow, two children, both of whom are failing in their reading classes, differentially discoordinate with the publicly available scripted activity, permitting differential diagnosis of their specific difficulties.

At the start of the transcripts, the two boys, Billy and Armandito, are starting to read the second paragraph of the day. Katie is their teacher and Larry is an additional competent reader. Evidence for internalization of the scripted activity is provided by instances in which the children's talk and actions presuppose a next step in the procedure without overt provocation from the adults.

1. *Katie:* OK, lets go on to the second paragraph then.
2. *Billy:* How did they find them?
3. *Armandito:* The Eskimos.
4. *Katie:* I think it was an accident (as she says this, she begins to pass out the role cards, face down).
5. *Billy:* (Taking a card from the stack). How come, what kind of accident?
6. *Billy:* (Looking at his card). That's the same card again.

In line 2, Billy's question is an internalized version of the "what's going to happen next" role in the script that no one has specifically stimulated. He takes the card handed to him, asks a relevant question about the text, and comments on the relationship between his role in the previous segment of interaction and what he is about to do. He is coordinated through the script.

Armandito's participation is of a different order. His comment in line 3 is relevant to the topic at hand, but opaque. He does not take one of the role cards and has to be stimulated by Katie while Billy continues to show evidence of coordination:

7. *Katie:* Armandito! (He looks up and takes a card.)
8. *Billy:* We each get another one (referring to the cards; there are only four participants and Katie has not taken one, so someone will get an extra).

In a number of places in the transcript we see Armandito discoordinating within the activity which the other three participants maintain, permitting him to recoordinate from time to time. These discoordinations are of several types. The most obvious are such actions as drawing a picture instead of reading, or feigning abandonment of the activity altogether. But repeatedly, Armandito presupposes the scripted activity sufficiently to motivate quite specific analyses of his difficulties. The next example illustrates his aversion to the question about the main idea and provides information (corroborated in many examples) about his core difficulty:

9. *Larry:* (He has the card which says to pick the answerer.) Armandito. What's the main idea?
10. *Armandito:* I want to ask mine. I want to ask what happens next.
11. *Larry:* No. I know what you want, but I am asking. I pick the answerer.
12. *Armandito:* The main idea is . . . how these guys live.

Armandito is both accepting the joint task of Question-Asking-Reading ("I want to ask mine" ) and attempting to avoid the role that is at the heart of his problem (figuring out the main idea) by skipping that part of the scripted sequence. When he accepts his role (12) and attempts to state the main idea, his answer is not only vague, it is about the *previous* paragraph.

Through an accumulation of many such examples over several sessions, we were able to obtain a consistent pattern. This pattern showed that Billy found it difficult to come "unglued" from the letter-sound correspondences when he attempted to arrive at the main idea. When asked about the main idea, he repeatedly returned to the text and sought a "copy match" in which some word from the question appeared in the text. He then read the relevant sentence aloud, and puzzled over meaning. Armandito's problem was of a quite different order: he continually lost track of the relevant context, importing information from his classroom activities that day or previous reading passages which had no relevance.

The first conclusion to be drawn from this exercise is that we succeeded in creating a structured medium of activity which allowed diagnostically useful information about which part of the structure depicted in Figure 9.5 was deficient in the children with whom we worked. However, we also wanted to establish that QAR is an effective procedure for the acquisition of reading. Both Billy and Armandito did in fact improve their reading abilities, and Armandito's general behavior in the classroom changed so markedly that he won an award from the school recognizing his unusual progress. However, such individual change could not be attributed to QAR both because it was part of the larger activity system of Field College and because we had no proper control group.

To remedy these shortcomings, Catherine King (1988) replicated the small-group reading procedures in a follow-up experiment. Her study included appropriate control conditions, more stringently quantified pretest and posttest measures, and was conducted as the sole activity in a school prior to the start of regular classes.

In addition to testing the effectiveness of Question-Asking-Reading against a no-treatment control group, King included a group of children who were provided with the kind of structured intervention that Marlene Scardamalia and Carl Bereiter (1985) call "procedural facilitation," to assess whether the dynamic, dialogic characteristics of QAR were any more effective than workbook exercises in which children completed each of the tasks corresponding to the role cards individually in written form. The children in this experiment, like those in the original work illustrated in the transcript fragment, were selected from the upper elementary grades because of their difficulties in learning to read.

King found that both QAR and her version of the procedural facilitation technique boosted children's reading performance. How-

ever, children in the Question-Asking-Reading group retained significantly more material from the training passages than did those in
the procedural facilitation group. The students in the QAR group also
spent more total time actively engaged with the task and demonstrated a greater interest in the content of the readings, indicating an
intimate link between the motivational, social-interactional, and cognitive aspects of activity-in-context.

These results, although only sketchily presented here, provide support for the approach to reading I have summarized in this chapter.
Reading, we can conclude, is an emergent process of meaning making
that occurs when information topicalized by the text is synthesized
with prior knowledge as part of a general process of mediated interaction with the world. The acquisition of reading provides an excellent example of the social nature of developmental change.

As a means of bringing together the different parts of the overall
system of activity represented by QAR, consider Figure 9.7, a reinterpretation of Engeström's expanded model of mediation and activity
(Figure 5.3, p. 140). Here the individual triangles in Figures 9.2–9.6,
which focused exclusively on an assumed diadic relationship between child and adult, are expanded to represent the fact that several

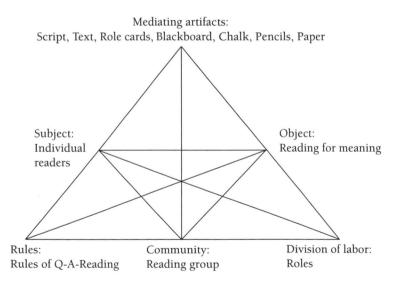

Figure 9.7.   Question-asking-reading represented in terms of the expanded activity system model.

participants in QAR were part of a larger set of ongoing afterschool activities. By interpreting QAR in terms of this expanded, social representation, we can represent the script and procedures as embodiments of the social rules, and the shifting division of labor enters explicitly into the overall schema. Looking upon the activity in this way reveals many resources for coordination that are only implicit in the individual analyses provided earlier.

## Re-mediation Reconsidered

I believe it is useful to conceive of the overall process of learning to read in developmental terms, as a process of *re*-mediation, mediating the behavior of the group and each individual within it in a qualitatively new way. Emphasizing the *re* in re-mediation also serves to remind us that the children were not blank slates at the start of instruction. Their behavior was mediated by language and other cultural artifacts and embodied social rules at the start; the challenge was to develop a new system of mediation adequate to the new demands of mediating action through print (literacy). Where this instructional process differs from other developmental approaches to reading acquisition is in its emphasis on the special role of the teacher in arranging the medium that coordinates preexisting systems of mediation in a single system of joint activity subordinated to the goal of comprehension.

Overall, I judge Question-Asking-Reading to be a successful application of cultural-historical theory to the problem of differential diagnosis and remediation of reading difficulties. The resulting system, when tested against a plausible alternative approach, proved more effective. In one respect, however, it was a failure. Once the research monies that had supported the "basic" aspect of the work ran out, the fact that it actually might work in practice was of no consequence.

However, a different fate awaited the other half of Field College, the half that involved computers. The story of how the computer-mediated activities survived and flowered is the topic of Chapter 10.

# 10 ⑥

# A Multilevel Methodology
# for Cultural Psychology

ONE OF THE MOST interesting lessons from our work at Field College arose from the fact that we began to take responsibility for "culturing" the children with whom we worked. We had, in terms of the garden metaphor of culture, started out in the role of the agronomist who visits the garden, and then added to it the role of the gardener who tends the garden. Theory and practice became different moments in a single process of inquiry.

As our prior analyses of the processes of teaching and learning had suggested, being responsible for implementing an educational activity provides privileged access to the processes at work. As a practitioner I constantly found myself using theoretical principles to guide my interactions. When I subsequently observed tapes of those interactions, my theoretically motivated interpretations were heavily influenced by knowledge gained in my "co-constituter's role" as teacher.

In this regard I think it symptomatic that when Emily Cahan and Sheldon White (1992) described the research programs that characterize the second psychology, they noted that its practitioners were likely to be found in schools and clinics, "doing things for people." The research of the "second psychologists" combined the goals of theoretical understanding and practical results. It seemed a "soft" form of inquiry in comparison with the "hard," quantitative, experimental approach it sought to displace. Question-Asking-Reading fits well within the tradition of the second psychology.

The project to be discussed in this chapter shares this dual orientation to theory and practice. On the one hand, it is intended to deepen our understanding of the cultural mediation of mind and processes of cognitive development. On the other hand, it is designed to produce a change in everyday practices. It goes beyond our work at Field College by including the development of the activity system, as well as the children who participate in it, within its overall scope.

When we began, we organized our inquiry around an intensely practical question. Why is it that so many "proven" educational innovations fail to survive? Why can't they be sustained?

## Why Focus on Sustainability?

My interest in sustainability as a goal of educational reform was piqued by my early work in West Africa. It was not difficult to identify shortcomings of Liberian schools from the perspective of an American developmental psychologist or educator. Teachers used sing-song rote procedures to teach children superficial aspects of literacy and numeracy; most of the children were being taught in a language they barely knew; the hand-me-down texts were largely inappropriate to local cultural and social circumstances; drop-out rates were phenomenally high. As often as not the most visible consequence of schooling was alienation of the young from their parents and from the community's traditional forms of economic life.

The solution, I thought, was to create new forms of schooling that taught knowledge and skills vital to participation in modern economic, social, and political practices in the context of local skills, knowledge, and concerns. So obvious did this approach seem that I was surprised that I saw no such schools in my travels around the countryside.

Subsequent library research only deepened my puzzlement. I found a number of accounts of schools built along principles I thought appropriate (for example, Murray, 1929). The curriculum in these schools was a prudent mixture of training in local agricultural and craft skills and folklore, into which literacy and numeracy were introduced as tools of inquiry, record keeping, and communication. The schooling seemed an excellent embodiment of Dewey's ideas about making authentic experience the foundation of education. And the schools seemed to work; those who ran them reported that the children mastered the curriculum, including its more traditional, European-based aspects. But when I sought to determine what had subsequently happened to these schools, I found that they had, without exception, "gone back to bush."

While we were beginning to contemplate life after Field College, my interest in the question of sustainability was rekindled in the process of preparing a monograph for the National Research Council (Cole, Griffin, and LCHC, 1987). Our task was to identify barriers to the participation of women and minorities in technological fields of study.

Part way through that exercise an NRC staff member sent me a report prepared by the American Association for the Advancement of Science about successful technological education programs targeting women and minorities, the very topic we were supposed to be re-searching (AAAS, 1984). On the basis of an evaluation of 168 exper-imental programs, the report identified sixteen characteristics of the successful programs. Why, then, was our report necessary? Why were new programs, many of which lacked the essential characteristics identified in the AAAS report, being reinvented every year, including programs at my own university? Why, in short, were proven, effective, programs not sustained?

The simple answer in both the American and Liberian cases is that the effective programs were tolerated by the social institutions around them only so long as they "paid their own way": when outside funding dried up, they could not compete successfully for internal resources.

Obviously *all* innovations don't go away. Some come and stay for a long time, such as the use of IQ-like tests as measures of academic achievement or Thorndikean drill-and-practice methods to teach ba-sic academic skills. What factors determine whether an educational innovation is taken up or rejected?

## Model Activity Systems as a Research Tool

Recall from my description of Field College that Question-Asking-Reading was only half of the action. The other half was the specially constructed computer-mediated activity called the Fifth Dimension (5thD). In the course of the work at Field College, the 5thD proved to be a flexible activity with the power to engage children, undergraduates, and researchers in long periods of intense interaction. Although we could not devote as much time to it as we wished, we did videotape several sessions and found that we were able to capture many theoretically interesting teaching/learning events for later analysis (see Griffin and Cole, 1984, 1987).

On the basis of our limited experience with the 5thD, we believed it might be an effective tool for investigating the process of *sustaining* innovations. Its peculiar combination of education and play seemed a good candidate for the kind of activities many afterschool institutions might like to take on. We were also pretty sure the 5thD was not unique in showing promise in afterschool settings. We knew there were a variety of ways to attract children and engage them in intellectual activities after school (Moll, Anderson, and Diaz, 1985; Riel, 1985). But we did not know what the dimensions of that variety were, either with respect to potential host community institutions, child populations, or kinds of computer-mediated activity.

A research plan was born. We would create four afterschool computer-mediated programs in four institutions in a single community. We would run a practicum course in child development at UCSD as a source of "older siblings." We would trace each system over time to observe the processes of development that we were attempting to create. During this same period we would learn as much as we could about the history of the institutions we worked with and their current organization and practices. We specified the goal of sustainability as the continuation of community-university collaboration modeled on the 5thD after the special research funds ran out.[1]

We planned for the project, which began in 1986, to last four years. Year one would be devoted to goal formation—staff at each community institution, in collaboration with the project staff, would investigate a broad range of potential computer-mediated activities for children suitable to their site. Years two and three would be devoted to designing and running the system. Year four would be the "uptake year" during which each institution would work with the project staff to make adjustments needed to continue the project once the startup funding had been terminated. Analyzing the patterns of success and failure (assuming there was at least one success), we thought, would give us something interesting to say about the dynamics of innovation at the institutional level.

Of course our interest in development was not restricted to the "macro" level of the institutions. We knew the 5thD provided rich opportunities to study the microgenesis of development. We believed that if some children stayed with the program for two or three years we might be able to gather enough data at different levels of the overall system of activity to say something about the interconnections between development at the microgenetic, ontogenetic, and cultural-historical levels.

## The Basic Structure of the Fifth Dimension

A combination of practical and theoretical concerns shaped our goals in designing the 5thD computer-mediated activities. Practically speaking, we needed to design an activity that children wanted to participate in. We immediately were confronted with the need to merge children's interests in play and arcade-style games with our interest in educationally effective games.

A second goal was to create an activity thick in opportunities for written and oral communication about the goals and strategies used in problem solving. Whether we looked to Piaget who emphasized the importance of reflective abstraction, or Vygotsky who emphasized that thoughts are completed in the act of communicating, we found theoretical justification for making communication instrumental at every turn.

Third, aware of repeated findings that girls engage in computer-based activity less than boys and preferred different content, we sought to create a set of activities with a lot of variety in it. Both our concern to promote reading and writing and our concern to attract girls as well as boys motivated us to include telecommunication in the activity, since communicative writing was one area of computer involvement to which girls seemed to be attracted.

Fourth, we wanted to avoid a situation where access to particular games became a way of bribing children to do what we wanted. Insofar as possible, we wanted the rewards for engaging in a particular game or striving for a particular level to be intrinsic to the activity itself. To this end we sought to design the activity so that the most pervasive reward for success is greater choice of action within the broad set of specific activities in the system.

Figure 10.1 provides a schematic overview of the 5thD in one of its institutional settings. The basic structure of these core elements has remained relatively constant across generations, so I will speak of them in the ethnographic present. I will deal with historical change and variation in due time.

The central coordinating artifact at the heart of the 5thD is a maze divided into twenty-one "rooms," each of which (symbolically) contains two activities. The actual maze is usually constructed of cardboard and is about one square meter wide and three inches high. The rooms of the maze are connected by doors through which children

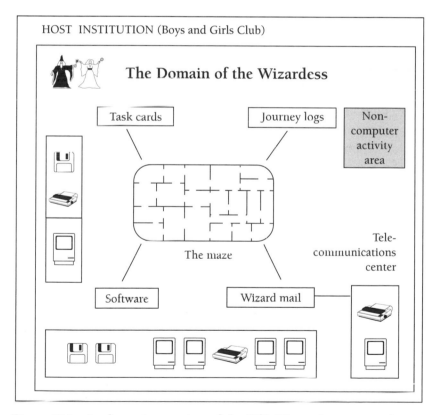

Figure 10.1. A schematic overview of the Fifth Dimension maze and other artifacts.

move tokens designating their location. Most, but not all, of the activities are instantiated as computer programs, including arcade and educational games; the remainder include arts and crafts and physical exercise.

The 5thD includes a variety of other standard artifacts in addition to computers and computer games:

A constitution with all of the rules printed on it.

A box containing record-keeping folders for each child.

At least one computer linked to a modem to enable children to communicate with distant places and with the Wizard.

Task cards that specify what one has to do to pass various levels of the game and give hints about ways to proceed.

A consequence chart that specifies "next rooms" which children can enter when they complete an activity at a specified level of expertise.

Tokens called "cruddy creatures" with children's names attached which are moved from room to room to mark the children's progress.

A "hints book" where good tips and strategies about playing the games are stored for others to consult.

A twenty-sided die used to make decisions about what room to go to in some circumstances.

According to the rules of the 5thD (contained in its constitution) the children make progress through the maze by completing the tasks associated with each game. In addition to the local goals of completing each game at one of its three levels, the 5thD provides for a variety of other goals, designed to appeal to a variety of children. For example, by traversing a path that takes them in one entrance and out another, they may "transform their cruddy creature" and obtain a more desirable figurine. Or they may choose to follow a path that will get them to a favorite game. Completion of the maze and "graduation" to higher status in the 5thD is achieved by completing half the games at the excellent level and the other half at the good level. This achievement is rewarded with a special t-shirt, often a party, and ascent to the status of Young Wizard's Assistant, which entails greater access to telecommunications and complex programs, as well as new duties and responsibilities.[2]

Two other features of the life-world of the Fifth Dimension require mention. The first is that ambiguous figure, the Wizard. It is said that the 5thD was a gift from a Wizard (or Wizardess) as a place for children to learn and play. The constitution was written by the Entity, who was available through e-mail or online chat to assist children in achieving their goals, to kibitz, and to arbitrate disputes.

Some of those disputes are about the Wizard Itself. There are ongoing discussions about who the Wizard is, where the Wizard lives, and what Its gender might be. The Entity, whatever It is, has a disorienting habit of changing genders in mid-sentence. That has led to the idea that It is a double entity, both male and female. There are also disputes about interpretation of the rules, about task card requirements, and about the quality of the games.

Disputes about the Wizard's personal being are never settled, but they allow recurring discussions about gender and power and responsibility. Disputes about rules tend to get settled by consensus. The Wizard admits to Its fallibility, and appreciates good arguments for improving the 5thD, which are incorporated as things go along. When children graduate to become Wizard's Assistants, the Wiz allows them to choose a new game for the 5thD, which the Wiz supplies as a gift to the activity as a whole.

Because the Wiz is in charge of the welfare of the system, the children and adults write to It when things go wrong (a game won't boot up, a task card is obscure). As a rule It is helpful, but It is often flaky in fulfilling responsibilities, and It has a terrible sense of humor. Because It is forgetful, necessary tasks (such as repairing computers) are neglected and things go wrong. In such circumstances, the participants criticize the Wizard and send It sharply worded letters of complaint.

The other feature requiring special comment is the content and organization of the maze. Figure 10.2 provides a more detailed schematic drawing of the Fifth Dimension maze with a listing of software in use during the 1995–1996 academic year. Notice that because there are two activities in each room, as well as multiple paths through the maze, children are confronted with choices at every step of the way. They can choose to continue playing the game at the same or a higher level or go to a new game in the same room. They can go to another room. Or they can go play elsewhere. In this manner we sought to allow them to satisfy their own goals within the con-

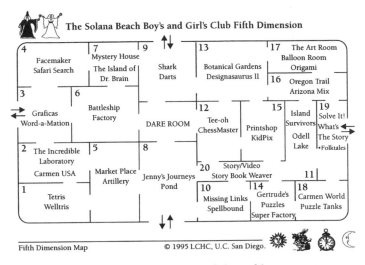

Figure 10.2. A schematic representation of the Fifth Dimension maze containing software used in the 1995-1996 academic year.

straints provided by the Fifth Dimension as a whole and to treat participation as genuinely *voluntary.*

One set of constraints was motivated by our experience with kids' tendency to gravitate to their favorite games and ignore the others. A major goal was to create a system that would get them to explore a wide variety of games. We also wanted to encourage attempts to get to higher levels of involvement even if the entering level was difficult. Several features of the Fifth Dimension address this problem. For example, at the top of Figure 10.3 we see the trajectories of activity children would experience if they completed all tasks at the beginner level. Note that by and large beginner-level achievement quickly leads to a dead end, where the child oscillates between two rooms. At the bottom of Figure 10.3 are the consequences of achievement at each level. This arrangement of pathways was chosen to make control over what game to play next the major institutional reward for completing difficult levels of the games; higher levels of achievement increase children's freedom of choice within the maze. They can use this freedom either to return to a favorite game or to pursue one of the other goals inhering in the 5thD.

Figure 10.4 illustrates the way that children's interactions within a game are structured using task cards. In this case the game is an

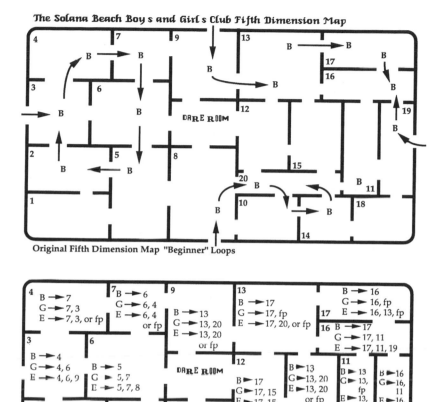

Figure 10.3. (top) Pathways through the Fifth Dimension if children choose to remain at the beginner level. (bottom) Choices open to children achieving at beginner, good, and expert levels. Note that the level of choice increases with the level of performance (fp = free pass).

# FACTORY

Welcome to Willy Wonka's Wacky factory! As the new supervisor in charge of new product development, it is your job to create new things!!!! You have various machines you can use to do this! These machines can punch holes in your product, rotate your product to a variety of angles, and even stripe your product with various sizes of stripes. The purpose of your factory is to design some cool new products. In fact, your job as supervisor depends on it. You had better get STARTED!!!!!!!!

**BEGINNER:** Begin by testing the machines. To do this, type #1. At the bottom of the screen you have the choice to punch, rotate or stripe. Select punch. Then choose circle, then one. You will see the board enter the machine and the result will be a square with a circle punched in the middle. Test all the machines. Then make a product that is a square, with a cross made of two medium stripes, with a round hole right in the middle.

**GOOD:** Do the Beginner Level. Then go on and do some CHALLENGES! Do EASY level challenges with "Make a Product" until you get three right on your first try!! Write to the **Wizard** and describe what your challenge products looked like and tell the **Wiz** how many machines it took you to create the product. (HINT: Better keep track by writing some things down!!)

**EXPERT:** Pick "Make a Product" to try to figure out how to make the products that the computer challenges you to do!! Figure out how to make three different products at the ADVANCED LEVEL! Write to the **Wizard** and describe for **ME** what each product looked like and the machines you used to make them!! Or write to a child at another 5th Dimension with a Factory Challenge! Describe for them one of your products and challenge them to make an Expert level product of their own and write to YOU about it!

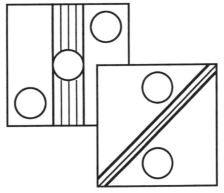
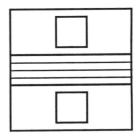

Figure 10.4. Sample of a task card used to structure a child's interactions with a game. In this example, the game is Factory, produced by the Sunburst Corporation.

embodiment of a Piagetian formal operations problem. In reading through the task cards, note that the beginning level provides the child with a relatively accessible goal that remains entirely within the predesigned computer program structure. But for both the "good" and "expert" levels the child must not only complete actions specified by the software but write about the strategies used and knowledge gained. Sometimes this writing is for a "hints" box to be used by others, sometimes to children at other sites, and sometimes to the Wizard.[3]

## Social Organization of the Fifth Dimension

The prior section conveys some idea of how the 5thD "works" as an activity system. But it is insufficient to describe the artifacts of a culture without saying something about the social relations they mediate. A double articulation is required: attention must also be paid to the social rules that mediate the way the artifacts mediate social relations.

From our experience with organizing the reading groups at Field College, we had already come to appreciate the powerful role of the undergraduates in their interactions with children. Routinely they played with the children in a way that involved a lot of mediation of actions through print. We counted on the fact that the undergraduates occupy a "real life" position between the researchers and the children. They are like the researchers in being "big people" who come from the university. They are like the children in that they are still in school, still being graded, and still struggling with adult authority.

We refer to the undergraduates as Wizard's Assistants, who are there to be the children's friends and helpers. This role assignment seems to work well. The undergraduates, no less than the children (and the researchers!) have a lot to learn to be skillful players of many of the games and users of the telecommunications facilities. But compared with the children, they know a lot about reading and about trying hard in the face of adversity in school. By virtue of their intermediate status between the researchers and the children, the undergraduates change the power dynamics of the interactions between adults and children.

The normative rule of thumb that guides pedagogical practices in the 5thD is to provide the children with as little help as possible, but as much help as necessary to ensure that both the students and the children have a good time (this heuristic will be recognized as a possible "rule of thumb" implementation of Vygotsky's notion of interactions in the zone of proximal development). After every session of the 5thD the students write detailed fieldnotes about their interactions with the children, the Wizardess, the software, and the life of the 5thD. These fieldnotes are primary data about the workings of this cultural system.

The participants in the 5thD are a heterogeneous lot, not only in terms of age but in terms of the length of their participation and expertise. At UCSD, which divides its academic year into three ten-week quarters, the 5thD goes through three eight-week sessions per year. The undergraduates enroll in a course entitled Practicum in Child Development, which they are allowed to repeat for credit. Children are allowed to attend year after year. Consequently, participants include a mix of children from roughly six to twelve years of age, undergraduates, and researchers, some of whom are "old timers," others "newcomers."

An interesting feature of this arrangement is that cultural knowledge, status, and age are not tightly linked: very often the children have more knowledge about the computers, games, and norms of the 5thD than the undergraduates. This unusually heterogeneous distribution of knowledge and skill is a great resource for reordering everyday power relations, thereby creating interesting changes in the typical division of labor.

In the fall of 1987 we "planted" the 5thD in three different community institutions: a library, a daycare center, and a boys and girls club (hereafter BGClub) in a coastal town near the UCSD campus. Then we sought to nurture these programs and cultivate their growth while we observed what happened.

## Theorizing the Fifth Dimension

Several of the metaphors about culture, context, and artifact-mediated activity discussed in earlier chapters provide useful tools for thinking about the 5thD and the forms of development it embodies. I have already invoked the garden metaphor and will do so as I go along.

I also think about the 5thD as a tertiary artifact in which the reality of everyday life is put slightly askew. The various primary artifacts (computers, pencils, modems, and so on) and secondary artifacts (including the constitution, the task cards, and special rituals for children who graduate to becoming Young Wizard's Assistants) come to life when they are taken up by the participants and used to mediate actions as a part of the overall activity. Each 5thD session requires the adults (researchers and undergraduates) to collude with one another and the children in the pretense that they are playing games provided by a Wizard of doubtful gender who can only be reached through a computer network. The children, many initially attracted by computer games, quickly sense that playing in the 5thD is not the same as playing the arcade game available for a quarter in the next room. It is a place where you have to read and write a good deal but where the grownups must be playing let's pretend because they talk about a wizard and argue about its gender. The pretending makes the grownups more fun to play with than usual.

Considered as a tertiary artifact, the 5thD is instrumental in different senses, depending upon one's place in the system and hence one's perspective and experience. All participants in this "alternative reality" experience interpersonal interactions which, while not without conflict, are emotionally satisfying because the participants are licensed to have fun with others. It is instrumental to the staff of the club and to parents because they approve of the activities the children are engaged in. In addition to accumulating course credits, participation is instrumental for the undergraduates, both in terms of mastering valued technical skills and for reevaluating their interest in working with children once they leave college. The 5thD is instrumental to the researchers because it provides a rich medium of research. And finally, it is instrumental to the children as a place to play with computers and prestigious young adults who are genuinely interested in them.

As a practical heuristic for keeping straight the different levels and threads of analysis, I have found it useful to think of the overall system using the 5thD in terms of the "embedded contexts" representation of ecological psychology and contextualism. Figure 10.5

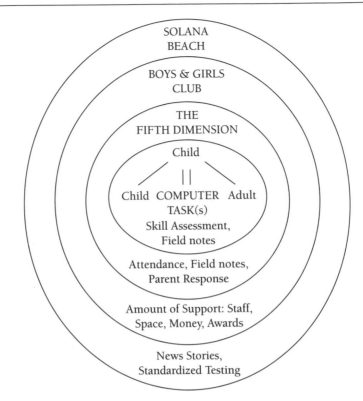

Figure 10.5. The "culture as garden" metaphor of context applied to the Fifth Dimension. The innermost circle corresponds to the level of face-to-face interaction between adults and children engaged in computer-mediated activities. The next circle represents the activity as a whole. Successive circles represent higher levels of context. Each level of context is evaluated according to criteria specific to it.

uses this framework to schematize the levels of context involved in a single 5thD activity system in a single institutional setting. Using this approach it seems natural to view one or two children and an undergraduate playing a computer game together as the innermost unit of analysis, the level where face-to-face joint mediated activity occurs. It is here that we observe the process of microgenetic change. Our evidence about the working of the system at this level comes from videotapes, fieldnotes, children's records of achievement, and assessment tests built into the task cards. At the level of the 5thD as a whole, the "cultural-historical" level, the same set of data sources is relevant, but so are simple social indicators such as the number of children who appear each day, the relative proportion of boys and girls, and accumulation of new artifacts, ranging from rituals (the Wizard's birthday) to maps, lists, and new computer games. Evaluation at the level of the institution includes assessment of the resources provided for running the activity and the ways in which the activity is, or is not, incorporated into the bureaucratized routine and budget of the institution.

In principle, as I emphasized in Chapter 5, each level of such a system both constitutes and is constituted by the level above it and below it. The ways in which games are played both affects and is affected by the quality of the 5thD as an overall activity system. The quality of the 5thD, in turn, affects and is affected by the way it is constituted in relation to its institutional context. Showing such connections between data features at different levels of the system as well as interactions among features over time that embody the levels is a major long-term goal of the analysis.

Our focus on sustainability adds a new dimension to the system we had created that is not present in the embedded contexts diagram—time. Analysis of change in the 5thD includes studying with the children in the microgenetic and ontogenetic time domains, while simultaneously studying the growth of the activity system and coordination among institutions in "mesogenetic" time, a few years of cultural-historical time.

## The Fifth Dimension as a Cultural System

One ordinarily thinks of cultures in terms of some relatively large social group, such as "all the people on Manus island when Margaret Mead arrived there for a visit in the 1920s" or even "all the people in a large nation-state" (French culture). But according to the definition of culture given in Chapter 5, culture comes into being wherever people engage in joint activity over a period of time. We recognize this fact intuitively through our experience of the "microcultures" we encounter in gymnasiums, car dealerships, schools, and hospitals, where we enter as strangers into ongoing social worlds with their own ways of doing things and ways of talking.

The minimal requirements for the emergence of culture were studied several decades ago by Rose and Felton (1955), who created small groups to work together to complete an idiosyncratic and somewhat complicated task. They found that members quickly begin to invent new vocabulary and ways of doing things, primary and secondary artifacts. When new members were introduced to an already established group, they quickly acquired its special ways, while perhaps introducing innovations of their own.

This process at work in the 5thD is apparent to anyone who walks into the room while the activity is in progress: at first it seems chaotic and formless: there are children and adults engaged in a wide variety of tasks; they move around in hard-to-understand patterns; they are excited by invisible events; they say odd things ("Wildcat is down!"; "Right 45 degrees"; "Katmandu"; "I hate the Wizard"); and so on.

In thinking about the 5thD as a cultural system I have drawn upon the ideas of Gary Alan Fine (1987), who participated in and wrote about the culture of Little League baseball. Fine remarks "Culture includes the meaningful traditions and artifacts of a group; ideas, behaviors, verbalization, and material objects" (p. 124). He calls the cultural formation that emerges in a small group an *idioculture,* which he defines as a "system of knowledge, beliefs, behaviors, and customs shared by members of an interacting group to which members can refer and that serve as the basis of further interaction. Members recognize that they share experiences, and these experiences can be referred to with the expectation they will be understood by other members, thus being used to construct a reality for the participants" (p. 125). This description fits as if it were designed with the 5thD in mind.

The shared culture that grows up over time in the 5thD may not, initially, be evident to a casual observer. Many visitors to the 5thD have reported reactions like this: "At first it seemed pretty chaotic with kids coming and going, and arguments in progress, and computers blinking. Pretty soon I noticed that almost everyone seemed to know what to do. No one was bumping into or fighting with anyone else, the children seemed to be enjoying themselves, and they were doing a lot of academic stuff."

Engagement in the activities creates a heightened awareness of the culture. Routinely the initial fieldnotes written by the undergraduates express their conviction that they are entering a system of shared understandings that is mysterious to them. Because they are not casual observers, but novice participants, the recognition that they have to learn the culture of the 5thD generally evokes anxiety and an expressed desire to figure out what it takes to become a member:

> As I looked into that room through the windows I had many questions running through my head. How does this program work? What am I supposed to do here? How can I possibly be a leader here when I don't know the first thing about computer games? (Fieldnotes, JG, 01/20/92)

> It was really odd having a young adolescent guiding us through the game. I sort of felt helpless in a way, considering that knowledge is power in this society. Here we were, elders who would soon take on the challenge of helping children develop their minds and to help them get through the fifth dimension and we couldn't even finish the first round! Boy was I humiliated in a fun way! (Fieldnotes, CM, 10/04/91)

With equal frequency, undergraduates report in their end-of-course evaluations that their understandings undergo a marked change during their sessions at the 5thD:

> I got to know everyone at the site very well. We were almost like a little family, because we helped each other and shared ideas about the children. I never would have expected this type of bonding.

> My notes started to include statements like, "I asked what I should make . . . When I explained that . . . I suggested . . . I told her that . . ." I think these statements show that I had begun to define my role in the Fifth Dimension, even though I know this was not a conscious decision.

A second, slightly more subtle indicator of the process of enculturation can be found in a predictable shift in the way in which the artifacts of the 5thD mediate the activities of undergraduates once they become familiar with the system. Participants typically reference fundamental artifacts like the Wizard, maze, constitution, and task cards in their daily fieldnotes, which describe their experiences as they learn to become functioning citizens.

Analysis of the fieldnotes reveals the presence of the three modes of interacting with these artifacts. The first mode might be called "orientational," in which the person treats the artifacts as "things in themselves." The second mode might be called "instrumental" because the artifact is incorporated as a mediator in some kind of goal-directed action. The third mode might be called "reflective" because it indicates a particular form of mindfulness in working with the artifacts.

What makes this distinction particularly interesting in the present circumstances is that there is a shift in the relative use of orientational, instrument/mediational, and reflective patterns as participants become familiar with the cultural system. At first, fieldnote references to 5thD artifacts are primarily oriented toward interpreting and understanding one's role in the 5thD:

> Scott proceeded to tell us more about the program: what our role with the children would be, how to use the maze as a guide, the task cards . . . We then split into small groups in order to use the computers and different games. (LA, 10/1/91)

> Here, we learned about the task cards, the hint box, the journey log, the all knowing Wizard and his Wizard's assistants, the Fifth Dimension map, the constitution . . . Even the Task Cards didn't give you that much advice. (JG, 1/14/91)

Later, as the participants begin to appropriate the culture, they use the term "task card" in an instrumental fashion:

> Since he didn't read the instructions, I read him the task card and then asked him to tell me the objective of the game and what he needed to do in order to finish the game successfully. (LA, 10/31/91)

> The Task Card mentions that you should start off with all levels at five and gradually increase one of the variables to see which level they belong to, to eventually reach the requested growth of 100cm (Botanical Gardens). (CM, 12/5/91)

Analysis of the frequency and usage of the orientational and instrumental kinds of reference to various key artifacts such as the task cards provides a quantitative picture of the shifting understandings that accompany acculturation. As shown in Figure 10.6, in the first weeks of their participation in the 5thD, students use of "task card" is primarily orientational, but toward the end of the eight-week session, instrumental uses come to outnumber orientational uses.[4] Reflective uses of "task card" are rare when students take the class only once. Students who continue in the program display more reflective/critical functional uses of the term, in which they comment on the way novices understand (or fail to understand) their uses and on ways in which the artifacts could be improved: "The day began with a visit from Romy. She wanted me to tell her whether the task card for Golden Mountain was a good one or a bad one . . . [Later she wrote] I think that if I had read him the task card straight through I would have lost him . . . The task card was not challenging for the children" (CM, 11/5/91).

These results suggest that the 5thD is indeed interpretable as a cultural system. Enculturation into this system involves simultaneously the acquisition of knowledge, changing role structures, and new ways of mediating one's interactions through the artifacts the culture makes available.

## Cross-cultural Research in the Fifth Dimension

I did not start this project believing that it would be possible to carry out cross-cultural research. I only had experience with a single 5thD and had no idea of how it would vary from one set of institutional circumstances to another. I was so focused on the issue of sustainability that it didn't occur to me that when the different centers adopted the 5thD we had created a variation of the "same task, different settings" strategy we had been using for a long time.

The "same task" in this case refers to the fact that all of the centers started with the same "starter kit" of primary and secondary artifacts with which to construct their 5thD. The undergraduates who participated in the different systems all came from the same course, had the same background readings, and were taught "the official" way of conducting the 5thD as part of their coursework. To the best of their

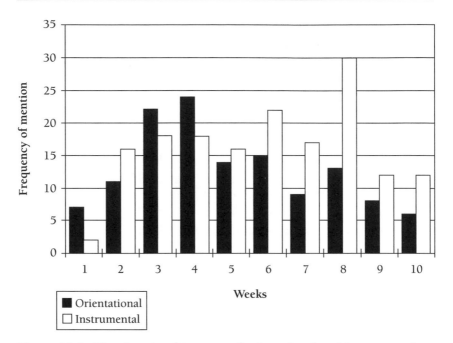

Figure 10.6. The changing frequency of orientational and instrumental uses of the term "task card" in the written discourse of the undergraduate participants in the Fifth Dimension.

abilities, they, along with me and the rest of the staff, tried to make "the" 5thD happen at each site.

Our prior experience had shown that "same tasks" implanted in "different settings" didn't remain the same for long. That was certainly true of the different 5thDs in their institutional settings. Each formed a unique and recognizable pattern.

My sense of each 5thD as a distinctive cultural system originated in the comments that students made whenever they went from their habitual 5thD site to another one. Visitors routinely remarked how different the "other" 5thD was. The way was open to "cross-cultural research."

Ageliki Nicolopoulou and I carried out a "cross-cultural" analysis of children's performance in the 5thDs at the BGClub and the Library (Nicolopoulou and Cole, 1993). Fieldnotes generally described the 5thD at the BGClub as loud and chaotic. Children came and went for reasons that were difficult to fathom. The children worked with undergraduates and played games, but they often did not seem to know each other well and interactions were characterized by a relatively contentious atmosphere and a good deal of horseplay. The various rules of the 5thD often seemed to be honored only in the breach.

By comparison, the Library group seemed intimate, law abiding, and concentrated; children came on time and stayed to the end of the session, often having to be dragged away by their parents or pushed out the door by the librarians. Intense friendships grew up between undergraduates and the children.

A key to understanding the differences between the two 5thD activity systems is to step outside them to examine their local ecologies. The BGClub outside the 5thD is a boisterous place with rock music blaring, teenagers hanging out, and pool games usually in progress. Elsewhere children are playing basketball and varieties of run-around games such as tag, or swimming, or eating snacks and gossiping with their friends. Outside the 5thD the leading activities in the BGClub are play and peer interaction.

The Library, expectedly, is a quiet place where decorous behavior is expected at all times; education, not play, is the leading activity. When children left the 5thD in BGClub, as they were free to do at any time, there were many different activities they could begin to engage in. The children could even go home if they liked. But when the children left the 5thD in the Library, they were expected to read quietly and wait for their parents, who expected them to spend the full hour-and-a-half session there.

When we combine information on the differences between what goes on inside the two 5thDs with information on the different relations of each 5thD to its institutional setting, we immediately grasp the way in which the culture of each activity (text) is co-constituted with its con-text (Figure 10.7). Using the crude variable of "noise level" as a proxy for the qualitatively complex differences between the two locations, we see that at the same time that the 5thD in the BGClub is noisier than the 5thD in the Library, the 5thD in the Library is noisier than its institutional context while the 5thD in the BGClub is quieter than its institutional context. The qualitative features of each 5thD are created in the relationship of "text" to "context," or "activity system" to "institutional setting."

Each 5thD mixes several leading kinds of activity—affiliation, peer,

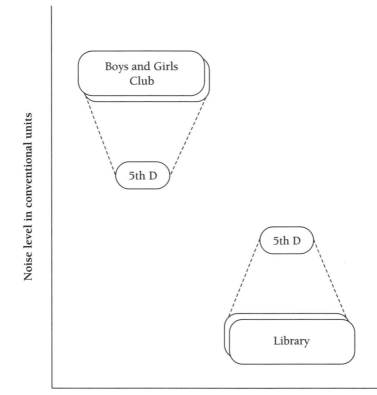

Figure 10.7. A schematic representation of the boisterousness of activity in the Library and Boys and Girls Club Fifth Dimensions. While the BGClub is noisier than the Library and the Fifth Dimension in the BGClub is noisier than its counterpart in the Library, the Library Fifth Dimension is noisy relative to its context while the BGClub Fifth Dimension is quiet relative to its context.

education, and play—but the nature of the culture to emerge from this mixture differs. When placed in the institutional context of the BGClub, where play dominates, the educational features of the 5thD render it relatively more serious and education-like (quieter). When placed in the institutional context of the Library, the play feature of the 5thD makes it more play-like than its sober-minded educational setting (noisier).

As a way of testing the cognitive correlates of cultural differences between 5thD systems, Nicolopoulou compared the degree to which two of the systems fostered the development of shared knowledge and levels of individual children's achievements. As evidence she used the copious fieldnotes describing the children playing a computer game called Mystery House (see Nicolopoulou and Cole, 1993). Figure 10.8 shows the changes in performance on Mystery House over the course of the year in the two settings. Note that in the BGClub there is no overall growth in the level at which the game is played; performance at the beginning of the year is low, yet better, on average, than at the end of the year. By contrast, performance improves with the growth of the culture of shared knowledge in the Library. These and a number of measures of the density and growth of the cultures of the two 5thDs confirmed that there was little cultural growth during the year at the BGClub, but marked and sustained growth in the Library.

## Change in Face-to-Face Interaction

If, for purposes of discussion, we take performance on Mystery House to reflect a broader range of children's accomplishments, and we combine that information with evidence of qualitative differences in participation patterns in the two sites, the BGClub 5thD might appear to be a pretty barren garden for promoting cognitive growth. Yet the Club personnel thought it was worth supporting for that purpose. Were they blinded by their desire to have children occupied with computers, or is there evidence that learning valued by adults went on there?

For evidence concerning the day-to-day activities in the BGClub I turn again to student fieldnotes. I will present two examples, one from a case where a child is playing a game designed to promote phonetic analysis, the second where the game is designed to build skill in navigating the number line. I have placed interpretive comments in brackets within the text where special artifacts and practices of the 5thD are crucial to interpreting the notes.

### A Lesson in Phonics

This fieldnote excerpt describes an interaction involving the game Word Munchers. Word Munchers challenges the players to identify a particular sound within given words, displayed on a five-by-six matrix. The player must manipulate the keyboard effectively in order

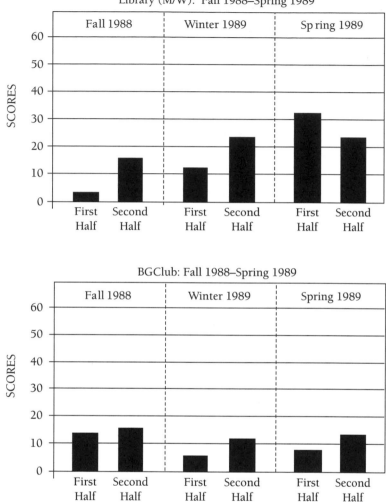

Figure 10.8. Changes in performance when children play a game in the Library and in the BGClub over the course of one year. Note that the improvement is greater in the library, indicating a denser culture of shared learning.

to move the character up, down, left, and right in order to escape a
bad guy (referred to as a troggle) that appears intermittently. It is not
an easy game for beginners to win, not even UCSD undergraduates.
The notes were written by Teri Moore, playing with eight-year-old
Adam (all children's names are pseudonyms).

> Adam got Word Munchers with no problem and started to play
> at the first level. Word Munchers is divided into different cate-
> gories according to vowel sounds—"e" as in tree, "ou" as in
> mouse. The first one was "e" as in tree. He sounded out a lot of
> the words correctly, but not all of them. Even when he sounded
> them out right, he often "munched" words that weren't in the
> same category. It was hard for Adam to distinguish between long
> and short vowel sounds and he repeatedly stumbled over close
> pronunciations. An example was in the category "oo" as in book.
> I have to admit that the categories can be quite tricky some-
> times, with only subtle differentiations between the words. For
> example, "hook" and "rope" both have a long-ish sounding "o"
> but they are not the same sound. This case was hard for Adam,
> and I think that he is just starting to get the grasp of phonics
> in school. Between munching the wrong words and not getting
> them right and his friend Charlie next to him yelling at him to
> munch certain words, Adam was unable to finish even five levels
> [It is necessary to complete five levels in the game to complete
> the beginner level according to the task card]. I decided to help
> him out.
>    I told him that he had to finish five levels to complete the
> beginner level. By this time, Adam was frustrated and was often
> losing all three men in one level. "I can help you complete five
> levels," I told him. "I'm an expert." We switched chairs and I
> started to play.
>    Instead of just letting him watch me though, I got him and
> Charlie both to verbalize the target words. This was Adam's LAST
> man and I promised him that I wouldn't let it die. I wouldn't
> munch on the words unless they told me to and for words they
> were uncertain of, I would linger on it, pronounce it a couple
> of times and then pronounce the category a few times. This

repetition seemed to work and help Adam, especially, distinguish between long and short vowel sounds.

An example that I particularly remember [of the difficulty in distinguishing long and short vowels] was in the category "ou" as in "mouse." The boys thought that we had munched all the words, but we hadn't. There were a lot left, with spellings different than "ou" but with the same pronunciation. I went to the word "clown." "Clown?" I asked, and Adam said "No." "Listen again: clooowwn. And now mooouuuse. They don't have to be spelled the same to sound the same." Adam eventually accepted this idea, though reluctantly. He assumed that they had to be spelled the same, but I said the words didn't have to. They just had to sound the same. We made it to level four with me munching and the two of them giving me feedback on the words.

"Ok, now YOU have to finish," I told Adam. "You can make it to level five." This was the last man. I told him I'd help.

Adam did OK with prompting from both Charlie and me but he was eaten by a troggle again. Often, Adam lost control of his man and sent it careening back and forth on the maze. I warned him about troggles, but sometimes they came out of the walls and ate him. Anyway, he lost this man so I assumed it was the end of the game. He thought it was over, too, but then he realized that we had gotten a "free" man. I'm not sure how we got it, maybe because the score was so high now. Anyway, with this man Adam was able to reach level seven and complete the beginner level.

He went to Amy who told him that he had to get the task card from me. I told him that he still needed to fill it out. He wrote down the five vowels—almost forgetting "a"—and then he had to distinguish between long and short vowel sounds. This was what Adam had been struggling over the whole game, so I was curious to see how he'd do. There were five words. Next to them you had to identify the vowel and write next to it "long" or "short." He identified the vowels, no problem. He knew "cake" and "tree" were long, but he stumbled over a word (red) which was clearly a short "e." I helped him out by contrasting the sound to the "e" in tree. He saw the difference but after much prompting. He handed the completed task card to Amy to get his star.

These notes describe an undergraduate engaging two children in a reading task and providing assistance for one of them in particular. They illustrate several features of the 5thD that could be expected to win favor with adults.

There is no doubt that instruction is going on here, but it is different from school instruction in several ways. The undergraduate supports the boys in a flexible manner that is regulated by her interpretation of what they know and her knowledge of the task. Although there are three participants, the division of labor that the undergraduate negotiates allows her to pinpoint one child's biggest problem (vis-à-vis phonics)—the contrast between long and short vowel sounds.

Using the possibilities provided by the rules of the 5thD and the structure of this particular game, the undergraduate provides encouragement by actually helping the child achieve *his* goals: she takes over part of the task while getting the boys to chip in and then turns the task back to the boy she is concentrating on and adopts the role of helpful spectator. Along the way she discovers a conceptual confusion that could be expected to prolong Adam's difficulties if not corrected—his belief that for words to sound alike they must be spelled alike.

The final segment in which the child must complete the task card provides a diagnostically relevant "post-test." Adam still has difficulties distinguishing vowel length, but we can conclude he has gotten a first-rate lesson in analyzing the contrast between long and short vowels and that he has learned something in the process. However, his understanding is still fragile and requires a good deal of further consolidation.

### Estimation Using Cartesian Coordinates

My second example describes an instance of Brian, age nine, playing the game "Shark," created by James Levin. The fieldnotes are written by Emily Rubin. Figure 10.9 provides the display confronting children when they reach the third and higher levels of the game (on the

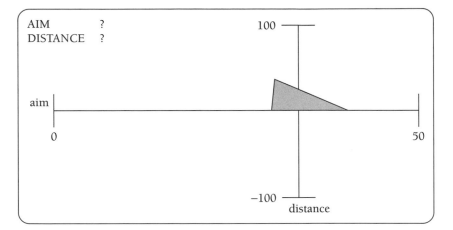

Figure 10.9. Example of Shark game screen at a high level of the game.

first level, only the abscissa, labeled "aim," is presented; on the second level, only the ordinate, labeled "distance," is presented).

> I found the task card and joined Brian at the computer. I had noticed his name when he wrote it on the journey logs on the wall. When I wrote his name on the task card, he was very surprised. "How did you know my name?" he asked. I told him that I saw him write it under the game "Shark" on the wall. He laughed and put the disk into the computer and shut the latch. I told him that he could turn the computer on and gestured to the corner that the switch was on. He turned on the computer and I turned on the monitor, because he said he couldn't reach. The first question that the computer asked was "Who wants to play this game?"
>
> He asked me if there was a way to tell the computer that two people were playing. I told him it was a one person game and that he should type his name in. He typed his name slowly while mouthing the letters out loud, "B-R-I-A-N." I told him that I had only briefly played this game, so we should probably read the directions on the task card.
>
> I read the description of the game from the task card. Before I had finished, he had begun the first level. For the first five levels or so, I used the task card to keep track of the guesses he

made at harpooning the shark. He wasn't very aware that I was doing this until I told him that he had only made two, three, two, and one misses and he was well on the way to becoming an expert at this game. He then began paying attention to what I was writing down. Every now and then he even asked me what his last guess had been.

During the first level of Shark, he was fumbling with the concept of the number line. He had not grasped the concepts of "aim" and "distance" yet, rather he was just filling in the numbers which he felt corresponded to the lines on the screen. The first level was just an "aiming" level. He noted the numbers on either end of the number line and said, "This is huge!", referring to the distance between 0 and 50. He did much of his thinking out loud. "I'm gonna put . . ." he mumbled out loud, "I'll put 45." I would explain to him how his shot was too far to the right and he needed a lower number. He quickly shot the shark within two tries.

The second level was more difficult. It included distance as well as aim. He typed in a number for the first line and pushed return. He sat back in his chair expecting the harpoon to fly, but instead the computer read, "Type a number?" "Type a number!!!???" he read aloud. "I just did . . ." I told him that he would have to guess the distance as well. I motioned to the second number line on the screen. "You not only have to type where the shark is [horizontally], but how high to shoot the harpoon," I said. He guessed the distance incorrectly. He was about to guess the second distance lower than the first when the shot had been too low. I remarked, "Remember last time? You guessed 33 . . ." He quickly changed his input to 35 and harpooned the shark within three tries.

By the third level, he was prepared to enter both aim and distance. His first shot, which he made without my assistance, he exclaimed was "Too high!!!" (referring to the distance number line). He began making the observations that I had previously made in the first two levels. On his next shot, he commented, "It was too high again! and too far that way!!" These directional comments were similar to the ones I had made on the previous levels.

As we made our way through the next few levels, he became more independent when making the decisions. For instance, when we were narrowing down a shot, I suggested that the aim should be 17, but he quickly responded by saying, "No, I'll do something . . . (He was thinking of what to type) . . . I'll do 16" He was right on the dot with the aim, but the distance was still off. "So, I'll change the distance . . ." This was the first time I had heard him refer to the number line by saying "the distance," rather than pointing to the line and guessing. Although he clearly was becoming more independent with his decisions, the game was getting harder and he was more than willing to accept my advice. On level five, for instance, he said out loud, "I'm gonna do 16." I told him that the number line was from 0 to 50 and that 16 would be too far to the left. "OK," he said, "25, no 29 and (for the distance) − 70." He shot the harpoon and it was a little off line. He analyzed it without my help. "Oh, it's perfect (referring to the distance) . . . Ooops just a little to the right. It has to be 26!!" He had harpooned the shark and we were now on level six. "I'm on level six," he screamed as he examined the task card, "Sheesh!"

The number lines were becoming more difficult as they began to incorporate more negative numbers and smaller gradients. He seemed very enthusiastic about the game and the increasing difficulty did not slow him down at all. His knowledge of the number lines was superb. Even when the line went from − 100 to + 100, he was able to adjust. In one circumstance, he even explained to me why a shot must be corrected. I told him that my guess would be 30. When he entered this into the computer it responded, "Smaller . . ." "Smaller!!!!" he yelled, "Oh, it's negative 32!!! It would have to be − 40, because that's getting lower" (he was pointing to the distance line). He was able to notice the negative gradient before I did.

By level eight, Brian was really excited, "I can't believe how far I've got!!!" He had become very comfortable with using the terms aim and distance and was able to narrow the shots down with relatively little help. "A little bit higher, a little to the left," he mouthed out loud, "Let's see . . . I had 39 that time, so 40 (for the aim) and I had 39 (for the distance) . . . so let's see . . .

49! This might be close." Although his deductions were not adequate to harpoon the shark, he did not lose hope. "[The] aim is closer and so is the distance," he said. He quickly finished level eight and nine and we had finished the game. I told him that he had completed all the computer levels and should be an expert at the game.

He jumped up to choose another game, before I had a chance to encourage him to finish the task card. Teri helped me motivate Brian to finish the card and become an official expert. One of the first questions on the task card was "What is the difference between aim and distance?" I wrote his answer down as a way of easing him into the task card. He replied, "Aim is where the shark is, and distance is how high . . ." I then had him draw some pretend number lines for the aim and the distance. He especially enjoyed guessing the numbers on the number lines toward the back of the task card. He counted the marks between the numbers out loud. One number line was from 10 to 80. He counted, "10, 20, 30, 40, 50 . . . (all the way to 80)" to be sure that the gradient was by 10. He then said the answer was 50. He had already developed a mental strategy for solving the problems and it was only the second one.

This example is somewhat less explicit about the child's difficulties with the number line, which do not seem particularly acute. But it provides an excellent account of the way his mastering of the increasingly complex sub-tasks of the game is part and parcel of his interaction with his undergraduate companion. (The fact that the child spontaneously talks aloud is an important resource for analysis of this example.) Several moments stand out in this account:

Initially the child takes no note of the adult keeping a record of progress, but then he starts to use the adult's contributions to mark his progress.

Initially the child has difficulty understanding the specialized vocabulary of the game, but he soon picks it up.

As the game progresses, the child overtly appropriates the special pointers and adult verbal formulaic speech patterns.

The child becomes more independent as the game progresses despite the increasing difficulty of the subtasks.

Eventually the child adopts the role of "more competent peer,"
  instructing the adult in how to interpret the meaning of larger
  negative numbers.
The way in which the child's increasing excitement and satisfaction
  are intertwined with his increasingly accurate and complicated
  behavior is evident throughout the fieldnotes.

Despite the relatively loose structure of the 5thD at the Boys and
Girls Club, interactions of these kinds are a routine occurrence. By
contrast, the children's activities outside of the 5thD at the BGClub
were very unlikely to contain so much educational content. The fact
that children come to the 5thD and spend time there, and that adults
routinely encounter them engaged in activity that is noticeably educational, is reason enough for the BGClub staff and parents to approve of it.

## What about Sustainability?

For purposes of discussion, I will assume that the 5thD is, in some
sense, good for children—the kind of thing the BGClub would like
to promote and support. Does that settle the problem of sustainability?

When we turn to the question of sustainability we are addressing
change at the cultural-historical level. Following the basic principles
of the cultural-historical approach, we need to understand the history
of changes in the 5thD from as far back as possible. A convenient
beginning is the planning year, before we planted the activity system
in three institutions.

During the goal-forming year of the project (1986–87) the staff
held workshops periodically. Staff from the four institutions that had
agreed to start out with us attended these sessions, at which they
were familiarized with a variety of things they might do to get their
kids involved with computers and with UCSD students.

At the end of that year I actively entered the project. I conducted
interviews with the directors of each institution: the School, the
Childcare Center, the Library, and the BGClub. Whatever goal formation had gone on during the workshops, little was in evidence.
The School decided not to go ahead with their involvement because

they feared for the safety of their computers; they offered to help the Childcare Center. Staff from the other two locations had enjoyed the 5thD and thought their kids would like it too. The Library personnel expressed the hope that the 5thD could be implemented in a way that would involve the children with library functions, and we agreed it was a good idea. So, more or less by default, the 5thD became the common denominator of the activities.

## Childcare Center

The first 5thD to expire was at the Childcare Center, where our activities continued only two-thirds of the 1987–1988 academic year. The demise was not the result of the failure of the 5thD to please the children or the staff. In fact, not long after starting the program, at the request of the Center staff, we modified our procedures to allow access by more children so that all of the kids could get a chance to participate.

The stress point that led to the demise of the 5thD at the Center was fear of child abuse combined with the relatively rapid turnover of undergraduates (UCSD classes run for only ten weeks a quarter). As a result of publicity surrounding a preschool child abuse case in Los Angeles and a high level of concern about child abuse more generally, the agency that licensed the Childcare Center insisted that all adults working in daycare facilities register their fingerprints with the Department of Justice and take a TB test. Money was not a problem but time was; the quarter was well under way by the time all the paperwork was completed and the undergraduates could go to the site. As a consequence of these complexities, we suggested, prior to the start of the third quarter, that we suspend the project. The director of the Center was much relieved; she had wanted to back out of the project, as the continued appearance of unfamiliar adults at her facility was unacceptably nerve-racking. But she had hesitated to do so for fear of offending us.

## The Library

The Library 5thD was located in a back corner of the library. When it was not in session, the computers, the maze, and other paraphernalia were stored in an adjacent closet.

Because the library was located across a freeway from the elementary school, children who attended the 5thD there were generally dropped off and picked up by their parents, and it took a few weeks for the new activity to catch on. By midway through the first quarter we had a steady complement of six or seven children attending twice a week. We even tried to create a homework hotline to the Wizard on our off days in response to demand for activities on the days the 5thD was not open, but this idea did not catch on. In the second year, we accommodated increased demand by running two shifts of the 5thD for an average of eight or nine children per session, four days a week.

Despite its small size, the Library 5thD was the most successful of our systems from the perspective of its impact on the children. As I indicated when I explained its success in promoting better game performance, interactions at this site were marked by the high level of friendship that developed among the children and the undergraduates.

From early in the project we worked with the Library staff to build expertise in the running of the 5thD and helped them raise money for hardware and software. We created special activities that required the children to acquire library skills, and we met with the staff periodically to review progress in the program. The librarian was helpful in seeing that a phone line was placed near the 5thD to facilitate communication with the Wizard. Friends of the library provided equipment.

At the end of the third year of the project we met with the staff at the Library to discuss the future. We had gotten to the point where we had to shift more responsibility from the university to the community. We could guarantee that supervised undergraduates would keep coming, but we could not provide a site coordinator and we could not be responsible for computer uptake, purchases, and so on.

The Library staff decided not to continue the program. There were many reasons for this decision: the Library was short of space, the children sometimes got noisy when they became excited about a game they were playing, there were administrative difficulties in handling the money needed to pay a site coordinator, they did not have time to train people to work with the children. Each of these problems could have been solved, but the fact was that even if the money was available, even if volunteers stepped in to help, the librarians had come to the conclusion that the 5thD did not fit closely enough with their main goals as librarians. And that was the end of the 5thD in the Library.

## The Boys and Girls Club

The 5thD at the BGClub took place in a large room that well exceeded our initial, modest capacities to accommodate children. We slowly added to our four or five computers, undergraduates came in larger numbers, so we were gradually able to handle larger numbers of children. As soon as we had the person power, we kept the program open four days a week. Since the space was not being shared with other programs, we had the luxury of leaving things set up between sessions. We could also put the maze in a prominent place in the center of the room and put children's artwork and posters relevant to 5thD activities on the walls.

The number of children who sought admission to the 5thD each day fluctuated wildly from a low of 4–5 to a high of 12–13. However, even more important than total numbers were the facts that children came and went as they pleased, that many came only once a week while others were habitués and many came only once or twice altogether. The rapid flow of children, both within and between days, made it difficult for children and undergraduates to get to know each other. The undergraduates and researchers found it difficult to keep track of which games children had completed at each level. There were so many "cruddy creatures" in the maze that kids could get discouraged just looking for theirs. These conditions made it hard for the undergraduates to grasp and make use of the rules and conventions they and the children were supposed to follow. As a consequence, some children (and undergraduates) felt that the rules were coercive and external to them, so they either resisted or ignored them.

These difficulties induced us to try to simplify the operation of the 5thD during the last quarter of the first year. In place of the 5thD with its constraints on involvement with the games, we created a chart with forty games and spaces to mark a child as having completed beginner, good, or expert level. There were no restrictions on "next games" the children could play; they simply had to choose an activity and a level they had not yet completed.

This attempt at simplification was a total failure. Before long the children settled into playing whatever games suited their fancy at whatever level. The undergraduates themselves started to introduce new rules, but these were not related to one another and everyone felt they were arbitrary and unproductive.

That summer we ran a special summertime 5thD at the BGClub in which we returned to the original structure, elaborating new artifacts to deal with the complexities of the BGClub setting (record-keeping devices, a carefully worked out organization of the games within the maze, improved task cards, for example). When the 5thD reemerged in its elaborated form, it proved a gratifyingly sturdy tool.

I should note that whatever *our* discontent with the 5thD, the children kept on coming. During the second year, ambitious undergraduates opened a new 5thD in one of the neighboring BGClubs, and soon thereafter a third BGClub asked for and got a 5thD. The clubs gave the program an award and embraced it as an important new addition to their program. Most important, they provided support for computers and telephone lines in addition to space.

When we met with the directors of the Boys and Girls Club at the end of the third year they were committed to continuing the program. They did not shy away from responsibility for paying a site coordinator part time. For a while we ran 5thDs at three clubs in the area, but when the recession of the early 1990s caused cutbacks at both the clubs and at UCSD we cut back to the "main 5thD" at the original club.

For the next two years, the 5thD at the BGClub treaded water. The practicum class continued to be taught at UCSD and we continued to send students to the BGClub. But I shifted my attention and research money to new 5thDs created as part of a separate project with a group of Russian psychologists.[5] Left more or less on its own, the 5thD at the BGClub continued to attract children and to provide undergraduates an excellent opportunity to confront their bookish knowledge with practical experience. But it was also run down and somewhat tired looking.

Then, unexpectedly, the 5thD became the focus of another round of research, this time to see if it was possible to scale up our initial experiment to include several institutions of higher learning and as many community partners. A new generation of 5thDs came into being. Once again all of them created valued opportunities for children to learn alongside undergraduates. Once again some of them prospered, some of them did not. At the end of another three-year round of research, seven 5thDs were in operation (see Cole, 1995b; Nicolopolou and Cole, 1993; Schustak et al., 1994; Woodbridge, Olt, and Cole, 1992). The BGClub 5thD prospered.

## Preliminary Lessons about Sustainability

As I write these words the 5thD is still in existence. There are currently a dozen offspring from that first 5thD which came into being more than a decade ago. They are located in afterschool programs at elementary schools, BGClubs, a YMCA, and a church. The undergraduates who participate in them come from a broad range of colleges and universities. Several additional systems have been proposed at universities around the country. Despite the fact that the project is still in progress, enough time has elapsed and enough experience has accumulated to hazard some preliminary conclusions about factors associated with sustainability. I focus here on the BGClub system.

Overall, I am impressed by how difficult the process of creating a sustainable new system has been. Despite the fact that the 5thD provides activities that are valued by community institutions responsible for children after school, despite the fact that it provides university students with special research experiences at little cost to the university (a laboratory where students worked with white rats would be far more expensive), and despite ample good will on all sides, its ability to continue once external research funds are withdrawn must be considered problematic if not improbable. Why?

Several systemic impediments can be identified. The first difficulty manifested itself during the planning year of the first grant, although we could not evaluate its significance at the time. We noticed that different people represented the various community institutions at different workshops. This reflected that facts that many such institutions are chronically understaffed and that very few of the staff are career professionals. One reason for the failure of the institutions to form their own clear goals for an afterschool activity in the goal-forming phase of the project was that there was no one person at any of the institutions who had an overview of the possibilities, although we had tried hard to provide that overview.

Once we got under way, the lack of continuity of supervising personnel remained a prominent feature of the system. At all three of the institutions we worked in, the people responsible for implementing the 5thD were not the people who had been involved in the planning.

Continuity is also a problem on the university/college side of the system. Colleges and universities are involved in instruction only part of the year. They run on schedules dictated by whether they are on a semester system or a quarter system, whether they have a mid-winter or spring break, and so on. In my area, the university opens in the fall several weeks after the local schools, so that the 5thD starts late from the perspective of the BGClub. It is closed at times (Christmas holidays, for example) when the local institutions might like to have intensified 5thD activities.

Providing faculty to teach the requisite course twice or three times a year, depending upon the local academic schedule, poses additional problems. So long as the commitment of faculty is only for a short period (two or three years), other departmental needs can be held in abeyance. But if the activity is to be institutionalized, an entire department must agree to see that the course is staffed, even if the person who initiated the activity is on sabbatical or leaves for another job. Getting that kind of consensus in departments that are hard pressed to meet more routine teaching needs for large courses is a rare achievement, regardless of the value of the activity.

Another area of difficulty that community organizations face is to sustain the material base of the 5thD. Here I would include both the hardware and software associated with the computers, and the "firmware" we provided (the task cards, the maze, the Wizard), as well as personnel.

The lack of continuity among the contributing institutions makes it difficult to sustain the cultural knowledge needed to see that the activity runs smoothly. There are several aspects to this task. First, whoever supervises the 5thD needs a modicum of expertise in fixing minor problems with hardware on the spot and in knowing how to work around glitches. Second, that person has to see to it that the hardware is repaired and replaced when necessary, and to search out new software as it becomes available. Third, that person has to be familiar enough with the culture of the 5thD to help arrange for it to come to life in the fall, when school begins, and re-create itself during the school year. An analogous process applies to the university's role.

Will our local 5thD be sustainable in the long run? It is too early to tell. Whether or not the 5thD survives beyond the current round of research, it has provided a rich medium within which to apply and evaluate the ideas of cultural-historical psychology.

# 11 ⑥

# The Work in Context

Scientific observation is not merely pure description of
separate facts. Its main goal is to view an event from as
many perspectives as possible. Its real object is to see and
understand the way a thing or event relates to other things
or events.   *Alexander Luria*

I HAVE NOW taken the reader on a rather lengthy trip through
selected issues in the prehistory of psychology, several decades of
cross-cultural research, and a reconstruction of cultural-historical
psychology, ending with examples of my research in that tradition.
It's a long way from the Torres Straits to the Fifth Dimension.

Having made the journey, it is time to return to the questions with
which I began, viewing them now through the lens of my version of
a modern cultural psychology. In a sense we have come full circle.
The problems we end with are the problems we began with: the dual
nature of psychology and of the methodologies which organize its
investigation of human thought and action; and the implications of
this duality for a culturally informed theory of mind.

On the whole I am enormously impressed with the quality of
Wundt's thinking about the choices that faced psychology if it wanted
to become an autonomous science at the end of the nineteenth century. In proposing a dual science he was incorporating a long history
of thought about *Homo sapiens'* dual nature and the means by which
the resulting hybrid could be rigorously investigated. Moreover, his
analysis maps nicely onto divisions within the discipline between

those who seek to make a natural sciences approach extend to all of psychology and those who seek a second psychology, of which various forms of cultural psychology are one manifestation.

The main disappointment of Wundt's thinking about the two psychologies problem in the present context is that he provided so little guidance for how and where the two psychologies could be brought together. Well-worked-out attempts to resolve this problem remained a task for the next generation and, as it has turned out, later generations down to the current day. The problems of unifying in a single paradigm the "two psychologies" has by no means been resolved.

As was true a century ago, there remain three dominant positions among psychologists about how to deal with these problems. The first, which was the focus of my attention in Chapters 2 and 3, was to forge ahead on the basis of the first psychology. The second was to take the road suggested by Dilthey, and place psychology within the cultural sciences, allowing the study of human physiology and elementary psychological functions to be the province of the neurosciences and other natural scientific disciplines. Alternatively, the province of the first psychology could be reinterpreted as discourse and its facts as text.

I believe that the logic of the path I have been traveling leads to a third way, one which follows Mill, Wundt, and others in recognizing important differences between humans and other creatures associated with the unique environment of human life, culture. However, it goes beyond Wundt in suggesting how the two world views associated with the natural and cultural halves of Wundt's system can be united into a single scientific enterprise. I shall review the questions we started with from the perspective of the cultural-historical approach I have been developing in the last several chapters.

## Concerning Question 1

*Why has it proven so difficult for psychologists to keep culture in mind?*

A short answer might be: Because when psychology treated culture as an independent variable and mind as a dependent variable, it broke apart the unity of culture and mind and ordered them temporally—culture is stimulus, mind response. The entire history of cross-cultural psychology can be viewed as a long struggle to put back together that which was torn apart as a consequence of the division of the humane sciences into the social sciences and humanities. This is the source of the continuing discussions of methodology and theory involving psychologists and anthropologists, earlier phases of which I have discussed in prior chapters. (The appearance of a journal called *Psychology and Culture* in 1995 is one manifestation of current interest in these issues; see also Jahoda, 1982, 1992.)

The "long" answer to this question is given in Chapters 2 and 3, supplemented by discussion in later chapters where I undertook the process of theoretical reconstruction. I argued that it is difficult for psychologists to keep culture in mind because when psychology became institutionalized as a social/behavioral science, the constituent processes of mind were divided among several sciences: culture to anthropology, social life to sociology, language to linguistics, the past to history, and so on.

Each of these disciplines developed methods and theories appropriate to its domain. As we have seen, in psychology the major methods depended upon the use of standardized procedures (tests, experimental tasks, questionnaires) that permit randomized assignment of subjects to conditions, quantification of data, and the application of linear statistical models to determine the significance of variations among outcomes. In anthropology, by contrast, the major methods depended upon participation with people in their everyday activities and interviewing in a flexible, probing, and socially acceptable way. These methods were diametrically opposed with respect to the appropriateness of using artificial experiments on the model of the natural sciences and the grounding of data-collecting procedures in everyday life events.

The marginality to general psychology of the kinds of cross-cultural research conducted in the 1960s and 1970s was more or less predetermined by the requirements of the first psychology. The experimental, quantitative approach of methodological behaviorism assumes the generation of context-free laws, but the phenomena of interest can be explained in such terms only in a reduced fashion that does not remain true to the facts of everyday, lived experience and that has great difficulty accounting for the process of developmental change.

These same features of cross-cultural experiments made them unacceptable to anthropologists as well, but from a different perspective. The key objection was formulated neatly by Robert Edgerton more than two decades ago. In contrast to the normative experimental methods associated with methodological behaviorism, according to Edgerton, anthropological methods "are primarily unobtrusive, nonreactive ones; we observe, we participate, we learn, hopefully we understand . . . This is our unspoken paradigm and it is directly at odds with the discovery of truth by experimentation which, at least as many anthropologists see it, ignores context and creates reactions" (1974, pp. 63–64).

Edgerton knew about the efforts of cross-cultural psychologists to become more culture-sensitive, and he encouraged that movement. But he did not think it had created the paradigmatic revolution that seemed to be in the offing. It still "created reactions," behaviors that are not a part of people's natural repertoires.

This conclusion certainly applied to my own efforts to combine psychology and anthropology. As described in Chapters 2 and 3, despite our best intentions, my colleagues and I still had very few results based on a methodology starting from everyday activities.[1] Our methodological critiques of the way others reached conclusions were acknowledged to be useful, but our theorizing was dismissed as unproductive particularism—we could criticize the use of methodological behaviorism but we had no viable alternative to offer. Gustav Jahoda spoke for many psychologists when he wrote:

Cole set out to track down the causes of this poor performance in some detail. Some of the empirical work was in fact undertaken, but most of his account consists of listing various possibilities like a seemingly endless trail vanishing at the distant horizon . . . [This approach] appears to require extremely exhaustive, and in practice almost endless explorations of quite specific pieces of behavior, with no guarantee of a decisive outcome. This might not be necessary if there were a workable "theory of situations" at our disposal, but as Cole admits, there is none. What is lacking in [the context-specific approach] are global theoretical constructs relating to cognitive processes of the kind Piaget provides, and which save the researcher from becoming submerged in a mass of unmanageable material. (1980, pp. 124–126)[2]

It was an interesting Catch-22. Insofar as we moved toward satisfying the requirements of ecological validity, we moved away from standard forms of experimentation and toward the analysis of activity as the empirical basis for theorizing. But that route leads to an emphasis on the context-dependent and activity-dependent nature of psychological processes, and fails to satisfy the need for generalization. Nor did these deficiencies quickly disappear. As Jean Lave (1988, p. 173) was to comment some years later, activity- and context-specific approaches to cognition are still obligated to account for the sources of continuity in everyday life. It is against this background that we arrive once again at Question 2.

## Concerning Question 2

*If you are a psychologist who believes that culture is constitutive of mind, what can you do that is both academically acceptable and true to your sense of the complexities of the phenomenon?*

When I was an undergraduate I encountered the concept of a Zeitgeist in E. G. Boring's *History of Experimental Psychology.* Zeitgeist literally refers to "the current ways of thinking and feeling" or "the spirit of the times." Boring was speaking of the scientific, experimental spirit that animated the pioneers of a scientific psychology.

For a long time I viewed the idea of Zeitgeist as a remnant of prescientific spiritualism, the bad old days. However, having spent a good deal of my time in recent years reading the ideas of nineteenth-century scholars and simultaneously experiencing rapid changes in academic thinking about culture, context, and development, I find that the concept has acquired a certain appeal.

The general problematic of this new Zeitgeist in academia is a growing sense that the nineteenth-century division of the social and humane sciences, whatever its achievements, has run its course. All during the 1960s, 1970s, and 1980s new interdisciplinary combinations of social science and humanities sprouted up around the country. A common thread among these diverse explorations was the assumption that culture, language, and history play prominent roles in constituting human thought and action. The atemporal, positive social sciences were "cross-breeding" with the cultural-historical sciences.

The particular manifestation of this Zeitgeist that I have focused on is the one of which I have been a part, the effort to formulate a developmental psychology in which culture is accorded a co-constitutive role alongside, and intertwined with, phylogeny and ontogeny. As I noted in Chapter 4, there are many concurrent efforts to elaborate such a cultural psychology. Among the possible paradigms, it was the ideas of the Russian cultural-historical psychologists that served as my theoretical starting point. But the Russian approach could not serve usefully unless it was reconciled with the results of our cross-cultural work on the context-specificity of cognition. Chapters 5–10 describe my efforts to construct one, viable reconciliation.

## Rethinking Culture and Context

I began the task of constructing a second psychology in Chapter 5 by reexamining the theoretical primitives that emerge when one considers culture the species-specific medium of human life and artifacts as the elementary units of culture. Drawing upon a mixture of Russian and American traditions, I proposed that artifacts have a dual conceptual-material nature by virtue of their prior participation in goal-directed human activity. It is by being taken up into action as "auxiliary means" that culture "deforms" action and brings into being the "cultural habit of behavior." Artifacts are always involved in a dual mediation, with the nonhuman world and with other people.

As a means of thinking about the ways artifacts are organized into systems and networks, I turned to ideas in schema and script theory currently in wide use among psychologists, anthropologists, and sociologists. However, instead of interpreting scripts and schemas as inside-the-head mental entities, I treated them as distributed, conventional artifacts, constraining relations between what is in the head and what the head is in. If I am correct in the way I interpret current work in schema theory and discourse (D'Andrade, 1995; Holland and Cole, 1995; Strauss and Quinn, in press), the ideas presented here are part of a much broader stream of scholarly work in cognitive psychology and symbolic anthropology.

This much cultural apparatus allows us to think more broadly and systematically about mediated action, but it still is missing what I referred to generically as the "supra-individual envelope of development": context, activity, situation, practice, and so on. I would like to be able to provide a brief and exhaustive taxonomy of the ways these different terms are used and the theoretical choices that they index. Unfortunately, I remain uncertain about their interrelationships. Judging from my own behavior and the writings of those whose work I read, such terms are used in a mixture of commonsense and theoretically motivated ways. Moreover, these concepts are applied to such a wide array of empirical objects of analysis that I wonder if differences among them may not arise from the affordances of the particular phenomena scholars study and the means they use to study them rather than from deep theoretical disagreements.

## Some Unresolved Tensions

Certain issues recur in the discussions of those pursuing one or another form of cultural psychology. The first can be phrased in many ways. I have discussed it here as the tension between the senses of context-as-given and context-as-constructed. Jean Lave characterizes this same tension as follows:

> The major difficulties of phenomenological and activity theory in the eyes of the other will be plain: Those who start with the view that social activity is its own context dispute claims that objective social structures exist other than in their social-interactional construction in situ. Activity theorists argue, on the other hand, that the concrete connectedness and meaning of activity cannot be accounted for by analysis of the immediate situation. (1993, p. 20)

I doubt if this tension will go away any time soon. However, there has been a great deal of interaction among participants in these discussions in recent years, and research bridging the two traditions is beginning to appear (for example, R. Engeström, 1995; Goodwin, 1994; Hutchins, 1995; Nardi, 1996).

Another important tension, especially prominent in discussions among psychologists who draw heavily upon the Russians, has been

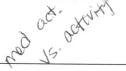

whether mediated action or activity is the appropriate level of analysis. This issue can be seen in the way James Wertsch and his colleagues summarize the shared assumptions of those who adhere to a sociocultural approach to mind (Wertsch, Del Rio, and Alvarez, 1995):

1. One of the basic ways in which sociocultural settings shape mental functioning is through the cultural tools employed.
2. Mediation provides the formulation of how this shaping occurs.
3. In order to specify how cultural tools exist and have their effects, it is essential to focus on human action as a unit of analysis.

While points (1) and (2) are easily recognized as compatible with the approach I have tried to develop here, the third statement requires discussion. At first glance it appears that Wertsch leaves out the supra-individual envelope of development. Where is activity? Where is context?

Wertsch and his colleagues are at some pains to insist that their notion of action applies to groups as well as individuals and is not subject to the charge of individual reductionism. Elsewhere in the same book they note that action must always be understood with respect to its context, and that one way to describe that context is as the level of activity. They offer an interesting discussion of Kenneth Burke's (1962) ideas about the elements of scene, act, and agency as a language for talking about mediated action in context. So the level of activity is present in Wertsch's formulation; it is simply backgrounded when he focuses on the process of mediated action.

An activity theorist such as Yrjö Engeström (1993) begins from a different direction by asserting that "the entire activity system is the unit of analysis." His analyses, while including individuals, artifacts, and mediated actions, also include the institutional contexts and history of the systems of activities he investigates. The danger with a focus on mediated action, from Engeström's point of view, is that context is not equally theorized. As a consequence, "individual experience is described and analyzed as if consisting of relatively discrete and situated actions" while the system, or "objectively given context," of which those actions are a part is either treated as an immutable given or barely described at all (p. 66).

This tension between context-as-given and context-as-constructed repeats in some respects the long-standing difference of opinion between Russian activity theorists who followed the line of Vygotsky and Leontiev and those who followed in the line of Sergei Rubenshtein, whose work derived from Marx and the German philosophical tradition (Brushlinskii, 1968; Van der Veer and Valsiner, 1991). Andrei Brushlinskii faults Vygotsky for "signocentricism," which means that in focusing on word meaning as the unit of analysis for uniting language and thought, he neglected the context (activity) through which consciousness is formed. Brushlinskii criticizes Leontiev for the opposite sin—giving too much weight to external activity and insufficient attention to mediation.

My longtime observations of the running argument on this matter among Russian psychologists have convinced me that this kind of dispute is rarely productive. Mediated action and its activity context are two moments of a single process, and whatever we want to specify as psychological processes is but a moment of their combined properties. It is possible to argue about how best to parse their contributions in individual cases, *in practice,* but attempting such a parsing "in general" results in empty abstractions, unconstrained by the circumstances to which they are appropriate.

## The Toolkit of Metaphors

It has probably not gone unnoticed that in Chapter 5 I used several different metaphors to index key phenomena such as culture, context, and activity. In my experience, metaphors are useful tools of thought. There is no such thing as an all-purpose (context-free) tool, so it is natural to invoke different metaphors depending upon the task at hand.

For example, the metaphor of context as concentric circles is a useful heuristic because it forces one to remember that any presumed level of phenomena is constituted by those "above" and "below" so that a methodology encompassing at least three levels is required. But this metaphor has a down side: it tempts one to assume the circumstances of action to be immutable and not dynamic (Bateson, 1972; Engeström, 1993).

At other times a "weaving together" metaphor is needed when different elements of two systems of constraints, two discourses, two

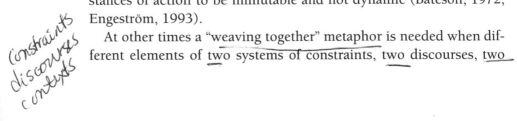

threads of context, recombine, reorganizing the system of which they are a part to create a new pattern when considered synchronically. Such weaving together seems essential to a co-constructive perspective. C. H. Waddington's statement that "each new level of development is a new relevant context" virtually demands a weaving-together perspective. He made the statement with respect to embryogenesis; I make it with respect to human development throughout the life course.

Many other metaphors are useful. It is helpful, for example, to map out the system I am studying in terms of Yrjö Engeström's expanded triangle (see Chapter 5), which has the Vygotskian (implicitly individualistic) triangle as a constituent "at the top," with "the bottom" expanded to include social rules, communities, and division of labor. Use of this analytic structure has the great virtue of including both individual and others in the basic unit of analysis; it is joint mediated activity we are discussing. But as I commented with respect to the Vygotskian semiotic triangle, the expanded triangular representation is a timeless ideal that functions analytically to provide the synchronic constraints on action. When Engeström introduces temporality into the analysis, however, the triangle metaphor gives way to a spiral metaphor, in which it is transformations in sociocultural events that are the focus of concern. One requires a combination of at least these two metaphors to represent the process of culturally mediated activity.

Other examples could be mentioned. My main point is that different metaphors provide access to different properties and moments of the overall process of sociocultural and individual change. One of the attractive aspects of a cultural-historical approach to constructing a second psychology is its underlying assumption that to understand behavior one must study the history of behavior. This same feature introduces a significant complication as well, because it requires a breadth of knowledge about different developmental domains that spills beyond the limits of existing disciplines or the competence of single individuals to master in a lifetime of work.

## Reconstructing the Account of Hominization

I will not dwell on my excursion into the genetic domain of phylogeny and its relation to cultural history because I am at the very best an amateur observer and it is clear that disagreements about the fine points can have enormous implications for how one thinks about the process of hominization as a whole. As I interpret the consensus of current thinking, in both paleontology and primatology, I am well advised to emphasize the symmetry of the social and nonsocial environments with respect to artifact mediation. The act of mediation always accomplishes a double coordination—with the physical world and with other people. It is not a question of one most and the other least.

Dichotomous views of the relation between nature and culture, whose demise has been greatly exaggerated by many psychologists in recent decades, do not apply within the cultural-historical framework I am proposing. We can, to be sure, make analytic distinctions for particular purposes under particular circumstances, but from a cultural-historical perspective, human nature is not the mechanical result of the interaction of two, independent, forces, like two marbles bumping into each other. It is the bio-social-cultural product of a long co-evolutionary process. As Clifford Geertz pointed out more than two decades ago, the normal human brain functions through culture, and if it cannot do so normal human development cannot occur.

Agreement on this general point still leaves ample room for serious disagreement and misunderstanding. Over and over again the discussion revolves around the relative contribution of cultural and phylogenetic constraints to individual human natures. The tradition that argues the functional autonomy of human behavior from phylogeny owing to the emergence of culture (Ratner, 1991) jousts with the tradition that argues the heavy dependence of individual psychological properties on biological constraints (Buss, 1994). This is another issue that will not go away. The nature of the hybrid that is human beings, and the inescapable limitations on our knowledge of our origins, will forever make points of origins and history a source of moral tension and political conflict.

The literature on hominization also provides a fascinating illustration of the danger of falling into arguments over continuity and discontinuity in development. As the current data on prehistorical humans and cross-species organization of development dramatically indicate, myriads of apparent continuities live side by side with differences in patterning that appear as marked discontinuities. It's a good lesson to remember when thinking about ontogenetic stage transitions.

## Culture, History, and Ontogenetic Development

When I look around me in the field of developmental psychology, I find ample evidence that a concern for culture and context is a part of a contemporary Zeitgeist. Discussion of cultural context was virtually absent from the developmental psychology of the 1960s and 1970s when we first began to publish our cross-cultural research. But in the 1990s, even those cross-cultural psychologists who have most severely criticized us for our particularism straightforwardly adopt "the individual in context as the unit of analysis" (Segall et al., 1990, p. 344).

Interest in cultural approaches to development has now spread well beyond the core of people associated with cultural psychology. Even such "neo-Piagetian" theorists as Kurt Fischer, Robbie Case, and their colleagues currently accord the cultural context of action an important role in development. Case (1992) argues explicitly for the inclusion of sociohistorical context in the developmental process and integrates this idea with his version of neo-Piagetian theory. Fischer and colleagues (1993) propose an expansion of Fischer's skill theory which appears to come very close to the theory being offered here, leading to an emphasis on the ongoing, dynamic relations between context and behavior.

I have felt a different manifestation of this same Zeitgeist in the child development text I wrote with my wife (Cole and Cole,1996). The basic narrative of the text is organized around the proposal that ontogenesis is a process of co-construction among factors conceived of as biological, social, and psychological that periodically gave rise to "bio-social-behavioral-shifts" which take place within the medium of culture. This process occurs over time and must be studied that way; hence the text is chronological in its organization. When we first began that project in the early 1980s the significant role attributed to culture and the notion that a high-level chronological text is possible were both oddities. In 1996 they are taken-for-granted propositions.

## Questions of Methodology

Unfortunately, agreement that "people acting in cultural contexts" is a basic unit of psychological analysis does not extend to agreement on the meaning of *context*, which, as we have seen, is a devilishly polysemic concept. Further clarification requires knowledge of what pattern of methods is used to relate theoretical claims on the one hand to empirical warrants on the other. This pattern of mediation in the process of inquiry is what I mean by a methodology. A methodology is a coordinated set of lenses through which to interpret the world.

When we set out on our methodological journey in the 1960s, I had never used the word *methodology* and did not understand that I was rediscovering the history of my scientific discipline through a new lens. In going to Africa I stumbled on a situation where the tools of my profession led to conclusions that radically contradicted my everyday experience. It was inconceivable to me that anyone with the "objective" deficiencies of nonliterate peoples as indicated by psychological tests could function effectively in the complex activities I watched them engage in. I was sure I couldn't function effectively if I were put in their shoes. That contradiction—between the evidence through the lens of my discipline's methodology and that through the lens of my commonsense response to attempting to live in their environment—posed the challenge: come up with a methodology that could reconcile the two different views.

### Analyzing Everyday Activities

Given its theoretical commitment to psychological analysis grounded in activity, one might expect the Russian cultural-historical school to be a rich source of analytic techniques for the study of cognition in all sorts of activity settings. Certainly the hope that cultural-historical psychology would help me ground analysis in everyday activities was an important reason for my interest in it. For better or for worse, it turned out that I misunderstood the nature of that commitment.

The Russian cultural-historical approach begins with everyday activity only in an abstract manner. Rather than concern themselves with concrete parameters of everyday scenes, the Russians focused on what they considered to be the central core of all activity—its mediated nature. Work of Vygotsky's published well after we concluded our cross-cultural research makes it clear that he was not particularly sympathetic to the kind of ethnographic approach which has been so important to us. Regarding strategies of experimentation, he commented: "It might seem that analysis, like the experiment, distorts reality—creates artificial conditions for observation. Hence the demand for closeness to life and naturalness of the experiment. If this idea is carried further than a technical demand—not to scare away that which we are looking for—it leads to the absurd. The strength of analysis is in the abstraction, like the strength of the experiment is in artificiality" (quoted in Van der Veer and Valsiner, 1991, p. 147).

While I agree with Vygotsky's general point that analysis is central to the scientific enterprise, my experience has led me to believe that he underestimated the intellectual task condensed into the idea of a "technical demand" not to "scare away" the phenomena of interest. This characterization of the problem overlooks the analytic achievement involved in specifying a cognitive task in its context, and overestimates the experimenter's ability to re-create a task in a new context and still have it remain the same task.

It may be that the settings within which Vygotsky and his colleagues worked were such as to support his confidence that ecological validity is only a technical problem. They conducted research in schools, clinics, and hospitals (or at home with their own children), where they had the right, both institutionally and from the point of view of their subjects, to define the context, in effect silencing other voices. Whatever the reasons, overgeneralization of this restricted set of possibilities could easily lead to belief in context-free experimentation.

It is interesting in this regard that one of Vygotsky's arguments for cross-cultural research on adults was that in adulthood, biological change is relatively stable. Assuming that natural human processes are universal (as he did), comparative studies of adults in different cultures become "pure" evaluations of the role of culture in mind. There appears to be little recognition in this work of the complexities of identifying cognitive processes characteristic of everyday life and of creating experimental circumstances where just those processes are exhibited for analysis, especially in alien cultural circumstances.

The difficulties of this approach are evident in Luria's Central Asian studies, which I criticized in Chapter 4. Adhering to Vygotsky's notion of proper caution, Luria tried to conduct the experimental sessions in familiar and comfortable circumstances and to use local culture as the content of many of his tasks. On the assumption that he had not "scared away" the forms of thinking people ordinarily engage in by these accommodations, he could then assume that their failure to engage in (say) hypothetical reasoning in his tasks bespoke something general about the way the people thought. But what if he had scared away the phenomenon? How would he know?

*Interdisciplinary Contributions*

It is at this juncture that the activity-based, context-sensitive approach favored by American and European social and behavioral scientists has made its most important contributions to the development of cultural-historical methodology. As I noted in Chapter 8, there are now many demonstrations that it is possible to carry out analyses of thinking in everyday activities and to test out the implications of such analyses through experimental models. It has even proven possible to combine experimental and ethnographic approaches to study the developmental dynamics of cognition.[3]

Although the number of highly elaborated examples that extend over multi-year periods is small, recent research in American sociocultural studies, broadly considered, also goes a long way toward dealing with the need to include the institutional context of activity in a cultural-historical analysis of culture in mind. When we reach this level of analysis we arrive at the borders of what is ordinarily counted as psychology. As a rule, the social-institutional context of action is treated as a (largely unanalyzed) dichotomized independent variable (formal schooling versus apprenticeship training, for example) or left to sociologists.

It might be argued that it is unreasonable to ask psychologists not only to take responsibility for studying cognitive tasks in context but also to concern themselves with the institutional settings of those activities-in-context. However, from a cultural-historical perspective this level of analysis is important as a site where large-scale factors such as social class articulate with individual experience. Consequently, cultural-historical psychologists must either educate themselves in requisite methods or work as part of interdisciplinary teams.

My own approach to this problem has been to work in interdisciplinary teams united around the issue of ecological validity and methods for identifying same tasks in different settings. This research makes it clear that the larger setting in which activities occur plays a crucial role in shaping the structure of the activities, individuals' goals, and the constraints on achieving those goals. These efforts have been only a small part of a growing body of research on mediated action and activity in their institutional contexts (Chaiklin and Lave, 1993; Engeström, 1993; Forman, Minnick, and Stone, 1993; Goodnow, Miller, and Kessel, 1995; Hutchins, 1995; Lave, 1988; Lave and Wenger, 1991; Rogoff, 1990). Among the institutional settings that have been analyzed with respect to the cognitive process involved are classrooms, medical centers, psychotherapy sessions, a job placement center, and the chart room of a naval vessel. These studies reveal pervasive aspects of mediated action and development that are obscured by experimental analyses based on the methods of the first psychology.

For example, Jean Lave's influential discussion of the different ways people use arithmetic when they are shopping and when they are in school emphasizes the way institutional constraints on mathematics in school are so focused on assessing problem solving that they obscure the essential process of problem finding. In the supermarket the problem-finding aspect of cognition emerges for analysis, leading Lave to reformulate the overall process involved. Instead of prepared problems to be solved, what one observes are dilemmas that need to be resolved. Lave's data reveal problem solving in the supermarket to be a process of iteration and transformation: "It involves, on the one hand, what the shopper knows and what the setting holds that might help and, on the other hand, what the solution or resolution looks like. The activity of finding something problematic subsumes a good deal of knowledge about what would constitute a (re)solution, or a method for arriving at one" (1988, p. 159). These conclusions dovetail nicely with the work described in Chapter 8 on the arithmetic practices of Brazilian child street vendors (Nunes et al., 1993; Saxe, 1991), and with Newman and colleagues' (1989) study of individual and small-group combinatorial reasoning.

Edwin Hutchins's (1995) analysis of the sort of thinking involved in navigating large ships or flying 747s forces attention to the ways

in which cognition is distributed among individuals and cultural artifacts. The complexity of the social arrangements and systems of
activities he studies raises a possibility which cultural-historical psychologists had not previously considered: there may be jointly
achieved, interpsychological functions which are sufficiently complicated that they never become independently realizable individual
psychological functions but can only be achieved as joint, mediated,
activity in context.

I think it is fair to say that despite their limitations, these new lines
of research provide more solid empirical possibilities of founding a
psychology on the study of everyday activity. With the further development of video-recording techniques and the fusion of video with
computer technology, we can anticipate new developments in research on multi-person joint activity in the context of its institutional
settings.

## Practice: The Unifying Methodological Element

Despite Vygotsky's belief that the experimental method is essential to
understanding uniquely human psychological processes, it is not
clear whether he believed it possible for any psychology to be entirely
a natural scientific enterprise. Insofar as the two kinds of psychology
can be reconciled, he argued, unification will come about through
uniting theory with practice: "most complex contradictions of psychology's methodology are brought to the field of practice and can
only be resolved there. Here the dispute stops being sterile, it comes
to an end . . . That is why practice transforms the whole of scientific
methodology" (quoted in van der Veer and Valsiner, 1991, p. 150).
He criticized eclectic, atheoretical approaches to practice, arguing
instead for a principled methodology of theory-driven practice that
he called "psychotechnics."

Vygotsky draws heavily on Hugo Münsterberg's ideas about unification in practices as the requirement for uniting the two kinds of
psychology. Münsterberg (1914; see Chapter 1) argued that the meeting point of the two psychologies "is reached in applied psychology
which speaks of the practical application of mental facts in the service
of human purposes. The selection of these purposes is a matter of
purposive psychology, the mental effects to be used a matter of causal

psychology. They are thus joined in that practical part which comes nearest to real life" (p. 16). According to Münsterberg, the study of pedagogical practice by the methods of causal psychology is helped by the fact that schoolchildren are glad to get away from their classrooms to participate in experiments, whereas studies of witnesses or artists is complicated by uncertainty about their purposes. Vygotsky makes a similar argument: psychotechnics operates in circumstances where purposes are known, so that the methods of causal psychology can be applied without problems of interpreting subjects' goals.

While I agree that the two ways of knowing have a natural meeting point in practice, years spent attempting to conduct studies of pedagogical practice make me extremely skeptical of the claim that practice itself reveals the purposes of individual action. In fact, the difficulties associated with knowing subjects' goals (in contrast with what the psychologist thinks their goals should be) underpin many of the arguments about interpreting poor performance in tests and experiments that I addressed in earlier chapters.

My preference is to look upon practice as the arena within which individual goals and knowledge come together with socially prescribed goals and constraints. It is perilous to claim that practice removes ambiguity about the purposive aspects of behavior (for example, that we know the individual's construal of the situation or her "psychological field," to use Lewin's terminology). However, in practice we at least have an opportunity to put different interpretations into dialogue with each other, and thereby to learn more about each "voice" in the dialogue.

## Luria's Romantic Science

Luria's and Vygotsky's views about theory and practice were similar in many respects. The earliest example of their joint attempts to apply their ideas was the report of the Parkinsonian patient who could walk when he mediated movement by incorporating artificial stimuli (paper squares) to walk on. But toward the end of his life Luria adopted a view of the relation of theory to practice, and a way to combine the two psychologies, that harked directly back to Dilthey's ideas about the need for psychology to account for real-life experience. He called this way of doing psychology "romantic science."

Luria (1979) begins his autobiography with a discussion of the science of psychology he inherited, the story I told in Chapter 1. From his earliest research, he sought a way to combine the two psychologies, one experimental/generalizing, one descriptive/particularizing. He concludes his narrative by proposing a particular way of combining the two psychologies in practice—by applying them to the life circumstances of an actual person.

Luria contrasted romantic science with what he called classical science:

> Classical scholars are those who look upon events in terms of their constituent parts. Step by step they single out important units and elements until they can formulate abstract, general laws . . . Romantic scholars' traits, attitudes, and strategies are just the opposite. They do not follow the path of reductionism, which is the leading philosophy of the classical group. Romantics in science want neither to split living reality into its elementary components nor to represent the wealth of life's concrete events as abstract models that lose the properties of the phenomena themselves. (p. 174)

In writing about romantic science, Luria quoted a line from Goethe's *Faust* in which Mephistopheles tells an eager student, "Grey is every theory, ever green the tree of life," expressing his skepticism for the golden promises of theory. While editing Luria's autobiography, I read *Faust* to see what other insights into Luria's ideas I could discover there. One such passage struck me forcefully for its power to contrast the two sciences. In it Mephistopheles advises the eager student on his future career, describing the consequences of following the path of science. The images he uses not only capture perfectly the difference between classical and romantic science, but do so in terms that make an explicit link to the metaphor of context as weaving together.

The conversation begins with Mephistopheles admiring the work of weavers, who create patterns, a process in which "A single treadle governs many a thread, / And at a stroke a thousand strands are wed." Quite different is the scientists' approach, and quite different the result. In light of my discussion to this point, it would not be amiss to think of the scientist as a psychologist who pursues the first psychology and a weaver who follows the path of the second.

> And so philosophers step in
> To weave a proof that things begin,
> Past question, with an origin.
> With first and second well rehearsed,
> Our third and fourth can be deduced.
> And if no second were or first,
> No third or fourth could be produced.
> As weavers though, they don't amount to much.
> To docket living things past any doubt
> You cancel first the living spirit out;
> The parts lie in the hollow of your hand,
> You only lack the living link you banned.
> (Goethe, 1988, p. 95)

Here we encounter in yet another form the idea that when we are talking about human life processes, declarations about "firsts," the ultimate causes from which consequences flow, must always be suspect. For the same reasons, romantic science as formulated by Luria does not allow a simple formulation such as "purposive psychology is concerned with goal formation, causal psychology is concerned with problem solution." Both principles are involved at different moments of one and the same psychological act. Analysis must seek to include both moments and their dynamics.

Luria illustrated his concept of romantic science in two longitudinal case studies involving people for whom ordinary ways of mediating action in the world were impossible (1968, 1972). One was a man with a superb but unusually organized memory. The other was a man who had suffered unusual disorganization of thought and memory owing to massive destruction of part of his brain. In each case Luria combined information from experimental studies of large groups of subjects with the peculiarities of this individual. His ideas about how the two kinds of processes combine were illustrated by the therapeutic regimes he prescribed.

In recent years the major champion of romantic science has been Oliver Sacks, whose deep involvement with his patients over a period of time is strongly reminiscent of Luria's approach and adds importantly to the range of abnormal brain-behavior relationships we can use to develop a more powerful theory of mind. According to Sacks, central to romantic science is that it treats analytic science and synthetic biography of the individual case as essentially complementary, "the dream of a novelist and a scientist combined" (1987, p. xii). Equally important in my view is that both Luria and Sacks are therapists who engage their patients as human beings and attempt to demonstrate through practical amelioration of suffering the truth of the basic premises of their theories.

At the time that I edited the translations of Luria's case studies I did not integrate their implications either with my cross-cultural work or with several of the other projects Luria describes in the autobiography (studies with mental retardates and twins, for example). But ever since I began to work with children in afterschool activities, his ideas have taken on special relevance for me.

Long-term involvement with a single group of children forces the analyst to recognize the individuality of each child and the difficulty of determining an analytic origin, a "first" from which it is possible to deduce conclusions logically. For example, on the first day that we held a cooking club session in our work on ecological validity, my assistant and I assigned children to work on baking a cake in boy-girl pairs. We were interrupting their collective actions. There ensued twenty minutes of what we first thought of as chaos, but which subsequent painstaking analysis revealed to be the children's successful efforts to rearrange the conditions of the assignment so that each child could work with a friend. Even after the children had settled down to do "the task," the spontaneous division of labor they invented and their other, simultaneously relevant goals cropped up too often to allow us to make simple sequential analyses of their behavior.

At the time that we first reported these findings in 1977–1978 they met with indifference from our colleagues in psychology, who struggled to place the work in some well-known category. Subsequently, thanks to the efforts of many colleagues, this sort of phenomenon came to be recognized as socially distributed cognition, which is a respectable object of study in cognitive science.

It was during the research on ecological validity that I undertook my first case study of a child diagnosed as learning disabled (see

Chapter 8). Over the period of a year, using information from the tests we administered, samples of classroom behavior, and his actions in our afterschool clubs, it became possible to build up a portrait of a child who actively organized the settings of his life to minimize the impact of the difficulties he experienced when asked to read. We not only learned a lot about the individual child and the social organization of the settings in which he appeared, we learned what the word "specific" means for the diagnostic category "learning disability."

Similarly, when we opened Field College to study learning disabled children we were dealing with an entire group of children who were having difficulties in their classes, only half of whom fit the standard diagnostic criteria of learning disabled. Nor did the standard diagnoses help in identifying what, in particular, made reading difficult for them. In the game-like activities we organized for the children, each emerged as an individual, with an individual pattern of strengths and weaknesses. Nevertheless, we were able to organize group activities with multiple roles that allowed us to apply "scientific knowledge" (microgenetic analyses motivated by principles of cultural-historical psychology) to all of the children for purposes of differential diagnosis and remediation. It was in the course of this work that we first came to understand what we were doing as a form of romantic science (LCHC, 1982).

## The Fifth Dimension as a Medium of Research

It should be clear from Chapter 10 that I consider the methodology of the research in the Fifth Dimension to be an extended example of romantic science, one that applies to the growth of systems of activity as well as to the growth of the children and undergraduates who inhabit them and give them life. But I also see it as a particularly useful tertiary artifact for thinking about and acting on issues associated with my identity as a developmental psychologist. These include such "micro" research questions as demonstrating conditions under which cooperative interaction around intellectual goals and means can be routinely arranged for and analyzed or the effectiveness of writing through e-mail in enhancing children's communicative skills. They also include more macro goals such as ways to understand better the impediments to fulfilling my community's goals for

children, particularly goals associated with mastery of modern technologies and the ability to work well with other people.

The 5thD is an especially useful medium within which to study
the interrelation of different genetic domains because in it we track
activity at the levels of the institution, the activity as a whole, and
face-to-face interaction among individual participants. Moreover,
since each 5thD quickly develops its own local cultural configuration,
it is also possible to conduct "cross-cultural" studies of children in
different Fifth Dimensions, such as that described in Chapter 10 with
respect to problem solving.

A methodological issue of special current interest to me is the
status of undergraduate fieldnotes as data. From the perspective of
methodological behaviorism, this method cannot be objective and
rigorous. From the perspective of cultural-historical theory, however,
the undergraduates are privileged observers of the interactions they
describe because they helped to make them.

Several features of undergraduate fieldnotes have especially impressed me. The first is that they resolutely fuse cognition and emotion. The students want to be liked, they want to have fun, they want
to help the child, they want good grades. The kids have a parallel set
of wants. Under these conditions, the interactions are interpreted by
the undergraduates, as it were, from the perspective of their affective
significance. But that evaluation depends on their own and their partner's cognitive achievements.

We are currently in the process of comparing information in undergraduate notes with analysis of videotapes of the same interactions. We are interested both in the way dialogue is recalled and in
ways of documenting the affective qualities of the interaction as they
relate to cognitive achievements and disappointments. Equally important will be documentation of those factors as they are linked to
the social relations between the participants.

Because the Fifth Dimension behaves in various ways like a sociocultural system, it is my belief that it can be used as a medium within
which to compare theoretical insights provided by various social and
cultural theorists as well as psychologists. Consequently, we are conducting analyses of the 5thD in terms of a number of theoretical
positions: Russian activity theory, Lave and Wenger's ideas of legitimate peripheral participation, Rogoff's ideas about planes of analysis,

Habermas's ideas about the conditions and consequences of ideal discourse, Foucault's concerns with power, and so on.

At the "cultural-historical level" of the 5thD we are currently carrying out a comparative analysis of several systems created in widely differing geographical locations. One such system has been taken up by both the local school system and the university to become a regular part of the curriculum, required of all future teachers. Others are in various stages of growth. Still others have died. These histories will provide us with the materials for a comparative analysis of the growth, death, and flowering of the systems, the development of children within them, and the conditions in which such hybrid systems can grow and flourish.

⑥ So there we have one particular answer to the question of how to go about implementing a second, cultural psychology. Consistent with the ideas of nineteenth- and early twentieth-century cultural psychologists, as well as the Russian cultural-historical school, I adopt a developmental approach to the study of human nature. Consistent with the broad, contextualist underpinnings of cultural psychology, I seek to derive its principles from activities located at the level of everyday practices and to return to those practices as a grounding for its theoretical claims.

My approach is, in a certain sense, old-fashioned. It fits well with Hugo Münsterberg's idea that the two psychologies can be productively combined in practice when the knowledge gained from the first psychology becomes the instrument of human purpose. I find Luria's idea of a romantic science to be a useful extension of Münsterberg's because it bridges the additional dichotomy between idiographic and nomothetic science, the science of the unique and the science of the general, which is implied by the "two sciences" formulation. At the same time, it requires the investigator to return time and again to become immersed in real life.

In the end, my version of a cultural psychology is simply stated: Adopt some form of cultural-historical psychology as your theoretical framework. Create a methodology, a systematic way of relating theory to data that draws upon both the natural sciences and the cultural sciences, as befits its hybrid object, human beings. Find an activity setting where you can be both participant and analyst. Enter into the process of helping things grow in the activity system you have entered by bringing to bear all the knowledge gained from both the cultural and natural sciences sides of psychology and allied disciplines. Take your ability to create and sustain effective systems as evidence of your theory's adequacy. The failures are sure to outnumber the successes by a goodly margin, making it certain that you will never run out of interesting things to do.

# Notes

## 1. Enduring Questions and Disputes

1. This attribution of paternity has been shown to be a myth (Blumenthal, 1975; Brock, 1993b). Equal credit might be given to other German scholars such as Helmholtz or to scholars in other countries such as William James in the United States, Francis Galton in England, and Vladimir Bekhterev in Russia.

2. Prospero spoke of Caliban thus: "Abhorred slave, / Which any print of goodness wilt not take / . . . I pitied thee, / Took pains to make thee speak, taught thee each hour / One thing or other: when thou didst not, savage, / Know thine own meaning, but wouldst gabble like / A thing most brutish, I endow'd thy purposes / With words that made them known" (*The Tempest* I.2).

3. However, this ecological view, complicated by theories of the economic practices and social institutions encouraged by different geographic-climatological conditions, has remained an important element in anthropological thought in the twentieth century (Harris, 1968, pp. 41ff). In modified form, it can also be found in theories of gene-culture co-evolution (Lumsden and Wilson, 1983).

4. For example, Carl Vogt in his *Lectures on Man*, published by the Anthropological Society of London in 1864, claimed anatomical evidence that the Negro is intermediary between the ape and the white man, offering such presumed facts as these: (1) the foot of the gorilla is more anthropoid than that of any other ape and the foot of the Negro more ape-like than that of the white man; (2) the Negro is as much distinguished from the white man, by the comparative thickness of the spinal cord and the nerve trunks, as the ape is from the Negro; (3) there is a "remarkable resemblance" between the brains of apes and of human beings of "the lower type."

5. In recent times a variety of more sophisticated criteria have been used to define levels of historical development and evolutionary sequence (Levinson and Malone, 1980). Leslie White (1959), for example, focused on the per-capita level of energy consumption; Carneiro (1973) used statistical analysis to establish sequences of increasing social complexity of social institutions. Common to these approaches, despite their differences, is the selection of a single criterion, or a small set of criteria, to characterize the level of development of a culture *as a whole.*

6. No better example of this process can be offered than Rudyard Kipling's famous lamentation on the "white man's burden": "Take up the White Man's Burden / Send forth the best ye breed / Go, bind your sons to exile / To serve the captive's need: /To wait in heavy harness, / On fluttered folk and wild / Your new-caught, sullen people, / Half-devil and half-child."

7. For a deeper analysis of Plato's contributions to contemporary psychological thought from the perspective of cognitive science, see Gardner (1985); for a deeper analysis of Plato's thought with respect to incorporating culture in mind, see Shweder (1991).

8. Later in this chapter I will discuss the concept of *Völkerpsychologie* in greater detail. Suffice it to say here that the concept is difficult to render satisfactorily in English. Blumenthal (1975), who has written extensively on the history of psychology, refers to *Völkerpsychologie* as cultural psychology. Discussing the problem of translation, he writes: "*Völkerpsychologie* is a unique German term, one that has generally been mistranslated as 'folk psychology.' However, the prefix, *Völker,* carries the meaning of 'ethnic' or 'cultural' " (p. 1081).

9. Mill was following in the tradition of David Hume, who had attempted to identify laws of association on the model of Newton's theory of gravitation. Noting physicists' success in determining the laws governing the movement of planets, he suggested that the same could be done for other parts of nature. There is no reason, Hume wrote, "to despair of equal success in our inquiries concerning the mental powers and economy if prosecuted with equal capacity and caution. It is probable that one operation and principle of mind depends on another" (1843/1948, section 1, pp. 14–15).

10. I am indebted to Bernd Krewer and Gustav Jahoda (1990) for their summary of the contents and context of the work of Lazarus and Steinthal. My discussion is derived from their work (see also Jahoda, 1992).

11. Recent historiography has shown that many of these criticisms were based upon far less substantial causes than officially remembered by psychologists (Brock, 1993b).

12. Cahan and White (1992) point to an interesting exception to this generalization in the ideas of E. C. Tolman, the most "cognitive" of the leading behaviorists. In defending the use of rats as suitable subjects upon which to base a general psychology, Tolman announced the following "confession of faith": "I believe that everything important in psychology (except perhaps such matters as the building up of a superego, that is everything save such matters as involve society and words) can be investigated in essence through the continued experimental and theoretical analysis of determiners of rat behavior at a choice point in a maze" (1938/1958, p. 172). Tolman's exceptions identify rather clearly the hallmarks of the second psychology that we have traced back to Mill, Wundt, and Münsterberg.

## 2. Cross-Cultural Investigations

1. William Kessen (1990, p. 12) provides a useful catalog of starting dates for the different social science disciplines: 1880, Academy of Political Science; 1884, American Historical Association; 1885, American Economic Association; 1892, American Psychological Association; 1899, National Institute of Social Science; 1902, American Anthropological Association; 1905, American Sociological Association.

2. I know of no outright attempts to replicate any cross-cultural psychological experiment using the same procedures and the same cultural groups. There have, however, been attempts to replicate findings by applying the same procedures to other groups for which the same underlying causal factors are assumed to be operative. For example, there have been several replications of A. R. Luria's (1976) research on syllogistic reasoning, most but not all of which have replicated his basic findings (Cole, Gay, Glick, and Sharp, 1971; Das and Dash, 1990; Scribner, 1977; Tulviste, 1991).

3. Titchener did not totally reject the idea of cross-cultural experimentation. In fact, he urged cooperation between laboratory researcher and field worker, and hazarded the guess that highly specific methods based on very precise instruments might make possible scientifically valid comparisons *for the study of elementary psychological functions.* However, when we consider that the researchers' measurements of sensory acuity were influenced by the ways in which subjects interpreted what they were supposed to be doing, it seems inescapable that elementary and higher psychological processes (those involving systems of meanings) are both involved.

4. I provide sufficient detail here only to follow the general logic of the research program and its major findings. An extended discussion of the original research and many follow-up studies can be found in Segall, Dasen, Berry, and Poortinga (1990). See also Wagner (1977) for an additional, carefully conducted study of visual illusions.

5. S. F. Nadel, an anthropologist who reviewed this topic about the same time, summed up the thinking of most anthropologists when he commented that not only were the test scores obtained in such studies completely out of line with the impressions of anthropologists who had worked with such people over extended periods of time, but "natives belonging to groups whose social efficiency and adjustment to environment cannot be doubted obtain a score so low as to seem absurd" (Nadel, 1939, p. 185).

6. Eells (1951) provides three criteria that a test would have to pass in order to be considered culture free: (a) the test must be composed of items which deal with materials common (or equally unfamiliar) to the various subcultures in which it is to be used; (b) it must be expressed in language and other symbols (or materials) which are equally familiar (or unfamiliar) to the different subcultures; (c) it must be so organized and administered as to stimulate equal degrees of interest and motivation from the different subcultures.

7. Many years later, Deregowski (1970) obtained similar results comparing rural and urban Zambian adolescents. He predicted, correctly, that the urban subjects would emphasize temporal items built into the stories more than their rural brethren because clock time and dates had become such a prominent aspect of their lives. For nontemporal aspects of the stories there were negligible differences in recall between

the groups, but for the key temporal items the urban subjects displayed superior recall.

8. Two earlier studies using stories as the to-be-remembered materials, one by Dube (1977) and the other by Ross and Millsom (1970), found somewhat better recall by African than by American subjects.

## 3. Cognitive Development, Culture, and Schooling

1. Within the span of a single year in the 1960s, more influential articles and monographs on culture and mind were published than at any comparable time in the prior eighty years of the discipline. These included the Segall, Campbell, and Herskovitz (1966) study of culture and perception discussed in Chapter 2, Witkin's (1967) theory of culture and cognitive style, Piaget (1966) writing about culture and cognitive development, and Greenfield, Bruner, and their colleagues' (1966) monograph on cognitive growth, culture, and schooling. The *International Journal of Psychology* led off its inaugural issue in 1966 with Piaget's summary of the cross-cultural evidence vis-à-vis his theory. This publication served as a major vehicle for research on culture and mind until the *Journal of Cross-Cultural Psychology* made its appearance in 1973. The next decade saw a veritable outpouring of cross-cultural, developmental research.

2. Participants in this project included Thomas Ciborowski, John Gay, Joseph Glick, Frederick Frankel, John Kellemu, David Lancy, and Donald Sharp. It was supported by the National Science Foundation.

3. Many years later, on the basis of detailed clinical interviews with skilled players from the Ivory Coast and computer simulations, Jean Retschitzski (1989) concluded that the strategies offered by players require the kind of thinking characteristic of formal logical operations.

4. This is not to say that such modeling is impossible. In later years anthropologists and psychologists (ourselves included) did build successful experimental models of a variety of indigenous practices. At the time, however, we did not properly integrate our observational studies of everyday practices with our experimental studies of the influence of schooling.

5. The effect of schooling on syllogistic reasoning has been found repeatedly, but Das and Dash (1990) failed to find superior syllogistic reasoning among Indian children because non-schooled children performed quite well.

6. Brown and French (1979) and Ginsburg (1979), in their commentaries on this monograph, expressed concern that our evidence not be taken to indicate that schooling is irrelevant to development. Then, as now, we agreed; but specifying the effects of schooling in cognitive-psychological terms remains a difficult challenge.

7. See LCHC (1982) for a discussion of this issue. Frijda and Jahoda (1966) considered the intertwined nature of culture-behavior relations so tangled as to make causal analysis impossible.

## 4. From Cross-Cultural Psychology to the Second Psychology

1. Scribner's (1985) paper on Vygotsky's uses of history presents a brilliant treatment of several difficult concepts in Vygotsky's treatment of historical change.

2. For an excellent summary of Vygotsky's writings on this subject, see Van der Veer and Valsiner (1991). For Luria's views see Luria (1979).

3. The Russian cultural-historical approach first appeared in English in a series of publications in the late 1920s and 1930s (Leontiev, 1932; Luria; 1928, 1932; Vygotsky, 1929). They have subsequently been supplemented by a large number of volumes (e.g., Leontiev, 1978, 1981; Luria, 1976, 1979; Vygotsky 1978, 1934/1987, Van der Veer and Valsiner, 1994).

4. The wording of this passage reveals an important commonality between the words "means" and "medium" in Russian. The Russian word translated here as medium in the phrase "by the medium of which" was almost certainly *sredstvo,* judging from similar statements in other articles written at this time. Sredstvo is often translated as "means," particularly in the phrase "by means of which." I note this confusion because the intimate relation between means and media is one of the central theoretical assumptions of the cultural-historical approach.

5. The Russian philosopher Pavel Florenskii (1990, p. 346), also writing at this time, referred to culture as the "medium that grows and nourishes the personality."

6. Van der Veer and Valsiner (1994) suggest that *Tool and Symbol* was also a joint Vygotsky-Luria publication.

7. Vygotsky and Luria quote Marx concerning the essence of labor: in labor "an object given by nature itself becomes an organ of man's activity, an organ which he annexes to the organs of his body, in the way extending, in spite of the bible, the natural dimensions of the latter" (p. 77).

8. In the case of Vygotsky the search for originals is particularly problematic because many presumed original papers are edited versions of stenographic notes and all of his work was the subject of ideological disputes that often affected what was presented as the original text. See Van der Veer and Valsiner (1991) for elucidation of this problem.

## 5. Putting Culture in the Middle

1. For a discussion of language as a system of artifacts and the homology between words and what we usually think of as material artifacts, see Rossi-Landi (1983, pp. 120ff).

2. In my experience it is difficult at first to grasp the notion that language is artifactual, perhaps because the materiality of language seems transparent. A simple demonstration makes the point clearly. When you hear a language that you do not understand, you are experiencing only its material manifestations. The meaning of the words, their "ideal" aspect, is missing because you lack a past history of interactions using those artifacts as mediational means.

3. Here again I need to note the affinity of this approach to artifact mediation and Dewey's notions. As Larry Hickman points out in his analysis of Dewey's "pragmatic technology," Dewey believed that "the tools and artifacts we call technological may be found on either side of what he argued was an extremely malleable and permeable membrane that separates the 'internal' from the 'external' with respect to the organism only in the loosest and most tentative senses" (Hickman, 1990, p. 12).

4. Richard Barrett (1989) provides an interesting discussion of White's symbolic/mediational views in relation to his better-known ideas concerning materialist social evolutionism.

5. Members of this seminar included Aaron Cicourel, Roy D'Andrade, Jean Mandler, George Mandler, Jay McClelland, Bud Mehan, and Donald Norman.

6. Dorothy Holland and Jaan Valsiner (1988) point out that the anthropological notion of "cultural models" is very similar to the cultural-historical notion of a mediator. Holland and Valsiner use the term "mediational device" and find it useful to limit mediational devices to "circumscribed, tangible activities or objects of sensory dimensions." I prefer to think of cultural models as systems of artifacts in order to emphasize the dual materiality/ideality of both cultural models and artifacts with more obvious sensory dimensions.

7. This limitation of scripts as mediators underpins Milan Kundera's remark: "We leave childhood without knowing what youth is, we marry without knowing what it is to be married, and even when we enter old age, we don't know what it is we're heading for: the old are innocent children of their old age. In that sense, man's world is a planet of inexperience" (1988, pp. 132–133).

8. Ray McDermott (1993) provides a striking illustration of the shifting boundaries between object and context that provides phenomenalistic access to a process that seems semi-mystical in abstract discussions such as this one. He uses a visual illusion that is created by slightly shifting the frame of a pattern of intertwining lines. Although we know that nothing has changed in the pattern, the pattern we see is no longer perceptually the same.

9. Bateson, who can be considered an expert on the topic, commented on the difficulty of thinking relationally about context: "Let me say that I don't know how to think that way. Intellectually I can stand here and give you a reasoned exposition of this matter; but if I am cutting down a tree, I still think, 'Gregory Bateson is cutting down the tree. *I* am cutting down the tree.' 'Myself' is to me still an excessively concrete object, different from the rest of what I have been calling 'mind.' The step to realizing—to making habitual—the other way of thinking, so that one naturally thinks that way when one reaches for a glass of water or cuts down a tree—that step is not an easy one" (1972, p. 462).

10. Readers familiar with contemporary sociological theories of action will readily recognize here a close affinity between the views about mediation derived from the writings of the cultural-historical school and those of Anthony Giddens (1984). For example, Giddens writes, "According to the notion of the duality of structure, the structural properties of social systems are both medium and outcome of the practices they recursively organize . . . Structure is not to be equated with constraint but is always both constraining and enabling" (p. 25).

## 6. Phylogeny and Cultural History

1. Sigmund Freud lucidly summarized the limitations inherent in retrospective analysis: "So long as we trace the development from its final stage backwards, the connection appears continuous, and we feel that we have gained insight which is completely satisfactory or even exhaustive. But if we proceed the reverse way, if we start from the premises inferred from the analysis and try to follow these up to the final result, then we no longer get the impression of an inevitable sequence of events which could not be otherwise determined. We notice at once that there might have been another result" (1920/1924, p. 226).

2. This is not to say that *australopithecus* did not engage in simple tool use of the kind found among modern chimpanzees. The difficulty is that only stone tools could be expected to survive to the present.

3. Some, like Donald (1991), claim that there was also myth and ritual, but in the absence of material remains this is probably best considered conjecture.

4. Neanderthals, who coexisted with *Homo sapiens*, did not have anatomically modern voice apparatuses, leading to speculation that differences in communication capacities were crucial to the development of *Homo sapiens* and the stagnation and eventual demise of the Neanderthal (Lieberman, 1991).

5. Whether the tools used by *Homo erectus* were complicated enough to require such teaching is in dispute. Wynn (1988) argues that they are not; Donald (1991), citing studies where modern humans take a good deal of time and instruction to learn to make early stone tools, argues that they are.

6. The graph in Figure 6.1 might also be interpreted as a depiction of Engels's statement: "The eternal laws of nature to an ever greater extent are changing into laws of history."

7. The Russians also used Thurnwald as an authority to argue against biological explanations of cultural variations and for the idea that the elementary psychological functions are common to all of humanity owing to their common phylogenetic heritage.

8. I spent the summer of 1966 in Moscow working through the Central Asian materials in preparation for the work that eventuated in *The Cultural Context of Learning and Thinking* (1971). I brought with me the most recent literature available at the time.

## 7. A Cultural Approach to Ontogeny

1. The opposite cases are also possible, as when a mutation brings about rapid change in ontogenetic change (usually with disastrous consequences), or when the advent of a new technology, or a war, transforms the process of ontogenetic change.

2. Note that this example implicates cultural influences in prenatal development. Such influences consist both of ways in which the mother's ingestion of various biological agents are shaped by cultural practices (Mead and Newton, 1967) and of exposure to language in various forms (Mehler et al., 1986; De Casper and Spence, 1986; see Cole and Cole, 1993, ch. 3, for a summary).

3. In addition, as life-span developmental psychologists emphasize, unique historical events (a war, a depression) may provoke great discontinuity in development (Baltes, Featherman, and Lerner, 1990).

4. For the large and growing literature on the developmental consequences of parental beliefs for children's development and the myriad of cultural formations that result, see Harkness and Super (1995).

5. The rather rigid schedule imposed by modern industrialized life may be pushing the limits of what the immature human brain can sustain; while the length of a longest sleep period may be a good indicator of physical maturity, pushing those limits may be a source of stress with negative consequences for children who cannot measure up to parental expectations (Konner and Super, 1987).

6. Whiting and Edwards also invoke the notion of a script. They report that the settings inhabited by children at different ages and in different communities are organized in terms of "scripts for daily life." These scripted activities become the primary locus of developmental change.

7. In the past decade there have been a variety of attempts to relate modules to

specific central nervous system mechanisms (Edelman, 1992) and to various forms of intelligence (Gardner, 1983).

8. One further bit of evidence about the circumstances necessary for the development of language comes from cases in which adults from two language groups interact through a pidgin language and their children, hearing only pidgin, which lacks many features of normal language, create and speak a creole, which has the basic features of a normal language (Bickerton, 1990).

9. The similarity of Bruner's formulation of the basic cultural unit required for language acquisition and Savage-Rumbaugh's use of this same unit in her work with chimpanzees, and their common similarity to Nelson's ideas about scripts/generalized events, should not go unnoticed.

10. Barbara Rogoff makes the same point: "Biology and culture are not alternative influences but inseparable aspects of a system within which individuals develop" (1990, p. 28).

## 8. The Cognitive Analysis of Behavior in Context

1. This discussion draws heavily on the unpublished monograph by Cole, Hood, and McDermott (1979).

2. Other important sources of ideas about ecological validity include Roger Barker, whose work on the effects of social setting on behavior retains its influence to the present day, and J. J. Gibson, who claimed that the crucial questions in the study of perception are to be resolved not so much by an attention to the perceiver as by the description of how the environment in particular everyday-life arrangements "affords" a person perceptual information.

3. Consider what kind of difficulties Brunswik would have faced had he been forced to proceed without any of these resources for interpretation. If he had obtained equivocal results with respect to constancy based on proximal or distal cues, he would have been in a quandary. He might have wanted to conclude that real-life perception depends upon a mix of distal and proximal cues; he might have pleaded that his subject was in some way atypical. He might have begun to worry about the efficacy of his question as a means of inducing the subject in a real-world environment to engage in a task that he had successfully posed in the laboratory.

4. This point was made not long after we began our work by Schwartz and Taylor (1978) in their discussion of validating standardized achievement and IQ tests: "Does the test elicit the same behavior as would the same tasks embedded in a real non-contrived situation? . . . Reality is a difficult notion. Both physics and the psychology of perception tell us that human interactions with the real world are usually—some would say exclusively—mediated by models that inform the vision of the beholder. Further, even to speak of the same task across contexts requires a model of the structure of the task. In the absence of such a model, one does not know where the equivalence lies" (p. 54).

5. Support for this work came from the Ford Foundation and the Carnegie Foundation.

6. Survey work was carried out with the assistance of Ethan Golegor, Robert Schwartz, and Elizabeth Hurlow-Hannah. Michael Smith conducted the village ethnography of Vai literacy.

7. Lois Hood, Ray McDermott, and Ken Traupmann collaborated with me in this study, which was supported by the Carnegie Corporation.

8. For an account of another project which used this facility, see Miller (1977).

9. Jaan Valsiner and Laura Benigni (1986) argue (persuasively, in my opinion) that ecological research must start from the premise that biological organisms, of which *Homo sapiens* is an example, are *open systems* and that ecological research must study the ongoing exchanges between the organism and its meaningfully structured environment (its cultural context).

10. Joseph Glick (1991) provided a useful framework for thinking about this issue. He argued that there is a tradeoff between structuration in one's analytic tools and the structuring of the phenomena being analyzed: "If you have weak analytic devices then you need 'strong' data garnered in the most restrictive, closed system kinds of ways. However, if you have strong analytic devices, you can loosen up on the kind of data allowed into the system."

11. Our work contrasting preschoolers' use of language in their classroom and in the supermarket makes Reed and Lave's case for language.

## 9. Creating Model Activity Systems

1. The "we" in this case included Denis Newman and Peg Griffin, who took day-to-day responsibility for the project. The teachers who made this work possible were Marilyn Quinsaat, Kim Whooley, and Will Nibblet. Bud Mehan, Margaret Riel, Sheila Broyles, and Andrea Pettito made important contributions to different aspects of the project. For more details about this work see Newman, Griffin, and Cole, 1989.

2. A full report of this work has only appeared in Russian; see Peg Griffin, Esteban Diaz, Catherine King, and Michael Cole, "Re-mediating learning difficulties," in *A Socio-historical Approach to Learning and Instruction* (Pedagogika Publishing House, 1989). A more detailed account of the events surrounding this work can be found in LCHC (1982). The group that undertook this work included Ann Brown, Joe Campione, Bud Mehan, and Ken Traupmann. Brown and Campione were engaged at the time in creating new forms of reading activity and designing cognitive training regimes to help low-achieving children overcome their difficulties with school learning. Traupmann shared their interest in cognitive training studies. Mehan was beginning to study the factors associated with the decision to place children in special education classrooms and their fate once placed there. The Bureau of the Educationally Handicapped provided support.

3. The four models were based upon the following ideas: (1) increasing comprehension through increasing lexical access (based on the work of Isabel Beck and her colleagues at the University of Pittsburgh: Beck, Perfetti, and McKeown, 1982); (2) enhancing comprehension as internalized problem solving (from the Kamehameha Early Education Project, KEEP, 1981); (3) comprehension enhancement through the guided anticipation of meaning (Fillmore and Kay, 1983); (4) reciprocal reading instruction (Brown and Palincsar, 1982).

## 10. A Multi-level Methodology for Cultural-Historical Psychology

1. Funding for this research came from the Carnegie Corporation, the Mellon Foundation, and the Spencer Foundation.

2. In Leontiev's (1981) terms, the 5thD provides a variety of possible effective motives, in addition to motives (such as the need to master new information technologies) that are "merely understandable" to the children.

3. These materials are based upon software provided by the Sunburst Corporation for purposes of research.

4. This analysis was carried out by Vanessa Gack.

5. The 5thD proved to be an effective medium for conducting bi-national research on learning and development (Belyaeva and Cole, 1989). The additional centers were run by Catherine King in New Orleans, Gillian McNamee in Chicago, and members of the VEGA international laboratory in Moscow.

## 11. The Work in Context

1. This paradigmatic difference accounts for the anthropologist Harry Wolcott's reaction to our research among the Kpelle: "I'll expect more of a sensation when we reach the point at which such [experimental] observations provide the lift from the runways of contrived performance to the ethereal and illusive process of normal cognitive functioning" (1972, pp. 449–450).

2. The issue of a theory of situation has not gone away in the intervening years. Lauren Resnick has recently proposed a "situated rationalist" framework for understanding development. As Resnick puts it, a theory combining biological and sociocultural "prepared structures" "will require a theory that is now largely absent from psychological thinking and only loosely developed in other fields of social science, *a theory of situations*. Such a theory would define the dimensions—social, cognitive, and physical—of situations with an eye to how activity in one situation might prepare individuals to enter another. Developing such a theory, taking into account both biological and social constraints on learning, represents a major challenge for those who would apply the concept of situated rationalism to education" (1994, p. 491).

3. Recent work by Edwin Hutchins (1995; Hutchins and Hazlehurst, 1991) has shown that it is also possible to model culturally mediated cognitive development in the class of computer programs known as parallel distributed processing models.

# References

Adams, M. J. 1990. *Learning to Read: Thinking and Learning about Print*. Cambridge, Mass.: MIT Press.

Adamson, L. B. 1995. *Communication Development during Infancy*. Madison, Wis.: Brown and Benchmark's.

Altman, I., and Rogoff, B. 1987. World views in psychology: Trait, interactional, organismic, and transactional perspectives. In D. Stokols and I. Altman, eds., *Handbook of Environmental Psychology*, vol. 1. New York: Wiley.

American Association for the Advancement of Science (AAAS). 1984. *Equity and Excellence: Compatible Goals*. AAAS Publication 84–14. Washington: Office of Opportunities in Science.

Anderson, A. B., Teale, W. H., and Estrada, E. 1980. Low-income children's preschool literacy experiences: Some naturalistic observations. *Quarterly Newsletter of the Laboratory of Comparative Human Cognition, 2,* 59–65.

Antell, S. E., and Keating, D. P. 1983. Perception of numerical invariance in neonates. *Child Development, 54,* 695–701.

Austin, J. 1962. *How to Do Things with Words*. Oxford: Oxford University Press.

Baillargeon, R. 1987. Object permanence in 3 1/2- and 4 1/2-month old infants. *Developmental Psychology, 23,* 655–664.

Bakhtin, M. M. 1981. *The Dialogic Imagination: Four Essays by M. M. Bakhtin*. M. Holquist, ed. Austin: University of Texas Press.

——— 1986. *Speech Genres and Other Late Essays*. C. Emerson and M. Holquist, eds. Austin: University of Texas Press.

Bakhurst, D. 1991. *Consciousness and Revolution in Soviet Philosophy: From the Bolsheviks to Evald Ilyenkov*. Cambridge: Cambridge University Press.

Bakhurst, D., and Padden, C. 1991. The Meshcheryakov experiment: Soviet work on the education of the blind-deaf. *Learning and Instruction, 1*, 201–215.

Baltes, P. B., Featherman, D. L., and Lerner, R. M., eds. 1990. *Life-span Development and Behavior,* vol. 10. Hillsdale, N.J.: Erlbaum.

Barash, D. P. 1986. *The Hare and the Tortoise: Culture, Behavior, and Human Nature.* New York: Viking.

Baron-Cohen, S., Leslie, A., and Frith, U. 1985. Does the autistic child have a "theory of mind"? *Cognition, 21*, 37–46.

Bard, K. A. 1990. "Social tool use" by free ranging orangutans: A Piagetian and developmental perspective on the manipulation of an animate object. In Parker and Gibson, eds., 1990.

Barker, R. G., and Wright, H. F. 1951. *One Boy's Day: A Specimen Record of Behavior.* New York: Harper.

————— 1968. *Ecological Psychology.* Stanford: Stanford University Press.

Barkow, J. H. 1989. *Darwin, Sex, and Status: Biological Approaches to Mind and Culture.* Toronto: University of Toronto Press.

Barrett, R. A. 1989. The paradoxical anthropology of Leslie White. *American Anthropologist, 91*, 986–999.

Bartlett, F. C. 1923. *Psychology and Primitive Culture.* Cambridge: Cambridge University Press.

————— 1932. *Remembering.* Cambridge: Cambridge University Press.

————— 1958. *Thinking.* Cambridge: Cambridge University Press.

Bartlett, F. C., Ginsberg, M., Lindgren, E. J., and Thouless, R. H. 1939. *The Study of Society.* London: K. Paul, Trench, Trubner, and Co.

Bates, E. 1976. *Language and Context: The Acquisition of Pragmatics.* New York: Academic Press.

Bateson, G. 1936. *Naven.* Cambridge: Cambridge University Press.

————— 1972. *Steps to an Ecology of Mind.* New York: Ballantine.

Beach, K. 1995. Sociocultural change, activity, and individual development: Some methodological aspects. *Mind, Culture, and Activity: An International Journal, 2*, 277–284.

Beach, K. D. 1993. Becoming a bartender: The role of external memory cues in a work-directed educational activity. *Applied Cognitive Psychology, 7*, 191–204.

Beck, I. L., Perfetti, C. A., and McKeown, M. G. 1982. Effects of long-term vocabulary instruction on lexical access and reading comprehension. *Journal of Educational Psychology, 74*, 506–521.

Bellman, B. 1975. *Village of Curers and Assassins: On the Production of Fala Kpelle Cosmological Categories.* The Hague: Mouton.

Bellugi, U., Bihrle, A., Jernigan, T., Trauner, D., and Doherty, S. 1990. Neuropsychological, neurological, and neuroanatomical profile of Williams Syndrome. *American Journal of Medical Genetics Supplement, 6*, 115–125.

Belyaeva, A. V., and Cole, M. 1989. Computer-mediated joint activity in the service of human development: An overview. *Quarterly Newsletter of the Laboratory of Human Cognition, 11*, 45–97.

Bereiter, C. 1985. Toward a solution to the learning paradox. *Review of Educational Research, 55*, 201–226.

Bergson, H. 1911/1983. *Creative Evolution.* New York: Holt.

Berlin, I. 1981. *Against the Current: Essays in the History of Ideas.* Oxford: Oxford University Press.

Bernstein, R. 1971. *Praxis and Action: Contemporary Philosophies of Human Activity.* Philadelphia: University of Pennsylvania Press.

Berry, J. W. 1966. Temne and Eskimo perceptual skills. *International Journal of Psychology, 1,* 207–229.

——— 1971. Müller-Lyer susceptibility: Culture, ecology, or race? *International Journal of Psychology, 6,* 193–197.

——— 1976. *Human Ecology and Cultural Style.* New York: Sage-Halstead.

——— 1981. Developmental issues in the comparative study of psychological differentiation. In R. H. Munroe, R. L. Munroe, and B. B. Whiting, eds., *Handbook of Cross-cultural Human Development.* New York: Garland STPM.

Berry, J. W., and Bennett, J. 1989. Syllabic literacy and cognitive performance among the Cree. *International Journal of Psychology, 24,* 429–450.

Berry, J. W., Poortinga, Y. H., Segall, M., and Dasen, P. R. 1992. *Cross-cultural Psychology: Research and Applications.* New York: Cambridge University Press.

Berry, J. W., Van de Koppel, J. M., Sénéchal, C., Annis, R. C., Bahuchet, S., Cavalli-Sforza, L. L., and Witkin, H. 1986. *On the Edge of the Forest: Cultural Adaptation and Cognitive Development in Central Africa.* Lisse: Swets and Zeitlinger.

Betanzos, R. J. 1988. Dilthey: An introduction. In W. Dilthey, *Introduction to the Human Sciences: An Attempt to Lay the Foundations for the Study of Society and History.* Trans. R. J. Betanzos. Detroit: Wayne State University Press.

Bickerton, D. 1990. *Language and Species.* Chicago: University of Chicago Press.

Binet, A., and Simon, T. 1916. *The Development of Intelligence in Children.* Vineland, N.J.: Publications of the Training School at Vineland. Rpt. Nashville: Williams Publishing, 1980.

Blank, M. 1973. *Teaching Learning in the Preschool: A Dialogue Approach.* Columbus: Merrill.

Bloom, L. 1993. *The Transition from Infancy to Language: Acquiring the Power of Expression.* Cambridge: Cambridge University Press.

Bloom, L., Rocissano, L., and Hood, L. 1976. Adult-child discourse: Developmental interaction between information processing and linguistic knowledge. *Cognitive Psychology, 8,* 521–552.

Blumenthal, A. 1975. A reappraisal of Wilhelm Wundt. *American Psychologist, 30,* 1081–1088.

Bock, P. K. 1988. *Continuities in Psychological Anthropology: A Historical Introduction.* 2nd ed. New York: Freeman.

Boesch, C. 1993. Transmission aspects of tool use in wild chimpanzees. In T. Ingold and K. Gibson, eds., *Tool, Language, and Intelligence: An Evolutionary Perspective.* Cambridge: Cambridge University Press.

Boesch, E. E. 1990. *Symbolic Action Theory and Cultural Psychology.* Berlin: Springer-Verlag.

Bolton, R., Michelson, C., Wilde, J., and Bolton, C. 1975. The heights of illusion: On the relationship between altitude and perception. *Ethos, 3,* 403–424.

Bourdieu, P. 1977. *Outline of a Theory of Practice.* New York: Cambridge University Press.

Bousfield, W. A. 1953. The occurrence of clustering in the free recall of randomly arranged associates. *Journal of General Psychology, 49,* 229–240.

Bowen, E. 1964. *Return to Laughter.* New York: Doubleday.

Boysen, S. T. 1993. Counting in chimpanzees. In S. T. Boysen and E. J. Capaldi, eds., *The Development of Numerical Competence: Animal and Human Models.* Hillsdale, N.J.: Erlbaum.

Brace, C. L., Gamble, G. R., and Bond, J. T. 1971. *Race and Intelligence.* Washington: American Anthropological Association.

Bremmer, M. E. 1985. The practice of arithmetic in Liberian schools. *Anthropology and Education Quarterly, 16,* 177–186.

Brewer, S. M., and McGrew, W. C. 1989. Chimpanzee use of a tool-set to get honey. *Folia Primatalogia, 54,* 100–104.

Bringmann, W. G., and Tweney, R. D., eds. *Wundt Studies: A Centennial Collection.* Toronto: C. J. Hogrefe.

Brock, A. 1993a. Charles Hubbard Judd: A Wundtian psychologist in the United States. *Geschichte und Psychologie, 2,* 19–23.

———— 1993b. Something old, something new: The "reappraisal" of Wilhelm Wundt in textbooks. *Theory and Psychology, 3,* 235–242.

Bronfenbrenner, U. 1979. *The Ecology of Human Development.* Cambridge, Mass.: Harvard University Press.

———— 1986. Ecology of the family as a context for human development: Research perspectives. *Developmental Psychology, 22,* 723–742.

Brown, A. L. 1992. Design experiments: Theoretical and methodological challenges in creating complex interventions in classroom settings. *Journal of Learning Sciences, 2,* 141–178.

Brown, A. L., and French, L. A. Commentary. *Monographs of the Society for Research in Child Development, 44,* ser. 178, 101–109.

Brown, A. L., and Palincsar, A. S. 1982. Inducing strategic learning from text by means of informed, self-control training. *Topics in Learning and Learning Disabilities, 2,* 1–17.

Brown, J. S., Collins, A., and Duguid, P. 1989. Situated cognition and the culture of learning. *Educational Researcher, 18,* 32–42.

Bruner, J. S. 1982. Formats of language acquisition. *American Journal of Semiotics, 1,* 1–16.

———— 1983. *Child's Talk.* New York: Norton.

———— 1990. *Acts of Meaning.* Cambridge, Mass.: Harvard University Press.

———— 1996. *The Culture of Education.* Cambridge, Mass.: Harvard University Press.

Brunswik, E. 1943. Organismic achievement and environmental probability. *Psychological Review, 50,* 255–272.

Brushlinskii, A. V. 1968. *The Cultural-Historical Theory of Thinking* (in Russian). Moscow: Vysshyaya Shkola.

Burke, K. 1945. *A Grammar of Motives.* New York: Prentice-Hall.

———— 1962. *The Grammar of Motives and a Rhetoric of Motives.* Cleveland: World Publishing Co.

Buss, D. M. 1994. *The Evolution of Desire.* New York: Basic Books.

Butterworth, G. E. 1991. The ontogeny and phylogeny of joint visual attention. In A. Whitten, ed., *Natural Theories of Mind.* Oxford: Blackwell.

Butterworth, G., and Jarrett, N. 1991. What minds have in common in space: Spatial mechanisms serving joint visual attention in infancy. *British Journal of Developmental Psychology, 9,* 55–72.

Cahan, E. D., and White, S. H. 1992. Proposals for a second psychology. *American Psychologist, 47,* 224–235.

Call, J., and Tomasello, M. 1996. The role of humans in the cognitive development of apes. In A. E. Russon, ed., *Reaching into Thought: The Minds of the Great Apes.* New York: Cambridge University Press.

Campos, J. J., and Sternberg, C. G. 1981. Perception, appraisal, and emotion: The onset of social referencing. In M. E. Lamb and L. R. Sherrod, eds., *Infants' Social Cognition: Empirical and Social Considerations.* Hillsdale, N.J.: Erlbaum.

Carey, S., and Gelman, R., eds. 1991. *The Epigenesis of Mind: Essays on Biology and Cognition.* Hillsdale, N.J.: Erlbaum.

Carneiro, R. L. 1973. The four faces of evolution: Unilinear, universal, multilinear, and differential. In, J. J. Honigmann, ed., *Handbook of Social and Cultural Anthropology.* Chicago: Rand McNally.

Carraher, T. N. 1986. From drawings to buildings: Working with mathematical scales. *International Journal of Behavioral Development, 9,* 527–544.

Carraher, T. N., Carraher, D. W., and Schliemann, A. D. 1985. Mathematics in the streets and in schools. *British Journal of Developmental Psychology, 3,* 21–29.

Carroll, J. B. 1982. The measurement of intelligence. In R. J. Sternberg, ed., *The Handbook of Human Intelligence.* Cambridge: Cambridge University Press.

Case, R. 1992. *The Mind's Staircase.* Hillsdale, N.J.: Erlbaum.

Cazden, C. B. 1981. Performance before competence: Assistance to child discourse in the zone of proximal development. *Quarterly Newsletter of the Laboratory of Comparative Human Cognition, 3,* 5–8.

—— 1992. *Readings of Vygotsky in Writing Pedagogy.* Paper presented at the University of Delaware, October 1.

Chaiklin, S., and Lave, J., eds. 1993. *Understanding Practice: Perspectives on Activity and Context.* New York: Cambridge University Press.

Chall, J. 1983. *Stages of Reading Development.* New York: McGraw-Hill.

Chamberlain, A. F. 1901. *The Child: A Study in the Evolution of Man.* London: Walter Scott.

Cheney, D. L., and Seyfarth, R. M. 1990. *How Monkeys See the World.* Cambridge: Cambridge University Press.

Childs, C., and Greenfield, P. M. 1980. Informal modes of learning and teaching: The case of Zinacanteco learning. In N. Warren, ed., *Studies in Cross-cultural Psychology,* vol. 2. New York: Academic Press.

Cicourel, A., Jennings, K. H., Jennings, S. H. M., Leiter, K. C. W., MacKay, R., Mehan, H., and Roth, D. R. 1974. *Language Use and School Performance.* New York: Academic Press.

Cohen, L., and Oakes, L. 1993. How infants perceive a simple causal event. *Developmental Psychology, 29,* 421–433.

Cohen, R., and Siegal, A. W. 1991. *Context and Development.* Hillsdale, N.J.: Erlbaum.

Cole, M. 1976. Introduction. In A. R. Luria, *Cognitive Development.* Cambridge, Mass.: Harvard University Press.

—— 1979. Afterword. In A. R. Luria, *The Making of Mind.* Cambridge, Mass.: Harvard University Press.

———— 1985. The zone of proximal development: Where culture and cognition create each other. In J. Wertsch, ed., *Culture, Communication, and Cognition*. New York: Cambridge University Press.

———— 1988. Cross-cultural research in the sociohistorical tradition. *Human Development, 31*, 137–151.

———— 1990. Cultural psychology: A once and future discipline? In J. J. Berman, ed., *Cross-cultural Perspectives. Nebraska Symposium on Motivation, 1989*. Lincoln: University of Nebraska Press.

———— 1992. Culture in development. In M. H. Bornstein and M. E. Lamb, eds., *Developmental Psychology: An Advanced Textbook*. 3rd ed. Hillsdale, N.J.: Erlbaum.

———— 1995a. From the perspective of the individual. *Communication Review, 1*, 129–132.

———— 1995b. Socio-cultural-historical psychology: Some general remarks and a proposal for a new kind of cultural-genetic methodology. In J. V. Wertsch, P. Del Rio, and A. Alvarez, eds., *Sociocultural Studies of Mind*. New York: Cambridge University Press.

Cole, M., ed. 1989. *Sotsialno-istoricheskii podkhod v obuchenii* (A social-historical approach to learning). Moscow: Pedagogika.

Cole, M., and Cole, S. R. 1996. *The Development of Children*. 3rd ed. New York: Scientific American Books.

Cole, M., Dore, J., Hall, W. S., and Dowley, G. 1978. Situational variability in the speech of preschool children. *Annals of the New York Academy of Science, 318*, 65–105.

Cole, M., Gay, J., and Glick, J. A. 1968. A cross-cultural study of information processing. *International Journal of Psychology, 3*, 93–102.

Cole, M., Gay, J., Glick, J. A., and Sharp, D. W. 1971. *The Cultural Context of Learning and Thinking*. New York: Basic Books.

Cole, M., Griffin, P., and The Laboratory of Comparative Human Cognition. 1987. *Contextual Factors in Education*. Madison: Wisconsin Center for Education Research.

Cole, M., Hood, L., and McDermott, R. 1979. Ecological niche picking: Ecological invalidity as an axiom of experimental cognitive psychology. Technical Report, Laboratory of Comparative Human Cognition, Rockefeller University, New York.

Cole, M., and Means, B. 1981. *Comparative Studies of How People Think*. Cambridge, Mass.: Harvard University Press.

Cole, M., and Traupmann, K. L. 1981. Learning from a learning disabled child. In W. A. Collins, ed., *Aspects of the Development of Competence: The Minnesota Symposia on Child Psychology*, vol. 14. Hillsdale, N.J.: Erlbaum.

Condorcet, J. 1822/1955. *Sketch for a Historical Picture of the Progress of the Human Mind*. London: Weidenfeld and Nicolson.

Crowder, R. G., and Wagner, R. K. 1992. *The Psychology of Reading*. 2nd ed. New York: Oxford University Press.

Curtiss, S. 1977. *Genie: A Psychological Study of a Modern-day Wild Child*. New York: Academic Press.

D'Andrade, R. 1984. Cultural meaning systems. In R. A. Shweder and R. A. Le Vine, eds., *Culture Theory: Essays on Mind, Self and Emotion.* New York: Cambridge University Press.

———— 1986. Three scientific world views and the covering law model. In D. W. Fiske and R. A. Shweder, eds., *Metatheory in Social Science: Pluralisms and Subjectivities.* Chicago: University of Chicago Press.

———— 1989. Cultural sharing and diversity. In R. Bolton, ed., *The Content of Culture: Constants and Variants: Essays in Honor of John M. Roberts.* New Haven: HRAF Press.

———— 1990. Some propositions about the relationship between culture and human cognition. In J. W. Stigler, R. A. Shweder, and G. Herdt, eds., *Cultural Psychology: Essays on Comparative Human Development.* New York: Cambridge University Press.

———— 1995. *The Development of Cognitive Anthropology.* New York: Cambridge University Press.

D'Andrade, R., and Strauss, C. 1992. *Human Motives and Cultural Models.* New York: Cambridge University Press.

Danziger, K. 1990. *Constructing the Subject: Historical Origins of Psychological Research.* New York: Cambridge University Press.

Darwin, C. 1859/1958. *The Origin of Species.* New York: Penguin.

Das, J. P., and Dash, U. N. 1990. Schooling, literacy, and cognitive development. In C. K. Leong and B. S. Randhawa, eds., *Understanding Literacy and Cognition: Theory, Research, and Application.* New York: Plenum.

Dasen, P. R. 1972. Cross-Cultural Piagetian research: A summary. *Journal of Cross-cultural Psychology, 3,* 29–39.

———— 1974. The influence of ecology, culture, and European contact on cognitive development in Australian Aborigines. In J. W. Berry and P. R. Dasen, eds., *Culture and Cognition.* London: Methuen.

———— 1975. Concrete operational development in three cultures. *Journal of Cross-cultural Psychology, 6,* 156–172.

———— 1977a. *Piagetian Psychology: Cross Cultural Contributions.* New York: Gardner.

———— 1977b. Are cognitive processes universal? A contribution to cross-cultural Piagetian psychology. In N. Warren, ed., *Studies in Cross-cultural Psychology,* vol. 1. London: Academic Press.

———— 1984. The cross-cultural study of intelligence: Piaget and the Baoulé. *International Journal of Psychology, 19,* 407–434.

Dasen, P. R., Berry, J. W., and Witkin, H. A. 1979. The use of developmental theories cross-culturally. In L. H. Eckensberger, W. J. Lonner, and Y. H. Poortinga, eds., *Cross-cultural Contributions to Psychology.* Lisse: Swets and Zeitlinger.

Dasen, P. R., and deRibaupierre, A. 1987. Neo-Piagetian theories: Cross-cultural and differential perspectives. *International Journal of Psychology, 22,* 793–832.

Dasen, P. R., and Heron, A. 1981. Cross-cultural tests of Piaget's theory. In H. C. Triandis and A. Heron, eds., *Handbook of Cross-Cultural Psychology,* vol. 4: *Developmental Psychology.* Boston: Allyn and Bacon.

Dasen, P. R., Lavallée, M., and Retschitzki, J. 1979. Training conservation of quantity (liquids) in West Africa (Baoulé) children. *International Journal of Psychology, 14,* 57–68.

Dasen, P. R., Ngini, L., and Lavallée, M. 1979. Cross-cultural training studies of concrete operations. In L. H. Eckenberger, W. J. Lonner, and Y. H. Poortinga, eds., *Cross-cultural Contributions to Psychology*. Lisse: Swets and Zeilinger.

Dawson, G., and Fischer, K. W. 1994. *Human Behavior and the Developing Brain*. New York: Guilford Press.

d'Azevedo, W. 1962. Uses of the past in Gola discourse. *Journal of African History, 1,* 11–34.

De Casper, A. J., and Spence, M. J. 1986. Prenatal maternal speech influences newborn's perception of speech sounds. *Infant Behavior and Development, 9,* 133–150.

deLemos, M. M. 1969. The development of conservation in Aborigine children. *International Journal of Psychology, 4,* 225–269.

Deregowski, J. 1970. Effect of cultural value of time upon recall. *British Journal of Social and Clinical Psychology, 9,* 37–41.

—— 1989. Real space and represented space: Cross-cultural perspectives. *Behavioral and Brain Sciences, 12,* 51–119.

de Villiers, J. G., and de Villiers, P. A. 1978. *Language Acquisition*. Cambridge, Mass.: Harvard University Press.

Dewey, J. 1916. *Human Nature and Experience*. New York: Holt.

—— 1938/1963. *Experience and Education*. New York: Macmillan.

Dilthey, W. 1923/1988. *Introduction to the Human Sciences: An Attempt to Lay the Foundations for the Study of Society and History*. Trans. R. J. Betanzos. Detroit: Wayne State University Press.

Dobzhansky, T. 1951. Human diversity and adaptation. *Cold Spring Harbor Symposia on Quantitative Biology, 15,* p. 385.

Dollard, J. 1935. *Criteria for the Life History*. New Haven: Yale University Press.

Donald, M. 1991. *The Making of the Modern Mind*. Cambridge, Mass.: Harvard University Press.

Donaldson, M. 1978. *Children's Minds*. New York: Norton.

Dore, J. 1978. Conditions for acquisition of speech acts. In I. Markova, ed., *The Social Concept of Language*. New York: Wiley.

—— 1979. Conversational acts and the acquisition of language. In E. Ochs and B. B. Schieffelin, eds., *Developmental Pragmatics*. New York: Academic Press.

Dreyfus, H. L., and Dreyfus, S. E. 1986. *Minds over Machines*. Oxford: Blackwell.

Dube, F. 1977. A cross-cultural study of the relationship between "intelligence" level and story recall. Ph.D. diss., Cornell University.

Dunbar, R. I. M. 1993. Coevolution of neocortical size, group size and language in humans. *Behavioral and Brain Sciences, 16,* 661–736.

Duranti, A., and Goodwin, C., eds. 1992. *Rethinking Context: Language as an Interactive Phenomenon*. New York: Cambridge University Press.

Durham, W. H. 1991. *Coevolution: Genes, Culture, and Human Diversity*. Stanford: Stanford University Press.

Durkheim, E. 1912/1947. *The Elementary Forms of Religious Experience*. Glencoe, Ill.: Free Press.

Eckensberger, L. 1990. From cross-cultural psychology to cultural psychology. *Newsletter of the Laboratory of Comparative Human Cognition, 12,* 37–52.

Eckensberger, L., Krewer, B., and Kasper, E. 1984. Simulation of cultural change by cross-cultural research: Some metamethodological considerations. In K. A. McCluskey and H. W. Reese, eds., *Life-span Developmental Psychology: Historical and Generational Effects*. New York: Academic Press.

Eckensberger, L., Lonner, W., and Poortinga, Y. H. 1979. *Cross-cultural Contributions to Psychology*. Lisse: Swets and Zeitlinger.

Edelman, G. 1992. *Bright Air, Brilliant Fire: On the Matter of the Mind*. New York: Basic Books.

Edgerton, R. 1974. *The Cloak of Competence*. Berkeley: University of California Press.

Edwards, D. 1995. A commentary on discursive and cultural psychology. *Culture and Psychology*, 1, 55–65.

Edwards, D., and Middleton, D. 1986. Conversation with Bartlett. *Quarterly Newsletter of the Laboratory of Comparative Human Cognition, 8*, 79–89.

Eells, K. 1951. *Intelligence and Cultural Differences*. Chicago: University of Chicago Press.

Emerson, C. 1981. Bakhtin and Vygotsky on internalization of language. *Quarterly Newsletter of the Laboratory of Comparative Human Cognition, 5*, 9–13.

Emmorey, K., Grant, R., and Ewan, B. 1994. A new case of linguistic isolation: Preliminary report. Paper given at the Boston University Conference on Language Development, January 8.

Engeström, R. 1995. Voice as communicative action. *Mind, Culture, and Activity, 2*, 192–215.

Engeström. Y. 1987. *Learning by Expanding*. Helsinki: Orienta-Konsultit Oy.

———— 1993. Developmental studies on work as a testbench of activity theory. In Chaiklin and Lave, eds., 1993.

Erikson, F., and Shultz, J. 1977. When is a context? Some issues and methods in the analysis of social comparison. *Quarterly Newsletter of the Institute for Comparative Human Development, 1*, no. 2, 5–10.

Ermath, M. 1978. *Wilhelm Dilthey: The Critique of Historical Reason*. Chicago: University of Chicago Press.

Evans-Pritchard, E. E. 1963. *Essays in Social Anthropology*. New York: Free Press.

Farr, R. M. 1983. Wilhelm Wundt (1832–1920) and the origins of psychology as an experimental and social science. *British Journal of Social Psychology, 22*, 289–301.

Feldman, D. H. 1994. *Beyond Universals of Cognitive Development*. 2nd ed. Norwood, N.J.: Ablex.

Ferguson, C. 1977. Baby talk as a simplified register. In C. E. Snow and C. Ferguson, eds., *Talking to Children*. New York: Cambridge University Press.

Fernald, A. 1991. Prosody in speech to children: Prelinguistic and linguistic functions. In R. Vasta, ed., *Annals of Child Development*, vol. 8. London: Jessica Kingsley.

Fillmore, C. J., and Kay, P. 1983. Final report to NIE: text semantic analysis of reading comprehension. Berkeley: Institute of Human Learning, University of California.

Fine, G. A. 1987. *With the Boys*. Chicago: University of Chicago Press.

Fischer, K. W., and Bidell, T. 1991. Constraining nativist inferences about cognitive capacities. In S. Carey and R. Gelman, eds., *The Epigenesis of Mind: Essays on Biology and Cognition*. Jean Piaget Symposium Series. Hillsdale, N.J.: Erlbaum.

Fischer, K. W., Knight, C. C., and Van Parys, M. 1993. Analyzing diversity in developmental pathways: Methods and concepts. In W. Edelman and R. Case, eds., *Contributions to Human Development*, vol 23: *Contructivist Approaches to Development*. Basel: Karger.

Florenskii, P. A. 1990. *U vodorazdelov mysli* (At the watersheds of thought), vol. 2. Moscow: Pravda.

Fodor, J. 1983. *Modularity of Mind*. Cambridge, Mass.: MIT Press.

Forman, E. A., Minnick, N., and Stone, C. A., eds. 1993. *Contexts for Learning: Sociocultural Dynamics in Children's Development*. New York: Oxford University Press.

Franco, F., and Butterworth, G. E. 1991. Infant pointing: Prelinguistic reference and co-reference. Paper presented at Society for Research in Child Development Biennial Meeting, Seattle, April.

Freud, S. 1920/1924. The psychogenesis of a case of homosexuality in a woman. Trans. B. Low and R. Gabler. *Collected Papers*, vol. 2. London: Hogarth Press.

———— 1930. *Civilization and Its Discontents*. In J. Strachey, ed. and trans., Standard Edition of the Complete Psychological Works of Sigmund Freud, vol. 21. London: Hogarth Press.

Friedman, N. 1967. *The Social Nature of Psychological Research: The Psychological Experiment as Social Interaction*. New York: Basic Books.

Frijda, N., and Jahoda, G. 1966. On the scope and methods of cross-cultural research. *International Journal of Psychology, 1,* 110–127.

Frith, U. 1989. *Autism*. Oxford: Oxford University Press.

Gallistel, R., and Gelman, R. 1992. Preverbal and verbal counting and computation. *Cognition, 44,* 43–74.

Galton, F. 1883. *Inquiries into Human Understanding and Its Development*. London: Macmillan.

Gardner, H. 1983. *Frames of Mind*. New York: Basic Books.

———— 1985. *The Mind's New Science*. New York: Basic Books.

———— 1991. *The Unschooled Mind: How Children Think and How Schools Should Teach*. New York: Basic Books.

Geertz, C. 1973. *The Interpretation of Cultures*. New York: Basic Books.

———— 1983. *Local Knowledge: Further Essays in Interpretive Anthropology*. New York: Basic Books.

Gelman, R. 1978. Cognitive development. *Annual Review of Psychology, 29,* 297–332.

———— 1990. Structural constraints on cognitive development: Introduction to a special issue of *Cognitive Science. Cognitive Science, 14,* 3–10.

Gelman, R., and Baillargeon, R. 1983. A review of some Piagetian concepts. In P. Mussen, ed., *Handbook of Child Development,* vol. 3: *Cognitive Development*. New York: Wiley.

Gelman, R., and Greeno, J. G. 1989. On the nature of competence: Principles for understanding in a domain. In L. B. Resnick, ed., *Knowing and Learning: Essays in Honor of Robert Glaser*. Hillsdale, N.J.: Erlbaum.

Gergen, K. J. 1994. *Realities and Relationships*. Cambridge, Mass.: Harvard University Press.

Gesell, A. 1945. *The Embryology of Behavior*. New York: Harper and Row.

Gibbs, J. 1965. The Kpelle of Liberia. In J. Gibbs, ed., *Peoples of Africa*. New York: Holt, Rinehart and Winston.

Gibson, J. 1979. *The Senses Considered as Perceptual Systems*. Boston: Houghton Mifflin.

Gibson, K. R. 1993. Tool use, language, and social behavior in relation to information processing capacities. In Gibson and Ingold, eds., 1993.

Gibson, K. R., and Ingold, T., eds., 1993. *Tools, Language, and Intelligence in Human Evolution*. Cambridge: Cambridge University Press.

Gick, M. L., and Holyoak, K. J. 1980. Analogic problem solving. *Cognitive Psychology,* 12, 306–355.

Giddens, A. 1979. *Central Problems in Social Theory: Action, Structure, and Contradiction in Social Analysis.* Berkeley: University of California Press.

—— 1984. *The Constitution of Society.* Berkeley: University of California Press.

Ginsburg, H. P. 1979. Commentary. *Monographs of the Society for Research in Child Development, 44,* ser. 178, 93–100.

Glick, J. A. 1991. Notes on a query. Note posted to XLCHC electronic mail discussion, Feb. 22.

Goethe, J. W. von. 1988. *Faust: Part 1,* trans. P. Wayne. London: Penguin.

Goffman, E. 1959. *Strategic Interaction.* Philadelphia: University of Pennsylvania Press.

Goldin-Meadow, S. 1985. Language development under atypical learning conditions. In K. E. Nelson, ed., *Children's Language,* vol. 5. Hillsdale, N.J.: Erlbaum.

Goldin-Meadow, S., and Mylander, C. 1990. The role of parental input in the development of a morphological system. *Journal of Child Language, 17,* 527–563.

Goodall, J. 1986. *The Chimpanzees of Gombe: Patterns of Behavior.* Cambridge, Mass.: Harvard University Press.

Goodenough, F. L. 1936. The measurement of mental functions in primitive groups. *American Anthropologist, 38,* 1–11.

Goodman, Y. M., and Goodman, K. S. 1990. Vygotsky in a whole-language perspective. In L. C. Moll, ed., *Vygotsky and Education.* New York: Cambridge University Press.

Goodnow, J. J. 1962. A test of mileu differences with some of Piaget's tasks. *Psychological Monographs, 76,* 36.

—— 1990. The socialization of cognition: What's involved? In J. S. Stigler, R. A. Shweder, and G. Herdt, eds., *Cultural Psychology: Essays on Comparative Human Development.* Cambridge: Cambridge University Press.

Goodnow, J. J., Miller, P. J., and Kessel, F., eds. 1995. *Cultural Practices as Contexts for Development.* New Directions for Child Development, 67. San Francisco: Jossey-Bass.

Goodwin, C. 1994. Professional vision. *American Anthropologist, 96,* 606–633.

Goodwin, C., and Duranti, A. 1992. Rethinking context: An introduction. In Duranti and Goodwin, eds., 1992.

Goody, J. 1977. *Domestication of the Savage Mind.* Cambridge: Cambridge University Press.

—— 1987. *The Interface between the Oral and the Written.* Cambridge: Cambridge University Press.

Gossett, T. F. 1965. *Race: The History of an Idea in America.* New York: Shocken.

Gottlieb, G. 1992. *Individual Development and Evolution: The Genesis of Novel Behavior.* New York: Oxford University Press.

Gould, S. J. 1977. *Ontogeny and Phylogeny.* Cambridge: Harvard University Press.

—— 1980. *The Panda's Thumb.* New York: Norton.

—— 1981. *The Mismeasure of Man.* New York: Norton.

—— 1987. *An Urchin in the Storm: Essays about Books and Ideas.* New York: Norton.

Greenfield, P. M. 1966. On culture and conservation. In J. S. Bruner, R. P. Olver, and P. M. Greenfield, eds., *Studies in Cognitive Growth.* New York: Wiley.

———— 1976. Cross-cultural Piagetian research: Paradox and progress. In K. F. Riegel and J. A. Meacham, eds., *The Developing Individual in a Changing World: Historical and Cultural Issues,* vol. 1. Chicago: Aldine.

Greenfield, P. M., Brazelton, T. B., and Childs, C. P. 1989. From birth to maturity in Zinacantan: Ontogenesis in cultural context. In V. Bricker and G. Gossen, eds., *Ethnographic Encounters in Southern Mesoamerica: Celebratory Essays in Honor of Evon Z. Vogt.* Albany: Institute of Mesoamerican Studies, State University of New York.

Greenfield, P. M., and Bruner, J. S. 1966. Culture and cognitive growth. *International Journal of Psychology, 1,* 89–107.

Greenfield, P. M., and Childs, C. P. 1977. Weaving skill, color terms, and pattern representation: Cultural influences and cognitive development among the Zinacantecos of Southern Mexico. *Interamerican Journal of Psychology, 2,* 23–48.

Greenfield, P. M., and Savage-Rumbaugh, S. 1990. Grammatical combination in Pan paniscus: Processes of learning and invention in the evolution and development of language. In Parker and Gibson, eds., 1990.

Griffin, P., and Cole, M. 1984. Current activity for the future. In B. Rogoff and J. Wertsch, eds., *Children's Learning in the "Zone of Proximal Development."* New Directions for Child Development, 23. San Francisco: Jossey-Bass.

———— 1987. New technologies, basic skills, and the underside of education: What is to be done. In J. Langer, ed., *Language, Literacy, and Culture: Issues of Society and Schooling.* Norwood, N.J.: Ablex.

Griffin, P., and Mehan, H. 1981. Sense and ritual in classroom discourse. In F. Coulmas, ed., *Explorations in Standardized Communication Situations and Prepatterned Speech.* The Hague: Mouton.

Gumperz, J. 1992. Contextualism and understanding. In Duranti and Goodwin, eds., 1992.

Habermas, J. 1971. *Knowledge and Human Interests.* Boston: Beacon.

Haddon, A. C., ed. 1901. *Report of the Cambridge Anthropological Expedition to the Torres Straits,* vol. 2. Cambridge: Cambridge University Press.

Haller, J. S. 1971. *Outcasts from Evolution: Scientific Attitudes of Racial Inferiority, 1859–1900.* Urbana: University of Illinois Press.

Hallpike, C. P. 1979. *The Foundations of Primitive Thought.* Oxford: Clarendon Press.

———— 1986. *The Principles of Social Evolution.* Oxford: Clarendon Press.

Harkness, S. 1992. Human development in psychological anthropology. In T. Schwartz, G. M. White, and C. A. Lutz, eds., *New Directions in Psychological Anthropology.* New York: Cambridge University Press.

Harkness, S., and Super, C. 1977. Why African children are so hard to test. *Issues in Cross-cultural Research. Annals of the New York Academy of Sciences, 285,* 326–331.

———— 1995. *Parents' Cultural Belief Systems: Their Origins, Expressions, and Consequences.* New York: Guilford.

Harris, M. 1968. *The Rise of Anthropological Theory.* New York: Crowell.

Harris, P., and Heelas, P. 1979. Cognitive processes and collective representations. *Archives Européennes de Sociologie, 20,* 211–241.

Hatano, G. 1995. Cultural psychology of development: The need for numbers and narratives. Annual Meeting of the Society for Research in Child Development, April.

Havelock, E. 1963. *Preface to Plato.* Cambridge, Mass.: Harvard University Press.

Hayes, K. J., and Hayes, C. 1951. The intellectual development of a home-raised chimpanzee. *Proceedings of the American Philosophical Society, 95,* 105–109.

Heltne, P. G., and Marquardt, L. A., eds. 1989. *Understanding Chimpanzees.* Cambridge, Mass.: Harvard University Press.

Herder, J. G. 1966. *Outlines of a Philosophy of the History of Man.* New York: Bergman Publishers.

Herskovitz, M. 1948. *Man and His Works: The Sciences of Cultural Anthropology.* New York: Knopf.

Hickman, L. A. 1990. *John Dewey's Pragmatic Technology.* Bloomington: Indiana University Press.

Hicks, L. H. 1956. An analysis of number-concept formation in the rhesus monkey. *Journal of Comparative and Physiological Psychology, 49,* 212–218.

Hilgard, E. R. 1956. *Theories of Learning.* 2nd ed. New York: Appleton-Century-Crofts.

Hirschfeld, L. A., and Gelman, S. A., eds. 1994. *Mapping the Mind: Domain Specificity in Cognition and Culture.* New York: Cambridge University Press.

Hodgen, M. T. 1964. *Early Anthropology in the Sixteenth and Seventeenth Centuries.* Philadelphia: University of Pennsylvania Press.

Holland, D., and Cole, M. 1995. Between discourse and schema: Reformulating a cultural-historical approach to culture and mind. *Anthropology and Education Quarterly, 26,* 475–489.

Holland, D., and Quinn, N., eds. 1987. *Cultural Models in Language and Thought.* New York: Cambridge University Press.

Holland, D., and Valsiner, J. 1988. Cognition, symbols, and Vygotsky's developmental psychology. *Ethos, 16,* 247–272.

Hume, D. 1777/1975. *Enquiries Concerning Human Understanding.* L. A. Selby-Bigge, ed. Oxford: Oxford University Press.

Humphrey, N. 1976. The social function of intellect. In P. P. G. Bateson and R. Hinde, eds., *Growing Points in Ethology.* Cambridge: Cambridge University Press.

Hutchins, E. 1986. Mediation and automation. *Quarterly Newsletter of the Laboratory of Comparative Human Cognition, 8,* 47–58.

——— 1995. *Cognition in the Wild.* Cambridge, Mass.: MIT Press.

Hutchins, E. and Hazlehurst, B. 1991. Learning in the cultural process. In C. Langton, C. Taylor, J. D. Farmer, and S. Rasmussen, eds., *Artificial Life.* Redwood City, Calif.: Addison-Wesley.

Hydén, L.-C. 1984. Three interpretations of the activity concept: Leontiev, Rubinshtein and critical psychology. In M. Hedegaard, P. Hakkarainen, and Y. E. Engeström, eds., *Learning and Teaching on a Scientific Basis.* Arhus: Psykologisk Institut.

Ilyenkov, E. V. 1977. The problem of the ideal. In *Philosophy in the USSR: Problems of Dialectical Materialism.* Moscow: Progress.

——— 1979. Problema ideal'nogo (The problem of the ideal). In two parts. *Voprosy filosofii (Questions of Philosophy), 6,* 145–158 and 7, 128–140.

Ingold, T. 1986. *Evolution and Social Life.* Cambridge: Cambridge University Press.

Irvine, J. 1978. Wolof "magical thinking": Culture and conservation revisited. *Journal of Cross-Cultural Psychology, 9,* 300–310.

Irvine, S. H., and Berry, J. W., eds. 1983. *Human Assessment and Cultural Factors.* New York: Plenum.

—— 1988. *Human Abilities in Cultural Context*. Cambridge: Cambridge University Press.

Isaacs, S. 1930/1966. *Intellectual Growth in Young Children*. New York: Schocken.

Ivanov, V. V. 1974. The significance of M. M. Bakhtin's ideas on sign, utterance, and dialogue for modern semiotics. In H. Baran, ed., *Semiotics and Structuralism: Readings from the Soviet Union*. White Plains, N.Y.: International Arts and Sciences Press.

Jakobson, R., and Halle, M. 1956. *Fundamentals of Language*. The Hague: Mouton.

Jahoda, G. 1980. Theoretical and systematic approaches in cross-cultural psychology. In H. C. Triandis and W. W. Lambert, eds. *Handbook of cross-cultural psychology*, vol. 1. Boston: Allyn and Bacon.

—— 1982. *Psychology and Anthropology*. London: Academic Press.

—— 1992. *Crossroads between Culture and Mind: Continuities and Change in Theories of Human Nature*. New York: Harvester/Wheatsheaf.

James, W. 1916. *Pragmatism: A New Name for Some Old Ways of Thinking*. New York: Longmans, Green.

Jerison, H. 1981. The evolution and ontogeny of intelligence. In R. J. Sternberg, ed., *Handbook of Intelligence*. New York: Cambridge University Press.

Judd, C. H. 1926. *The Psychology of Social Institutions*. New York. Macmillan.

Kail, F. 1990. *The Development of Memory in Children*. 3rd ed. New York: Freeman.

Kantor, J. R. 1982. *Cultural Psychology*. Chicago: Principia Press.

Kaplan, B. 1983 Genetic-dramatism: Old wine in new bottles. In S. Wapner and B. Kaplan, eds., *Toward a Holistic Developmental Psychology*. Hillsdale, N.J.: Erlbaum.

Kaplan, H., and Dove, H. 1987. Infant development among the Ache of Eastern Paraguay. *Developmental Psychology, 23,* 190–198.

Karmiloff-Smith, A. 1991. Beyond modularity: Innate constraints and developmental change. In Carey and Gelman, eds., 1991.

—— 1992. *Beyond Modularity: A Developmental Perspective on Cognitive Science*. Cambridge, Mass.: MIT Press.

Kawatoko, Y. 1995. Social rules in practice: "Legal" literacy practice in Nepalese agricultural village communities. *Mind, Culture, and Activity, 2,* 258–276.

Kaye, K. 1982. *The Mental and Social Life of Babies*. Chicago: University of Chicago Press.

KEEP. 1981. Educational perspectives. *Journal of the College of Education*, University of Hawaii at Manoa, 20 (1).

Kellogg, W. N., and Kellogg, L. A. 1933. *The Ape and the Child*. New York: McGraw-Hill.

Kendler, H. H., and Kendler, T. S. 1962. Vertical and horizontal processes in problem solving. *Psychological Review, 69,* 1–16.

Kessen, W. 1990. *The Rise and Fall of Development*. Worcester, Mass.: Clark University Press.

Kidd, D. 1906. *Savage Childhood: A Study of Kafir Children*. London: A. and C. Black.

King, C. 1988. The social facilitation of reading comprehension. Ph. D. diss., University of California, San Diego.

Klein, A., and Starkey, P. 1987. The origins and development of numerical cognition. In J. A. Sloboda and D. Rogers, eds., *Cognitive Processes in Mathematics*. Oxford: Clarendon Press.

—— 1988. Universals in the development of early arithmetic cognition. In G. B.

Saxe and M. Gearhart, eds., *Children's Mathematics*. New Directions for Child Development, vol. 41. San Francisco: Jossey-Bass.

Koch, S., and Leary, D. E. 1985. *A Century of Psychology as Science*. New York: McGraw-Hill.

Köhler, W. 1925. *The Mentality of Apes*. London: Routledge and Kegan Paul.

Konner, M., and Super, C. 1987. Sudden infant death syndrome: An anthropological hypothesis. In C. Super, ed., *The Role of Culture in Developmental Disorder.* New York: Academic Press.

Krauss, R. M., and Glucksberg, S. 1969. The development of communication: Competence as a function of age. *Child Development, 42,* 255–266.

Krewer, B. 1990. Psyche and culture: Can a culture-free psychology take into account the essential features of the species, homo sapiens? *Newsletter of the Laboratory of Comparative Human Cognition, 12,* 24–36.

Krewer, B., and Jahoda, G. 1990. On the scope of Lazarus and Steinthal's "Völkerpsychologie" as reflected in the "Zeitschrift für Völkerpsychologie und Sprachwissenschaft," 1860–1890. *Quarterly Newsletter of the Laboratory of Comparative Human Cognition, 12,* 4–12.

Kroeber, A. 1917. The superorganic. *American Anthropologist, 19,* 163–213.

Kundera, M. 1988. *The Art of the Novel*. New York: Grove Press.

La Barre, W. 1954. *The Human Animal*. Chicago: University of Chicago Press.

La Barre, W. 1970. *The Ghost Dance; Origins of Religion*. New York: Doubleday.

LCHC (Laboratory of Comparative Human Cognition). 1978. Cognition as a residual category in anthropology. *Annual Review of Anthropology, 7,* 51–69.

———— 1979. What's cultural about cross-cultural psychology? *Annual Review of Psychology, 30,* 145–172.

———— 1982. A model system for the study of learning disabilities. *Quarterly Newsletter of the Laboratory of Comparative Human Cognition, 1,* 39–66.

———— 1983. Culture and cognition. In P. Mussen, ed., *Handbook of Child Psychology,* vol. 1: *History, Theory, and Methods.*, ed. W. Kessen.

Labov, W. 1972. The logic of non-standard English. In F. Williams, ed., *Language and Poverty*. Chicago: Markham.

Lancy, D. F. 1983. *Cross-cultural Studies in Cognition and Mathematics*. New York: Academic Press.

Latour, B. 1994. On technical mediation: Philosophy, sociology, genealogy. *Common Knowledge, 3,* 29–64.

Latour, B., and Strum, S. C. 1986. Human social origins: Oh please, tell us another story. *Journal of Sociological and Biological Structures, 9,* 169–187.

Lave, J. 1977a. Tailor-made experiments and evaluating the intellectual consequences of apprenticeship training. *Quarterly Newsletter of the Laboratory of Comparative Human Cognition, 1,* 1–3.

———— 1977b. Cognitive consequences of traditional apprenticeship training in West Africa. *Anthropology and Education Quarterly, 8,* 177–180.

———— 1980. What's special about experiments as contexts for thinking? *Quarterly Newsletter of the Laboratory of Comparative Human Cognition, 2,* 86–91.

———— 1988. *Cognition in Practice*. Cambridge: Cambridge University Press.

———— 1993. The practice of learning. In Chaiklin and Lave, eds., 1993.

Lave, J., Murtaugh, M., and de la Rocha, O. 1984. The dialectics of arithmetic in grocery shopping. In B. Rogoff and J. Lave, eds., *Everyday Cognition; Its Development in Social Context*. Cambridge, Mass.: Harvard University Press.

Lave, J., and Wenger, E. 1991. *Situated Learning.* New York: Cambridge University Press.

Leakey, R. 1981. *The Making of Mankind.* London: Michael Joseph.

Leontiev, A. N. 1931. *Razvitiye pamyati: Eksperimental'noe issledovanie vysshikh psi-khologicheskikh funksii* (The development of memory: experimental studies of higher psychological functions). Moscow-Leningrad: Uchpedgiz.

—— 1932. Studies of cultural development of the child, 3: The development of voluntary attention in the child. *Journal of Genetic Psychology, 37,* 52–81.

—— 1978. *Activity, Consciousness, and Personality.* Englewood Cliffs, N.J.: Prentice-Hall.

—— 1981. *Problems in the Develoment of the Mind.* Moscow: Progress.

Leontiev, A. N., and Luria, A. R. 1956. Vygotsky's outlook on psychology. In L. S. Vygotsky, *Selected Psychological Works.* Moscow. Academy of Pedagogical Sciences Press.

Lerner, D. 1958. *The Passing of Traditional Society.* Glencoe, Ill.: Free Press.

Lerner, R. M. 1991. Changing organism-context relations as the basic process of development: A developmental contextual perspective. *Developmental Psychology, 27,* 27–32.

Leslie, A. M. 1994. To MM, To By, and Agency: Core architecture and domain specificity. In L. A. Hirschfeld and S. A. Gelman, eds., *Mapping the Mind.* New York: Cambridge University Press.

Levin, J. L., and Souviney, R. 1983. Computers and literacy: A time for tools. *Quarterly Newsletter of the Laboratory of Comparative Human Cognition, 5,* 45–68.

Le Vine, R. A., and Price-Williams, D. R. 1974. Children's kinship concepts: Cognitive development and early experience among the Hausa. *Ethnology, 13,* 25–44.

Levinson, D., and Malone, M. J. 1980. *Toward Explaining Human Culture.* New Haven: HRAF Press.

Levitin, K. Y. 1982. *One Is Not Born a Personality.* Moscow: Progress.

Levy-Bruhl, L. 1910/1966. *How Natives Think.* New York: Washington Square Press.

Lewin, K. 1943. Defining the "field at a given time." *Psychological Review, 50,* 292–310.

Lewontin, R. C. 1982. *Human Diversity.* New York: Scientific American Books.

—— 1992. *Inside and Outside: Gene, Environment, and Organism.* Worcester, Mass.: Clark University Press.

Liberman, P. 1991. *Uniquely Human: The Evolution of Speech, Thought, and Selfless Behavior.* Cambridge, Mass.: Harvard University Press.

Linnaeus, C. 1735/1806. *A General System of Nature, through the Three Grand Kingdoms of Animals, Vegetables, and Minerals.* London: Lackington, Allen, and Co.

Lippmann, W. 1922. *Public Opinion.* New York: Harcourt, Brace.

Lipset, D. 1980. *Gregory Bateson: The Legacy of a Scientist.* Englewood Cliffs, N.J.: Prentice-Hall.

Litowitz, B. E. 1993. Deconstruction in the zone of proximal development. In E. A. Forman, N. Minnick, and C. A. Stone, eds., *Contexts for Learning: Sociocultural Dynamics in Children's Development.* New York: Oxford University Press.

Lucariello, J. 1995. Mind, culture, and person: Elements in a cultural psychology. *Human Development, 38,* 2–18.

Lumsden, C. J., and Wilson, E. O. 1983. *Promethean Fire.* Cambridge, Mass.: Harvard University Press.

Luria, A. R. 1928. The problem of the cultural development of the child. *Journal of Genetic Psychology, 35,* 493–506.

―――― 1928/1978. The development of writing in the child. In M. Cole, ed., *The Selected Writings of A. R. Luria.* White Plains, N.Y.: Sharpe.

―――― 1931. Psychological expedition to Central Asia. *Science, 74,* 383–384.

―――― 1932. *The Nature of Human Conflicts.* New York: Liveright.

―――― 1936/37. The development of mental functions in twins. *Character and Personality, 5,* 35–47.

―――― 1968. *Mind of a Mnemonist.* New York: Basic Books.

―――― 1971. Towards the problem of the historical nature of psychological processes. *International Journal of Psychology, 6,* 259–272.

―――― 1972. *Man with a Shattered World.* New York: Basic Books.

―――― 1976. *Cognitive Development: Its Cultural and Social Foundations.* Cambridge, Mass.: Harvard University Press.

―――― 1979. *The Making of Mind.* Cambridge, Mass.: Harvard University Press.

―――― 1981. *Language and Cognition.* Washington: V. H. Winston; New York: J. Wiley.

Luria, A. R., and Yudovich, F. Y. 1959. *Speech and the Development of Psychological Processes.* London: Staples.

Mandler, G. 1985. *Cognitive Psychology: An Essay in Cognitive Science.* Hillsdale, N.J.: Erlbaum.

Mandler, G., and Dean, P. J. 1969. Seriation: The development of serial order in free recall. *Journal of Experimental Psychology, 81,* 207–215.

Mandler, J. 1980. *Structural Invariants in Development.* University of California, San Diego: Center for Human Information Processing, no. 96, September.

Mandler, J. M., Scribner, S., Cole, M., and DeForest, M. 1980. Cross-cultural invariance in story recall. *Child Development, 51,* 19–26.

Marsella, A. J., Tharp, R., and Ciborowski, T. 1979. *Perspectives on Cross-cultural Psychology.* New York: Academic Press.

Marx, K. 1845/1967. Theses on Feurbach. In L. D. Easton and K. H. Guddat, eds., *Writings of the Young Marx on Philosophy and Society.* Garden City, N.Y.: Doubleday, Anchor Books.

Matsuzawa, T. 1994. Field experiments on use of stone tools in the wild. In Wrangham et al., 1994.

McClelland, J. L., and Rumelhart, D. E. 1981. An interactive activation model of context effects in letter perception, 1: An account of basic findings. *Psychological Review, 88,* 375–407.

McDermott, R. P. 1980. Profile: Ray L. Birdwhistell. *Kenesis Reports, 2,* 1–4, 14–16.

―――― 1993. The acquisition of a child by a learning disability. In C. Chaiklin and J. Lave, eds., *Understanding Practice: Perspectives on Activity and Context.* New York: Cambridge University Press.

McGrew, W. C. 1992. *Chimpanzee Material Culture.* Cambridge: Cambridge University Press.

Mead, G. H. 1934/1956. *The Social Psychology of George Herbert Mead.* A. Strauss, ed. Chicago: University of Chicago Press.

Mead, M. 1932. An investigation of the thought of primitive children, with special reference to animism. *Journal of the Royal Anthropological Institute, 62,* 173–190.

―――― 1935. *Sex and Temperament.* New York: William Morrow.

―――― 1978. The evocation of psychologically relevant responses in ethnological field work. In G. D. Spindler, ed., *The Making of Psychological Anthropology.* Berkeley: University of California Press.

Mead, M., and Newton, N. 1967. Cultural patterning of perinatal behavior. In S. Richardson and A. Guttmacher, eds., *Childbearing: Its Social and Psychological Aspects.* New York: Morrow.

Mehan, H. 1979. *Learning Lessons.* Cambridge, Mass.: Harvard University Press.

Mehler, J., Lambertz, G., Jusczyk, P., and Amiel-Tison, C. 1986. Discrimination de la langue maternelle par le nouveau-né. *Comptes rendus de l'Academie de Science, 303,* 637–640.

Mertz, E., and Parmentier, R., eds. 1985. *Semiotic Mediation: Sociocultural and Psychological Perspectives.* New York: Academic Press.

Meshcheryakov, A., 1979. *Awakening to Life.* Moscow: Progress.

Middleton, D., and Edwards, D. 1990. *Collective Remembering.* London: Sage.

Mill, J. S. 1843/1948. *A System of Logic.* London: Longmans.

Miller, G. A. 1977. *Spontaneous Apprentices: Children and Language.* New York: Seabury Press.

⸻ 1988. The challenge of universal literacy. *Science, 241,* 1293–1299.

Miller, P. H. 1993. *Theories of Developmental Psychology.* 3rd ed. New York: Freeman.

Miller, P. J. 1982. *Amy, Wendy, and Beth: Learning Language in South Baltimore.* Austin: University of Texas Press.

Moll, L. C., Anderson, A., and Diaz, E. 1985. Third College and CERRC: A university-community system for promoting academic excellence. Paper presented at the University of California's Linguistic Minority Conference, Lake Tahoe.

Moll, L. C., and Diaz, S. R. 1987. Change as the goal of educational research. *Anthropology and Education Quarterly, 184,* 300–311.

Morford, J. P., and Goldin-Meadow, S. 1994. Communication about the Non-Present Child-Generated Language. Manuscript.

Morton, J. and Johnson, M. H. 1991. CONSPEC and CONLEARN: A two-process theory of infant face recognition. *Psychological Review, 98,* 164–181.

Müller-Lyer, F. C. 1920. *The History of Social Development.* London: Allen and Unwin.

Munroe, R. H., Munroe, R. L., and Whiting, B. B. 1981. *Handbook of Cross-cultural Human Development.* New York: Garland.

Münsterberg, H. 1914. *Psychology.* New York: D. Appleton.

Murray, A. V. 1929. *The School in the Bush: A Critical Study of the Theory and Practice of Native Education in Africa.* London: Longmans, Green.

Myers, J. L. 1953. *Herodotus, Father of History.* Oxford: Clarendon Press.

Nadel, S. F. 1937a. Experiments in culture psychology. *Africa, 10,* 421–425.

⸻ 1937b. A field experiment in racial psychology. *British Journal of Psychology, 28,* 195–211.

⸻ 1939. The application of intelligence tests in the anthropological field. In F. C. Bartlett, ed., *The Study of Society.* Cambridge: Cambridge University Press.

Nardi, B., ed. 1996. *Context and Consciousness: Activity Theory and Human-Computer Interactions.* Cambridge, Mass.: MIT Press.

Neimark, E. D. 1975. Longitudinal development of formal operational thought. *Genetic Psychology Monographs, 91,* 171–225.

Neisser, U. 1976a. *Cognition and Reality.* San Francisco: W. H. Freeman.

⸻ 1976b. General, academic, and artificial intelligence. In L. B. Resnick, ed., *The Nature of Intelligence.* Hillsdale, N.J.: Erlbaum.

—— 1976c. *General, Academic, and Artificial Intelligence.* Hillsdale, N.J.: Erlbaum.

Nelson, K. 1981. Cognition in a script framework. In J. H. Flavell and L. Ross, eds., *Social Cognitive Development.* Cambridge: Cambridge University Press.

—— 1986. *Event Knowledge: Structure and Function in Development.* Hillsdale, N.J.: Erlbaum.

Newman, D., Griffin, P. and Cole, M. 1989. *The Construction Zone.* New York: Cambridge University Press.

Nicolopoulou, A., and Cole, M. 1993. Generation and transmission of shared knowledge in the cultural of collaborative learning: The Fifth Dimension, its play-world, and its institutional contexts. In E. A. Forman, N. Minnick, and C. A. Stone, eds., *Contexts for Learning: Sociocultural Dynamics in Children's Development.* New York: Oxford University Press.

Norman, D. A. 1990. Cognitive artifacts. In J. M. Carroll, ed., *Designing Interaction: Psychology at the Human-Computer Interface.* Cambridge: Cambridge University Press.

—— 1991. Approaches to the study of intelligence. *Artificial Intelligence, 46,* 327–346.

Nunes, T., Schliemann, A. D., and Carraher, D. W. 1993. *Street Mathematics and School Mathematics.* New York: Cambridge University Press.

Odom, H. 1967. Generalizations on race in 19th century physical anthropology. *Isis, 58,* 9.

Oliver, R. A. C. 1933a. The adaptation of intelligence tests to tropical Africa, I. *Overseas Education, 4,* 186–191.

—— 1933b. The adaptation of intelligence tests to tropical Africa, II. *Overseas Education, 5,* 8–13.

Olson, D. 1994. *The World on Paper.* Cambridge: Cambridge University Press.

Ord, I. G. 1970. *Mental Tests for Pre-literates.* London: Ginn and Co.

Ortner, S. 1984. Theory in anthropology since the sixties. *Comparative Studies of Society and History, 26,* 126–166.

Palincsar, A. S. 1989. Less charted waters. *Educational Researcher, 18,* 5–7.

Parker, S. T. 1990. Origins of comparative developmental evolutionary studies of primate mental abilities. In Parker and Gibson, eds., 1990.

Parker, S. T., and Gibson, K. R., eds. 1990. *"Language" and Intelligence in Monkeys and Apes: Comparative Developmental Perspectives.* New York: Cambridge University Press.

Pepper, S. 1942. *World Hypotheses.* Berkeley: University of California Press.

Petitto, A. L. 1985. Division of labor: Procedural learning in teacher-led small groups. *Cognition and Instruction, 2,* 233–270.

Piaget, J. 1928/1995. Genetic logic and sociology. In J. Piaget, *Sociological Studies,* ed. L. Smith. London: Routledge.

—— 1952. *The Origins of Intelligence in the Child.* New York: Norton.

—— 1966/1974. Need and significance of cross-cultural studies in genetic psychology. In J. W. Berry and P. R. Dasen, eds., *Culture and Cognition: Readings in Cross-cultural Psychology.* London: Methuen.

Piatelli-Palmerini, M., ed., 1980. *Language and Learning: The Debate between Jean Piaget and Noam Chomsky.* Cambridge, Mass.: Harvard University Press.

Pinker, S. 1994. *The Language Instinct.* New York: Morrow.

Plomin, R. 1990. *Nature and Nurture: An Introduction to Human Behavioral Genetics.* Pacific Grove, Ca.: Brooks/Cole.

Pollack, R. H. 1970. Müller-Lyer illusion: Effect of age, lightness, contrast and hue. *Science, 170,* 93–94.

—— 1989. Pictures, maybe; illusions, no. *Behavioral and Brain Sciences, 12,* 92–93.

Pollack, R. H., and Silvar, S. D. 1967. Magnitude of the Müller-Lyer illusion as a function of pigmentation in the fusus oculi. *Psychonomic Science, 8,* 83–84.

Porteus, S. 1937. *Primitive Intelligence and Environment.* New York: Macmillan.

Posner, J. 1982. The development of mathematical knowledge in two West African societies. *Child Development, 53,* 200–208.

Povinelli, D. J. 1994. Why chimpanzees (might) know about the mind. In R. W. Wrangham, W. C. McGrew, F. B. M. de Waal, and P. G. Heltne, eds., *Chimpanzee Cultures.* Cambridge, Mass.: Harvard University Press.

Premack, D. 1971. On the assessment of language competence in the chimpanzee. In A. M. Schrier and F. Stollnitz, eds., *Behavior in Non-human Primates,* vol. 4. New York: Academic Press.

—— 1986. *Gavagai.* London: Cambridge University Press.

—— 1990. The infant's theory of self-propelled objects. *Cognition, 36,* 1–16.

Price-Williams, D. R. 1961. A study concerning concepts of conservation of quantities among primitive children. *Acta Psychologia, 18,* 297–305.

—— 1975. *Explorations in Cross-cultural Psychology.* San Francisco: Chandler and Sharp.

—— 1979. Modes of thought in cross-cultural research: An historical review. In Marsella, Tharp, and Ciborowski, eds., 1979.

—— 1980. Toward the idea of a cultural psychology: A superordinate theme for study. *Journal of Cross-cultural Psychology, 11,* 77–88.

Price-Williams, D. R., Gordon, W., and Ramirez, M. 1969. Skill and conservation: A study of pottery-making children. *Developmental Psychology, 1,* 769.

Quinn, N., and Holland, D. 1987. Culture and cognition. In D. Holland and N. Quinn, eds., *Cultural Models in Language and Thought.* New York: Cambridge University Press.

Rabinow, P., and Sullivan, W. M., eds. 1987. *Interpretive Social Sciences: A Second Look.* Berkeley: University of California Press.

Raeithel, A. 1994. Symbolic production of social coherence. *Mind, Culture, and Activity, 1,* 69–88.

Ratner, C. 1991. *Vygotsky's Sociohistorical Psychology and Its Contemporary Applications.* New York: Plenum.

Reed, H. J., and Lave, J. 1979. Arithmetic as a tool for investigating the relations between culture and cognition. *American Ethnologist, 6,* 568–582.

Resnick, L. B. 1994. Situated rationalism: Biological and social preparation for learning. In Hirschfeld and Gelman, eds., 1994.

Retschitzki, J. 1989. Evidence of formal thinking in Baoulé airele players. In D. M. Keats, D. Munro, and L. Mann, eds., *Heterogeneity in Cross-cultural Psychology.* Amsterdam: Swets and Zeitlinger.

Reynolds, P. C. 1982. The primate constructional system: The theory and description of instrumental object use in humans and chimpanzees. In M. Von Cranach and R. Harré, eds., *The Analysis of Action: Recent Theoretical and Empirical Advances.* Cambridge: Cambridge University Press.

Riel, M. 1985. The computer chronicles newswire: A functional learning environment for acquiring literacy skills. *Journal of Educational Computing Research, 1*, 317–337.

Rivers, W. H. R. 1901. Vision. In A. C. Haddon, ed., *Report of the Cambridge Anthropological Expedition to the Torres Straits,* vol. 2. Cambridge: Cambridge University Press.

Rogoff, B. 1981. Schooling and the development of cognitive skills. In Triandis and Heron, eds., *Handbook of Cross-cultural Psychology,* Vol. 4. Boston: Allyn and Bacon.

———— 1990. *Apprenticeship in Thinking: Cognitive Development in Social Context.* New York: Oxford University Press.

Rommetveit, R. 1974. *On Message Structure.* London: Wiley.

Rose, E., and Fenton, W. 1955. Experimental histories of culture. *American Sociological Review, 20,* 383–392.

Ross, B. M., and Millsom, C. 1970. Repeated memory of oral prose in Ghana and New York. *International Journal of Psychology, 5,* 173–181.

Rossi-Landi, F. 1983. *Language as Work and Trade: A Semiotic Homology for Linguistics and Economics.* South Hadley, Mass.: Bergin and Garvey.

Rubin, J. Z., Provenzano, F. J., and Luria, Z. 1974. The eye of the beholder: Parents' views on sex of newborns. *American Journal of Orthopsychiatry, 44,* 512–519.

Rumbaugh, D. M., Savage-Rumbaugh, E. S., and Sevcik, R. A. 1994. Biobehavioral roots of language: A comparative perspective of chimpanzee, child, and culture. In Wrangham et al., 1994.

Rumelhart, D. 1978. Schemata: The building blocks of cognition. In R. Spiro, B. Bruce, and W. Brewer, eds., *Theoretical Issues in Reading Comprehension.* Hillsdale, N.J.: Erlbaum.

Rumelhart, D. E., and Norman, D. A. 1980. *Analogical Processes in Learning.* University of California, San Diego, Center for Human Information Processing, 97.

Sacks, O. 1987. Foreword to the 1987 edition. In A. R. Luria, *The Man with a Shattered World: The History of a Brain Wound.* Cambridge, Mass.: Harvard University Press.

Sahlins, M. D. 1976. *Culture and Practical Reason.* Chicago: University of Chicago Press.

Sahlins, M. D., and Service, E., eds. 1960. *Evolution and Culture.* Ann Arbor: University of of Michigan Press.

Salomon, G., ed., 1993. *Distributed Cognitions: Psychological and Educational Considerations.* Cambridge: Cambridge University Press.

Savage-Rumbaugh, E. S. 1986. *Ape Language: From Conditioned Response to Symbol.* New York: Columbia University Press.

Savage-Rumbaugh, E. S., Murphy, J., Sevcik, R. A., Brakke, K. E., Williams, S. L., and Rumbaugh, D. M. 1993. Language comprehension in ape and child. *Monographs of the Society for Research in Child Development, 58,* nos. 3–4, serial no. 233.

Saxe, G. B. 1981. Body parts as numerals: A developmental analysis of numeration among a village population in Papua New Guinea. *Child Development, 52,* 306–316.

———— 1982. Developing forms of arithmetic operations among the Oksapmin of Papua New Guinea. *Developmental Psychology, 18,* 583–594.

———— 1985. The effects of schooling on arithmetical understandings: Studies with Oksapmin children in Papua New Guinea. *Journal of Educational Psychology, 77,* 503–513.

—— 1991. *Culture and Cognitive Development.* Hillsdale, N.J.: Erlbaum.

—— 1994. Studying cognitive development in sociocultural contexts: The development of practice-based approaches. *Mind, Culture, and Activity, 1,* 135–157.

Saxe, G. B., Guberman, S. R., and Gearhart, M. 1987. Social processes in early number development. *Monographs of the Society for Research in Child Development,* no. 216, 52.

Scardamalia, M., and Bereiter, C. 1985. Fostering the development of self-regulation in children's knowledge processing. In S. F. Shipman, J. W. Segal, and R. Glaser, eds., *Thinking and Learning Skills: Research and Open Questions.* Hillsdale, N.J.:Erlbaum.

Scarr, S. 1981. *Race, Social Class and Individual Differences in I. Q.* Hillsdale, N.J.: Erlbaum.

Schank, R. C., and Ableson, R. P. 1977. *Scripts, Plans, Goals, and Understanding: An Inquiry into Human Knowledge Structures.* Hillsdale, N.J.: Erlbaum.

Schieffelin, B. B., and Ochs, E. 1986. *Language Socialization across Cultures.* Cambridge: Cambridge University Press.

Schustack, M. W., King, C., Gallego, M. A., and Vásquez, O. A. 1994. A computer-oriented after-school activity: Children's learning in the Fifth Dimension and La Clase Mágica. In F. A. Villarruel and R. M. Lerner, eds., *Promoting Community-based Programs for Socialization and Learning.* San Francisco: Jossey-Bass.

Schwartz, J. L., and Taylor, E. F. 1978. Valid assessment of complex behavior: The Torque approach. *Quarterly Newsletter of the Laboratory of Comparative Human Cognition, 2,* 54–58.

Schwartz, T. 1978. The size and shape of culture. In F. Barth, ed., *Scale and Social Organization.* Oslo: Universitetsforlaget.

—— 1990. The structure of national cultures. In P. Funke, ed., *Understanding the USA.* Tubingen: Gunter Narr Verlag.

Scribner, S. 1975a. Recall of classical syllogisms: A cross-cultural investigation of error on logical problems. In R. Falmagne, ed., *Reasoning: Representation and Process.* Hillsdale, N.J. :Erlbaum.

—— 1975b. Situating the experiment in cross-cultural research. In K. F. Riegel and J. A. Meacham, eds., *The Developing Individual in a Changing World: Historical and Cultural Issues.* The Hague: Mouton.

—— 1977. Modes of thinking and ways of speaking: Culture and logic reconsidered. In P. N. Johnson-Laird and P. C. Wason, eds., *Thinking: Readings in Cognitive Science.* Cambridge: Cambridge University Press.

—— 1984. Cognitive studies of work. *Quarterly Newsletter of the Laboratory of Comparative Human Cognition, 6,* nos. 1 and 2.

—— 1985. Vygotsky's uses of history. In J. V. Wertsch, ed., *Culture, Communication, and Cognition: Vygotskian Perspectives.* New York: Cambridge University Press.

Scribner, S., and Cole, M. 1981. *The Psychology of Literacy.* Cambridge, Mass.: Harvard University Press.

Searle, J. R. 1975. A taxonomy of illocutionary acts. In K. Gunderson, ed., *Language, Mind, and Knowledge.* Minneapolis: University of Minnesota Press.

Segall, M. H., Campbell, D. T., and Herskovitz, M. J. 1966. *The Influence of Culture on Visual Perception.* Indianapolis: Bobbs-Merrill.

Segall, M. H., Dasen, P. R., Berry, J. W., and Poortinga, Y. H. 1990. *Human Behavior* in *Global Perspective: An Introduction to Cross-cultural Psychology.* New York: Pergamon.

Serpell, R. 1976. *Culture's Influence on Behavior.* London: Methuen.

—— 1982. Measures of perception, skills and intelligence: The growth of a new perspective on children in a Third World country. In W. W. Hartup, ed., *Review of Child Development Research,* vol. 6. Chicago: University of Chicago Press.

—— 1990. Audience, culture, and psychological explanation: A reformulation of the emic-etic problem in cross-cultural psychology. *Quarterly Newsletter of the Laboratory of Comparative Human Cognition, 12,* 99–132.

—— 1993. *The Significance of Schooling.* New York: Cambridge University Press.

Sharp, D., Cole, M., and Lave, C. 1979. Education and cognitive development: The evidence from experimental research. *Monographs of the Society for Research in Child Development, 44,* nos. 1–2, serial no. 178.

Shweder, R. A. 1977. Likeness and likelihood in everyday thought: Magical thinking in judgments about personality. *Current Anthropology, 18,* 637–648.

—— 1984. Preview: A colloquy of culture theorists. In R. A. Shweder and R. A. LeVine, eds., *Culture Theory: Essays on Mind, Self, and Emotion.* New York: Cambridge University Press.

—— 1990. Cultural psychology: What is it? In J. W. Stigler, R. A. Shweder and G. Herdt, eds., *Cultural Psychology: Essays on Comparative Human Development.* New York: Cambridge University Press.

—— 1991. *Thinking through Cultures.* Cambridge, Mass.: Harvard University Press.

Shweder, R. A., and D'Andrade, R. G. 1980. The systematic distortion hypothesis. In R. A. Shweder, ed., *Fallible Judgment in Behavioral Research.* San Francisco: Jossey-Bass.

Shweder, R. A., and Le Vine, R. A., eds., 1984. *Culture Theory: Essays on Mind, Self and Emotion.* New York: Cambridge University Press.

Shweder, R. A., Mahapatra, M., and Miller, J. G. 1987. Culture and moral development. In J. Kagan and S. Lamb, eds., *The Emergence of Morality in Young Children.* Chicago: University of Chicago Press.

Siegal, M. 1991. *Knowing Children: Experiments in Conversation and Cognition.* Hillsdale, N.J.: Erlbaum.

Siegel, A. W., and Cohen, R., eds. 1991. *Context and Development.* Hillsdale, N.J.: Erlbaum.

Simon, H. A. 1969. *The Sciences of the Artificial.* Cambridge, Mass.: MIT Press.

—— 1976. Discussion: Cognition and social behavior. In J. S. Carroll and J. W. Payne, eds., *Cognition and Social Behavior.* Hillsdale, N.J.: Erlbaum.

Slobin, D. I., and Welsh, C. A. 1973. Elicited imitation as a research tool in developmental psycholinguistics. In C. A. Ferguson and D. I. Slobin, eds., *Studies in Child Language Development.* New York: Holt, Rinehart and Winston.

Slobodin, R. 1978. *W. H. R. Rivers.* New York: Columbia University Press.

Smolka, A. L. B., De Goes, M. C., and Pino, A. 1995. The constitution of the subject: A persistent question. In J. V. Wertsch, P. del Rio, and A. Alvarez, eds., *Sociocultural Studies of Mind.* New York: Cambridge University Press.

Snow, C. E., Arlman-Rupp, A., Massing, Y., Jobse, J., Jooseken, J., and Vorster, J. 1976. Mothers' speech in three social classes. *Journal of Psycholinguistic Research, 5,* 1–20.

Snow, C. E., and Ferguson, C. A., eds., 1977. *Talking to Children*. Cambridge: Cambridge University Press.

Spelke, E. S. 1990. Principles of object perception. *Cognitive Science, 14,* 29–56.

Spencer, H. 1886. *The Principles of Psychology.* vol. 5. New York: D. Appleton.

Starkey, P., Spelke, E. S., and Gelman, R. 1990. Numerical abstraction by human infants. *Cognition, 36,* 97–127.

Stern, D. 1977. *The First Relationship.* Cambridge, Mass.: Harvard University Press.

Stern, E. 1916/1990. Problems of cultural psychology. *Quarterly Newsletter of the Laboratory of Comparative Human Cognition, 12,* 12–24.

Stevens, J. 1990. An observational study of skilled memory in waitresses. Laboratory for Cognitive Studies of Work, CUNY Graduate Center.

Stevenson, H. 1982. Influences of schooling on cognitive development. In D. A. Wagner and H. Stevenson, eds., *Cultural Perspectives on Child Development.* San Francisco: Freeman.

Stone, A., and Wertsch, J. V. 1984. A social interactional analysis of learning disabilities. *Journal of Learning Disabilities, 17,* 194–199.

Stone, C. A. 1993. What is missing in the metaphor of scaffolding? In E. A. Forman, N. Minnick, and C. A. Stone., eds., *Contexts for Learning: Sociocultural Dynamics in Children's Development.* New York: Oxford University Press.

Strauss, C., and Quinn, N. In press. A Cognitive Theory of Cultural Meaning. New York: Cambridge University Press.

Suchman, L. A. 1987. *Plans and Situated Actions: The Problem of Human-Machine Communication.* Cambridge: Cambridge University Press.

Super, C. M., and Harkness, S. 1972. The infant's niche in rural Kenya and metropolitan America. In L. Adler, ed., *Issues in Cross-cultural Research.* New York: Academic Press.

—— 1986. The developmental niche: A conceptualization at the interface of society and the individual. *International Journal of Behavioral Development, 9,* 545–570.

Taylor, C. 1987. Interpretation and the sciences of man. In P. Rabinow and W. M. Sullivan, eds., *Interpretive Social Sciences: A Second Look.* Berkeley: University of California Press.

—— 1989. *Sources of the Self.* Cambridge, Mass.: Harvard University Press.

Terrace, H. 1979. *Nim.* New York: Knopf.

Tharp, R. G., and Gallimore, R. 1988. *Rousing Minds to Life: Teaching, Learning and Schooling in a Social Context.* New York: Cambridge University Press.

Thurnwald, R. 1922. Psychologie des primitiven Menschen. In I. G. Kafka, ed., *Handbuch der vergleichenden Psychologie. Band 1.* Munich: Verlag von Ernst Reinhardt.

Titchener, E. H. 1916. On ethnological tests of sensation and perception. *Proceedings of the American Philosophical Society, 55,* 204–236.

Tolman, E. C. 1938/1958. The determiners of behavior at a choice point. In *Behavior and Psychological Man: Essays in Motivation and Learning.* Berkeley: University of California Press.

Tomasello, M. 1990. Cultural transmission in the tool use and communicatory signalling of chimpanzees? In Parker and Gibson, eds., 1990.

—— 1994. The question of chimpanzee culture. In Wrangham et al., 1994.

Tomasello, M., Davis-Dasilva, L., Camak, L., Bard, K. 1987. Observational learning of tool use by young chimpanzees. *Human Evolution, 2,* 175–183.

Tomasello, M., Kruger, A. and Ratner, H. 1993. Cultural learning. *Behavioral and Brain Sciences, 16,* 495–552.

Tomasello, M., Savage-Rumbaugh, S., and Kruger, A. 1993. Imitative learning of actions on objects by chimpanzees, enculturated chimpanzees, and human children. *Child Development, 64,* 1688–1705.

Toth, N., and Schick, K. 1993. Early stone industries and inferences regarding language and cognition. In K. R. Gibson and T. Ingold, eds., *Tools, Language, and Cognition in Human Evolution.* Cambridge: Cambridge University Press.

Toulmin, S. 1980. Toward reintegration: An agenda for psychology's second century. In R. A. Kasschauand and F. S. Kessel, eds., *Psychology in Society: In Search of Symbiosis.* New York: Holt, Rinehart and Winston.

—— 1990. *Cosmopolis: The Hidden Agenda of Modernity.* New York: Free Press.

Trevarthan, C. 1980. The foundations of intersubjectivity: Development of interpersonal and cooperative understanding in infants. In D. Olson, ed., *The Social Foundations of Language and Thought.* New York: Norton.

Triandis, H. C. 1980. Introduction. In Triandis and Lambert, eds., 1980.

Triandis, H. C., and Lambert, W. W., eds., 1980. *Handbook of Cross-cultural Psychology,* vol. 1. Boston: Allyn and Bacon.

Tronick, E. Z., Thomas, R. B., and Daltabuit, M. 1994. The Quechua manta pouch: A caretaking practice for buffering the Peruvian infant against the multiple stresses of high altitude. *Child Development, 65,* 1005–1013.

Tulviste, P. 1986. Ob istoricheskoi getergennosti verbal'nogo myshleniya (The historical heterogeneity of verbal thinking). In Y. A. Ponomarev, ed., *Myshlenie, obshchenie, praktiki: Sbornik nauchnykh trudov* (Thinking, communication, practice: A collection of scientific works). Yaroslavl: Yaroslavl Pedagogical Institute.

——1988. The historical development of thought. *Soviet Psychology, 25,* 3–21.

—— 1991. *The Cultural-Historical Development of Verbal Thinking.* Commack, N.Y.: Nova Sciences Publishers.

Tylor, E. B. 1865. *Researches into the Early History of Mankind and the Development of Civilization.* Edited rpt. Chicago: University of Chicago Press, 1964.

—— 1874/1958. *Primitive Culture.* Vol. 1. Rpt. London: J. Murray, 1929.

Ueno, N. 1985. The social construction of reality in the artifacts of numeracy for distribution and exchange in a Nepalese bazaar. *Mind, Culture, and Activity, 2,* 240–257.

——1995. Reification of artifacts in ideological practice. *Mind, Culture, and Activity,* 2, 240–257.

UNESCO. 1951. *Learn and Live: A Way out of Ignorance for 1,200,000,000 People.* Paris.

van de Koppel, J. M. H. 1983. *A Developmental Study of the Biaka Pygmies and the Bangandu.* Lisse, Netherlands: Swets and Zeitlinger.

Valsiner, J. 1987. *Culture and the Development of Children's Action: A Cultural-Historical Theory of Developmental Psychology.* New York: Wiley.

—— 1988. *Developmental Psychology in the Soviet Union.* Bloomington: Indiana University Press.

Valsiner, J., and Benigni, L. 1986. Naturalistic research and ecological thinking in the study of child development. *Developmental Review, 6,* 203–223.

van de Koppel, J. M .H. 1983. *A Developmental Study of the Biaka Pygmies and the Bangandu.* Lisse, Netherlands: Swets and Zeitlinger.

Van der Veer, R., and Valsiner, J. 1991. *Understanding Vygotsky.* Oxford: Blackwell.
——— 1994. *The Vygotsky Reader.* Oxford: Blackwell.
Van Hoorn, W., and Verhave, T. 1980. Wundt's changing conception of a general and theoretical psychology. In W. G. Bringmann and R. D. Tweeney, eds., *Wundt Studies: A Centennial Collection.* Toronto: C. J. Hogfrefe.
Van Rensberg, P. 1984. *Looking Forward from Serowe.* Gaborone, Botswana: Foundation for Education with Production.
Vernon, P. E. 1969. *Intelligence and Cultural Environment.* London: Methuen.
Vico, G. 1725/1948. *The New Science,* trans. T. G. Bergin and M. H. Fish. Ithaca: Cornell University Press.
Vogt, C. 1864. *Lectures on Man.* London: Longman.
Vygotsky, L. S. 1929. The problem of the cultural development of the child, II. *Journal of Genetic Psychology, 36,* 414–434.
——— 1930/1956. *The Genesis of Higher Psychological Functions* (in Russian). Moscow: Academy of Pedagogical Sciences.
——— 1930/1971. The development of higher psychological functions. In J. Wertsch, ed., *Soviet Activity Theory.* Armonk, N.Y.: Sharpe.
——— 1930/1994. Tool and Symbol in Child Development. In R. van der Veer and J. Valsiner, eds., *The Vygotsky Reader.* Cambridge, Mass.: Blackwell.
——— 1934/1987. *Thinking and Speech.* New York: Plenum.
——— 1978. *Mind in Society.* Cambridge: Harvard University Press.
——— 1981. The genesis of higher mental functions. In J. V. Wertsch, ed., *The Concept of Activity in Soviet Psychology.* Armonk, N.Y.: M. E. Sharpe.
——— 1983. *Sobranie sochinenii, Tom tretii. Problemi razvitiya psikhiki* (Collected works, vol. 3: Problems in the development of mind). Moscow: Pedagogika.
Vygotsky, L. S., and Luria, A. R. 1930/1993. *Studies on the History of Behavior: Ape, Primitive, and Child.* Hillsdale, N.J.: Erlbaum.
Wagner, D. A. 1977. Ontogeny of the Ponzo illusion: Effects of age, schooling, and environment. *International Journal of Psychology, 12,* 161–176.
Wagner, D. A. 1993. *Literacy, Culture, and Development: Becoming Literate in Morocco.* New York: Cambridge University Press.
Walden, T. A., and Baxter, A. 1989. The effect of context and age on social referencing. *Child Development, 60,* 1511–1518.
Wanner, E., and Gleitman, L. 1982. *Language Acquisition: The State of the Art.* Cambridge, Mass.: Harvard University Press.
Wartofsky, M. 1973. *Models.* Dordrecht: D. Reidel.
Washburn, S. L. 1960. Tools and human evolution. *Scientific American,* Sept., 63–75.
Washburn, S., and Howell, F. C. 1960. Human evolution and culture. In S. Tax, ed., *The Evolution of Man.* Vol. 2. Chicago: University of Chicago Press.
Wassman, J., and Dasen, P. R. 1994. Yupno number system and counting. *Journal of Cross-cultural Psychology, 25,* 78–94.
Wellman, H. 1990. *The Child's Theory of Mind.* Cambridge, Mass.: MIT Press.
Wentworth, W. 1980. *Context and Understanding: An Inquiry into Socialization Theory.* New York: Elsevier.
Werner, E. E. 1979. *Cross-Cultural Child Development: A View from the Planet Earth.* Monterey, Calif.: Brooks/Cole Publishing.
Werner, H. 1926/1948. *Comparative Psychology of Mental Development.* New York: International Universities Press.

Wertsch, J. V. 1985. *Vygotsky and the Social Formation of Mind.* Cambridge, Mass.: Harvard University Press.

—— 1991. *Voices of the Mind.* Cambridge, Mass.: Harvard University Press.

Wertsch, J. V., Del Rio, P., and Alvarez, A., eds. 1995. *Sociocultural Studies of Mind.* New York: Cambridge University Press.

White, L. 1942. On the use of tools by primates. *Journal of Comparative Psychology,* 34, 369–374.

—— 1959. The concept of culture. *American Anthropologist, 61,* 227–251.

Whiting, B. B., and Edwards, C. P. 1988. *Children of Different Worlds: The Formation of Social Behavior.* Cambridge, Mass.: Harvard University Press.

Whiting, J. W. M. 1977. A model for psychocultural research. In P. H. Liederman, S. R. Tulkin, and A. Rosenfeld, eds., *Culture and Infancy: Variations in the Human Experience.* New York: Academic Press.

Whiting, J. W. M., and Whiting, B. B. 1960. Contributions of anthropology to the methods of studying child rearing. In P. H. Mussen, ed., *Handbook of Research Methods in Child Development.* New York: Wiley.

Whitman, J. 1984. From philology to anthropology in mid-nineteenth-century Germany. In G. W. Stocking, ed., *Functionalism Historicized.* Madison: University of Wisconsin Press.

Whitten, A., and Byrne, R. W. 1988. Tactical deception in primates. *Behavior and Brain Sciences, 11,* 233–244.

Whitten, A. and Ham, R. 1992. On the nature and evolution of imitation in the animal kingdom: Reappraisal of a century of research. In P. Slater and J. Rosenblatt, eds., *Advances in the Study of Behavior.* New York: Academic Press.

Williams, R. 1973. *Keywords.* Oxford: Oxford University Press.

Witkin, H. A. 1967. A cognitive-style approach to cross-cultural research. *International Journal of Psychology, 2,* 233–250.

Witkin, H. A., Dyk, R. B., Paterson, H. F., Goodenough, D. R., and Karp, S. 1962. *Psychological Differentiation.* New York: Wiley.

Wober, M. 1975. *Psychology in Africa.* London: International African Institute.

Wolcott, H. F. 1972. Cognitive development of primitive peoples. *Phi Delta Kappan,* 53, 449–450.

Woodbridge, S. W., Olt, A. S., and Cole, M. 1992. Documenting children's problem solving behaviors using fieldnotes of participant observers. Paper presented at the American Educational Research Meeting.

Woodworth, R. S. 1910. Racial differences in mental traits. *Science, 31,* 171–186.

Wozniak, R., and Fischer, K., eds. 1993. *Development in Context: Acting and Thinking in Specific Environments.* Hillsdale, N.J.: Erlbaum.

Wrangham, R., McGrew, W., de Waal, F., and Heltne, P. 1994. *Chimpanzee Cultures.* Cambridge, Mass.: Harvard University Press.

Wundt, W. 1921. *Elements of Folk Psychology.* London: Allen and Unwin.

Wynn, K. 1992. Addition and subtraction by human infants. *Nature, 358,* 749–750.

Wynn, T. 1988. Tools and the evolution of human intelligence. In R. W. Byrne and A. Whitten, eds., *Machiavellian Intelligence: Social Expertise and Evolution of Intellect in Monkeys, Apes, and Humans.* Oxford: Clarendon Press/Oxford University Press.

Zinchenko, V. P. 1995. Cultural-historical psychology and the psychological theory of activity: Retrospect and prospect. In Wertsch, Del Rio, and Alvarez, eds., 1995.

Zinchenko, V. P., and Nazarov, A. I. 1990. Reflections on artificial intelligence. In
    O. I. Larichev and D. M. Messick, eds., *Contemporary Issues in Decision Making*.
    Amsterdam: North-Holland.
Zuckerman, M. 1993. History and developmental psychology: A dangerous liaison:
    A historian's perspective. In G. H. Elder, Jr., J. Modell, and R. D. Parke, eds.,
    *Children in Time and Place: Developmental and Historical Insights*. New York:
    Cambridge University Press.

# Acknowledgments

THE WORK summarized in this book could not have been completed if not for the extraordinary support provided me by several government and private foundations, the academic institutions within which I have worked, and the many colleagues and friends whose contributions I have tried to indicate at appropriate places in the text. Owing to their efforts, I have been able to sustain a single course of inquiry over a period of thirty years, a rare privilege indeed.

John Gay is to blame for my involvement in cross-cultural research. Had he not realized that something was radically wrong with importing American educational forms unchanged into the lives of Liberian children, it is exceedingly unlikely that I would ever have begun to study culture and thought. The fact that Joe Glick and William Kessen introduced me to the study of child development during the same period made it possible for me to put together two pieces of the puzzle I had begun to work on.

It is to my colleagues at the University of California at Irvine that I owe the opportunity to obtain on-the-job-training in methods of ethnography and field linguistics and to begin to accumulate knowledge from other social science disciplines required for making people's everyday activities the foundation of work on culture in mind. At Irvine I was allowed to teach courses in any subject I chose, which immediately included child development and cross-cultural studies. It was there that I met Charlie and Jean Lave, economist and anthropologist, with whom I was lucky enough to conduct joint research and teaching. Irvine was also home to Duane Metzger and Volney Stefflre, two charismatic characters of immense knowledge about culture and mind who provided concrete tools for attempting to reconcile, if not integrate, psychology and anthropology.

My move to The Rockefeller University in 1969 opened up un-paralleled opportunities to organize interdisciplinary research and to pursue the question of culture in mind wherever it might take me. New York is not a place where you can ignore the fact that culture, ethnicity, and development are highly charged political topics. At the time it was a place where minority-group neighborhoods were off grounds to Anglo researchers. The local populations had concluded, not without reason, that letting psychologists in did more harm than good, and the local people had the political power to back up their views. At the same time, foundations were still deeply involved in programs to improve children's educational performance as a means of overcoming chronic poverty. The country was experiencing a period of governmental "benign neglect" of issues of race and poverty, although no one thought that would solve any problems.

Some saw the work my colleagues and I had conducted in Africa and Mexico as offering hope for uncovering the hidden competence of poorly performing minority-group children and perhaps as a tool for organizing more effective educational efforts. In effect, I was faced with the question of deciding how to apply the lessons learned among the Kpelle to the analysis of development in New York City.

It was in this context that the organization currently called The Laboratory of Comparative Human Cognition (LCHC) came into being. It was clear that the effort to create a cultural approach to human development would require the long-term cooperation of a diverse group of researchers working on a set of research projects with over-lapping theoretical and methodological interests. The program included training in interdisciplinary research for scholars representing different ethnic and professional backgrounds. It received support through grants from Rockefeller University, the Carnegie Corporation, the Ford Foundation, and the National Institute of Child Health and Development. In this way, LCHC grew up as a consortium of interdisciplinary scholars working out different paths to better methods for describing people in their everyday settings and then connecting those observations back to theory and where possible to experimental manipulation.

In 1978 I moved to the University of California at San Diego and re-created the laboratory, which again gathered an ethnically diverse, interdisciplinary group of scholars. While I was conducting the research described in this book, other members of LCHC were initiating ethnographic and intervention studies of bilingual education (Moll and Diaz, 1987), comparative observational studies of literacy experiences in the homes of poor Latino, African American, and Anglo children (Anderson, Teale, and Estrada, 1980), and the process of joint activity mediated by computer networks (Levin and Souviney, 1983). Each of these lines of work extended and enriched my own empirical and theoretical efforts.

Over time, the composition of LCHC and the particular projects that served as the sites for research have continued to change to fit the intellectual issues that confront us, the expertise and interests of individual lab members, and funding opportunities. But a concern with the cultural mediation of development in context has remained constant. Thanks to modern telecommunications facilities, LCHC has become an international, distributed laboratory, allowing us to pursue the possibility of arriving at less ethnocentric conclusions about culture in mind. Cultural psychology is an undertaking too vast for any one person to encompass. Collectively, there is hope for continued progress.

Over all of its history, LCHC has been blessed by the dedicated participation of a sympathetic staff. It is certain that I could not have written this book without the help of Karen Fiegener and Peggy Bengel, who have held the effort together at times when no one else could.

Support for writing this book came from several sources over the course of a decade of intermittent effort. I am indebted to Mogens Larsen, Aksel Mortensen, Ingre Bernth, and their colleagues in Copenhagen for inviting me to give the Alfred Lehmann Memorial Lectures in which I first tried out many of the ideas presented here. John Morton and his colleagues at the Child Development Unit of the Medical Research Council in London provided me with an intellectual home during a sabbatical leave. The James McKeen Catell Foundation provided financial support for that leave. A year spent at the Center for Advanced Study in the Behavioral Sciences at Stanford, supported in part by the Spencer Foundation, gave me the time and space for writing and library research.

Last, and closest to home, I thank my wife Sheila, my partner in life and work, whose sense of adventure and endurance have made all things seem possible.

# Index